STEPHEN BELL is Associate Professor of Geography and History at the University of California, Los Angeles. He is the author of *Campanha Gaúcha: A Brazilian Ranching System, 1850–1920* (Stanford University Press, 1998), which was awarded the 1999 Warren Dean Memorial Prize.

A Life in Shadow

Portrait of Aimé Bonpland at São Borja, Brazil, c. 1845.
Drawn on site by Alfred Demersay and lithographed by Achille Devería.
SOURCE: Reproduced from Demersay, *Histoire physique . . . du Paraguay*. Atlas. General Research Division, The New York Public Library, Astor, Lenox and Tilden Foundations.

A Life in Shadow

AIMÉ BONPLAND IN SOUTHERN
SOUTH AMERICA, 1817–1858

Stephen Bell

STANFORD UNIVERSITY PRESS
STANFORD, CALIFORNIA

Stanford University Press
Stanford, California

© 2010 by the Board of Trustees of the Leland Stanford Junior University. All rights reserved.

No part of this book may be reproduced or transmitted in any form or by any means, electronic or mechanical, including photocopying and recording, or in any information storage or retrieval system without the prior written permission of Stanford University Press.

Printed in the United States of America on acid-free, archival-quality paper

Library of Congress Cataloging-in-Publication Data
Bell, Stephen, 1956-
 A life in shadow : Aimé Bonpland in southern South America, 1817-1858 / Stephen Bell.
   p. cm.
 Includes bibliographical references and index.
 ISBN 978-0-8047-5260-2 (cloth : alk. paper)
 1. Bonpland, Aimé, 1773-1858--Travel--South America. 2. Botanists--South America--Biography. 3. Naturalists--South America--Biography. 4. French--South America--Biography. 5. South America--History--19th century. I. Title. F2235.B765B45 2010
 982'.03092--dc22
 [B]
                         2009050492

Typeset by Bruce Lundquist in 10.5/14 Adobe Garamond

For Sandra Mabritto

Contents

List of Illustrations — ix
Acknowledgments — xi

Introduction — 1
1. Return to the Americas — 20
2. Prisoner in Paraguay — 64
3. From Paraguay to Pago Largo — 88
4. Somber Years of Civil War — 131
5. The Challenges of Peace — 164
6. Journey's End — 208
   Conclusion — 220

Abbreviations — 231
Notes — 233
Bibliography — 295
Index — 311

Illustrations

Figure I.1.	Humboldt and Bonpland Near the Foot of Mount Chimborazo in the Andes	5
Figure 1.1.	A Fragment of Ms. Biography by Bonpland	24
Figure 1.2.	The Plaza de Toros, Buenos Aires	32
Figure 1.3.	The Preparation of Yerba	57
Figure 2.1.	José Gaspar de Francia, Dictator of Paraguay	66
Figure 3.1.	Portrait of Bonpland at Buenos Aires, 1837	110
Figure 4.1.	The Landing Place at Montevideo, 1836	141
Figure 4.2.	Bonpland's Home at São Borja, c. 1845	158
Figure 4.3.	The Ruined Mission at São Miguel, c. 1845	159
Figure 5.1.	The Natural Vegetation Regions of Southern Brazil	169
Figure 5.2.	A Riograndense Rural Property, c. 1852	170
Figure 5.3.	Porto Alegre, c. 1852	172
Figure 5.4.	A Daguerreotype Image of Bonpland from the 1850s	204
Figure 6.1.	Bonpland's Rustic Home at Santa Ana, Corrientes, 1858	213

Acknowledgments

The writer Sybille Bedford argued that to remain monolingual reduced the mind to the confines of a tramline. The subject of this book was somebody who most certainly broadened his cultural experience as a young man through learning Latin and Spanish, and through much pondering of the significance of Native American words. His trajectory laid out research challenges which it has been a distinct pleasure to navigate. My first major debt goes to the Social Sciences and Humanities Research Council of Canada. The bulk of the financial support for archival research in Europe and in South America came from this institution. In addition, the support of the University of California proved crucial for filling in gaps as the research unfolded.

I extend my thanks to all those who helped shape this work in their various ways. The seed of the project germinated while I was still a graduate student, when consulting the tantalizingly imprecise category of "diverse documents" in the Arquivo Histórico do Rio Grande do Sul, Brazil. A conversation with Jock Galloway, my graduate mentor at the University of Toronto, brought the response that there might be a book in it. As often, he was right, and his encouragement is gratefully noted. In terms of method, I worked from the better cataloged to the lesser known, beginning in Paris and La Rochelle. In France, I especially appreciated the guidance of the late Frédéric Mauro, who invited me to participate in his seminar on the economic history of Latin America. In addition, the late Charles Minguet made many useful suggestions. Guy Martinière was always enthusiastic about the project, and his Bonplandista graduate students, Nicolas Hossard and Cédric Cerruti, both offered much spirited discussion.

Working across many countries (Argentina, Brazil, Canada, France, Germany, the United States, and Uruguay), any attempt to list those who helped can only fail by serious omission. I particularly appreciate that all my requests to view material met with respectful attention, even if establishment of credentials sometimes took a little time. A key moment in the research came during my first visit to Buenos Aires, when the late Prof. José L. Amorín conceded permission to consult the extensive Bonpland manuscript materials held in the institution he directed, the Museo de Farmacobotánica "Juan A. Domínguez." He and his staff, working with modest resources, deserve my heartfelt thanks. The atmosphere of work in the museum was special and enjoyable. I am particularly indebted to Liliana Maetakeda, who did all she could to squeeze out additional hours in which I could work uninterrupted.

Much of the research was done while I was still working within the Department of Geography at McGill University. I retain a deep affection for that department. But of all my former colleagues there, my thanks are due most especially to Sherry Olson. A keen Francophile, she helped my scholarship grow in ways neither of us probably fully realized. And outside the academy in Montreal, my thanks go to Ann Dadson, who accompanied me along parts of the French portion of the research trail. In the Department of Geography of the University of California at Los Angeles, all my colleagues have supported this research in different ways and I am thankful to them, but most especially to Chase Langford for his cheerful preparation of the maps and figures. At UCLA, I have particularly enjoyed the enthusiasm for all things Latin American shown by Larry Lauerhass, an ardent bibliophile and a true friend.

Prof. Thomas Whigham of the Department of History at the University of Georgia accompanied this project from its inception, thus from a time that we were both part of a very small international contingent consulting the archives of southernmost Brazil. I have greatly valued his sage comments on the manuscript. All translations as well as errors in this work are mine. I thank the Institute of Latin American Studies (now part of the Institute for the Study of the Americas), University of London, for permission to draw on material earlier published there. In addition, my thanks are due to the LuEsther T. Mertz Library, New York Botanical Garden, Bronx, New York, for allowing me to draw on the William Baldwin papers.

Finally, I remain indebted to Stanford University Press, and most especially to Norris Pope. For some of us, he has become synonymous with that publisher and its ongoing reputation for the maintenance of high standards. I also wish to thank Mary Barbosa for the care she has taken in editing this book.

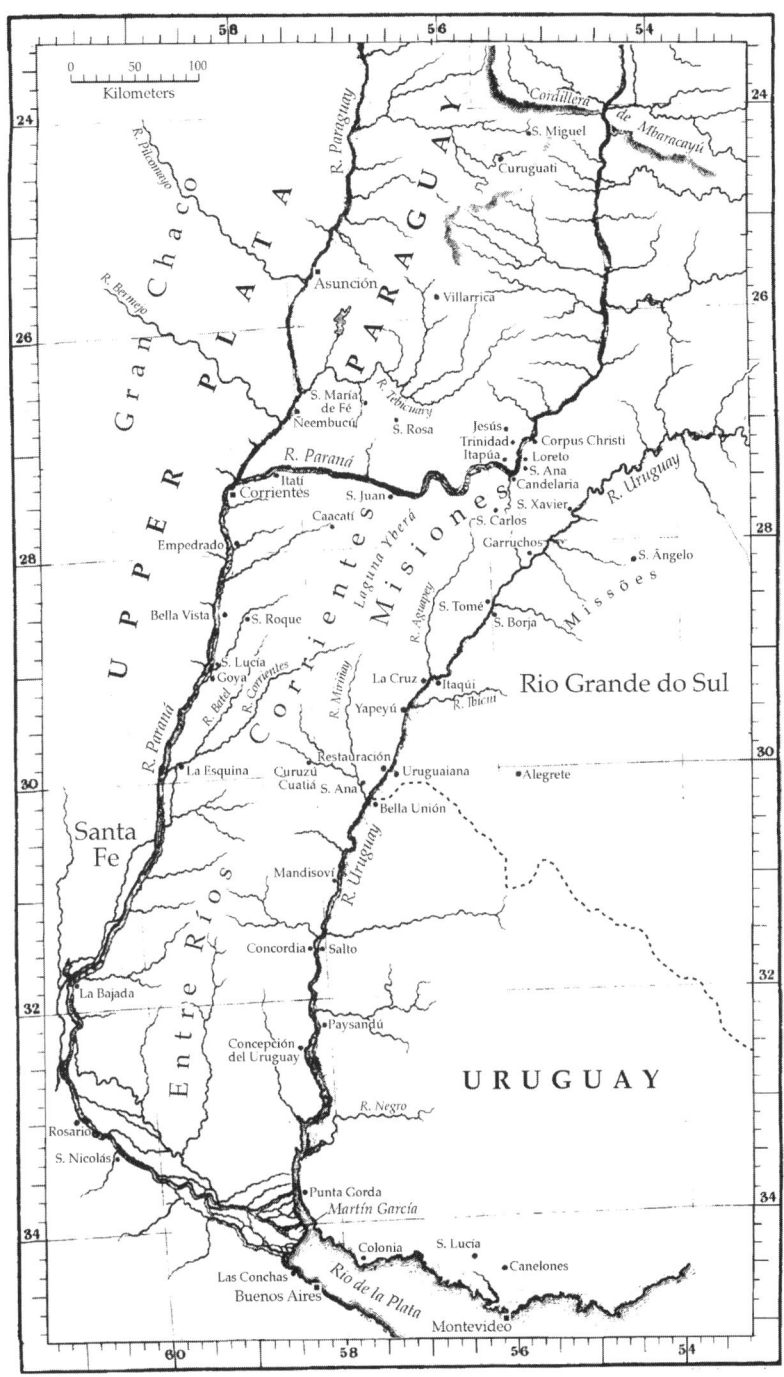

Regions of southern South America explored by Bonpland.
SOURCE: Prepared by Chase Langford, Department of Geography, UCLA. After John Arrowsmith, *The Republic of Paraguay and the Adjacent Countries with the Courses of the Rivers Paraguay, Parana and La Plata*. London: John Murray, 1838. Printed in Robertson and Robertson, *Letters on Paraguay*, vol. 3, frontispiece.

A Life in Shadow

Introduction

This book treats the southern South American career of the French naturalist Aimé-Jacques-Alexandre Goujaud-Bonpland, better known simply as Aimé Bonpland (1773–1858). Its main purposes are to clarify the post-1817 South American achievements of his life and to set aside some of the sense of disappointment and confusion that has built around him since his death. In the nineteenth century, Bonpland was famous. For example, the botanical journal *Bonplandia* began to be published in 1853 from Hannover, Germany, as the official organ of the Academia Caesaro-Leopoldina, one of the oldest academies in Europe (founded in the late seventeenth century).[1] The source of the honor was mainly the fame of the botanical work Bonpland achieved while working with Alexander von Humboldt (1769–1859). While the name Bonpland is affixed to such things as a genus of American plants, small towns in Argentina, streets of some major South American cities, a mountain in Venezuela, and, briefly, Lake Tahoe in California, among other memorials, it is not one that carries much resonance today outside of some limited portions of southern South America. When remembered at all, it is usually as a footnote to the immensely famous Alexander von Humboldt. Thus, before moving into Bonpland's own South American career, his links with Humboldt need to be briefly reviewed.

The development of geography in the nineteenth century has been interpreted by one authority as a gathering of tension between the "world of action and discovery, and that of the lecture theatre and library."[2] The contrasting careers of the distinguished travelers Bonpland and Humboldt, after their celebrated scientific journey through equinoctial America (1799–1804), represent a particularly stark illustration of this idea. Humboldt, who spent decades systematically publishing in Paris and Berlin from the field results, is venerated (an academic chair was named after him in the Department of Geography of the University of California at Los Angeles); in contrast,

Bonpland—who made extensive further field researches in South America (1817–1858) and wrote a good deal yet published very little—has fallen from view, to the point that a distinguished modern Brazilian bibliographer could complain that everything about his career is obscure.[3]

While the critical literature on Humboldt, often termed the "father of modern geography," is extensive, Bonpland has been largely forgotten. Modern accounts of the famous journey through equinoctial America frequently do not bother even to mention Bonpland's presence on the trip, although Humboldt himself laid careful stress on the critical role that the former played in the research. Many biographical sketches of Bonpland appear in the older literature, but most of these works written in Europe are thoroughly confused as to his motives and status in South America. The leading theme in the existing literature is that Bonpland met a tragic fate in South America, in my judgment a rather Eurocentric idea that does nothing to explain why he chose to stay—borrowing Mary Louise Pratt's phrase—in the "contact zone," or what was then commonly viewed as the periphery.[4] Any examination of Bonpland's manuscripts will show that, while he might be considered obscure from the perspectives of Paris, Berlin, or London, the argument will never hold for South America. In fact, Bonpland maintained a voluminous correspondence (including with scientists, politicians, entrepreneurs, and diplomats) for periods of his residence in Argentina and Brazil. His earlier fame as an explorer was recognized by figures who loom very large on the political map of South America of the early nineteenth century (Simón Bolívar and Bernardino Rivadavia, for example). As a resident in South America with clear intellectual gifts, almost all the leading political figures seem to have been prepared to grant Bonpland an audience, José Gaspar Rodríguez de Francia, the infamous dictator of Paraguay, being a conspicuous exception.

Before launching Bonpland into the Americas, some brief comment on his background is in order. Aimé Bonpland was born at La Rochelle in 1773 to a bourgeois family. A number of interests can be traced along the line of his ancestors, including the ownership of land and the commanding of sea vessels. There is at least one direct link to the Americas in the family tree, to an ancestor born in Québec. His parents had investments in the Caribbean colonies, as did many Rochellais bourgeois families. The predominant occupation of his forbears, however, was as apothecaries, an interest Bonpland would continue in southern South America. His father, Simon-Jacques (alias Jean), was trained in medicine, becoming the chief surgeon in the

La Charité hospital at La Rochelle. Simon-Jacques was the first member of the family to add the appendage Bonpland to the surname Goujaud. It was supposedly applied by his own father at his birth in a moment of affection as a corruption of "bon plant," conveying the idea of the baby as a fine seedling. Wherever the origins lie in a today murky family tradition, the name stuck as Bonpland, although French orthographers would probably have preferred Bompland. The name has frequently been presented incorrectly in the latter form, including by native-born French authors and others. Given Aimé Bonpland's American destiny, it seems apposite that his name is more easily pronounced in Spanish than in French.

Aimé was the youngest of three children to survive from his parents' marriage. Michel-Simon (1770–1850), the elder brother, would eventually follow his father into a medical career at La Rochelle. He alone seems to have retained the surname Goujaud-Bonpland. His sister, Élisabeth-Olive (1771–1852), married a lawyer, Pierre-Philippe-Amable-Honoré Gallocheau, remaining all her life in the Charente region of France. The two brothers, who can be differentiated as Goujaud-Bonpland and Bonpland, a habit that may have been present at Paris already by the 1790s, both gained access to a superior quality of higher education, certainly one of the best available in their era. By 1791, Aimé had joined his elder brother at medical school in Paris. The teachers included the major medical innovators Pierre-Joseph Desault (1738–1795), Jean Corvisart (1755–1821), and Xavier Bichat (1771–1802). Bonpland appears to have gained his knowledge of comparative anatomy from the last. The progress of his education along parts of the 1790s remains hazy. There is some evidence that he accomplished military service in the navy, beginning from Rochefort, where he may have continued his medical studies in the naval medical school.[5] Surviving letters to his sister confirm that Bonpland was at Rochefort in 1794.[6] Much later, Bonpland recounted orally from Montevideo that he completed his military service by serving as a ship's surgeon on the vessel *Ajax* from Toulon.[7] By early 1795, he rejoined his brother in Paris, where he continued his education along the next years by frequenting clinics and medical courses. However, a passion for botany and other branches of natural science also registered its presence early with both brothers. For example, they botanized together around La Rochelle, and they long held to the plan, never realized, of publishing together. Perhaps, according to Aimé Bonpland's own memory, some inner vocation pushed him in his spare time toward the Jardin des Plantes in Paris, "where he contemplated with a curious intelligence the numerous treasures assembled in this vast collection of the natural productions of all the countries."[8] The study of botany suited his capacity for close observation (his memory for earlier sightings of plant materials would become prodigious during his long South American residence). He completed his education under some of the leading teachers at the Jardin des Plantes. Under the influence of Jean-Baptiste Lamarck (1744–1829), Antoine-Laurent de Jussieu (1748–1836), and René-Louiche Desfontaines (1750–1833), he "developed a deep interest in natural history, chiefly botany, which needed only a little encouragement to flare out marvelously."[9] These were the talents that brought him famously into the company of Humboldt in 1798. However, another facet of Bonpland's education should not be forgotten—its socialization. His studies brought him friendships with a number of individuals who would go on to have distinguished careers in the French scientific establishment during the first half of the nineteenth century. The surgeon baron Guillaume Dupuytren (1777–1835) and the chemist baron Louis Jacques Thénard (1777–1857) are but two good examples of this; both began life with more modest social origins than Bonpland. Some of these relationships are of central importance for understanding the conduct of his later life in South America. They represented a type of social capital that enhanced his reputation in the region.

The careers of Bonpland and Humboldt were thrown inextricably together through the fame of the journey through the Americas from 1799 to 1804. Bonpland was Humboldt's assistant, responsible mainly for the botanical work, although he also worked in other fields. We have been left with a somewhat opaque vision of his contributions. Researchers today do not always remember that four-fifths of the botanical manuscripts written along the journey are Bonpland's work, nor, sometimes, do they even remember his presence along the journey.[10] In Douglas Botting's widely read biography, an illustration of "a page from the journal Humboldt kept on board the *Pizarro*" happens to be one in which all the script is clearly that of Bonpland.[11] Jason Wilson has noted how little of Bonpland comes through in the published travel account.[12] Humboldt's descriptions in his travel diaries are more immediate, never more so than in his account of when the canoe advancing up the Orinoco was on the point of capsizing, and Bonpland was the hero of the moment: "Don't be afraid, my friend, we shall save ourselves."[13] Humboldt could never forget that his traveling companion was ready to swim, if necessary carrying him on his back. George Sarton pointed out that Bonpland may have faced even more challenges than Humboldt:

"It is probable that in his search for plants in dismal places Bonpland exposed himself more than his friend."[14]

The evidence is abundantly clear in Humboldt's letters written from the Americas that he was delighted with Bonpland's knowledge, courage, and enthusiasm.[15] Given the range of Humboldt's correspondents—from distinguished scientists to such politicians as Thomas Jefferson and James Madison—the frequent mentions of Bonpland's work added to the latter's fame upon his return to Europe. Humboldt also worked to enhance his companion's reputation in France. After Humboldt's donation of a large portion of the American herbarium to the Paris museum, Napoleon granted Bonpland in 1805 an annual state pension of 3,000 francs.

The working relationship between Bonpland and Humboldt during the period from 1804 until 1816 still requires closer research. When Humboldt was away in such cities as Rome and Berlin, Bonpland was heavily involved with Humboldt's business affairs at Paris, especially in relation to

Figure I.1 Friedrich Georg Weitsch's painting from 1806–7 of Humboldt (standing) and Bonpland (seated) on the plain at the foot of Mount Chimborazo in the Andes.
SOURCE: Reproduced by permission of the Bildarchiv Preussischer Kulturbesitz/Art Resource, New York. In connection with Weitsch's painting, Humboldt wrote to Bonpland on 3 October 1806 from Berlin, asking his friend to send a drawing of himself in profile: "It is not a woman but the king who wishes this" (Schneppen, Bonpland: Humboldts vergessener Gefährte? p. 37). Humboldt informed Bonpland that he was on the way to immortality. Today, the painting hangs at the Schloss Bellevue in Berlin, the residence of the presidents of the Federal Republic of Germany.

publication matters.[16] In April 1805, for example, Humboldt urged Bonpland to think about melastomes, arguing that their joint fame depended on this.[17] Difficulties flowed from the fact that the work of botanical publication advanced only very slowly. It is widely recognized that Humboldt underestimated the time and work involved in bringing his raw research to fruit. Even the narrative of the travel experiences took decades to prepare, and remained incomplete. But the botanical aspect of the project, which was a huge portion of the overall endeavor, was hindered by 1809–10 as Bonpland was drawn more and more into administration, working for the Empress Joséphine as the administrator of her property at Malmaison. George Sarton identified the opposition between these two men following his observation that "with less generosity on either side they would have easily become enemies."[18]

The potential for tensions between Bonpland and Humboldt over the character of the botanical publications was deep even along the actual journey. For example, Humboldt had already invited the Berlin botanist Karl Ludwig Willdenow (1765–1812) to serve as the editor of the botanical publications in 1801.[19] The use of German collaborators was not something that Bonpland readily accepted, especially when certain of their specimens at Berlin were not present in Paris.[20] As Bonpland's rate of production stalled to a trickle along the second half of the decade, in part an understandable development given the level of his work commitments for Joséphine at her Malmaison and Navarre residences, Humboldt turned back to Willdenow in 1810, asking him to come to Paris from Berlin to assist with and advance the work. In his letter of invitation, Humboldt argued that neither he nor Bonpland himself had any influence over Bonpland's actions.[21] Willdenow died suddenly in 1812 and the work then passed to Karl Sigismund Kunth (1788–1850). Ulrike Leitner has argued that Bonpland ceased doing botanical work for Humboldt in 1813, but there is considerable evidence to the contrary.[22] There are also numerous indications from Bonpland while resident in southern South America that he saw his project there as the completion of Humboldt's work, most importantly in botany but also in other branches of science.

The Humboldt-Bonpland working relationship was one of uncommon intensity. The shifting phases of how they viewed each other would be a worthy theme for intense research scrutiny. Bonpland set the model for Humboldt of close research collaborations with other male scientists. There is no doubt that Humboldt's deep collaboration with the physicist Joseph-

Louis Gay-Lussac (1778–1850) rankled on some level with Bonpland. What level of intimacy Humboldt ever achieved with his research partners remains, as Aaron Sachs points out, something impossible to resolve.[23]

If the personal connections are impossible to recover in their entirety, other things seem clearer. The Humboldt and Bonpland journey between 1799 and 1804 was of key importance in the development of an affirmative view of at least parts of the tropical world. David Arnold has argued recently that "Humboldt surely did more than any other individual to 'invent' the tropics as a field of scientific enquiry and an aesthetic domain and to feed a positive perception of the tropics into wider environmental debates."[24] Important differences prevailed between Humboldt and Bonpland in their relationships to tropical environments. The appeal of these environments seems to have seized hold of Bonpland in the most tangible way. His early reaction of sensory overload on arriving with Humboldt in the tropics, "a cacophony of sense impressions bordering on insanity," as one author has phrased it, has been much repeated in the literature.[25] In the early nineteenth century, Bonpland had shown considerable pride in the material furnishings of his Paris apartment, writing to his sister and brother-in-law about parquet floors and marble chimneys.[26] Along the remainder of his life, the appeal of nature took hold of him and a passion for field studies became the guiding force of his life.

Bonpland clearly stood in Humboldt's shadow. His reputation was also affected by the distance he lived removed from metropolitan scientific institutions. In many ways, his life can be interpreted as an often desperate effort to maintain his own scientific authority in the face of Humboldt's immense and growing reputation. He certainly held to the ambition of publishing some of the results of his southern South American research. As late as 1849, when traveling across the mountains of southern Brazil, he told his old friend the French botanist Alire Raffeneau-Delile in a letter that he still wished to publish the plants that were properly his, that is things collected separately from Humboldt.[27]

Although Bonpland never saw France in person again after he left Le Havre for Buenos Aires in 1816, he made repeated promises to return. Following the importance of his work with Humboldt between 1799 and 1804, his imprisonment for almost a decade in Paraguay during the 1820s added a new layer of fame. By the middle of the nineteenth century, still in written contact with many of the surviving members of the scientific community of his generation in Europe, he was widely viewed in South America as a type of walking relic. Even so, his friendship was greatly appreciated by many younger people interested in science, to whom he offered much encouragement. In 1907, one of Bonpland's relatives offered the impressions, still "*très vive et très precise*," of meeting his ancestor over a half-century earlier at Montevideo. He retained the memory that, throughout southern South America, Bonpland was "the object of a kind of cult on the part of everybody, rich and poor, urban dwellers or gauchos."[28]

. . .

The complicated movement patterns of Bonpland's final years hindered knowledge of the whereabouts of his papers at his death. This has been a major source of confusion in the historiography. The Comte de Brossard, the French diplomatic representative to Paraguay, summarized the state of knowledge for the French minister to Argentina in August 1858. Four volumes of Bonpland's botanical registers, containing the descriptions of 2,449 species, and his geology catalog, giving an account of 357 mineral specimens, were at Corrientes, in the hands of Pastora Périchon, a long-standing family friend. The location of other papers, including "an extensive study on the woods of South America, a work to which he attached great value," was unknown.[29] Brossard held that Bonpland had left his manuscripts in São Borja, Brazil, when he moved his residence definitively to Santa Ana in southeastern Corrientes. He said he had "reasons to presume," though none were given, that the remaining manuscripts, at least, were in the hands of Jean-Pierre Gay, the French-born priest of that small Brazilian town since February 1850, and a close friend of Bonpland. The governor of Corrientes, Juan Pujol, saw things otherwise, maintaining that Bonpland's entire scientific heritage was on Correntino soil.[30] Based at Asunción, Brossard was in no position to question Gay directly. In addition, the inventory of what Bonpland had left at Santa Ana had still to appear. Suspicion thus fell on Gay, in the form of vague charges that he worked hard to dispel. Brossard was working to trade Bonpland's materials at Corrientes for books and instruments from France, thinking that these could serve as the beginning of a public library at Corrientes.

The administrators of the Muséum d'Histoire Naturelle at Paris staked their claim to Bonpland's heritage in a letter to the Ministry of Public Instruction in October 1858. The key evidence they used to make their case was a portion of the letter Bonpland had written to Humboldt from Corrientes on 7 June 1857. It contained an explicit statement that he wished to see his scientific heritage left to France. Humboldt was prepared to give the museum the original copy of his letter, should that prove necessary.[31]

Faced with requests for clarification about the whereabouts of Bonpland's manuscripts coming from French diplomats based at Paraná, Entre Ríos (Argentina), Porto Alegre (Brazil), and Asunción (Paraguay)—all considerable distances from the places where Bonpland had lived—Gay had to work hard to clear his reputation. He wrote a long manuscript (nineteen numbered pages) from São Borja to the French Minister of the Interior in August 1859 expressing his reluctance to see Bonpland's "treasures," meaning his collections and manuscripts, lost for the scientific heritage of France.[32] He held firm to his conviction that everything concerning Bonpland's scientific heritage was held in the province of Corrientes. Gay was concerned that the declining physical state of the plant specimens required urgent publication of Bonpland's southern South American flora. He received an eyewitness report about the state of Bonpland's herbarium in early 1859 from Louis de Luchi, the secretary of the Sardinian legation to the Argentine Confederation, who reported that the herbarium was kept in a very humid room and would presumably soon be lost to science.[33] By August 1859, Gay reached the conclusion that while Bonpland's plant collections were no longer in a perfect state, they were still in a fit condition from which to prepare illustrations. This was not something, he said, within the publishing resources of Corrientes, but work that needed to fall to the learned societies of Europe. Bonpland's flora of Paraguay, the Jesuit missions, the province of Rio Grande do Sul, and the republics of the Plata represented in Gay's opinion "a prize of boundless value for botany." At the time he wrote, however, the French diplomats posted in southern South America seemed to be reaching the conclusion that Bonpland had left no legacy, although Gay knew the manuscripts existed, partly at Corrientes and partly in the southeastern corner of that province. He placed the weight of responsibility with Juan Pujol to make sure Bonpland's work was posthumously published. Gay had worked since 1850 encouraging his friend to complete his work, or at least to take his collections to France. But Bonpland had come to identify with the customs and ways of the missions; he feared the idea of launching himself again into high society. Gay seems to have been disturbed by the patterns of Bonpland's daily life, and tried to recruit him into his own home, saying Bonpland was customarily surrounded "only by Indians and children." Gay took an extremely positive view of Bonpland's merits. He hoped a more skilled writer than himself would take on the task of writing his friend's biography.

It took the French authorities some time to prevail in their claim, to locate remaining material, and to move it from the South American interior to Paris. Some of Bonpland's French collateral relatives also made a claim, but they soon desisted. The French government was also aware that Bonpland had left "several natural children" in the Plata, whom he recognized. By 1860, two boxes had arrived at Paris and the bureaucrats then set to work, deciding what they could retrieve from Bonpland's South American legacy. In July 1860, a commission, which included the geologist Jules Desnoyers (1800–1887), the librarian at the Jardin des Plantes, was working to assess the contents of two cases of books and manuscripts. The commission met on Saturday, 7 July, and it was not impressed. The inventory described around thirty books, most of them in poor physical condition. These were mainly volumes relating to botany, zoology, and natural history more generally.[34] The books were seen as without importance and value. While they were items readily accessible at Paris, the same could certainly not be said for the interior of South America. The manuscripts were also a source of disappointment; they did not correspond at first sight with what could be expected "from the extended sojourn of the famous traveler in these countries so distant and so little explored."[35] This was hardly a judgment likely to stimulate scholarship, but the commission had worked with only a portion of Bonpland's papers. Much more would turn up almost a half-century later in South America.[36]

Despite the disappointment registered at Paris in the years following Bonpland's death, a considerable amount of literature on him exists, especially in French and Spanish. Essays by George Sarton and Jason Wilson excepted, there is remarkably little in print in English. Very little in any of the existing treatments is thematic. Most accounts center on the drama, which does not always further analysis.[37]

Bonpland's life holds considerable interest for the general reader.[38] Numerous articles have appeared in South American newspapers about his life, some of them highly informative.[39] His close association with Joséphine in Napoleonic France, work on behalf of South American revolutionaries in Europe, and imprisonment by Francia in Paraguay during most of the 1820s have all supplied much raw material for writing romantic fiction. It came as no surprise when Gabriel García Márquez drew on Bonpland within his work on the life of Bolívar.[40] He is also an important character in Augusto Roa Bastos's distinguished and innovative 1974 novel *Yo, el Supremo* (*I, the Supreme*) about Francia's life. Constructed in Jason Wilson's analysis around "documents, letters, fragments, and Francia's own punning mind-flow," this book shows a close sense of Paraguay's historical development.[41] Four years later, the Argentine novelist Luis Gasulla published a strangely titled historical novel of approximately six hundred pages directed squarely toward Bonpland's career in the Río de la Plata; it is heavily based on the Bonpland archives.[42] Philippe Foucault's French-language work of historical fiction went in the same direction, but it is built over a wider temporal span.[43] More will have heard of Bonpland from Daniel Kehlmann's recent novel about Humboldt and Gauss than any other single source.[44] Fiction builds interest in Bonpland, but it is not always helpful for our knowledge of his life while academic research has lagged so far behind. However great the temptations and appeal of creative writing, to say nothing of film, this study is confined to things seen in the archives.

The earliest biographies of Bonpland were mainly written from South America itself by some of his contemporaries. The first of these, a much-reproduced brief account, was published in sections in the periodical *Revista del Plata* in 1854. It was authored by Pedro de Angelis (1784–1859), a major figure in the intellectual history of South America, while he was based at Buenos Aires.[45] Another biography came from Montevideo, penned by Adolphe Brunel, a French medical doctor resident there. Brunel and Bonpland were also in direct contact during the latter's visits to Montevideo during the 1850s. Both of these authors' works are of interest partly because they contain elements of oral history. For example, Brunel opened the 1859 edition of his biography with the observation that most of it came from Bonpland's mouth. But neither de Angelis nor Brunel can have known much for sure about the conditions of Bonpland's life in the interior. Buenos Aires and Montevideo were probably closer in elite ways of life to Paris than to Bonpland's principal residences. The account provided by Alfred Demersay, a member of the central commission of the Société de Géographie at Paris, is different in this respect. Assigned in 1844 by the government of France to report on the state of Paraguay following the demise of Francia, Demersay spent several months as a guest of Bonpland at São Borja, tarrying on account of the politics in the neighboring regions. Encouraged by his host to draw, this visit also resulted in the greater part of the very limited iconography we have for Bonpland's long South American career.[46]

The best existing biography of the broad scope of Bonpland's career remains the work by Ernest-Théodore Hamy (1842–1908), stimulated by his preparation of a volume of Humboldt's letters around the time of the centenary of the journey to the Americas.[47] This research was intimately linked with Hamy's active involvement in directing the Congrès International des Américanistes (International Congress of Americanists). Even at the time of its publication (1906), however, the book provided an incomplete treatment. Hamy worked from Paris by correspondence, making little direct use of Bonpland's other archives.[48] As a result, he could provide only a pallid description of long stretches of Bonpland's South American career. He did not set Bonpland's activities in South America into broader context or assess their significance. A great strength of his work is that he was able to publish so many of Bonpland's letters. But any perusal of the chronology of those letters quickly reveals lacunae. From leaving Europe in late 1816 to emerging from Paraguay in 1831, only two letters by Bonpland are printed in Hamy's book. It would be foolish to expect letters during the Paraguayan confinement, but we are bound to question the silence on experiences of setting up life in the Americas. Another major gap when reading Hamy is during the 1840s. This is a reflection of political instability in South America, when letters were not reaching Europe. The focus of the subject's preoccupation then was much more regional than international. Whatever its weaknesses, Hamy's important book has long represented the bedrock for studies of Bonpland. Scholars ignore it at their peril, as demonstrated by the publication of materials claimed as new when they are not.[49]

A few years later, Henri Cordier published his account of Bonpland's unpublished papers that were conserved at Buenos Aires.[50] This effort was also linked to a meeting of the International Congress of Americanists, this time one held in Buenos Aires. Here, Juan A. Domínguez read a paper outlining how the museum he headed in that city had come into possession of material relating to the French naturalist. News of extensive papers still present at Santa Ana in Corrientes came south in 1905 with Pompeyo Bonpland, a grandson, who was studying medicine at the University of Buenos Aires. In accounting for the continued existence of the papers at Bonpland's former Argentine home, Cordier pointed the finger of suspicion at Gay once again, probably unaware of the detailed accounting the latter had provided for the French authorities back in 1859.[51] Cordier also wrote somewhat pedantically on the drawbacks of Hamy's treatment, making the argument that if the latter had drawn on the large store of manuscripts preserved in the Americas, he could have written the definitive biography of Bonpland. Given the limited time available to him, Cordier worked hard to produce a twenty-four–page summary of the contents of the archive at Buenos Aires.

He concentrated less on American themes than on links to famous scientists resident in Europe, starting with Humboldt, but also including other names of world reputation, such as Sir Joseph Banks and William Jackson Hooker. Cordier offered a most tantalizing glimpse of the content of the Buenos Aires archive, but not a measured reflection on it.

The arrival of the Bonpland collection at Buenos Aires was a subject of newspaper comment in Europe, mainly because it contained extensive correspondence with Humboldt.[52] At the University of Buenos Aires, the museum of pharmacobotany was aware that it was sitting on a type of historical treasure. Under Juan Domínguez's energetic direction, a start was made on organizing the contents, work entrusted to Eugène Autran, a Swiss botanist working in Argentina. The greatest strength of the slow publishing program at Buenos Aires has been the fact that the museum has worked thematically. Autran first organized and transcribed 28 letters from Humboldt to Bonpland, which were published as facsimiles of the manuscripts.[53] Even today, researchers turn to these, and doubtless they regret the rigors of reading Humboldt's hand. Autran died in 1912, which slowed the work of bringing the manuscripts to print. All further volumes produced at Buenos Aires have been facsimiles of manuscripts, accompanied by brief introductions. One volume provided a published version of the latter part of Bonpland's botanical registers.[54] The remainder of the series has political overtones. An extremely interesting volume published in 1940 demonstrated Bonpland's extensive links with the Spanish American revolutionaries based in London, documenting his services to them in the period 1814–1816. The year of publication of this work was significant; in part, the preparers had the didactic purpose of reminding people in Argentina of the important role that Britain, especially London, played in the mounting of the independence struggle against Spain. Another folio transcribed Bonpland's correspondence with the politicians connected with his journey into the Upper Plata that began in 1820. It provides a useful reminder of his optimism and energy shortly before he was dragged into captivity in Paraguay near the end of 1821. The final volume dealt with Bonpland's medical services to the army of Justo José de Urquiza, shortly before this latter and his allies toppled the famous dictator Juan Manuel de Rosas.[55] These works demonstrated effectively how Bonpland, while working in the shadows, sometimes played political roles of great consequence for Argentina.

In 1943, the distinguished historian of science George Sarton published an essay on Bonpland in *Isis*. This was a clear effort to resurrect his subject's reputation in the history of science. While Sarton's synthesis contains much of value, he could see "no point in following the activities of the final period of [Bonpland's] life . . . which were largely agricultural, financial, political."[56] Yet Bonpland had always mixed concerns for agriculture with his scientific observations in South America. In addition, finances are something it would be most helpful to know more about. The literature has been overwhelmingly uncritical about the patterns of payment and receipt of the state pension granted by Napoleon in 1805. It is also worthwhile remembering that Bonpland gathered new plant species more rapidly in his late seventies, during his 1849 journey across the Serra of Rio Grande do Sul, than at any other stage of his southern South American career. Reliance solely on secondary material has led to numerous errors of fact and interpretation in treatments of Bonpland, a trap even Sarton was unable to avoid. Take Sarton's assertion that Bonpland "reverted to native standards" in later life, for example.[57] This simply does not square with much of Bonpland's activities in the 1850s as revealed in his own manuscripts, but it does help to build the idea of a "tragic fate," the interpretation used by Hanno Beck in his major biography of Humboldt.[58]

In 1960, Wilhelm Schulz published a brief biography of Bonpland's career in South America (53 pages), the research for which was stimulated by the centenary of Humboldt's death.[59] Schulz laid useful emphasis on Humboldt's letters written to Bonpland in South America. Translating the facsimile manuscripts from French into German, he rendered these easily readable for the first time, a valuable contribution in its own right, language barriers apart. But again, Schulz's extended essay included no sustained examination of the primary sources. In short, the research linking Bonpland's divided archival records in western Europe and southern South America still remained to be done a century after his death, and even more recently.

Although some brief published account of the contents of the Bonpland archive at Buenos Aires has been available for nearly a century, thematic research has been slow to emerge from it. Most of the existing work treats aspects of the Humboldt-Bonpland working relationship or concentrates on specific regions of Bonpland's long southern South American residence.[60] A high degree of repetition occurs in the literature, while some important aspects remain weakly researched. In particular, Bonpland's links with Brazil have never attracted the close scrutiny they deserve, possibly because he lived in such a peripheral location within that vast country. However, there are welcome signs of renewed activity. Since the publication of Philippe Foucault's book, based on research originally intended for a television documentary, French scholars have shown a renewed interest. Nicolas Hossard's recent brief study, a synthesis of Bonpland's southern South American career, has shown the wealth of material available at Buenos Aires. His study is especially interesting for publishing documents relating to Bonpland's family for the first time.

The present study is the first detailed treatment of Bonpland in English. It lays special emphasis on what is least understood, his later career in southern South America. While the possibility is always real that new material will turn up in the archives, the study has worked to reconnect Bonpland's divided archival records in western Europe and southern South America.[61] It charts his activities in the context of the historical and geographical development of Argentina, southern Brazil, Paraguay, and Uruguay during the first half of the nineteenth century. Bonpland spent the last forty-one years of his life in this broad region, where he lived from a wide range of occupations, including medical doctor, pharmacist, farmer, rancher, government scientific explorer, and political conspirator. In the political context of the first half of the nineteenth century—that is, in the disturbed process of moving from colonies to nations—none of these diverse interests developed smoothly. The numerous interests are interlinked and all have received attention in my research. However, this book places its closest attention on the three themes of rural economy that stand in bold relief in Bonpland's thought and action: experimental cultivation in general; the cultivation of yerba maté, or Paraguayan tea (a staple in the southern South American diet) on a sustainable basis; and the breeding of merino sheep for wool. The sources for these pioneer interests on Bonpland's part are deep, extending back to Europe. They include the period he spent working for the Empress Joséphine as the scientific manager of her properties Malmaison and Navarre in Napoleonic France.

This book has been written keeping the following objectives in mind. First, it aims to provide a critical assessment of a significant but neglected historical figure in his own right. Academic interest in the French intellectual contribution to nineteenth-century Latin America has been growing.[62] It is already recognized that travelers with greater or lesser degrees of "obscurity" have played a significant role in the description of the earth, especially through their contributions to the formation of the world's major scientific collections. In addition, study of these travelers offers a valuable window for the reconstruction of the social and economic conditions of Latin America during the first half of the nineteenth century. Taking the totality of Bonpland's long career, it is doubtful whether any other individual in the nineteenth century witnessed directly more of Latin America than he did, thus his capacity for comparative observations was immense. The bicentenary of the Humboldt-Bonpland journey (1999–2004) did much to renew interest in these figures, with numerous conferences and exhibitions in both Europe and Latin America.[63] This seems an apposite time to attempt again the objective for Bonpland raised by George Sarton in his essay published in 1943: "Let us now turn our attention to that companion, snatch him out of the obscurity wherein he has sunk, and put him back in the center of the stage with Humboldt."[64]

More than Humboldt, however, the center of the stage should be South America itself. By concentrating on what Bonpland was doing in South America rather than what he was not doing in Europe—following Humboldt into decades of study of the research results from the equinoctial journey from 1799–1804, there is some potential to help redress Eurocentric biases in the historiography of exploration. Although European in background and training, it is known that Bonpland grew increasingly ambivalent about Europe after the Empress Joséphine's death, yet the developing character of this ambivalence still needs clarification. Given the strength of his reputation in Europe, we are bound to wonder why he did not return there. In historical fiction, the distinguished Uruguayan writer Eduardo Galeano has performed the useful service of viewing Bonpland as a figure who identified with the Americas.[65] In order to make sense of him, he implies, we need to understand the development trajectories of southern South America.

Those development trajectories include the matter of French influence. While Bonpland never made his way back to France, the period of his long residence in South America was one in which French interests developed considerably there.[66] He started life at Buenos Aires in a place where France had not yet established consular agents nor formal recognition of the government. The explicit support for monarchism coming from the Bourbons placed French residents in Spanish South America under a general cloud of suspicion in the new and still unstable republics, something that carried practical consequences for Bonpland when he first arrived on the frontiers of Paraguay. Although Spanish America was generally a backwater for official French policy, the temperate parts of the region attracted significant immigration from France after independence, with the heaviest geographical concentrations occurring in the Buenos Aires region and in southern Uruguay. This was usually couched within the language of a civilizing mission, one that continued to see value in the efforts of Argentina's Bernardino Rivadavia and his Unitarian party to build a centralized government and to attract European immigrants.[67] Around seventeen thousand French subjects were estimated to be on Uruguayan soil by 1844.[68] Redress claims from settlers and exaggerated claims about the strategic importance of the Plata fostered by local French diplomats drew Orléanist France more and more into the region, first alone and then in concert with Britain. This was especially the case for the Montevideo region, where the French supported the Argentine Unitarians in exile in their opposition to the Argentine leader Rosas. As many as six thousand French sailors eventually served in the anti-Rosas campaigns of the Plata. In 1850, a British diplomat could describe Montevideo as having "now quite the appearance of a French possession."[69] Just what part Bonpland played in France's civilizing mission for the region is not easily determined, not least because some of the most intriguing aspects remain undocumented. But if French policy concerned many layers—including the local policies of diplomats in regional postings, questions involving settlers, and policy issues framed by intellectuals, for example—Bonpland had links with his compatriots engaged in all these spheres. For example, two French South American residents who made the trip back to France in order to argue the plight of fellow residents in the Plata, Frédéric Desbrosses and Benjamin Poucel, were both known to Bonpland.[70] The former had even contemplated a business partnership with him during the 1830s. Given a residence pattern focused on the Upper Plata, Bonpland's political intelligence was of most potential interest at times when France was seeking to assemble coalitions of support from interior regions against the dictatorship of Rosas. The overall impression is of a shadowy figure, one that was never far from where French policy was being made on the ground in the region. At the same time, as a holder of property at several locations in an unstable interior, Bonpland was extremely careful not to jeopardize his position by revealing his political sympathies too overtly in his writing. Things changed for him under the Second Empire, when the government of Napoleon III showed more overt ambition in relation to the region. By taking on a project of seed transfer from South America to North Africa, he was able to serve French imperial interests in an open manner, a task he accepted with alacrity and enthusiasm.[71]

Finally, this study aims to add to our knowledge of the southern South American environments, both physical and human, in the first half of the nineteenth century. In a region where knowledge of the human impact on the physical environment remains extremely thin for this period, Bonpland's detailed written concern for impeding destructive forms of land use holds great historical interest. His manuscripts contain numerous descriptions of changing appraisals of physical resources. Some of the most significant come in the eleventh hour of his life from southern Brazil. He wrote, after all, on the eve of massive vegetation change there, the near total deforestation of the southern Brazilian plateau associated with non-Iberian European colonization.[72] Official efforts to preserve the vestiges of the once immense South Atlantic forest have been taken in Brazil only during the past few years.

Bonpland stands apart from most of the travel-account literature, on which the historical study of South America has relied very heavily, in at least two ways. First, he managed to bring only a very little of what he wrote into print. Taking the field of paleontology alone as an example, however, the earth scientist Eduardo Ottone has recently argued that Bonpland's findings and collections "are worthy of the highest consideration and respect."[73] Second, he gave land use and environmental issues in specific regions his attention over decades, not days or weeks. Concerns for sustainable development are not new. Historical geography has a contribution to make to this important field of enquiry.

The remainder of this book has been structured following the shape of Bonpland's long career in South America. Like much of the plant material that he studied there, his life opened and closed in reflection of the external circumstances. Chapter 1 takes up the theme of his arrival in the city of Buenos Aires early in 1817. This reflected the bold decision to chance a career in the Americas in the early phase of the formation of nations there. Despite recognition of his talents from multiple quarters, the unstable politics soon undermined the potential of his scientific work. Still, this was a time for making new connections, of trying new things, including a journey to the former Jesuit missions. In December 1821, Bonpland's life took on an emphatically new direction as he was dragged into confinement in Paraguay. Chapter 2 treats a phase that is clearly one of a life in shadow, when Bonpland was a prisoner in Paraguay for the greater part of a decade. Here the scope for any bridging of regions, countries, or even continents was lacking. Bonpland's experiences in Paraguay have long been a subject of interest to scholars. In Chapter 3, Bonpland's life opened once more, especially through his visits to Buenos Aires during the 1830s. By 1838, there were signs that he was achieving a firmer material base, with the filing of a land claim for an estancia in southeastern Corrientes. Yet all these efforts were abruptly undone in the following year at Pago Largo, when the military forces of Corrientes were defeated. The decade of the 1840s was one of deep instability in southern South America. Ongoing civil war prevailed in Rio Grande do Sul, Uruguay was in turmoil, and governments rose and fell with depressing frequency in Corrientes. This was clearly no time for resource appraisal. In Chapter 4, the book accounts for Bonpland's main actions during this turbulent period, one in which he was pulled more directly into the politics of his American life. Chapter 5 deals with what almost looks like Bonpland's third South American career. The greater degree of political stability of the 1850s meant that he saw scope yet again to seek the development of rural resources. Readers will not fail to be struck by the astonishing level of his ongoing activity during the final decade of his life. Chapter 6 examines the circumstances of Bonpland's late life and of his death; it shows how he sought to continue his work until almost the very end of his long life. A brief concluding chapter summarizes the main findings and suggests themes for further research.

CHAPTER ONE

Return to the Americas

> I am glad to hear that you have alterd your intention of visiting South america again at present, we wish & you need not be surprised that we wish, to Reap the benefit which Science must deserve from your Past Labors before you engage in new ones.
>
> LETTER FROM SIR JOSEPH BANKS
> TO BONPLAND, 1810[1]

> Desde el viaje qe. hice en la america meridional con humboldt he tomado un afecto todo particular à los americanos. [Since the journey I made with Humboldt in South America, I have developed a particular liking for the Americans.]
>
> FRAGMENT OF A LETTER BY BONPLAND
> ABOUT THE EMANCIPATION OF THE AMERICAS[2]

Before he left Europe in 1816, Bonpland worked at what some have called a center of calculation. He had an international scientific reputation. Five years later, he was dragged in irons into Paraguay, an event that removed him indefinitely from contact with the learned world. This chapter surveys the circumstances under which Bonpland left Europe, and his plans for the Americas while based at Buenos Aires. Between arriving at Buenos Aires in early 1817 and the beginning of his long captivity near the end of 1821, a great deal of work was accomplished on multiple fronts. Parts of this work have remained unclear, not least through the loss of materials deposited by Bonpland before 1821 at Buenos Aires and Corrientes. In his painstaking efforts to collect Bonpland's correspondence, Hamy was able to publish only two letters relating to Bonpland's southern South American career before his confinement in Paraguay. This absence of letters reaching Europe serves as a marker that the character of the career was now intensely American as much as European.

The evidence survives that along the first decades of the nineteenth century Bonpland held an independent set of scientific connections and a separate judgment from Humboldt. Bonpland felt a strong attachment to the American cause. He was an explicit supporter of Bolívar's project, as Humboldt himself recognized. The decision to leave Europe seems to have been both drawn out and relatively sudden. In other words, Bonpland held to the idea of emigration long before he was prepared to take action. As early as 1810, Sir Joseph Banks, thinking explicitly about the future of the fieldwork accomplished with Humboldt, tried to dissuade Bonpland from his ambition of returning to the Americas.[3] Humboldt's correspondence with Bonpland contains similar intimations.

While at Malmaison, Bonpland appeared to have an assured future. His income in this period was considerable and he may have equaled the liquidity of Humboldt, who was bankrupting himself in the massive venture of publishing the results from their American journey. The death of Empress Joséphine on 29 May 1814 brought an abrupt change to Bonpland's circumstances. The idea of returning to America was soon a theme that loomed large in his correspondence with his relatives in and around La Rochelle. Bonpland announced to his brother Michel-Simon in July 1814 his wish to go to America in the following spring. He was tracking the political happenings: "I would prefer the Spanish colonies, but at this moment they are in combustion."[4] He was offered the chance to travel to Cayenne in September 1814, but this date was coming too soon to allow him the time to finish work on the volumes of botany for Humboldt and on the description of the rare plants on Joséphine's properties.[5] He saw staying in Europe as a sure route to stagnation.[6] Michel-Simon did not want his brother to leave Europe. And if he must, the elder brother wanted his sibling to have some concrete ideas about what he planned to do in the Americas.[7] Aimé Bonpland knew that his sister Olive was worried, and he confessed his own fear of crossing water, but he told her the following in June 1815: "Above all, the article on *arrivals* and *departures* in English newspapers is an admirable thing to read."[8] In his letters to the La Rochelle region, Bonpland relished the intellectual prospects offered by South America, telling his brother-in-law, the lawyer Gallocheau, "while you will study the antiquities of Saintonge [presumably meaning Roman influence in the Charente], I shall investigate those of the Incas and of the people who live from Chile as far as the Strait of Magellan."[9] By April 1816, Bonpland confessed to his sister that the work of finishing some publications and of settling important business (left unspecified in his letter) meant that he was forced to divide his time between Paris and London.[10]

In the years 1814, 1815, and 1816, Bonpland made various trips to London. These had mixed motives. He traveled ostensibly for scientific reasons, making comparative observations in major British herbaria and developing his links with English scientists. However, London was also the center of the Spanish American movements toward independence.[11] Bonpland's motives for visiting London included the aim of making his "relations with Bolívar more frequent and more useful to America."[12] The evidence survives of an impressive broader range of contacts with South American revolutionaries, and Bonpland carried out a broad range of services on their behalf in relation to the movement of books, a printing press, and even weapons. These people kept him informed in considerable detail about the geography of the progress of the revolution in the different parts of South America through their letters, some of which display considerable intimacy.[13] For example, in September 1814, Vicente Pazos relayed the news that revolutionaries had finally taken Montevideo, the key to the Río de la Plata: "We are all mad with happiness, and I believe you, like every other liberal person, will be too."[14] By 1815, the revolutionaries were competing for Bonpland's services. Francisco Antonio Zea, the vice president of Gran Colombia, wanted Bonpland to come to Bogotá to continue the work of the Botanical Expedition headed by José Celestino Mutis. Following Mutis's death, a quarrel developed between his nephew, Sinforoso Mutis, and Francisco José de Caldas (the Colombian lawyer, naturalist, and geographer who would be executed in 1816). Bonpland was informed that the botanical work was suspended on account of a shortage of specialized talent.[15] The representatives in London from the Río de la Plata had other plans. Mariano de Sarratea held the plan to bring Bonpland to Buenos Aires, where he would found and direct a botanical garden.[16] Zea carried word of Bonpland's interest in emigration back to northern South America, and Manuel Palacio, the young revolutionary from what is now Venezuela, wrote Bonpland the following: "Since Zea has spoken of your project of passing to America, everybody there is impatiently waiting for you—with your patriotism and your understanding, they think you will bring happiness."[17]

It is doubtful whether Bonpland had fixed ideas about which part of Hispanic America would serve best to make his fortune; through the long journey accompanying Humboldt, he had accumulated an impressive knowledge of the geography of the Americas. Although his most developed American connections lay with northern South America, most visibly in his friendship and support of Simón Bolívar, he was ultimately drawn southward toward the Río de la Plata, where his connection to Bernardino Rivadavia proved especially important. In the period from 1815 to 1819, Rivadavia undertook a broad-ranging diplomatic mission to Europe on behalf of the United Provinces of the Río de la Plata, a project that was intent on bringing Europe to South America. During his mission, Rivadavia developed very close ties with intellectuals in both Britain and France.[18]

Bonpland was one of these. He crossed the English Channel in the company of Rivadavia on 18 November 1815, giving the latter room for expounding on the attractions of life in the Río de la Plata, although the political reality of those provinces at the time was that they had become "no more than a loose confederation of semi-independent, imperfectly organized, and even semihostile states."[19] On arrival in France, they toured the port of Calais together, and they went on to help each other mutually in various ways at Paris. For Bonpland, the most important thing was that Rivadavia wrote a letter of recommendation on 21 October 1816 to Juan Martín de Pueyrredón, the supreme director of the United Provinces since 3 May. In it, he made reference to Bonpland's reputation for having traveled with Humboldt, to his merit in botany, and to his moral qualities. While Rivadavia wrote a considerable number of recommendations for European intellectuals bound for the Plata, in Bonpland's case he pointed out that the emigrant was a particular friend, somebody worthy of especially close attention.[20]

There is no evidence that Bonpland planned to settle permanently in South America when he left Europe in 1816. While he was to arrive at Buenos Aires well prepared, that does not mean he intended to stay in the region for good. More likely he sought to replicate the paths of other Rochellais bourgeois families by making his fortune in agriculture overseas, thus assuring an independence to pursue projects in France that reflected his taste.[21] Some of this comes through in the letter he wrote to Humboldt from Le Havre in November 1816. In his own account for Humboldt, Bonpland said that he went to South America looking to gain his financial independence: "If I do not succeed, I shall stay there buried on some hill or other, or in a beautiful valley."[22] That turned out to be a prophetic forecast. Writing to a French friend in 1850, Bonpland stated that he had not planned to be away from France for more than five years. It is unlikely he was quite as optimistic in the 1810s about the time frame needed to make his fortune.[23] In 1814, he had predicted to his brother that it would take eight to ten years.[24]

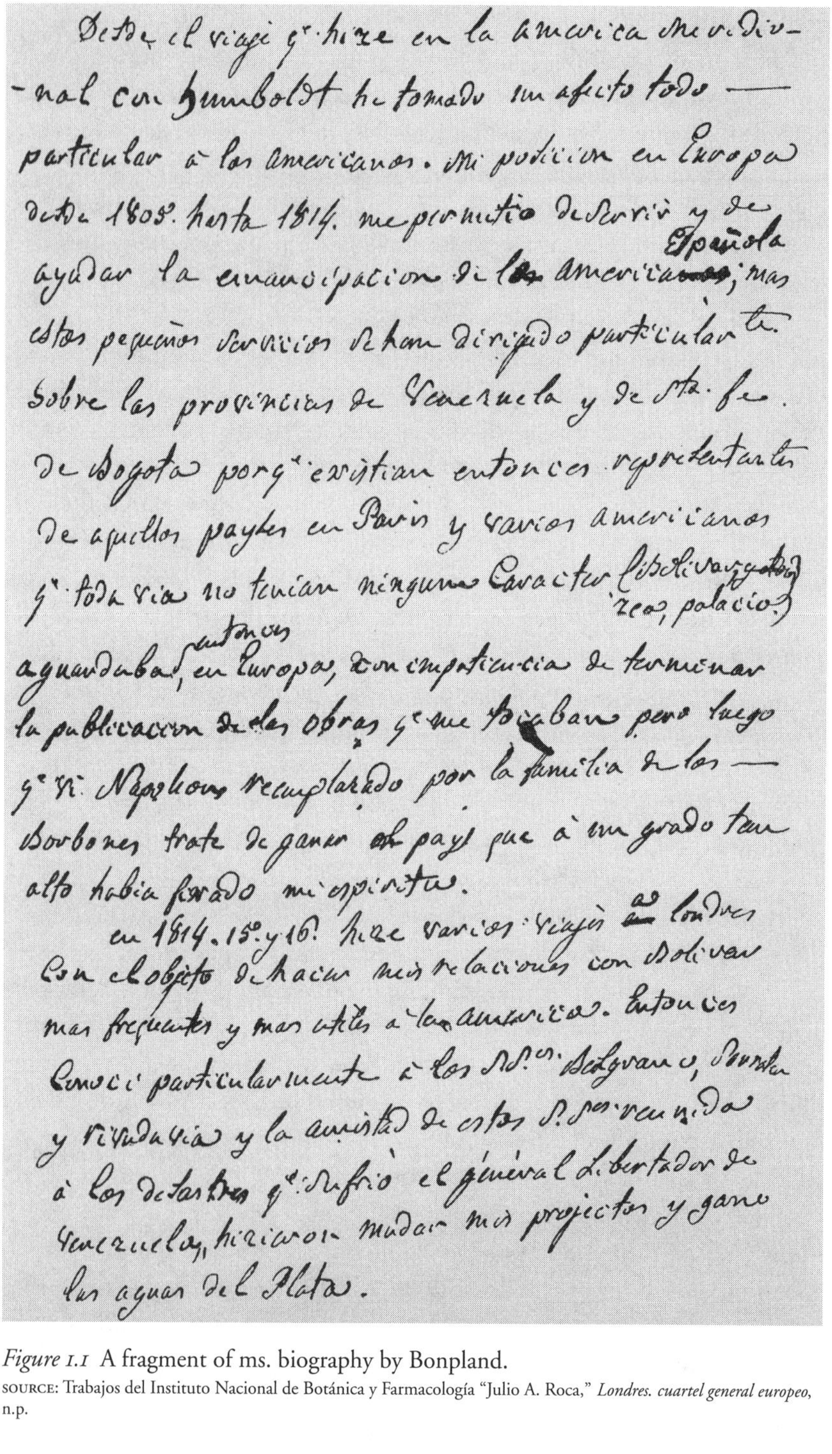

Figure 1.1 A fragment of ms. biography by Bonpland.
SOURCE: Trabajos del Instituto Nacional de Botánica y Farmacología "Julio A. Roca," *Londres. cuartel general europeo*, n.p.

Before Bonpland could quit Europe for the Americas, there was considerable business to resolve, including the tangled skein of affairs in connection with his wife Adeline.[25] In connection with publications, this related to both Humboldt and to Malmaison. There were also financial issues. A leading theme of the letters Michel-Simon Bonpland wrote to his younger brother in the period 1812 to 1815 is money, relating to the settlement of their parental estate. There are signs of strain in this correspondence, with Michel-Simon working to justify his management of the family financial affairs.[26] In 1815, Aimé Bonpland drew almost 8,000 francs from the preliminary settlement.[27] Before Bonpland left France, there was the matter of his account with Malmaison, where he received a third from Joséphine's heirs of what he reckoned he was due.[28] He also assumed a large debt at Paris for books destined for what the South American revolutionary Bernardino Rivadavia planned to be Argentina's national library, ultimately a stillborn project. When he quit Europe for South America, Bonpland left ongoing business behind him. Understandably, he left a proxy with legal authority at Paris, just as he would shortly do when absenting himself from Buenos Aires for what was designed to be a reconnaissance of limited duration of the Upper Plata. It is certain that Bonpland's finances were soon in a mess at Buenos Aires. It is usually assumed in the literature that Bonpland always had the benefit in South America of drawing on his annual French state pension, but this was emphatically not always the case.

Entering the Plata

Bonpland was an interesting catch for Argentina, and we can easily imagine the initial excitement both he and Buenos Aires society would have shared on his arrival. But what exactly was he going to do in a place where, though full of revolutionary spirit, "economic dislocation and social disintegration proceeded hand in hand"?[29] Incipient initiatives were already taken in this period toward the development of higher education, and here a Paris-educated botanist and medical doctor could play a useful role. For various reasons, this promise was never realized. The general nature of politics was not conducive. Add to this the spice of local jealousies, and the mixture did not take.

Work with Humboldt and then for Joséphine prepared Bonpland to think on a grand scale. Joséphine's properties of Malmaison and Navarre, both of which were developed after 1804, were by 1814 the leading repositories of the cultivation of rare plants in France, work in which Bonpland had been intimately involved.[30] The tendency to think big would never leave him, no matter how tightly external constraints stood in the way. This was surely the chief feature of his arrival at Buenos Aires, a sentiment echoed in the language of the local newspapers. Thus when the *Saint-Victor* anchored in the less than appealing muddy estuary of the Plata in early 1817, Bonpland did not step ashore alone. He was accompanied by his wife Adeline and her daughter from a previous marriage, Emma, as well as two assistants, Auguste Banville and Gabriel Lechêne. He also brought much other living material, notably plants drawn from Paris collections and nursery gardens in and around Le Havre. In making all this happen, the modern reader may gain the impression that the ship had sailed across a sea of red ink.

Bonpland's arrival at Buenos Aires was met by high expectations of what he could achieve there. A newspaper report noted in February 1817 that he enriched the country from the time of his first arrival "with a multitude of seeds, and with two thousand living plants."[31] All these were judged valuable "in a country where the vegetable kingdom is in its first infancy," a comment that reads strangely today. It reminds us that the political struggle for independence was perhaps seen as having an ecological counterpart—and that immigrants came in more than human form. There is no doubt that Bonpland was viewed as an especially valuable arrival, belonging to the "class of men" who held themselves apart from political controversies. He would not succeed in doing so for long, however. In a country of immense and fertile lands, here was an individual devoted to adorning nature with even more alluring qualities through the addition of even more plant life. Part of the dividend would come through medicinal plants. Another component of his efforts was agricultural, such that Bonpland was expected to "put into execution a method of practical agriculture, the fruit of all his observations in England, France, and America."[32] In addition, the authorities at Buenos Aires held in mind a plant conservatory, to be based on species introduced by Bonpland, those native to the region, and those that he could acquire through future research. Given the political upheavals that would shortly follow, such idealism makes almost painful reading today.

We do not learn of all the plant materials that accompanied Bonpland to the Plata from the contemporary newspaper account. But even a summary description points to a vast labor, which included fruit trees, vegetables, medicinal plants, pasture grasses, 150 species of vines from the Jardin du Luxembourg, and various types of willow useful for making baskets. In addition, the material included the Spanish carob tree (*Ceratonia siliqua*), commonly known as St. John's Bread, whose fruits were much appreciated for feeding livestock, especially horses, and all the sour-fruit trees of France. The newspaper editors opined, "we hope that our compatriots will know how to make use of this rich acquisition and propagate it in all the provinces."[33]

A few days later came a further newspaper summary outlining Bonpland's "eminent" scientific background in Europe, mainly on account of the work he had accomplished in the Americas with Humboldt. Botany was his forte, but the country would have made a "singular acquisition" if Bonpland were to communicate his researches to other sciences, "especially medicine, with which botany has an immediate connection."[34] The sentiment was clear that Buenos Aires had gained the talents of an immigrant of great scientific merit, with concrete achievements in both Europe and the Americas. As a friend of Simón Bolívar, Bonpland was also viewed positively as the first botanist and zoologist to visit Argentina since it declared its independence.

If Bonpland wrote his initial impressions of Buenos Aires, they have not survived. The British diplomat Woodbine Parish, who arrived a few years later, drew a sharp contrast between the negative impression of landing on the mudflats and the character of the city itself. In contrast to his unfavorable impression of Rio de Janeiro, Parish was struck by "the general cheerfulness of the white-stuccoed houses, and especially with the independent contented air of the people."[35] He also noted the dispersed nature of settlement in the city, claiming that it covered twice the area of any European center with an equivalent population.[36] The population was still relatively small, at around thirty-five thousand, but travelers stressed its international character.[37] There is good material on the social character of expatriate life in this period in the letters of the Scottish merchant William Parish Robertson. He makes the point that native and foreign society intermingled, especially during the first decade following his arrival there in 1818. The pioneers in the British community "mingled more with the Buenos Ayreans than did any of their successors."[38] In Robertson's view, social life was enlivened in this period by the British naval personnel of the River Plate station. Casting his eye more broadly across the foreign community, Robertson found "very few, scarcely any foreign families of note, except English, resident in the capital."[39] Bonpland and his wife constituted one of only two foreign families to receive specific mention in Robertson's account:

> I think it is so long ago as the year 1817, that Monsieur and Madame Bonpland arrived in Buenos Ayres from France. The fame, the talents, and the science of the one,—the accomplishments and fascinating manners of the other,—and the *savoir faire* and unaffected urbanity of both,—made their society to be generally sought in the capital of the provinces of the River Plate. From the early period mentioned, my own acquaintance with Monsieur and Madame Bonpland commenced.[40]

William Parish Robertson also noted the importance of the *tertulias,* or salons, in the social life of Buenos Aires. The Bonplands were part of this fashionable society. Along with other French residents or visitors, including the merchants Dominique Roguin and his partner, known today only as Meyer, Bonpland was closely connected with the salon run by Mariquita Sánchez. The famous Mariquita, subject of a widely read biography, was closely linked with French political matters. In the 1820s, Jean-Baptiste Washington de Mendeville, her second husband, became the French consular agent at Buenos Aires.[41] Bonpland knew both, though he was to become less fond of the latter. He also frequented the literary gatherings that took place in the city.[42] Vicente Fidel López left an interesting description of the literary salon of Don Tomás de Luca, an informed reader, at Buenos Aires. People would gather

> to hear what he had to say about the latest tract by Mr. de Pradt in favor of America and against Spain. . . . At other times he spoke about Benjamin Constant or Bentham, in favor of liberty and representative government. Or Mr. Bompland [*sic*], with his blue tailcoat, white tie and yellow vest, after placing his umbrella in a corner, often by the side of San Martín's sword, would enter with his air of angelical kindness, and was surrounded at once as the celebrated *iniciador* (initiator) of the beauties of our natural history. Every night he enchanted his listeners by describing some new useful and valuable herb he had discovered in his morning outings.[43]

The anonymous British author of *A Five Years' Residence in Buenos Ayres,* which deals with the period from 1820 to 1825, found prosperous Frenchmen in the city.[44] The idea existed (of which there are still echoes at Buenos Aires) that the Gallic settlers were more popular members of *porteño* (Buenos Aires) society than the Anglo-Saxons. However, the French community was politically divided between refugees from the Napoleonic system and supporters of the Bourbons.

The records that survive point to much energy on Bonpland's part. He was botanizing by February 1817.[45] The marginal notes in French in his botanical registers are rich in detail on the historical geography of plants. At Buenos Aires, for example, he noted that the blacks smoked marijuana in their pipes as a substitute for tobacco.[46] Asparagus had been cultivated at Buenos Aires for only two years, grown from seeds introduced from London.[47] And the registers are thick in comparative considerations about earlier botanical work undertaken with Humboldt. By 17 March 1817, he was planting seeds, many of them gathered at Malmaison two or three years earlier.[48] Others were given by individuals—great and small—resident at Buenos Aires. Within a year, Bonpland was able to send a consignment of southern South American seeds to Paris through the hands of Roguin & Meyer, the leading French merchant house at Buenos Aires in the period. Other shipments sent through Hullet Brothers were presumably destined for London.[49]

During his early period of residence at Buenos Aires, Bonpland considered various sites for the installation of a botanical garden, one of the leading features that had drawn him to the Río de la Plata. On 16 June 1817, he took up residence at the Quinta de los Sauces (in a district known as Hueco de los Sauces) on the fringes of the city, where he immediately began experimenting with the cultivation of indigenous plants.[50] Although the government at Buenos Aires was favorable to his plan of establishing a botanical garden there, Bonpland's decision to take on this particular property soon became highly problematical. The Bethlehemite fathers, who were the previous owners, did not wish to cede control. This drew Bonpland into a long and bitter legal struggle.[51] While he stayed in the conviction that he had bought the property outright for 10,000 pesos, the representatives of the Bethlehemite order claimed the right to charge an annual rent of 500 pesos. Neither side in the dispute showed any flexibility. Bonpland was determined to achieve a title to the property, as he had agreed with the government of the United Provinces. This insecurity over land tenure helps to explain Bonpland's readiness to travel beyond Buenos Aires as soon as political conditions enabled this.[52]

Another ongoing financial wrangle concerned books. There was clearly much misunderstanding about the circumstances under which Bonpland provided these for the public library at Buenos Aires.[53] On 15 May 1817, a meeting of the *cabildo* (city government) reviewed the state of progress in regard to the development of the public library. An agreement was made for a patriotic subscription destined to buy "the collection of useful works" offered for sale by Bonpland.[54] How much success he had with placing books by this means is not clear today. It is known that he had much further work to do. When he thought he had exhausted the possibilities of ready sale close to hand, he appears to have considered other locations, including across the estuary of the Plata at Montevideo. His key contact there was the scholar-priest Damaso Antonio Larrañaga, remembered today partly for the speech he made on the occasion of the opening of the public library at Montevideo on 26 May 1816.[55] Larrañaga was an admirer of Bonpland's work and of that being accomplished by Auguste de Saint-Hilaire. He claimed that Bonpland's work in South America surpassed any exaggerated notion of it. Every time he examined it, his admiration grew.[56] Bonpland wrote to Larrañaga from Buenos Aires on 13 February 1818.[57] He explained that on leaving Europe "several friends," left unspecified, had counseled him to bring books to the Plata, among which were many dealing with aspects of natural history. At base, Bonpland was using the commercial connections of the Roguin & Meyer French merchant house to develop a market for books. Thus he sent a list of titles across the estuary. Bonpland warned Larrañaga not to delay in his decisions since he had sent "a very considerable list of the works" to Chile. Larrañaga's reply is interesting on the character of the work he was undertaking (the Linnaean system). He did buy some of Bonpland's natural history books, including the zoology and comparative anatomy volume of the Humboldt and Bonpland journey and the *Tableaux de la nature*.[58] Two items that Larrañaga wanted, but that Bonpland was unable to send, were a book on barometric measurements (*Nivelaciones*) and a conspectus on longitude. The timing for book sales to Montevideo was awkward. The public library there was closed immediately after the occupation of the city by Portuguese troops in January 1817. It would not reopen before 1838.[59] This presumably closed a promising avenue for unloading Bonpland of books in quantity.

While resident at Buenos Aires, Bonpland began a long tradition of providing learned advice to South American governments. For example, he was asked to comment on the manuscript of an agricultural manual written by Tomás Grigera, "farmer in the suburbs of the capital of the United Provinces of South America," a work dedicated to the supreme director Pueyrredón. Grigera's work seemed calculated to interest Bonpland because it followed an emphatically practical bent. The minister Gregorio Tagle sought Bonpland's opinion of the study in a note to him of 27 December 1817. He wanted to know how the findings squared with the general rules of agriculture and with what Bonpland himself had found in Argentina. Bonpland reported his positive opinion on 13 January 1818. The value of Grigera's work, he stated, was not only to instruct local cultivators; it also instructed foreigners about the agricultural possibilities of the Río de la Plata. Bonpland recommended that the government should publish the work and then send copies to the learned societies of Europe, in the hope that they would send the necessary items for the agricultural development of Argentina. He did recommend changes to the manuscript, wishing to see some of the data organized in the form of analytical tables, which should include both the common and the scientific names of the plants in question.[60] In the following year, José Joaquín de Araújo, the minister of finance, visited Bonpland at his home, seeking his opinions about the work of the famous polymath, Félix de Azara.[61]

Bonpland had further scope to consider the regional possibilities for agriculture with the arrival of the South American Commission from the United States to South America in 1817–18, on board the frigate *Congress*. Sent to report on politics, the American party also included William Baldwin (1779–1819), the surgeon on the vessel as well as a trained botanist.[62] Baldwin's work collecting seeds and plants represented the first occasion that a trained botanist from the United States had undertaken official work in South America, "and it aroused much interest in the introduction of seeds and plants."[63] He was backed for the mission by the Columbian Institute for the Promotion of Arts and Sciences, the first learned society established in Washington. Baldwin came from Pennsylvania, a part of the United States with which Bonpland had gained some limited direct experience when returning from Latin America in 1804. There are a number of points of similarity in their careers. Both undertook botanical work of high caliber but published little. They shared medical training. Both had limited financial supplies, and both worked on government missions. One significant difference was to be that Baldwin would die young in 1819, while taking part in an expedition from Pittsburgh to the Rocky Mountains. Asa Gray maintained that "if he had lived, he would have outstripped all his contemporaries."[64]

Part of the official party from the United States arrived at Buenos Aires on 28 February 1818. Henry Marie Brackenridge, the secretary to the Commission, left an extensive published description of his impressions of the city in the volumes he published at Baltimore in 1819; these can be usefully supplemented by Baldwin's account in his unpublished journals. Like Brackenridge, Baldwin also quickly breathed in the revolutionary spirit of the city: "While at *Rio*, I could feel no interest in any thing but *plants*, &c. Here, I have unavoidably caught the enthusiasm of a people struggling for their long lost rights; and am involuntarily compelled to feel a deep interest in it."[65] Brackenridge and Baldwin were very quick to investigate the environs of Buenos Aires, making a Sunday afternoon excursion in search of open land where the latter could undertake botanical research. Starting out by passing through the Plaza de Toros, an important public space at Buenos Aires (two of Bonpland's French contemporaries would be executed there in the following year), they advanced to find evidence of a considerable degree of cultivation around the city. In 1818, it was already not an easy walk from the center of the city into open country: "We continued our walk about two miles beyond the town, but appeared to be no nearer the open fields, being completely enclosed on all sides, by what are here called quintas, which are large gardens of several acres, with abundance of fruit trees and vegetables."[66] This trip must have taken the two Americans into the vicinity of Bonpland.

On 4 March 1818, Baldwin met up with Bonpland for the first time. Given the latter's later preoccupations, it comes as no surprise that the first

Figure 1.2 The Plaza de Toros, Buenos Aires, c. 1820.
SOURCE: Reproduced from Vidal, *Picturesque Illustrations of Buenos Ayres and Monte Video*, frontispiece. Rare Books Division, The New York Public Library, Astor, Lenox and Tilden Foundations.

plant Baldwin mentioned in his journal is Paraguayan tea, described by Bonpland as "still a desideratum in botany."[67] Baldwin also spent part of 6 March with the Bonpland family, where communication was probably helped by the fact that Adeline and Emma were specifically recorded as speaking English, presumably a linguistic dividend from the time they spent living in London prior to their emigration with Bonpland to South America. Impressive though Bonpland's botanical resources seemed to Baldwin ("he has not less than 20,000 plants!"), he emphasized the key point that the Frenchman was not yet established, describing his herbarium as "in confusion, remaining in boxes & loosely tied up [with] no paper."[68] Bonpland showed Baldwin the land allocated for his garden and greenhouses, probably during a botanical excursion they undertook together during the afternoon.[69] Although time was limited, the two botanists clearly found plenty to discuss. First, Bonpland examined Baldwin's specimens drawn from Rio de Janeiro and around Montevideo, finding several new genera and many new species.[70] Another major theme of discussion was the resource potential of the pampas, and specifically the issue of whether trees would grow there. This was a current topic of debate at Buenos Aires. Brackenridge summarized the thinking as follows:

> It has been thought by the ignorant, and those wanting enterprise, that forests cannot be cultivated in this country; either because the winds, or pamperos, are so powerful as to blow them up by the roots, or because some one has fancied that the soil is incumbent on a rock so near the surface, as to prevent the roots from penetrating: but actual experiments are the best refutations of these absurd theories.[71]

Bonpland informed Baldwin that it was possible to grow trees on the pampas with success, outlining some of the specific types that worked.[72] Agriculture also received attention: "Baldwin learned from Bonpland that no iron ploughs were in use, that the ground was very soft, and that irrigation was not necessary."[73] Where ploughs were concerned, this comment reveals Bonpland was still thinking in terms of European farming. In the Upper Plata, cultivators turned to regional hardwoods in order to fashion their implements.

Baldwin and Bonpland parted with an agreement to continue their acquaintance by correspondence and to exchange botanical specimens. Although Bonpland did not spend much time with Baldwin at Buenos Aires, the latter clearly considered their meetings productive. He noted from on board ship that if an opportunity had presented itself to return to Buenos Aires, "this would have been principally to have spent a little more time with M. Bonpland, of whose knowledge I should have been glad to have availed myself."[74] Shortly before the *Congress* left the waters of the Plata, Bonpland sent Baldwin a large collection of plants. Interestingly, he also appears to have written a letter of recommendation for Baldwin to Bolívar at Caracas.[75] Subsequent to the visit by the commission from the United States, a number of exchanges took place. For example, the commissioner Caesar Augustus Rodney delivered on his promise to send Bonpland seeds of sea-island cotton, grown mainly in Georgia. Baldwin also sent 138 specimens of plants south to Bonpland in October 1818.[76] News of these interesting exchanges across the Americas had reached print by 1820 in a brief article on Bonpland published in the periodical *The American Farmer* at Baltimore. Had Bonpland remained at Buenos Aires during Rivadavia's administration, we are bound to wonder how much else could have been achieved. But his correspondent Baldwin was dead by September 1819. Rodney was appointed the first United States minister to Argentina, but he died soon after arriving at Buenos Aires in 1824.[77]

While the commissioners from the United States provided Bonpland with some new links, some long-existing ones also were maintained. When Humboldt wrote from Paris in 1818, he informed Bonpland in detail about the circumstances of his election as a corresponding member of the French Académie des Sciences. He also lamented the lack of contact, noting he had received only a single brief letter, while others had seen more.[78] The inference to be drawn here is that Bonpland was closer to some other individuals in France than to Humboldt. However, the 1873 Karl Bruhns biography of Humboldt used only extracts of Humboldt's 1818 letter, summarizing it in such a way that Bonpland appears negligent. However short and basic Bonpland's missive to Humboldt had been, it did announce, as the recipient knew, that his earlier traveling companion had written other letters from South America. While preferable to work with the French version of the complete letter, published by Hamy in his biography of Bonpland, English-language readers will have long been more influenced by the more accessible though misleading excerpts in the Bruhns biography of the much more famous Humboldt.

On 22 June 1818, Bonpland asked for the chair in natural history left vacant by the sudden death of Tadeus Haenke at Cochabamba.[79] He laid out his objectives in three parts. First, he promised to conclude the work of gathering all the plants indigenous to Buenos Aires and its environs. Then he would begin the work of publishing a description of the regional flora based on dry specimens. He would take his model from the volumes on American plants published in collaboration with Humboldt. These had appeared in a vastly expensive folio edition.[80] It is known from the budget Bonpland presented to the Congress of Tucumán at Buenos Aires that his plans for a "Flore des Provinces Unies de la Plata" (Flora of the United Provinces of the Plata) also involved a folio format, with the illustrations to be engraved on copper plates.[81] As a concession to cost, however, the engravings would not appear in color. On the other hand, this volume would differ from Bonpland's earlier work by printing the observations on plant properties in Spanish, so that local readers without command of French or Latin could draw benefit from the work. As a final point, he announced his readiness to begin journeys to the interior. By this means, he could increase the number of species present in his garden, designed to become the future botanical garden of the United Provinces (an ambition he would never realize). Collections of dried plants, minerals, insects, birds, shells, and fossils could be deposited in the national library, the university, or wherever else the government saw fit. He concluded with the observation that work of this nature would motivate him to fix his residence "forever in this country."[82]

Bonpland was appointed to the chair in natural history, but there was no salary.[83] Although he would never meet his publication objectives, there is no doubt that he held to a design building on the work accomplished earlier with Humboldt and at Malmaison. Earlier biographers maintain that Bonpland supported himself from the sale of fruits and vegetables. It is wise to preserve this practical vision of his life, although his interest in planting ran far beyond the immediate matter of earning a living. Plant description and plant geography were themes of constant interest throughout his South American career, not something he turned toward when other aspects of life seemed disappointing. From the outset, Bonpland botanized in and around the city of Buenos Aires. He also quickly built up his network of contacts who brought him interesting plant materials from parts of South America that he had not yet had the chance to visit. Most tempting of all were those brought down the major rivers in commerce from the Upper Plata. Just as Humboldt repeatedly emphasized his friend's extraordinary energy for botanical work, this also held true for Bonpland's later and independent career. We have impressive evidence of an active scientific career while at Buenos Aires. First, there are the botanical registers, which contain the raw materials for his flora of the United Provinces. Then there are the surviving drawings of insects and butterflies at Buenos Aires, prepared for Bonpland by his assistant Pierre Benoit.[84] These records are testimony of concrete achievements from his early work at that city. We have only cryptic references about how much manuscript material was lost from Buenos Aires during the period when Bonpland was later held prisoner in Paraguay. There is no ground to disbelieve his claim in 1821 to a French colleague, the botanist Alire Raffeneau-Delile, that he was ready to publish the flora of the United Provinces (presumably meaning of the Buenos Aires region and of the Upper Plata).[85] However, like much else in his career, the fruit of this enterprise was robbed by politics. We know this for sure through Bonpland's comments when he emerged from Paraguay.

Bonpland's manuscripts also point to a vigorous program of seed exchanges, with a high degree of internationalism. While earlier authors may be partly correct in claiming that he sold fruit and vegetables for his survival, it is clear that much more than market gardening was taking place in his life at Buenos Aires.[86] Many of the names in his records of seed exchanges are easily traceable. As earlier at Malmaison, there is a heavy focus on elites. The list of recipients includes a who's who of major politicians from Argentina (such as Juan Martín de Pueyrredón, Manuel Belgrano, and José de San Martín), England (Robert Staples, the unofficial British consul, and William Bowles, commander of the South Atlantic squadron of the Royal Navy), France (including General Dauxion Lavaysse, a high-profile Napoleonic refugee at Buenos Aires, and the naturalist Félix Louis L'Herminier at Guadeloupe), and elsewhere. We learn that Bonpland received pineapples from Rio de Janeiro from a letter he wrote in November 1818, in which he announced his plans to construct a greenhouse at Buenos Aires, yet another echo of life at Malmaison.[87] He also received indigo from Rio de Janeiro.[88] He would publish a description of this plant from the Upper Plata at Buenos Aires.[89] By means of such exchanges, Bonpland established a network in which people widely recognized his authority and brought him natural history materials, from locations as diverse as the battlefield at Chacabuco and the Atlantic coast of what is now Uruguay.[90] Oral accounts often kindled curiosity to see particular species in situ. In 1818, Bonpland was given seeds of the giant water lily brought down from Santa Fe. Although he would soon observe this plant for himself, he worked immediately from a verbal description to arrive at a sense of how to classify this most striking of South American plants.[91] A few decades later, the degree of public interest in this plant was massive. It was named *Victoria regia* in honor of Queen Victoria and became one of the wonders of the Royal Botanic Gardens at Kew. The South American giant water lily was an object of great curiosity for travelers along the Paraná River during the nineteenth century.

Another aspect of Bonpland's practical interests was industrial chemistry, which was not something that began with his southern South American career. For example, it was Humboldt and Bonpland who introduced guano to Europe. In the same year Bonpland prepared to leave Europe, he conducted experiments with Nicolas-Louis Vauquelin (1763–1829), who had been one of Humboldt's many correspondents along the American journey.[92] At Buenos Aires, he threw himself into the tanning business, a logical use of his talents. Here was the regional staple par excellence, and the standards of tanning were open to improvement. He became especially interested in Curupay (*Piptadenia rigidia*) trees, whose bark yielded tannic acid. The source of bark from these trees at Buenos Aires was Corrientes, but bark of superior quality came from the settlements in Misiones. A considerable incidence of this timber also occurred farther north, in the Gran Chaco and Paraguay. Although Bonpland was not pioneering the use of this species, he was seeking to improve the use of its major product. By November 1818, he was engaged in making tanning experiments; the detailed paper he wrote on these compared methods in use in Argentina with those in Europe and with what he had seen along the Guaira coast near Caracas when traveling with Humboldt.[93] Bonpland also wrote out the prospectus for a tannery in 1818. It was initially planned to be located in Córdoba, although the rationale for that place is never made apparent. His partners for this venture were to be Lozano, resident at Buenos Aires and the source of the necessary capital, and Chevalier, a fellow Frenchman and a tanner by profession. Bonpland was to deal with the accounting and the provision of raw materials, but above all he was to continue his research on the tanning principles of various vegetable materials, with the aim of speeding the overall process. The business began to function on a small scale on 15 October 1819 on borrowed premises, and the *quinta*, or factory, along with the services of three black slaves skilled in tanning, was leased on 1 December 1819. The establishment also used the wage labor of six peons. Taking over an existing tannery, the partners turned a profit very quickly. The initial capital for the business was 3,000 pesos, and by the fourth quarter of operation the surplus stood at 15,533 pesos, meaning that Lozano received his capital back and each of the three partners seems to have been in a position to draw around 4,000 pesos from the business late in 1820. The details remain hazy, but the tannery venture provides a potential explanation of how Bonpland was financing himself in this period at Buenos Aires.

We sense that life must have been turning more difficult for the Bonpland family by 1818. While Bonpland's own projects had not proceeded smoothly, there was also the issue of his wife Adeline's activities. She did not share the vast Spanish American field experience of her husband, and it is conceivable that life at Buenos Aires was rather isolating for her. The Bonpland home became a center of social life for the French community at Buenos Aires, at least for the immigrant faction that was loyal to Napoleon.[94] Adeline meddled in the domestic politics of the United Provinces, something that brought repercussions for her family. Through his wife's political actions, Bonpland was also compromised with the authorities at Buenos Aires. On 28 July 1818, he received a warning from the government about the "scandalous meetings" he permitted to take place in his house, where the measures and plans of the Argentine government were criticized openly by foreigners.[95] Some of Bonpland's own thinking comes across in letters he wrote to French emigrés while based at South American locations other than Buenos Aires. One of these was written in August 1818 to Montevideo, the current base of Charles Robert de Connaut, a former habitué of Adeline's salon and the publisher of the first French-language newspaper in Argentina, the ephemeral *L'Independant du Sud*. Bonpland commented on the challenges faced by French emigrés in South America. He thought Brazil probably offered the best economic prospects for them, when seeking to accumulate the resources to return to France: "What greater happiness for us than to free ourselves from all that we see here?"[96] Bonpland told Robert about arrests made at Buenos Aires in connection with an attempted coup. By this time, the Bonpland family was living in a small house closer to the core of Buenos Aires, thick by the San Francisco church.[97] A further sense of the challenges is revealed in a letter Bonpland wrote in November to Joachim Lebreton, the head of the French Artistic Mission at Rio de Janeiro.[98] He felt that his life at Buenos Aires could have been productive, but that it was damaged by party dissension. Those who did not embrace politics cared only for trade. Too much of the social fabric, he said, was about buying for two and selling for four. The instability of the government hindered his projects, and widespread plotting against the government made for unsatisfactory society. Yet Bonpland appears to have derived at least some satisfaction from living at Buenos Aires. He praised the climate in particular, claiming that, if Lebreton knew of this in person, it would cause him to move south from Rio de Janeiro. The main things missing for Bonpland at Buenos Aires were infrastructure and government.

It is probable that political instability motivated Bonpland to intensify his long-standing interest in fieldwork. No plant caught his attention more than yerba maté, or Paraguayan tea, the staple beverage of the region. In part, the interest was academic; when Bonpland left Europe, the scientific characteristics of the plant were, as he expressed it, "entirely unknown."[99] There was also, however, a major practical component. Originally planted by the Jesuits in their missions, following their expulsion from South America in 1767, supply of the tea depended on the ability to harvest it. In the few years since Francia's Paraguay held the virtual monopoly of this commodity, its supply was increasingly in question. Nonetheless, "interest in Upper Platine yerba remained avid in Buenos Aires."[100] There was a long-standing interest at Buenos Aires in the question of whether yerba grew closer to the city, with various claims current that it grew on islands in the Paraná and mentions of its presence close to the Uruguay River.[101] In particular, Bonpland learned toward the end of 1817 from Canon Francisco Belgrano that yerba plants were present on the Argentine island of Martín García. Reminiscent of his work with Humboldt on the various species of cinchona, the study of yerba had obvious strategic and commercial components. Visiting Martín García in December 1818, Bonpland found a small stand of yerba, though with no help from members of the local garrison, who were using the leaves for their domestic use.[102] Using Paraguayan workers, Bonpland turned some samples of the leaves into maté, which he claimed produced a beverage matching the quality of the best Paraguayan product. He also wrote the earliest scientific description of maté by a European scientist; based solely on part of the fruit, however, this description was incomplete, which can only have heightened his interest in observing the plant further.[103]

It is clear from his records that Bonpland was not the only person interested in yerba sightings close to the city of Buenos Aires. He summarized in considerable detail any efforts to transfer yerba from the Upper Plata to the environs of the city. For example, in 1786–87, the viceroy, Marqués de Loreto, had ordered the planting of two maté bushes from the Paraguayan missions inside the fort at Buenos Aires. They grew to the respectable height of eighteen feet, becoming, in time, an intolerable obstacle to the line of fire of a cannon. Based on what he learned from reading Félix de Azara, combined with contemporary opinion, Bonpland realized that the yerba of highest quality originated in the former planted *yerbales* (yerba plantations) of the missions. While the pueblo of Loreto had the best reputation, he observed, most of what passed as coming from there began, in fact, at Ñuguazu. The place he would fix on until the end of his life was San Xavier, in the valley of the Uruguay River. Subsequent to the Martín García visit, Bonpland communicated both orally and in writing with Pueyrredón about the prospect of bringing plants and seeds of yerba from San Xavier to Buenos Aires. While the government approved of the idea, politics stood in the way, something Bonpland could still not forget thirty-six years later.[104]

Near the end of 1818 Bonpland returned to Buenos Aires to find trouble in the form of the so-called "conspiracy of the French," the major political event of the year at Buenos Aires.[105] French notables of different types were present in various South American cities in the early nineteenth century. At Buenos Aires, a strong contingent was composed of a series of former French soldiers linked to Napoleon, implicated in a conspiracy to overthrow the government in Chile. They were tied in with the interests of the Chilean Carrera brothers, who were also seeking to inspire revolution in some of the interior provinces and plotting against the supreme director Pueyrredón. The conspirators left Buenos Aires on 14 November 1818, crossing South America by land on their way to Chile. But they were intercepted along their journey. Bonpland was questioned regarding his involvement by the judge José García de Cossio on 12 January 1819, an interrogation in which he demonstrated his innocence. However, some of his correspondence with people implicated in the plot was subject to multiple interpretations. There was also the issue of what had been discussed during the *tertulias* hosted by his wife. After a military trial, in which Robert de Connaut opted for Bonpland to make his defense, most of those accused were to be merely expelled from Argentina.[106] However, the commission asked for death by hanging for Robert de Connaut and for Jean Lagresse, which was cause for plenty of worry in the French community at Buenos Aires. A petition asking for clemency was organized, headed by the signatures of Antoine Leloir, who served as the unofficial French consul, and by Bonpland, widely recognized as the French resident of greatest moral authority at Buenos Aires.[107] Although Bonpland hoped until the last minute that the government would repeal its death sentences, this did not happen. Lagresse and Robert de Connaut were executed by firing squad on 3 April 1819. Daniel Hammerly Dupuy maintains that the changed mode of death resulted from the fact that the authorities could not find the hangman.[108] Bonpland was one of three French citizens called upon to reclaim the corpses and to organize the funeral arrangements in the church of La Merced.[109] The outcome of this case can have done nothing to elevate his appreciation of the politics at Buenos Aires.

Again the sense of strain emerges in a letter written in May 1819 to an old friend in Paris. The gardeners brought out from France were showing their dissatisfaction with life in South America. Gabriel Lechêne had quit. Auguste Banville needed chasing to accomplish any work. Bonpland made his common refrain that people did not work properly. Throughout his long South American career, he always had the highest expectations of those he employed, and they were rarely met. According to Bonpland, if Banville had done his job, both he and Bonpland would supposedly be at their ease.[110]

All the earlier accounts of Bonpland's life assume that he continued to draw the benefit of his French state pension of 3,000 francs per annum in South America. But this was not paid during the first years of his South American residence, a victim of transatlantic bureaucratic confusion. It is certain that the French pension was suspended in 1819 for bureaucratic reasons. Bonpland's legal representative at Paris, F. Forest, asked Humboldt to intervene with the French government, pointing out that the value of their joint "travels and literary works" were such that they placed Bonpland "in a truly particular exception in the eyes of the minister."[111] This was not to be the only time when Humboldt and his Paris circle of collaborators, notably the Delessert family (which combined interests in banking and natural history), were to play a critical role in securing the transfer of state funds from France to southern South America. Humboldt did intervene, although without success. News of the pension suspension went from Paris to Buenos Aires on 19 June 1819, but only reached Bonpland in person in the latter city over a decade later on 23 May 1832.[112] Bonpland was mired in the French bureaucracy, and the administrators of the Jardin des Plantes showed only a vague knowledge of his undertakings in South America. Colonel Maler, the French consul general to Brazil, claimed in October 1820 from Rio de Janeiro that Bonpland was receiving money from the government of Argentina.[113] This was incorrect. The consequences of the 1819 pension suspension played out until 1837.

The slowness of the French bureaucracy was never easily understood from the other side of the Atlantic. Somebody, possibly the French merchant Dominique Roguin, traveled from Buenos Aires to Paris in 1819 carrying legal papers on Bonpland's behalf.[114] This emissary made three unsuccessful attempts to see Humboldt; his negative impressions of the experience are contained in the Bonpland archive at Buenos Aires.[115] It is also noted there that by 1851 Humboldt took a very different stance toward his former traveling companion. Here are what George Sarton called "ugly suggestions," the idea that Humboldt sought the sole profit from Bonpland's work.[116]

Fieldwork of 1819 and the Journey to Paraguay

Following Bonpland's first visit to Martín García in December 1818, it is probable that an obsession with the characteristics of yerba was taking hold. He reviewed the folk knowledge at Buenos Aires about the locations where it was supposedly growing far south of Paraguay along various rivers and islands of the Paraná and Uruguay. He was certainly not the only person at Buenos Aires interested in the notion of planting yerba there. His manuscripts mention specific efforts to cultivate the plant around Buenos Aires, both in the late colonial period (1786–87) and in a contemporary effort undertaken by Pueyrredón since 1818.[117] Based on the various details, Bonpland resolved to visit the islands of the Paraná with care. While the popular imagination always connects Buenos Aires with the pampas, with good reason, it is important to remember that the city also represented the entrance to the immense amphibious region of the lower Paraná River, where the latter empties into the Río de la Plata. Using a vessel belonging to Francisco Belgrano (one of the numerous brothers of Manuel Belgrano, the distinguished politician), Bonpland traveled there in August–September of 1819. He spent around three weeks engaged in intensive work, motivated mainly by the search for yerba in locations other than on Martín García. Bonpland had gathered a great deal of oral testimony before engaging in this work, not least from a clerical member of the Pueyrredón family. He seems to have worked to offset the cost of the research by cutting wood for sale in the city.

The work began by revisiting Martín García, where Father Pueyrredón had prompted Bonpland to expect to find three maté trees. Bonpland and his party could find only two, presumably the same examples as those seen nearly a year earlier: "We scoured the island and found but two examples of the maté tree. Both of these are situated on the point of the island closest to Martín García Chico, where there used to be some huts. The big question is to know whether this plant grew there naturally, or whether it was introduced by one of the inhabitants of these huts."[118] He then visited the island's smaller neighbor, where he found nothing specific to his search. On the other hand, the vegetation of Martín García Chico made its own impression: "In a word, through the force of its vegetation and through the repeated cries of the parakeets, this little island has all the aspect of the tropical countries."[119] Navigating the narrow Río Melo in a canoe, the orange trees, bamboos, and multitude of lianas later reminded Bonpland of the dense forests of the Orinoco and the Casiquiare. He was always interested in the diversity of the vegetation and the animal life (noting that capybaras were abundant and served as food for jaguars, the South American big cats), but a clear sense of frustration is apparent in his field notes at not finding yerba. This is readily conveyed by the exclamation marks in the manuscript that follow references to unsuccessful researches. At least nine separate references indicate specific field surveys that failed to find yerba, when he clearly expected the opposite result. In order to gain a panoramic vision of the vegetation, Bonpland climbed to the top of the masts several times, where his dominant impressions were of bands of palms following the banks of the rivers and of the *pajonales* (grasslands subject to seasonal flooding). The party proceeded to the Botijas Islands (a protected area of the subtropical forest since 1958), another location where the search for maté was unsuccessful. A portion of these islands had already been logged, making it difficult to find woods such as willow close to the edges. Willows and laurels were used mainly as firewood at Buenos Aires, and also in the manufacture of chairs. Bonpland observed that a fortune was in store for the individual who could find an economic use for the many ceibo trees (*Erythrina crista-galli*).[120] In an elegy to the local nature, he wrote at length especially on the bamboos, the orange trees, and the birds. He maintained that the resources could be developed if the many creeks were cleared. But the dominant impression is of a huge research effort expecting to find maté that did not ultimately succeed. If the maté was not on the islands near the mouth of the Paraná, it was certainly somewhere else. The trip must have heightened Bonpland's wish to explore more of subtropical southern South America. His interest in the interior comes through in the manuscript by the fact that he was always questioning the passengers of any passing ships about the state of politics up the river.

Despite his interest in what he termed the "picturesque landscapes" of the Paraná islands, for one who had journeyed up the Orinoco, climbed Chimborazo, observed crocodile behavior from the vantage of tall furniture in Havana, and more, it is unlikely that Buenos Aires offered enough scientific stimulation to hold Bonpland's interest. The idea of extending the radius of his work into the pampas also had little to recommend it; Bonpland was always more interested in the plant life of the tropical than the temperate zones. In any case, hostile Indians still held sway over most of the pampas in this period. Waterborne carriage along the Paraná into the interior was an easier prospect, if not without its own complications. Paraguay appeared before him as a kind of mirage perhaps, and the key in all of that was yerba.[121] Not that yerba was the only plant that drew Bonpland's curiosity toward the north. For example, the raw materials he was using in the tanning business must have also kindled his interest in the resources of the Upper Plata.

By August 1820, the news had reached the United States that Bonpland was on his way to Paraguay "as soon as practicable." The source was presumably Bonpland himself, writing letters either to the former U.S. South American Commissioners or to individuals linked with these. Describing Bonpland as "a colossus of industry and science," an article in *The American Farmer*, published at Baltimore, related some of his recent news, which included the following most doubtful claim: "The Dictator, Francia, has granted him permission to visit the country which he governs, and of which everybody entertains high notions. He believes he will enjoy the high satisfaction of planting the cotton of the Fredonian states in the soil of Paraguay."[122]

In 1820, as rumors began to circulate in Buenos Aires that Bonpland was planning to quit the city for Paraguay, the Bethlehemites saw in this a tactic on his part to delay further the legal case, already slow. A new head of the order at Buenos Aires made an attempt to settle the land conflict with Bonpland directly, but the matter stalled over how to deal with the three years of occupation of the Hueco de los Sauces. Bonpland argued that a sum of 1,500 pesos sought as rent by the religious order should be applied toward the purchase price for the property. The struggle over land issues was an important facet of Bonpland's life at Buenos Aires; the legal case over the quinta left him in insecurity, and this no doubt impeded the full development of his botanical garden. Before leaving for the Upper Plata, Bonpland made José Manuel Galup his legal representative at Buenos Aires (23 September 1820), and this latter soon devolved the task to Manuel Joaquín de la Cuesta (26 March 1821). As so often in his South American career, the timing was not propitious. A few years later the context would change dramatically. Under the religious reforms of the Rivadavia government, the properties of the Bethlehemites fell under secular power. Bonpland's quinta reverted to the state by a judicial ruling of 17 July 1822.[123]

Bonpland probably saw before him a chance to mix science with commerce. He associated himself with the merchants Roguin & Meyer, the most important French commercial house in Buenos Aires at that period. Tulio Halperín-Donghi has noted that the adventurous phase of trade ended around 1820, but Bonpland's ideas for the Upper Plata certainly fall within this mold, as the correspondence of the Roguin & Meyer company and their associates makes abundantly clear.[124] It is not known for certain what motivated Roguin & Meyer to seek trade opportunities specifically in the Upper Plata. There is no doubt that Bonpland would have been an optimist about the possibilities. The explicit aim was to do business with Paraguay.

On 11 August 1820, Bonpland asked the authorities at Buenos Aires for a passport to go to the Upper Plata on a scientific journey.[125] This was issued by Marcos Balcarce, the interim governor, on 25 September 1820, a period when the political conflict abated.[126] The document authorized Bonpland to work "in the city of Paraguay," which ignored the lack of political control that the authorities held over this region. It also allowed for Bonpland to be accompanied by the illustrator Pierre Benoit, although this did not occur. While the political context at Buenos Aires was far from good—"1820 was the year of anarchy"—the resources were sitting there to be taken.[127] The French merchants probably hoped to emulate some of the high returns of the Robertson brothers. No doubt tired of the vicissitudes of life at Buenos Aires, Bonpland soon had a new patron in the offing in the form of Francisco Ramírez, declared supreme chief of the republic of Entre Ríos on 24 November 1820. This new political unit of brief life bound together the territories of current interest to Bonpland—Entre Ríos, Corrientes, and Misiones—the lands of the former Jesuit missions located between the Paraná and Uruguay Rivers. Bonpland left his family at Buenos Aires, plus books, papers, and collections. Much of these, he would never see again. While the decision to ascend the Paraná is sometimes depicted as an abandonment of his family, the evidence is not straightforward. It is probable that Bonpland left Adeline and Emma at Buenos Aires in a similar spirit as he had left them at London not many years earlier, surrounded by a circle of solicitous friends until his circumstances permitted the reconstitution of the family.

Bonpland left Buenos Aires to ascend the Paraná on 1 October 1820 (the low-water period in the river, with less exposure to storms), traveling on a sixty-ton vessel, the *Bombardera*.[128] He traveled in the company of two compatriots, Razac, from Bordeaux, and Breard, a native of Normandy. Navigating the sinuous rivers of the delta around Tigre brought positive impressions, reminiscent of "the most handsome English river that exists in our European gardens."[129] Human achievements rated a much less positive rating. The village surrounding the port of San Nicolás offered "le tableau de la misère le plus parfait" (the most complete picture of poverty).[130] When the *Bombardera* was temporarily embargoed there, it was Bonpland's legal representative Galup who took the measures necessary to raise the blockade. Roguin & Meyer warned the travelers from Buenos Aires that they would need strong reserves of patience to do business in the Upper Plata and to work in conjunction with the people there.[131] On the other hand, Bonpland received at least some written encouragement from Buenos Aires about the plan to approach Paraguay. It came from Victoriano Aguilar, a distinguished soldier who was close to Bonpland's family. In Aguilar's view, Bonpland had little to fear from Francia, despite the latter's reputation: "We do not doubt that the dictator Francia will extend every class of favor to you: He is an individual of grand talents, and an intellectual, whose objective is to leave his knowledge and enlightenment in this America."[132] These happy comments, doubtless well meant, must have given their recipient much cause for subsequent reflection.

The remainder of the journey to Corrientes is not covered in the manuscript, and any initial impressions Bonpland may have written of his first sojourn in that place appear not to have survived. Corrientes had suffered badly in the recent wars; two travelers who passed through in 1819 described it as "half in ruins" and "more like a deserted village, than an inhabited city."[133] Situated at the confluence of two major rivers, the Paraná and the Paraguay, around 750 miles from Buenos Aires, Corrientes had a population of around six thousand in 1820. It was the capital of a huge, sparsely settled province of marked ecological diversity, but it was poorly integrated with its hinterland. In contemporary descriptions, the lifestyle of the city reflected the slower pace of the subtropical heat. As William Parish Robertson, who saw it not many years before Bonpland, captured the local sensation of repose: "The custom in Corrientes, instead of *dressing* for dinner, is to *undress* for it."[134] The young Robertson also left an affectionate portrait of the Périchons, a South American family Bonpland met there in 1820, and with whom he maintained close links until his death in 1858.[135] They provided him with a secure domestic base, and a place to safeguard books and papers. As Bonpland later noted, the Frenchman Estebán Périchon had come to South America via Mauritius. He was the brother of the viceroy Liniers's mistress at Buenos Aires; perhaps to escape some of the scandal surrounding that connection, he became the postmaster general of the distant province of Corrientes. Périchon also held business interests, including links with the Roguin & Meyer company. While Bonpland left little written record of the Périchons, he was certainly very close to them. Dona Pastora Périchon continued to be solicitous about his domestic needs in the 1850s, thus it seems convincing for Bonpland to tell his sister Olive in 1840 that he felt like "the son . . . of the house," a comment reading more interestingly when we consider that the household contained six daughters.[136]

In January 1821, Bonpland made an excursion to the Indian village of Itatí, a place that he knew had a special profile in Corrientes. This was a modest journey. His retinue was made up of no more than a servant and a pack mule. Founded by the Franciscans in the late sixteenth century, Itatí was a *pueblo de indios*, or village of settled Indians, best known for its image of the virgin and her associated miracles. Kept in a humble church at the time of Bonpland's visit, today Nuestra Señora de Itatí is housed in an imposing basilica, receiving pilgrims in large numbers from across the Upper Plata and even beyond. The excursion gave Bonpland the opportunity to write extremely detailed portraits of the local agriculture.[137] For example, he described four types of manioc under cultivation and related six different methods of preparing them. At the time of his visit, the segregated Indian status of the settlement was under considerable stress, thus he found many examples of people taking advantage of indigenous rights. Bonpland wrote: "Poor virgin, how they abuse your innocence." Since the revolution, white people had been admitted to the settlement—people, Bonpland noted, who would have been classified as Spanish "even if they were Greeks or Turks."[138] Even so, the population had diminished. Bonpland left a very close portrait of a place in a general state of abandon. The impact of the revolution was such that agriculture was generally in difficulty. He detected little sense of improvement in how the crops were grown; tobacco, for example, a new commodity for the region, would have benefitted massively from the provision of irrigation when this proved necessary. The livestock resources of the region were also suffering, with an absolute shortage of horned cattle, sheep, and mules. Overall, he provided a strong sense of underdeveloped resource potential. In Bonpland's view, the key to greater production and regional wealth lay in a more just treatment of the Indians, the people doing the work.

Bonpland returned from Itatí to concern himself more with commerce for a spell, based at Corrientes. Near the beginning of February 1821, he wrote south to his colleagues, wishing to learn whether the *Bombardera* had reached Buenos Aires on its return voyage.[139] He also sought commercial intelligence from that city, seeking to know what, in specific, was worth sending downriver. Breard had left Corrientes on 19 January to return to Buenos Aires with a consignment of yerba.[140] This was a joint venture between Roguin & Meyer and the Frenchman Feliberto Voulquin. Mixing business with science, Bonpland also sent 107 species of seeds south with Breard, who was to give them to his wife Adeline, firm evidence that family ties had not yet fully broken.[141] In the draft of his letter, Bonpland crossed out the information that if he had known the sailing challenges of rafts formed from canoes before Breard's departure, he would have done all in his power to persuade him to exchange this type of vessel for a launch. Bonpland knew from a letter sent by Breard from Goya that sailing the raft was a matter of slow progress (it handled very poorly at times of strong winds).[142]

Bonpland presented a detailed set of accounts to Buenos Aires of the business undertaken since Breard's departure. The only item selling steadily from the company store at Corrientes was flour and a little sale of salt. There seems to have been an uncertain commitment to keeping a store open on a regular basis. Since Breard's departure from Corrientes, small ships and canoes had arrived from Paraguay carrying yerba (estimated quantity of ten thousand arrobas) and tobacco. Bonpland presumed that those with cash on hand would be able to buy at favorable prices within a few days. He was buying timber, including palms, and presented a report of five folio pages on the types of timber the Upper Plata offered for commerce at Buenos Aires. From the manifest details of the *Bombo*, a vessel that left Corrientes on 10 February 1821, it is clear that the company was sending south such items as beams, cart shafts, and axles. One specific timber identified is the hardwood Guayaibi (*Patagonula americana*). Other types included the closely related *palo de lanza* and *palo amarillo* (*Phyllostylon rhamnoides*). Bonpland also wrote of a *jangada de palmas* (log boom) at Ñeembucú in Paraguay. At opportune times in the flow of the river, he laid plans to move this to the port of Las Conchas, on the outskirts of Buenos Aires.[143] There, the boom would have been broken apart and the timber sold for furniture manufacture and construction.

A few days later, Bonpland noted people had been buying yerba and tobacco from the Paraguayans. The *Bombo* left Corrientes on 10 February as part of a convoy: "This evening or tomorrow the four small Paraguayan ships should depart and one of them will bring you my packages. The *Bombo* left in convoy on 10 [February]. That is to say with the Entrerriano squadron and several commercial ships. All are loaded with soldiers and they are returning, it is said, to Bajada." Bonpland believed that if he had money on hand, he could have done good business, with business conditions liable to change very suddenly. Presumably short of working capital, he had tried in vain to barter salt, flour, and oil (probably vegetable or animal) with the Paraguayans against their products. He predicted more goods would soon be arriving at Paraguay, and he hoped to be able to buy them this time. It would also be easy, he noted, to buy tobacco in the interior of Corrientes.[144]

Various letters were sent up the river from Buenos Aires, providing comments on the changing state of the commercial operations at the market. In January 1821, Razac, back at Buenos Aires, told Bonpland and Breard that while sales had not resulted in a profit to their projected degree, the objects brought down the Paraná had amply covered their costs. Roguin & Meyer were preparing ships to send to Corrientes, including a vessel capable of carrying nine thousand hides.[145] In February, Roguin & Meyer also commented on the products that Razac had brought to Buenos Aires. While timber had sold slowly, and handling costs were high, the company had shown a profit. The senior partners provided information on the movements of other French merchants. Chevalier (an earlier partner of Bonpland in the tannery business at Buenos Aires) was on his way to Corrientes in order to set up a similar establishment there. He was said to be a very bad payer. Roguin & Meyer had been able to obtain nothing from an Alexandre Duran, and they warned Breard to be "as hard as marble."[146] The following month, Roguin & Meyer wrote again from Buenos Aires. Roguin and Breard were awaiting repairs to a *sumaca* (a "smack," or sloop) prior to joining Bonpland in the Upper Plata. The yerba brought downriver by Breard was selling slowly. The firm seemed more interested in finding hides and specific kinds of timber; Breard was designated to brief Bonpland on the specific types sought at Buenos Aires once he rejoined him. Razac, who had recently brought products to Buenos Aires from the Upper Plata, was now at Montevideo in order to buy a brig, which he planned to load with salt-beef for Havana.[147]

The Roguin & Meyer merchant company was clearly not fixed on any single commodity, as the partners tried to respond to the shifting market conditions. Despite their frequent complaints about transport costs (and the handling costs of timber), they claimed to be making profits. They worked with a considerable network of Frenchmen, of which Bonpland was a part, but they also needed other reliable contacts. Thus they advised Bonpland to try doing business in regional products with Juan Andrés Veron, the proprietor of an estancia near Corrientes.

While based at Corrientes, Bonpland was projecting his plans for the missions, but also thinking back to the work left at Buenos Aires. Writing south in April to his friend José Joaquín de Araújo, then the Minister of the Treasury at Buenos Aires, the main themes of his letter were the fate of his quinta, the care of his collections, and the future of a projected natural history museum for the Río de la Plata. He outlined the considerable collections he had already made, and he sent seeds south, including those of the *algarrobilla* (*Prosopis affinis*), used to tint materials black. He asked Araújo to deliberate firmly about the location of the natural history museum at Buenos Aires. The minister should prepare to receive shipments of materials: "I have some fruits in spirits, a good number of minerals, some insects, good specimens of woods and a lot of plants."[148] Combining the collections Bonpland had brought from Europe with those already gathered in the Río de la Plata, the potential was present to develop *"un gabinete más que regular"* (a more than fair cabinet of collections). As always, finances were a problem, partly on account of the nonpayment of his salary as natural historian by the government of Argentina. Bonpland announced his plans to leave for the missions within a few days, where he planned to colonize. He described the country as calm, "and there is no risk whatever in going through there." In a spirit of blithe optimism, he estimated he would be in Misiones for around two months before returning to Buenos Aires with collections.

Although Bonpland was away from Buenos Aires, his name was much in discussion there during early 1821 in connection with the reorganization of medical teaching, which sought to move medical studies away from the military and its Instituto Médico Militar into civilian hands. The government at Buenos Aires enthusiastically proposed Bonpland to fill the chair in materia medica, at an annual salary of 1,000 pesos fuertes.[149] The matter was placed before a tribunal, with the government sensitive not to override the qualifications of any local candidates, if any existed. The tribunal reported very favorably on Bonpland on 22 February 1821, based not only on his good reputation with the medical authorities at Buenos Aires, but also on his fame among European intellectuals. The three members of the tribunal noted that the famous Jean-Louis Alibert had dedicated his celebrated study *Elementos de terapéutica y materia médica* to Francisco Zea and to Bonpland in gratitude for the knowledge they provided.[150] Bonpland's contributions soon became evident to anybody reading Alibert's book. On numerous grounds, the tribunal reported, there was no individual better suited to fill the post.[151] The findings of the tribunal were approved, but despite there being no one in the whole of Argentina whose medical fame compared with that of Bonpland, a campaign against his nomination to the chair was nonetheless mounted.[152] The year 1822 saw the beginning of the Faculty of Medicine in the newly formed University of Buenos Aires. By the time Bonpland received word of the recognition of his medical talents at Buenos Aires, he was probably heading from Corrientes to Misiones.[153] After exploring the settled parts of Corrientes as a naturalist, he sought a passport in May 1821 to continue his work in the former Guaraní missions, those situated on the left bank of the Paraná, which belonged in popular perception to Corrientes.[154] Bonpland explained the nature of his mission to Ramírez at Corrientes, and the latter provided practical support to his endeavors.[155] Ramírez's main instructions were that Bonpland should study with "*suma atención*" (close attention) the state of the *yerbales* and the numbers of Indians present in the region.[156]

Misiones in 1821 was a yerba-rich area of once-great wealth, but it was also something of a demographic vacuum. The bitterly contested region was of commercial interest to various parties and presented uncommon strategic significance. After Paraguay declared its independence, John Hoyt Williams notes, Misiones "was alternately despoiled by Artigas, *Litoral* caudillos, Indians, bandits and expeditions from Brazil."[157] He argues elsewhere that "the land bridge between Paraguay and Brazil [was] one of the most hazardous terrains in the hemisphere."[158] Francia had evacuated Candelaria by 1815, but in 1821 the administrative geography of Misiones was still in flux. Various political groups coming from the south (led by the Federalist regional leader José Gervasio Artigas and General Ramírez) and from Brazil disrupted the settlement patterns of the remaining Guaraní Indians after 1817, leading to their general dispersal.[159] At the time Bonpland contemplated traveling there, the missions formed an administrative department of the Entrerriano Republic. After the defeat of the Guaraní caudillo Francisco Xavier Sití at the Paso de São Borja, Brazil, on 13 December 1820, the indigenous presence in Misiones focused on the lands west of the Aguapey River. The former missions in the old Jesuit department of Candelaria were in the hands of an Indian leader (Nicolás Aripí, based at Santa Ana), who was backed by another Indian cacique, or chief (Juan Nicolás Christaldo, based at San Ignacio Miní).

Bonpland left Corrientes for the missions on 11 May 1821, traveling with his compatriot Voulquin. He described the country as truly dreadful in the winter, with water near continually under the feet. In summer, on the other hand, this part of Corrientes was dry and it suffered from excessive heat. This was a hazardous undertaking, in part because he was traveling into a disputed frontier area with Paraguay.

He traveled first to the expressively named Caacatí (the toponym means "stinkweed"), commenting on the agriculture along the journey. Based on his observation of the spontaneous presence of indigo, and the fact that sugarcane, cotton, and tobacco all did well, Bonpland concluded that everything pointed toward a fertile region, but he still held a negative impression of it: "Human arts have done nothing; nature and the climate are all. The people cultivate just enough to live on, and since manioc, potatoes and maize yield a lot, the inhabitants work extremely little."[160] In other words, the inhabitants focused only on subsistence needs, thus the climate was held responsible for any additional developments. A clear image is presented in Bonpland's travel account that agriculture was underperforming. In addition, his impressions of the settlement of Caacatí itself were not especially positive: "One finds there absolutely nothing for the necessities of life, and even less for the comforts. At this time, the residents are living from meat, milk and mandioti."[161] Surrounded by lakes at almost every turn, Bonpland commented on the high level of humidity of Caacatí even in the winter. Temperature readings he took along a week averaged twenty-five degrees Celsius. This suave climate even in the winter was identified as advantageous for the growth of subtropical crops. Part of the commercial appeal in Corrientes was the potential of substituting what had formerly come from Paraguay. The most common tree was the Yatay palm, of which there were entire forests. This species was taken as an indicator of superior soil quality, thus plantations of crops were usually established here. The newest crop around Caacatí was tobacco, something the cultivators had not been allowed to grow in the colonial period.

Bonpland spent a week at Caacatí, waiting to hear the results of an expedition headed by Captain Gregorio Gómez of more than one hundred troops sent in against around forty Indians, who were supposedly bothering people engaged in the collection of yerba. Evaristo Carriego, the military chief of Corrientes, warned Bonpland that it was too dangerous to advance into the missions before learning with certainty the outcome of the expedition.[162] News remained frustratingly imprecise, but the oral reports Bonpland gathered left him in no doubt there had been plenty of indiscriminate killing. In his notes, he questioned that such "sensitive missions" could ever be successful when they were confided to "men without knowledge, without morality, and above all without the slightest notion of human rights."[163] While waiting for solid news, an informant gave Bonpland an account of contemporary life in the missions, made from San Ignacio Miní, where Aripí made his camp: "The account this individual gave me is sad. These men cultivate nothing, and thus have nothing much to eat. They are living off oranges and horsemeat."[164]

Stranded at Caacatí, Bonpland wrote several times to the caudillo Francisco Ramírez.[165] He told Ramírez that he had left Corrientes for the missions, a journey he had wanted to make for several years. He intended to carry out the plan of work he had laid out earlier for Ramírez at Corrientes. Part of this was to assess the resource potential of the missions, optimistically described as without doubt "the most fertile" part of the republic of Entre Ríos and thus "the most susceptible for the enrichment of the country."[166] Not surprisingly, Bonpland was carrying seeds. He himself planned to sow cotton of superior quality, indigo, and tobacco, and he would give other seeds to the Indians, in an effort to animate them toward work. Once the initial reconnaissance in Misiones was completed, he planned to meet up at Corrientes with Roguin and Breard and the supplies they were bringing up from Buenos Aires.

On 5 June, Bonpland received oral news at Caacatí from Aripí. This came from soldiers returning from raids against Indians. Aripí sent word to Bonpland indicating how keen he was to see him arrive in the missions, which, Aripí maintained, were "very rich in plants useful to medicine."[167] In light of the uncertainty, such news should have stiffened Bonpland's resolve to move on. In a second letter to Ramírez from Caacatí, written shortly before the definitive departure, Bonpland told him he was taking steps to redress the food shortage in Aripí's camp. He carried maize and potatoes with him, for eating and for sowing, along with seeds of mandioti, a "most useful plant." The diet in the camp was described as reduced to the eating of mules and horses. Bonpland's aim was to have Aripí accompany him around the missions and the forests containing *yerbales*.[168]

Bonpland in Misiones

The definitive departure for the missions came on 9 June 1821. Bonpland and Voulquin traveled with 2 carts, 20 oxen, 4 milk cows with their calves, 8 cattle to serve for food, 10 mules, 12 horses, and 10 servants. After Caacatí, there were more signs of the dead than of the living, in the form of *taperas*, or places of earlier inhabitance marked by the sign of a cross. The journey began with descriptions of such former Jesuit missions as Santa María that no longer amounted to much. Within around a week of travel, however, there was a sense of changing vegetation:

> The country is becoming bit by bit greener, more wooded and more cheerful, the clumps of woods to the south and the east are increasing and becoming larger, and always to our left and the north we distinguish the course of the Paraná by the high canopy trees which cover its banks and the islands. In addition, we can see the Paraguayan shore which is more elevated than this one here.[169]

On 20 June, they could see a chain of hills in the distance, which included such places as Santa Ana and Candelaria. Bonpland took the Pindapoi as the entrance to the missions, a river that could suddenly rise by ten to fifteen feet, blocking the passage of travelers. He examined the "*grands restes*" (impressive remains) of a wooden port built in Jesuit times, something he considered useful to reestablish.

By 22 June, he was near Candelaria, and saw for the first time "the sad vestiges of one of the largest mission villages."[170] Burned by the Paraguayans, the buildings were in a state of ruin. Not a single house was in a truly habitable state. Bonpland took consolation in the state of the orange plantations, which had "resisted the axes and fire of the Paraguayans." On the afternoon of the following day, he found the yerba maté plantation, west of the village, which he surveyed with evident interest. He counted 50 rows, planted from east to west, with each containing 250 plants. This venture at Candelaria originally had held 12,500 trees, but now only a third were left. Given the uneven quality of what remained, plus the presence of invasive species, it would need considerable restoration before it could be worked. He was clear that any attempt to harvest from the Candelaria plantation in its current state would lead to its definitive loss. Finding a multitude of very tall trees that had escaped fire, notably in a deep ravine forming the part of the plantation opposite the Paraguayan fort, Bonpland argued that these could serve to supply the seeds for new plantings. He wrote an optimistic letter to General Ramírez about the attractions of Candelaria's location; it detailed the work of restoration necessary to bring the *yerbal* back into production, estimating that would bring a production of at least 1,200 arrobas.[171] The few people who knew the plantation had not been bold enough to work it, probably because of its position opposite the fort. In the journey from Caacatí to Candelaria, Bonpland had not met up with any Indians. He learned from oral testimony that although many indigenous people had taken to the woods through fear, they were keen to resettle and to work.

Accompanied by a Paraguayan guide, Bonpland went back into the Candelaria plantation on 24 June, a visit motivated by the search for the type of yerba known as *caa miní*, the finer quality yerba for which the Jesuit missions had been famous.[172] Shortly after entering the plantation, they came across a large *caa miní* tree, and the Paraguayan set to work cutting samples: "I was soon convinced that the manner of cutting yerba is very bad and bereft of all forms of knowledge. My man axed from right to left, splintering the greater part of the branches. We took nine bundles from this tree and to my great satisfaction we found there some truly mature seeds." These seeds gave him "the pleasure of describing the fruit of this precious plant of which there only remains the flower to distinguish."[173]

The further he advanced, the more impressed he seems to have been by the state of the Jesuit remains. But much was in a state of abandon: "In Jesuit times, you could go from Loreto to Santa Ana by carriage." This was certainly no longer true. Near Loreto, Bonpland visited an octagonal calvary, located at an elevated point. It connected with Loreto through an alley of bitter-fruit oranges, described as of an "admirable beauty." However, the absence of cultivation had rendered the path extremely difficult: "The multitude of parrots and macaws inconvenience the traveler by their shrill and disharmonious calls."[174]

Toward the end of June, the travelers arrived at Aripí's camp, the base of the Indian leader allied with Francisco Ramírez. While Bonpland worked hard to do business with the Indians, his impressions of anything relating to Aripí were mixed from the start. He seems to have been singularly unimpressed by the state of the material culture there, something for which he had received some forewarning from the oral reports on the state of the local food resources: "God, what a camp! On the side of a fairly high mountain, and where the trees have been cleared, there are twenty wretched *ranchos* made of straw. That is the camp. There is not a single man there who is completely dressed; the majority would be completely naked if they did not have a *chiripá*—dirty and often torn—to cover their sexual parts."[175] Finding Aripí absent, the party spent the evening close by San Ignacio Miní at the Capilla de la Concesión, where the peons joined in the dancing with the Indians. Bonpland was impressed at the skill with which some of his Indian staff handled the European dances of very complex choreography. His comment reveals his still limited sense of indigenous capabilities.

Bonpland's first meeting with Aripí in person came on 29 June 1821.[176] Arriving at his camp to find an escort of soldiers, a display of the flag, and a virgin girl dressed in new clothes and garlanded with leaves from the Peruvian peppertree (*Schinus molle*), Bonpland and Voulquin were received with the "greatest distinction." Entering into the chamber, Aripí sat down on a bench, his hat still on his head, and spoke by means of an interpreter. The meeting cannot have been an easy occasion for Bonpland, not just on language grounds, but because Aripí also chose the occasion to discipline a subordinate, who was condemned to three days of confinement in his room. Through the help of the *linguarace* (interpreter), Bonpland and Voulquin described the merchandise they had brought from Corrientes, and the terms they were prepared to adopt when exchanging these goods for yerba. Although negotiations required more time, they decided against spending the night at the camp: "It was growing late and since they eat nothing other than mule in the military headquarters, we judged it better to return to Santa Ana, where we had left the greater part of our people and our baggage."[177]

Following this initial meeting with the commander, Bonpland and his retinue continued the work of surveying the former missions, interested mainly in the state of the former planted *yerbales*, in an effort to decide which locale would work best for the establishment of a colony. Aripí helped with the provision of Indian guides in return, notably, for a visit to the port at Corpus Christi. At San Ignacio Miní, everything breathed an air of grandeur not seen in the other missions. The landscape between San Ignacio Miní and Corpus Christi was clearly striking, as Bonpland used the word "magnificent" twice within a few lines in his efforts to describe it. They could see in the distance a chain of very elevated "mountains" (more a series of hills, in fact), which Bonpland was sure would contain "thousands of treasures," thinking no doubt of botanical and mineral resources. Although much destroyed, he considered Corpus Christi even more beautiful than the previous missions visited: "What is still admirable is the view from the peristyle of the church. The eye penetrates very far into the mountains of Paraguay and it lords over the Paraná, which runs very close to Corpus."[178]

Bonpland was not quite so much the pioneer with yerba in Misiones as is sometimes presented. In his own later testimony, when he arrived at the missions, a considerable number of Correntinos and Indians had been working the *yerbales* for two years in Francia's full knowledge.[179] Some concrete evidence of this claim is found in Bonpland's travel account of the journey to Paraguay, in the 13 July description of the yerba plantation at the Jesús mission. He found there a yerba workshop operating on the instructions of the commander at Caacatí and made a brief description of the Indians who were doing the work.[180] By the middle of July, the circumstances of the field reconnaissance were growing very difficult on account of heavy rains. Bonpland spent the night of Bastille Day covered by a hide, sitting on his night sack with his back propped up by a fallen cedar.[181] Given the dismal weather prospects, he chose to journey back to Santa Ana, a trip he accomplished alone and by mule. It was a journey high in risks, which he confided very clearly to his diary. While he did not experience his fear of being attacked

Figure 1.3 The preparation of yerba. Drawn on site by Alfred Demersay.
SOURCE: Reproduced from Demersay, *Étude économique sur le maté*, opposite p. 15.

by a tiger, his mule gave considerable difficulties, not least by falling from beneath him onto a piece of flat sandstone. After numerous other trials with the animal, and with the route, he arrived at the end of the day at Santa Ana, wet to the bone.[182]

Back at Santa Ana, Bonpland was disappointed with the letters he received from Captain Aripí. The Indian cacique Juan Nicolás Christaldo, based near San Ignacio Miní, also wrote in the capacity of deputy to General Ramírez, offering to be of help. Bonpland theorized that Christaldo may have been responsible for the tone of Aripí's letters. The surviving correspondence between Bonpland and Aripí reveals strains of misunderstanding between these two individuals. Aripí seems to have taken the stance that Bonpland, on arriving in the missions, had not treated the commander in a way that his position merited, an issue that hinged on the manner of presentation of his passport. While Bonpland was optimistic that a meeting in person would clarify his intentions, his inability to speak Guaraní was a major obstacle to communication. Forced to work through an interpreter, he found it to be a problem, as he wrote to Christaldo, that he could not transmit directly to Aripí the ideas for improvement that had drawn him to the missions.[183] The chance for a direct meeting with the caciques came on 18–19 July, a time marked by very cold weather. The Indians arrived in the afternoon and stayed at Santa Ana overnight. From Bonpland's laconic notes in his travel journals, we sense this meeting was also not without its challenges: "After dining, we got them drunk, and the chief pissed in his bed, or, rather, on his table."[184]

Aiming to develop a steady flow of trade in yerba, Bonpland set out the terms he and Voulquin expected. Working steadily, Bonpland reckoned a man could gather three arrobas (approximately 75 English pounds) of yerba per day. Supposing it was only two, paid at the rate of one peso each arroba, this would give a rate of pay of two pesos daily. Working ten days a month would give an income of 20 pesos, "that is to say more than a *capataz* [ranch manager] in Buenos Aires, Corrientes, Caacatí, and any other part of the world who works all month."[185] Bonpland was trying to obtain two hundred arrobas of yerba as quickly as possible, so that their carts could leave the missions and return with the seeds (beginning with manioc) the colony would need for planting. In setting out their trade proposals, Bonpland and Voulquin also made presents to Aripí.

On Sunday, 22 July, the weather was cold, with the thermometer at Santa Ana registering a temperature of minus five degrees Celsius. Bonpland worked in the yerba plantation at the mission, finding there at least fifty yerba trees. He maintained that this plant could be propagated if planted in beds, and he planted cuttings in the garden at Santa Ana, knowing, however, that these were unlikely to work on account of the cold. Perhaps thinking back to the resources of Malmaison, he speculated that progress would be certain if he had on hand a greenhouse for the multiplication of the maté plant "as we multiply all the others that come to us in Europe from distant lands and from every type of climate."[186] Seeing lengthy shoots of maté, he concluded that the plant must have had a prompt vegetation when properly exposed to the light and carefully cultivated. On the same day, he chose what he described as a "superb" piece of land on which to establish a *chacra*, or small farm. His aims included the conservation of the existing maté plants at Santa Ana and the discovery of others hidden in the woods. He would then multiply the maté plants in order to establish a *yerbal* of considerable proportions.[187]

Bonpland arrived back in Corrientes from the missions on 3 August 1821, where he suffered from a bout of illness, probably a reflection of some of the winter weather he endured in the missions, coupled with the strenuous traveling conditions. His plans were affected by the shifting politics. Initially, he had planned to go back to Buenos Aires in order to bring his wife and stepdaughter into the missions. The recent assassination of Ramírez on 10 July 1821 changed this. He learned through letters coming from Buenos Aires that the ports were closed, thus he could not come south even to Paraná in order to give a report on the state of the mission *yerbales*. On 3 September, Bonpland informed José Ricardo López Jordán, the acting supreme chief of the Entrerriano Republic, that he expected to return to the missions within a few days. While this journey was partly for personal motives, Bonpland traveled "with the hope it will be useful to everybody."[188] He announced that he would count himself happy were he able to contribute something concrete to the restoration of some of the missions, seeing them as a source of future wealth for the inhabitants of Entre Ríos. Further details of the challenges of the work in the missions emerged in Bonpland's letter of the same date to José Ildefonso Castro, the secretary to the government of Entre Ríos.[189] Unrest had resulted when reports of Ramírez's demise reached the missions "in the first days of July." Through intervention with Aripí, Bonpland seems to have played some role in pacifying this. He clearly had to work to assuage suspicions in parts of Corrientes about the nature of his work in Misiones. Bonpland informed Castro that, in Caacatí, word circulated that the French had given two hundred cartridges to the

Indians. There was some truth in this. Convinced of Aripí's worthwhile intentions, Bonpland gave him a pound of gunpowder; he also helped him to make some forty cartridges before the chief proceeded against what were termed rebel Indians. The main issue seems to have been keeping credibility with Aripí, whether for Bonpland in particular, or the government of Entre Ríos more generally. Bonpland thought that the best way to proceed in the missions was to send a good priest and some settlers north to Santa Ana. This would supposedly induce harmony with the Indians.

It is not certain when Bonpland left Corrientes for the return to Santa Ana, but he did not meet his stated objective of departing a few days after 3 September, as reported in his letter to López Jordán. There were perhaps political developments under way worthy of consideration. For example, Corrientes regained its autonomy from the Entrerriano Republic on 12 October 1821. Around this time, Bonpland was undertaking botanical work along the banks of the Riachuelo River, south of the city of Corrientes.[190]

It was during this period while Bonpland was probably watching and waiting that Humboldt wrote to him again from Paris, once more lamenting lack of contact: "Your long silence has often caused me pain." Humboldt opined that he would never forget his friend's actions "in the most difficult circumstances of life."[191] He sent personal money to Bonpland. All this was motivated by intelligence received following the return of the Prussian minister to Brazil, news that things were not going well in Argentina. This financial subsidy came too late to have any immediate practical use to Bonpland.

By November, Bonpland was back at Santa Ana, working in conjunction with Aripí to develop the yerba resources and awaiting a visit from Dominique Roguin. This last wanted to examine the nature of Bonpland's colony in person before investing any of his resources in it. Decades later at Montevideo, Roguin admitted his skepticism about Bonpland's business plans.[192] A more optimistic, if highly romanticized, account of the yerba venture in Misiones came from the Scottish merchant William Parish Robertson:

> For about two years M. Bonpland prosecuted, in peace and retirement, but with all the energy of an active mind, his philosophic and useful avocations; and success the most complete promised to crown his judicious labours. His little colony was a model of industry, order, and happiness. The docile Indians were the Naturalist's labourers; and he pursued a system with them, which, with all the virtues, had none of the vices that characterized the rule of the Jesuits. A law inseparable from the nature of M. Bonpland, was the desire to elevate whatever portion of humanity surrounded him; and his

gentle manner, his unassuming deportment, and his fund of good sense . . . endeared him to those whom he employed in his service.[193]

Although Robertson had firsthand familiarity with both Bonpland and the region, his description raises a number of misconceptions. First, Bonpland's involvement with the Santa Ana colony was short lived. Whatever successes he had in attracting Indian labor, an enterprise that would begin and vanish within a six-month period, can only have been more the intention than the realization of "a model of industry." The claim that Santa Ana represented a model of peace hardly squares with the cultural challenges present in Bonpland's own manuscripts. In addition, in Robertson's account, all the kudos go to Bonpland, without any mention of Aripí's enabling infrastructure.

Although he must have been aware that he was working in contested territory, Bonpland appears to have been open with Francia about his presence. Bonpland wanted Francia to know his intentions, which he communicated in person to Paraguayan authorities and through the merchant José Tomás Isasi, who was then a figure holding the dictator's trust (Isasi would later fall afoul of Francia, fleeing Paraguay for good).[194] Isasi was sent by Francia to Buenos Aires as early as 1818 to act as commercial agent for Paraguay. Before 1815, he had been in charge of the Candelaria region, where Bonpland now proposed to settle.[195] It seems highly possible that Bonpland and Isasi would have conversed at Buenos Aires. And if their meeting was not direct, it is known for sure that Bonpland dealt with many in the Buenos Aires mercantile community, the object of Isasi's endeavors. Bonpland seems to have been highly optimistic about what to expect by way of treatment from Francia. He was no doubt bolstered by support from opinion in some quarters of Buenos Aires, and by his direct knowledge that Francia had permitted a considerable number of Correntinos and Indians to gather yerba for two years. Bonpland made several approaches to the Paraguayan authorities, informing them of his activities and seeking their cooperation. Reviewing the circumstances in 1834, he told the government of Corrientes that he had presented himself in person to the Paraguayan guard at Campichuelo, in front of the Candelaria mission, where supposedly three friendly interviews took place.[196] He was first interviewed by the Paraguayans on 20 November 1821 at the port of Candelaria. Twenty armed men, commanded by the officers Sebastian José Morínigo and Sublieutenant Proa, arrived there in two canoes. A week later, the Paraguayan resources for a second visit were reduced to ten armed men and a single craft.[197]

While Bonpland's overtures to Francia appear to have been open, William Parish Robertson compared the approach of the latter to the former with the "stealthy creep of the tiger."[198] In his instructions to Norberto Ortellado on 23 November 1821, Francia set out to deal with the Indians remaining from Artigas's forces who were earlier based around San Francisco Xavier on the Uruguay River. By establishing themselves "with their families and rabble" around San Ignacio Miní, they had come onto land belonging to Paraguay. Francia chose to take action quickly, fearing the Indians led by Aripí would only become more securely entrenched with time. In Francia's eyes, Bonpland was equally guilty to Aripí's people of working Paraguayan resources without the permission of his government. He gave Ortellado explicit instructions to mount a force. It should cross the Paraná by stealth and remove all the resources, human and otherwise, from Bonpland's Santa Ana colony. In particular, Francia wanted care to be shown in ensuring that Aripí fell into Paraguayan power, whether alive or dead.[199]

The attack, unexpected for Bonpland, came on 8 December, less than six months since he first established his pueblo at Santa Ana. On the preceding day, he was profiting from the hot weather to conduct chemical experiments on *caa obi* (wild indigo), mature plants about to bud, which he had cut in the fields around Santa Ana.[200] Writing from memory in 1834, he recalled that a division of five hundred to six hundred armed Paraguayans crossed the Paraná at night, attacking his colony at daybreak and treating his party as enemies.[201] No resistance was offered, and, supposedly, the Paraguayans did not fire a single shot. Nevertheless, nineteen men were killed by the sword, and sixty-three others taken prisoner, including Bonpland himself. In his account of the attack, Bonpland kept, as almost always, to the bare facts. A much more expressive account of the event was given by William Parish Robertson:

> Amid the cries and shrieks of the inmates, the soldiers *massacred* all the male Indians of the establishment; they beat and wounded the women; they set fire . . . to houses, implements, crops, plantations, - and reduced the whole to a heap of black and smouldering ruins; they stunned M. Bonpland with the blows of their sabres; they loaded him with irons; they dragged him from among the corpses of all the faithful servants, who, three hours before, had surrounded him in health, happiness and affection.[202]

Robertson's full account of Bonpland's sufferings is more extended than the above. He defended himself against the possible charge of exaggeration with the comment "hundreds of witnesses have attested the truth of my narrative."[203]

On his journey to examine the Santa Ana colony, the French merchant Roguin arrived in the territory of the missions at the time of the attack. He and his party had a narrow escape from the Paraguayan soldiers, saved only by a violent storm that rendered one of the tributaries of the Paraná impassable. Roguin soon met up with the escapees from Santa Ana, who had taken refuge in the woods, reduced to feeding themselves on roots. These people and two carts loaded with yerba were all that remained of the Santa Ana experiment. Roguin led them back to the province of Corrientes, where the news of the burning of Bonpland's establishment was treated as a public calamity. Bonpland had brought a new life to Corrientes, in commerce and in cultivation, that it had long lacked.[204] Within months, the unfortunate news of the demise of Bonpland's project had diffused to Buenos Aires; in a single stroke, the removal of Bonpland had broken the credit of the country of Paraguay.[205]

. . .

In reviewing the immense activity of Bonpland's first years in the Río de la Plata, the key impression is one of unfortunate timing, a judgment made of course with the benefit of hindsight. Soon after he left Buenos Aires for the interior, the political circumstances there turned, at least for a period, in ways that would have appealed to him. While admitting its pretension, María Sáenz Quesada argues that there was much at Rivadavian Buenos Aires in the first half of the 1820s to justify the contemporary use of the label "Athens of the Plata."[206] For example, the year 1821 saw the foundation of the university there. When Rivadavia laid the basis for an agricultural school on 7 August 1823, its emphasis was designed to be practical, and the institution was to include a garden for the acclimatization of plants—both subjects at the core of Bonpland's interests and experience. Three years later, when Domingo Olivera organized the Sociedad Rural Argentina in its earliest guise, Bonpland's close friend Roguin was one of the seven directors of this institution.[207] In short, during the 1820s there was vastly more in the spirit of useful improvement to engage him at Buenos Aires than in Paraguay. But now, for nearly a decade, his place of residence was no longer a matter of choice.

CHAPTER TWO

Prisoner in Paraguay

> Dr. Francia, the author, and, up to this hour, the inflexible upholder of the non-intercourse policy of Paraguay, is, doubtless, one of the most singular characters of his day.
> ROBERTSON AND ROBERTSON,
> *Letters on Paraguay*, 3:9

> On 26 February 1822, that is to say eight days after I had begun to observe the temperatures at Santa María [Santa María de Fé, the former mission where Bonpland lived for much of his time in Paraguay], the dictator [Francia] sent for my books and instruments. After two months, my books and instruments were returned, minus, however, my thermometer, some of the books and certain other instruments. Thus I could not continue my temperature readings.
> BONPLAND, 1822[1]

> During the nine years I was a prisoner in Paraguay . . . , my thoughts were often fixed on Paris while walking alone at night in the sweet-fruit orange groves. . . . I often visited the Jardin des Plantes, the Faubourg Saint Germain, where, it seems, you are still living . . . , and the fine property of Malmaison. How present these places remain engraved in my memory despite the years.
> LETTER FROM BONPLAND TO VICTORINE, COMTESSE DE CHASTENAY, 1840[2]

Bonpland spent nearly a decade (late 1821–early 1831) as a hostage of the famous José Gaspar de Francia, living in several Paraguayan rural locations. Along with the work achieved earlier with Humboldt, the drama of the confinement in Paraguay added greatly to his fame in Europe. A wide range of world authorities made efforts to secure Bonpland's release (including Bolívar, Humboldt, and Emperor Pedro I of Brazil), all without avail. After his release, he often claimed that he had done no writing while in Paraguay. While he was certainly cut off from his international circuit of correspondents, and both paper and ink were in desperately short supply, there are some written records from this period in Bonpland's manuscripts (including details of plantings and of medical matters). Whatever the privations, Bonpland summoned his energies to continue the work of resource assessment.

Although famously moderate in his subsequent comments about the circumstances of his removal to Paraguay, Bonpland expressed a considerable curiosity in the circumstances of how he came to be viewed so negatively by Francia. As seen, Bonpland tried to communicate with Francia directly through the intermedium of one of the latter's very few trusted collaborators. In initially setting up his approach to Paraguay, he had negotiated with José Tomás Isasi in the city of Corrientes and possibly earlier at Buenos Aires. Bonpland would retain suspicions of Isasi's conduct toward him throughout his imprisonment in Paraguay. Following his release from Paraguay, Bonpland had the chance for an interview with Isasi in person during his first visit to Buenos Aires. Isasi's appearance when giving answers to Bonpland's "multitude of questions" about Paraguay only further raised his doubts. More was learned about the Paraguayan's conduct during Bonpland's 1834 visit to his compatriot Breard at Caacatí. Based on what Breard had learned from a French third party, Isasi held the ambition to control all of Paraguay's commerce himself; thus he had distrusted Bonpland's industry: "Knowing the dispositions I was taking at Santa Ana, he feared this point would become such a center of commerce that it would necessarily destroy that of Paraguay."[3] At the least, any commercial success at Santa Ana would come at the detriment of Paraguayan prospects. Bonpland was firm in his belief that he had been undercut by false reports to Francia of his motives. In addition, a letter dictated by Aripí to the dictator that began with the undiplomatic wording "friend and companion" was hardly calculated to please Francia. There are signs Aripí was a stickler for the niceties of protocol with Bonpland. He seems to have been much less careful himself when composing a missive to the famously prickly Francia.

Often presented as an irrational act, Bonpland's imprisonment was probably not so much a matter of details as one of Francia's general policy of

Figure 2.1 José Gaspar de Francia, dictator of Paraguay.
SOURCE: Reproduced from Robertson and Robertson, *Letters on Paraguay*, vol. 1, frontispiece.

isolation for his country. In 1823, a French diplomat reported to his government how Francia had set up a system of isolation in order to spare Paraguay from "the moral contagion of the American Revolution." Paraguay was favored by its geographical location to be spared from many of the dissensions taking place farther south:

> It is difficult and even dangerous to cross the limits of this isolated province. When this despotic chief perceives a rare talent or a superior spirit in a foreigner, he keeps him, either as a useful acquisition for the country, or so that he will not uncover the methods and the secrets of his administration. It is following this principle that he had M. Bonpland kidnapped from the territory of the neighboring province of Corrientes.[4]

But in weighing the qualities and defects of Francia, Consul Barrère opined for the authorities at Paris that Paraguay was the only country in South America where one found "morals and virtues." In another French diplomatic report from the following year, the author remarked on how both Artigas and Bonpland had met with captivity in Paraguay, noting "[the Paraguayans] make it as soft as possible for them, but they are kept from view or sequestered in the convents."[5]

John Hoyt Williams has described Francia's management of Paraguayan foreign affairs as "redoubtable," but has also argued that this country's isolation was a reflection of geopolitics as much as of Francia's character.[6] After Paraguay's de facto independence in 1811 followed a history of a long period of hostility from its neighbors. Given that Paraguay's contact with the outside world was predominantly through the south, trade and other contacts in this direction called for careful management. The river system of the Paraguay-Paraná and the territory of the Misiones were important cultural filters. Despite their ambitions, the political authorities at Buenos Aires were unable to dominate Paraguay. But the many dissensions between the coast and the interior in what became Argentina brought many challenges to Paraguay's southern borders. The years before Bonpland arrived in Misiones had seen the depredations of Artigas and his allies. In addition, the Portuguese had crossed west of the Uruguay River in military campaigns. Francia feared an invasion by the forces of Ramírez. Removal of Bonpland was an important step in renewing Paraguayan control over the area around Candelaria. Control of Candelaria, in turn, was vital for giving the Paraguayan army the chance to patrol across the territory of Misiones, which it did, sometimes as far as the Uruguay River.

The year 1821 was a momentous one in the history of the consolidation of Francia's regime. When Bonpland was arriving in the missions in June 1821, Asunción was a city marked by death, as Francia worked to control the large-scale conspiracy he suspected against him. His policies saw the imprisonment of the European Spaniards and execution of many of the conspirators from the creole elite.[7] In addition, Juan Pérez Acosta argued interestingly that Bonpland was compromised by the activities of Pedro [Pierre] Saguier. Saguier was sent from France on a secret mission in 1818, the objective of which was to determine whether Francia was interested in establishing free trade with France. Given the sensitive nature of this undertaking, he traveled in the guise of a representative of mercantile enterprise. In any case, Francia held a deep suspicion of French motives in relation to Latin American independence movements. When detained at Asunción, Saguier's papers included a letter from Richard Grandsire, a Calais merchant and natural historian that served to compromise Bonpland. Grandsire claimed to have learned from the French immigrant Robert de Connaut that Bonpland was involved in something more than a simple commercial operation. He suggested that his work developing the resources of Misiones was part of a large-scale project involving various Frenchmen and designed to open up the commercial possibilities of Paraguay.

Francia sent his instructions about how to proceed regarding the Indians in Misiones to Ortellado on 23 November 1821. He seems to have feared an arms buildup within the remnants of the Indian communities that were left behind following Artigas's defeat. Well informed of Bonpland's circumstances at Santa Ana, Francia was not prepared to see the Santa Ana colony become the staging post for the southern invasion of Paraguay that he feared. Writing a half-century later, the famous traveler and writer Richard Burton showed some sympathy with Francia's motives: "When M. Aimé Bonpland . . . , settling on land claimed by Paraguay, began imprudently to cultivate the monopolized yerba, he was seized by order of the Dictator, and was carried prisoner across the frontier. This act has been held to be a violation of territory - has been called gross as the capture and execution of the Duc d'Enghien."[8]

While most of Francia's prisoners were confined to Asunción, Bonpland was given rather more latitude. Most of the time he lived in Paraguay was spent around two former Jesuit missions, Santa Rosa (1698) and Santa María de Fé (1651). Unlike his earlier mission experiences, these were places shielded from the physical destruction of the independence wars.[9] One contemporary account of the former mission maintained that it still contained "the richest and most beautiful temple in Paraguay," whose gold and silver ornaments had been "sufficient to attract the rapacity of Doctor Francia."[10] It seems certain that Bonpland was at Santa Rosa in January 1822 from the notes he left of tobacco cultivation there, a theme carried over from earlier work at Santa Ana.[11] He wrote a description of the *tabacal* (tobacco crop), maintaining that the planting was performed in such a manner that the plants were too close together. The ground was very sandy. Weeding was done in a superficial manner, accomplished with the shoulder blades of oxen or cows attached to long sticks. He became very interested in the different types of tobacco grown in South America. His closest attention was devoted to a dark variety, a type he inferred required more labor in the preparation than the red tobacco commonly grown in Paraguay.[12] Bonpland wrote detailed notes on how to prepare this dark tobacco, with references to the Dutch, to Brazil, to Corrientes, and to what he had seen in the Orinoco during his journey with Humboldt. He claimed that Villarrica was the most important point for tobacco cultivation in Paraguay. In January 1822, he also commented on the sundial placed by a Jesuit priest in the courtyard at Santa Rosa.[13] The following month he was at Santa María, where he began to take temperature readings on 18 February. This initiative was short lived. Around only a week later, his books and most of his instruments were removed on Francia's orders. The exact nature of the materials concerned was never specified, but this is interesting; it reveals Bonpland was not totally devoid of books when he arrived in Paraguay. Although most of them were later returned, the loss must have rankled. Trying to describe a plant in 1824, he noted he could not attempt a description of the sexual organs while bereft of his magnifying glass.[14] All this seems a fine specific example of the throttling of culture that marked the Franciata in Paraguay.[15] In March 1822, he took notes on the methods of tobacco cultivation at Santa María.[16] Among other crops, Bonpland also grew sugarcane at Santa María. In April 1822, he noted the presence of various species of soldier beetles (*Cantharida*) that were larger than the European varieties.[17] Elsewhere, he expressed his wish to visit the long-wooled sheep and the mercury mine at San Miguel. The fact that this mine is located only approximately forty kilometers NNW of Santa Rosa gives some sense of Bonpland's diminished radius of activity.[18] In February 1823, he made a note about an indigo substitute (*caa obi*) that used to be grown in Paraguay near Curuguati, a hamlet northeast of Asunción, and the place where the caudillo Artigas found refuge. It appeared, he said, that entire fields were formerly sown with this crop.[19] Through these many descriptive notes and planting records, the portrait emerges of a very busy man.

In August 1822, Bonpland ventured a letter to the *subdelegado* Romero, the head of the local authority at Santa María. He wanted to know if he was to remain in the missions, or whether he could hope to continue his researches on South America, with a view to making them public someday. Whether or not travel was possible, Bonpland wished to visit Asunción in search of "all the necessary things for a useful establishment."[20] In addition, he wanted to make arrangements regarding his family and business interests at Buenos Aires. However reasonable Bonpland's requests sounded, Francia's response showed that he was not prepared to consider them. For Francia, Bonpland had acted in bad faith. He should not be considered "a mere prisoner of war," but somebody who had encouraged factional politics with the bandits on Paraguay's frontiers, who were seeking to rob the resources of the *yerbales*. In Francia's view, Bonpland should consider himself very fortunate not to be behind bars or in even worse circumstances.[21] Considering the potential dangers surrounding a missive such as the above, it is interesting that Bonpland risked at least one letter written directly to Asunción, again designed to bring supplies into the missions. It was directed to the Swiss physician Johann Rudolph Rengger, another of Francia's foreign detainees, who served with his compatriot Marcel Longchamps as a surgeon to the Asunción garrisons. The reply, in Spanish, came from Rengger to Bonpland on 29 January 1823. It was written profiting from the knowledge that a cart was about to leave for the missions. Days before, Rengger had received a list of remedies to send to Bonpland, a mission it was "entirely impossible" to fulfill: "We are denuded of remedies and we see ourselves forced to make expectative more than active medicine." The only requested item Rengger hoped to find was a little opium. Other remedies, such as quinine, were nowhere to be found, even in the capital. Syringes were present, but only in private houses, whose occupiers did not wish to give up these instruments. Moreover, El Supremo was not an enthusiast for the results of the medical work undertaken by this "Swiss European atheist."[22] While Francia believed that Rengger had managed to poison many of his personal guards, any lack of medical success experienced by the two Swiss physicians can be partially ascribed to the lack of materials.

In return, Bonpland had succeeded in sending some bottles of patent medicine to Rengger, and the latter was aware that Escoffier, another hostage, was also receiving patent medicine from Bonpland.[23] Rengger's letter ended with some observations on the treatment of "Señor Don José," presumably Francia himself.[24] Apart from some early interviews with John Parish Robertson, Rengger and Longchamps were the only foreigners with whom Francia interacted in person.[25] Had they met, there seems no doubt that Bonpland and Francia, who had a donnish element as one side of his character, would have found much to discuss, beginning with the development of Paraguay's natural resources. They also shared an interest in reading some of the same French medical texts.[26]

Deprived of even the most modest medical resources of Asunción, Bonpland was thrown back to using and observing the pharmacobotanical resources of his area of captivity and study. Knowledge of this comes through from his planting records. In 1823, he was active in the hills adjacent to Santa María. Most of the crops he seeded were common ones, but the records also show some knowledge of indigenous species, such as araticu (the chirimoya), presumably planted for its fruit. The manuscripts now at Paris show that Bonpland continued his botanical work while resident in Paraguay. For example, he made very detailed notes on a type of large bamboo, yet "smaller than our *Bambusa guadua*," an oblique reference to work undertaken earlier with Humboldt in the Cauca Valley of modern Colombia.[27] Bonpland first observed this variety from the missions near San Ignacio Miní prior to being taken into Paraguay. He found a membrane in the interstices of the bamboo knots whose consistency he compared with the part of the sheep used to make English frock coats. In Paraguay, the large bamboos flowered after seven years of growth, producing a seed "the size of our fine European wheat." The flour made from the seeds had considerable food value; thus it was used for making bread, pies, and all kinds of paste. The Paraguayan *taquarales* (bamboo forests) flourished in 1821, but in 1822 and 1823 not a single example could be found for use in the construction of houses.[28] Presumably, this posed obstacles for his own building projects as he established himself in the missions of Paraguay. Bonpland built his knowledge through comparative observations. For example, he commented on a type of cedar (*cedro puyta*, or *Cedrella odorata*), described as very common at Campichuelo, Itapúa, Santa Rosa, and Santa María.[29] It was a red and very odoriferous cedar, superior to all the other varieties for woodworking. In October 1822, he described the plants in the garden of the mission at Santa María, beginning with the Chinese parasol tree (*Sterculia platanifolia*), of which there was a single example. He surmised that this must have been planted in the time of the Jesuits: "Nobody has had the curiosity to multiply it, either from its seeds, or by taking cuttings."[30] The contents of the garden seem to reflect the diversity of interests of the Jesuits. The plants included grenadines, bergamots, small bananas (the dominico type from the Antilles), and numerous types of citrus fruit. There were also "an enormous maté tree," figs, and palms. Another plant linked with the Jesuits that interested him was *urucu* (*Bixa orellana*): "The Jesuits brought this tree into the missions. Today, one sees several examples at Itapúa and a sole one at Santa María. This last is small and in very poor condition. The only use for its fruit they know here is to tint red the beads from *Curiy* [one of the several vernacular names for the Paraná pine (*Araucaria angustifolia*)] that serve to make rosaries." While the state of the urucu at Santa María had given pause for thought, Bonpland later added in pencil: "at the village of Trinidad, the Bixa orellana is growing very well and is covered each year in flowers and fruits." By the following year, as his knowledge grew, Bonpland had decided that urucu was indigenous to Paraguay. He claimed that it grew spontaneously near Asunción. The indigenous people brought cakes from there, made from the pulp surrounding the seeds. Yet the presence of the tree in the missions reflected convenience in its Jesuit function of dying beads a fine shade of red.[31] There is no doubt from his descriptions that Bonpland was in the hills of Santa María in November 1823.[32] Another focus of his work was *encienso*, used as a substitute for incense in all the churches.[33] He gave the Latin description in September 1825, then followed with the marginal comment in October: "Out of a thousand residents of the country, there is not a single one who has seen the 'encienso' in flower." Thirty years later, he would reflect that it had taken him seven years of continuous research to find this in flower and fruit. Other objectives were never met. During the nine years of captivity in Paraguay, the woods were full of *catigua*, but he never succeeded in finding its seeds.[34] In 1829 and 1830, he left further plant descriptions from the missions Jesús and Trinidad, and from the "hillocks" of Itapúa in December of the previous year.

During most of his stay in Paraguay, Bonpland was based at the Cerrito, located between the former missions of Santa Ana and Santa Rosa. He threw himself into a broad range of agricultural activities there. In some ways, confinement may have been beneficial for the development of Bonpland's projects. Travel so often diffused his energies. He prepared remedies and confectionery at the Cerrito, then left every week for Itapúa, where he attempted to sell these things from a rented room.[35] Accounts of how Bonpland fared while in Paraguay are understandably rare. In September 1824, the French traveler Richard Grandsire, who had unsuccessfully attempted to enter Paraguay, reported to Humboldt that Bonpland was doing well. This was based on the oral information of one of his Paraguayan neighbors, who affirmed that Bonpland was cultivating land provided to him by Francia. In addition, he was practicing medicine, distilling alcoholic drinks (eaux-de-vie made from the base of honey), and continuing his old passion for collecting and describing plants.[36] On leaving Paraguay the following year (1825), the Swiss physician Rengger claimed that Bonpland was deriving no more than subsistence from his various agricultural schemes; on the positive side, however, he was greatly respected in his district.[37] An 1827 newspaper report at Buenos Aires commented on how the success of his medical work had attracted "a numerous clientele."[38]

Several authors have maintained that Bonpland formed a new family during his long residence in Paraguay. The idea of a relationship with Maria, the daughter of an Indian chief, beginning with this young woman offering Bonpland fresh water sweetened with honey while he was still part of a group of prisoners, has obvious romantic appeal, and even plausibility. The medical base he established would certainly have brought him into sustained contact with the female gender, and it may be correct that Maria helped him with the work of running a dispensary. But the hard evidence for any of this, including the supposed birth of a son (Amado) and a daughter (Maria), is not yet forthcoming. Nicolas Hossard argues that the modesty of the period explains such limited details of Bonpland's private life, including the reserve of the subject himself. But Bonpland, a medical doctor among other roles, was by no means as reserved about matters of the body as some of those he lived around. His many observations about the causes of syphilis in some of his patients are alone testimony to this.

Bonpland's own accounts of his Paraguayan life were made subsequent to his release. The first, which was widely disseminated in both South America and Europe, was prepared for the French merchant Roguin, shortly after Bonpland arrived on Brazilian soil. He maintained that the nine years in Paraguay had passed as happily as was possible for an individual deprived of contact with country, family, or friends. Medicine was the bedrock of his existence, but agriculture was something that Bonpland embraced with great enthusiasm. It was an activity backed by a distillery, a carpentry shop, and a forge. Taken together, he reported, these activities provided the means for him to live "in great ease."[39] A much more detailed account of the agriculture came in a letter to his close friend Alire Raffeneau-Delile, written from Buenos Aires in August 1832. By this time, Bonpland had confronted considerable obstacles (financial and legal) in engaging anew with a broader world. Life in the establishment at the Cerrito was taking on a more positive gloss. Paraguay was now described as "an admirable country." Bonpland described himself as "a rich cultivator" when Francia gave him the order to leave, one who employed forty-five people. The crops he cultivated included cotton, sugarcane, various types of peanuts and potatoes, and yerba. It is surprising to find no mention of tobacco, a major focus of his research in Paraguay. He claimed to have established plantations of vines, various citrus fruits (especially oranges), and guavas. There were sufficient livestock to work the property at Cerrito properly, including four hundred cattle. Medicine had not been merely a matter of visiting patients, since Bonpland established a cottage hospital with four rooms. He claimed to be "as content and vigorous" as Raffeneau-Delile had known him at Navarre and Malmaison.[40]

Efforts to Bring Bonpland's Release

Famous already for his work along the American journey, a long confinement in Paraguay gained Bonpland fame of a different kind. Without ready supplies of paper and ink, writing became an extraordinary challenge. In any case, written contacts with the outside world were forbidden in Francia's Paraguay. Humboldt worked to mobilize efforts in Bonpland's favor, using both his diplomatic and his scientific connections. One obvious channel to pursue was his influence over Simón Bolívar. Bolívar wrote to Francia from Lima in October 1823.

> Since my earliest youth I have had the honor of cultivating the friendship of Monsieur Bonpland and Baron von Humboldt, whose knowledge has done more for America than all the conquistadors.
> I have learned, to my dismay, that my beloved friend M. Bonpland has been detained in Paraguay, for reasons unknown to me. I suspect that some false reports may have slandered that good and wise man and that the government over which Your Excellency presides has allowed itself to be misled concerning this noble gentleman. Two considerations impel me to plead urgently with Your Excellency for the release of M. Bonpland. The first is that I am the cause of his coming to America, since it was I who invited him to Colombia, and, after he had decided to undertake his voyage, the events of the war forced him to proceed to Buenos Aires. The second consideration is that this learned man could greatly enlighten my country with his genius, if

Your Excellency would graciously allow him to proceed to Colombia, whose government I head by the will of the people.

No doubt Your Excellency is not [un]acquainted with my name or with my services to the American cause; yet if I were to be permitted to pledge all that I value in order to obtain the release of M. Bonpland, I should venture to address this plea to Your Excellency: may it please Your Excellency to hear the cry of four million Americans who have been freed by the army that I command; they all join me in asking Your Excellency to show clemency for the sake of humanity, wisdom, and justice, and out of respect for M. Bonpland.

M. Bonpland can, before leaving your territory, give your Excellency his word that he will leave the provinces of the Río de la Plata, so that he cannot in any possible manner harm the province of Paraguay. Meanwhile, I shall await him with the anxiety of a friend and the respect of a pupil, for I would be capable of marching as far as Paraguay only to free this best of men and the most celebrated of travelers.[41]

Bolívar's letter reads as a splendid piece of bravado, but military threats fell on deaf ears with Francia. In a letter to Bonpland's wife Adeline on the same date, Bolívar claimed that her husband was a prisoner in Paraguay "with the innocence that characterizes martyrs."[42] Bolívar's references to Paraguay as a province also cannot have endeared him to Francia.[43]

An extended initiative came from Richard Grandsire, a Calais merchant and natural historian.[44] He had made a commercial visit to Buenos Aires in 1817, where he came to know Bonpland. Grandsire proposed to seek Bonpland's release from Paraguay while pursuing the geographical question of whether the Plata basin and the Amazon River were connected, an issue of concern to him since his first visit to South America. Along with the botanist Charles François Brisseau de Mirbel, Humboldt urged that the Académie des Sciences should use Grandsire's second journey to South America advantageously, in an effort to seek Bonpland's release from Paraguay. The botanist academicians armed Grandsire with a letter, drafted by Humboldt: "The intellectuals of Europe ardently wish for the return of this traveler."[45]

Arriving at Rio de Janeiro in May 1824, Grandsire found some support for his mission there, not least within the membership of the imperial family.[46] He announced to Pedro I that the purpose of his scientific journey was to find the link between the Paraná basin and the Amazon. He claimed that Empress Leopoldina was very familiar with Humboldt's writings. She too was a naturalist, with a particular interest in mineralogy. Grandsire moved along to Buenos Aires, where he was met only with suspicion. Since the only route open to Paraguay lay through Brazil (which included, at the time, the territory of what is now Uruguay), the authorities in Argentina could not readily understand what this French traveler was doing in their country. He was expelled. This was not necessarily an act of simple vengeance, as Bonpland's biographer Hamy interpreted the event.[47] The commander of the French naval station in South America, Rear Admiral du Campe de Rosamel, also doubted Grandsire's objectives, something he relayed in a dispatch to Paris.[48]

Whatever his strengths and defects of character, Grandsire worked hard to keep Humboldt informed of the state of his mission. He wrote from Montevideo, then twice from the borders of Paraguay, first in hope (18 August 1824), then in resignation (10 September), when Francia refused him admission to Paraguay.[49] Francia was full of suspicions about French political designs in South America. He did not accept the validity of Grandsire's claims to work as an explorer. While Grandsire related the varying character of Francia's doubts about the outside world, he painted a generally positive image about the social conditions that the dictator fostered in his country. Grandsire faced considerable trials of endurance along his mission. Writing from Curitiba in southern Brazil, he observed that things never came to such a useful point that he felt able to forward Humboldt's letter to Francia.[50] Fearing for their shelf life on account of the elevated humidity, Grandsire had jettisoned Humboldt's books sent out to Francia as a token of his esteem. Still conveying some optimism, he now proposed to approach Paraguay through the Brazilian fort at Nova Coimbra in Mato Grosso. This line of approach to Paraguay did not prove feasible. By July 1825, he was back at São Borja.[51]

Grandsire's efforts were complicated by Brazilian diplomacy, notably the mission of the diplomat Antônio Manoel Correa da Câmara, who represented imperial Brazil as consul and commercial agent before the government of Paraguay after May 1824.[52] Along his mission, Correa da Câmara followed the Riograndense route toward Paraguay.[53] While at São Borja, he was displeased to find Grandsire's presence there. Grandsire seems to have attracted very negative publicity from Correa da Câmara, who saw him as undermining his mission. In July 1825, Correa da Câmara informed the frontier commander of the Brazilian missions of the great danger the Frenchman posed. He gave instructions that Grandsire should be expelled from Rio Grande do Sul. However, the conde de Palmeira, the commander of the Brazilian missions, appears to have effected some of his own diplomacy; with his support, Grandsire managed to persist for several months around Santo Tomé on the other side of the Uruguay River from São Borja.[54] It stands to Grandsire's credit that he used his local contacts with the conde de Palmeira to help the British effort to free Bonpland, initiated by Woodbine Parish at Buenos Aires.[55] The British consul's official letter to Francia was forwarded through the hands of a British merchant who arrived at São Borja in November 1825. The mission was not successful. Caught up in international issues surrounding state formation, Grandsire stood in an impossible position. He was distrusted not only by the authorities at Buenos Aires but also by some of the Brazilians and even some of the French. Above all, he enjoyed no credit with Francia in Paraguay.

Correa da Câmara's arrival at Asunción on 25 August 1825 was a considerable event.[56] The Paraguayan capital had not seen any diplomatic visits since 1813. Correa da Câmara took up the cause of Bonpland following a successful lunch with Francia, when he presented him with a letter written in June 1824 by the Brazilian minister of foreign affairs, Luís José de Carvalho e Mello, the visconde de Cachoeira. Carvalho e Mello had written to Francia from Rio de Janeiro, making the case for Bonpland's release on family grounds. He told Francia that the former's family was in Rio de Janeiro "in the most pitiful state," resulting from the absence of the head of the family.[57] The request from Rio de Janeiro met with a negative response.[58] Correa da Câmara left Asunción on 1 December 1825. During the journey back to Itapúa, he met with Bonpland at Santa María, but treated him with great suspicion.[59] Bonpland asked for tea seeds and gave the Brazilian a letter, which the latter left in Paraguay.

By May 1826, Grandsire had found his way back to Rio de Janeiro, where he worked to mount yet another approach to Paraguay, this time through the Amazon. While revisiting the Brazilian capital, a letter he wrote to Cuvier contained the indirect news that Bonpland was doing well with his business in Paraguay.[60] Following further bureaucratic difficulties—he could not arrange sea transport to Cayenne—Grandsire then traveled to Martinique, from where he worked to correct some false impressions present in the European press. Francia did not hold Bonpland for reasons of enmity or caprice, he maintained. Reading in the Martinique newspapers of the Bolívarian threats to march on Paraguay, Grandsire claimed that the parties involved showed minimal understanding of what motivated Francia's policies. His position was that use of force could bring Bonpland to a position of catastrophe and that a high-level diplomatic mission from France was needed.[61] Grandsire died traveling somewhere along the Jari River, approaching Brazil from French Guiana. His iconic remains included "a pair of pistols, a compass and a portable dictionary."[62]

When Humboldt received Grandsire's disappointing news from the borders of Paraguay, he shifted his hopes to the British capacity to obtain Bonpland's release. He published in Europe the British diplomat Woodbine Parish's view that the only thing Francia held against Bonpland was the "prosperity of his Paraguayan tea plantations" at Santa Ana on his nation's frontiers.[63] The efforts by Woodbine Parish to write to Francia, not just as an act of humanity but as a service to science in general, did not go over well with the French rear admiral, Grivel.[64] They had no impact whatsoever on Francia, who returned the British diplomat's letter unopened.[65]

After his release, Bonpland was more appreciative of the British efforts taken on his behalf within South America than those of the French.[66] Jean-Baptiste Washington de Mendeville, the French consul at Buenos Aires, told Bonpland in 1832 that he had written directly to Francia on his behalf. By 1836, Bonpland had gained evidence to the contrary, managing to obtain a copy of the consul's letter (presumably from the archives of the diplomatic mission), which was written to Francia on 12 October 1828. Making no mention of any specific individuals by name, part of this letter asked for the release of French nationals who were held in Paraguay against their will. If Francia could not accept their presence elsewhere on South American soil for "political motives," Mendeville stated, he undertook to guarantee their removal directly to Europe. Bonpland was familiar with the route that the French diplomat's letter had taken on its way to Paraguay, arguing that there was no way Francia could have received it from its Correntino intermediary in less than six months (that is, April 1829). In 1833, Bonpland forwarded to Francia a second letter written by Mendeville (on 26 July 1832). Its leading purpose was to thank the dictator for expelling Bonpland from Paraguay and to "protest in general the French who vegetate in the so-called republic of Paraguay."[67] Writing at Buenos Aires on 6 December 1836, Bonpland observed that Francia had still to reply to either of Mendeville's two letters.

Efforts by Humboldt and others to free Bonpland from Paraguay had no useful impact in that vein. In the phrasing of John Hoyt Williams, "Francia would rather be branded an international criminal than allow a foreign government to grant permission for other foreigners to trespass on Paraguayan soil."[68] Bonpland was maintained as a topic of conversation in a breadth of intellectual circles. When Humboldt visited Goethe for dinner in December 1826, the items discussed included "fossils, biogeography and Dr. Francia."[69]

Efforts to Communicate with Bonpland in Paraguay

Various letters survive attesting to the efforts to reach Bonpland while he was held hostage in Paraguay. Since chances are remote that Bonpland saw any of these attempts on his behalf earlier than 1831–32, this begs the question of who preserved these letters for a period of some years.

On Christmas Day 1825, Louis-Augustin Guillaume Bosc (1759–1828), the professor in charge of cultivation at the Jardin des Plantes in Paris, wrote Bonpland a note accompanying a box of seeds sent to Buenos Aires. Although uncertain whether his letter would reach its destination, he thought it worth a try. Bosc informed Bonpland that he had not been forgotten in the scientific circles of Paris: "We often speak of you in our scientific meetings."[70] He claimed to have written to Bonpland before his entry into Paraguay, letters that appear to have been lost. The key point in the current news from 1825 was the claim that botany and natural sciences were prospering. Kunth had finished the *Nova genera et species plantarum*, the publication of the plants Bonpland brought back from the Americas during his journey with Humboldt. Humboldt himself was well. Among the Paris-based scientists known to Bonpland but no longer alive was Bosc's predecessor André Thouin (1747–1824), and Bosc forwarded the printed eulogy of Thouin to South America.[71] By the time Bonpland left Paraguay, Bosc himself was dead. In ignorance of that, Bonpland still followed the advice that they exchange plants and seeds, writing to him from Buenos Aires in 1832. He sent him a new species of lily indigenous to Buenos Aires, and questioned Bosc about the means to send a collection of living plants.[72]

While left unspecified, it is highly probable that Raffeneau-Delile was one of the scientists with whom Bosc discussed Bonpland. Although based at Montpellier, Raffeneau-Delile spent part of each year in Paris, where he consistently sought news of Bonpland, especially through the agency of the Delessert family. Raffeneau-Delile wrote to Bonpland from Montpellier in 1826, although he chose not to send his letter until six years later. He had read about Bonpland through a letter of Grandsire's published in *Le Moniteur*. The description of his detainment did not ring true for him, and he felt that Bonpland's prolonged sojourn must have had an element of choice in it. As he would for decades, Raffeneau-Delile painted a very negative picture of the life of an academic botanist. Salaries were insufficient even to buy the necessary books, he opined. Reflecting on his own professional future had brought him a thousand times to Bonpland. Describing his own scientific credentials as profound in certain branches of botany, Raffeneau-Delile reported that a M. de Villiers from Isle Adam (in the Paris Basin) was on his way to Montevideo. De Villiers was supposed to inform Bonpland about the current state of publishing in botany, a field of science "augmented so much by you and by our contemporaries."[73] Raffeneau-Delile wanted hard news of Bonpland, claiming that nothing was conclusive in Grandsire's report. Although Raffeneau-Delile was clearly concerned about Bonpland's fate, de Villiers's mission did not take place. Raffeneau-Delile held on to his 1826 letter for some years; it presumably accompanied the delivery of a later letter from him, written from Montpellier on 27 November 1832.

In 1827, Bonpland was made an honorary citizen of Mexico, recognizing his contributions to the philosophy and knowledge of the New World, especially in that republic. The decree was made on 28 September 1827, in the name of "Bonplant." In the deliberations of the Mexican authorities, three variant spellings of his name are employed, all of them wrong. "Humboldt," they knew how to spell correctly. The citizenship certificate, made out in the name "Amado Bomplant," was sent south from Mexico by Joel Roberts Poinsett (1779–1851), a diplomat and politician then serving as the U.S. minister to Mexico and mainly remembered today for introducing the poinsettia into the United States. Poinsett shared South American experience with Bonpland, having been sent to Buenos Aires in 1810 as a special commissioner investigating the political circumstances leading to independence.[74] Poinsett sent Bonpland's certificate to him, saying he hoped it would be "as useful as it was honorable." If he managed to leave Paraguay and come to Mexico, Poinsett reassured him, "you will be very well received."[75] This well-intentioned document probably languished at Buenos Aires for some years.

. . .

Despite the considerable constraints against him, Bonpland appears to have gained some prosperity in Paraguay. However, it cannot have been of much monetary value. Otherwise, he should have been able to pay the export taxes on his livestock upon receipt of the order to leave the country. In the analysis the Robertsons offer, once Bonpland prospered, back came Francia to torment him again:

> Useful as he was to the Dictator, the distrustful and envious ruler began to get jealous of the increasing popularity of his prisoner. He could not but

feel that his own proceedings offered a sorry, but a most startling contrast to those of Bonpland; and of Bonpland, therefore, he determined to get rid.

It is not easy to say, as regards that amiable man himself, whether his *capture* or his *dismissal* was the basest.[76]

Francia's order to release Bonpland was communicated in a letter of 10 May 1829 to José León Ramírez, the frontier commander at Itapúa.[77] Very soon after, the Brazilian diplomat Correa da Câmara, who was stifling at Itapúa while waiting for permission to proceed to Asunción, was quick to send a negative report about Bonpland to the government he served at Rio de Janeiro:

> This man makes a public profession of being a decided partisan of Napoleon and mourns while remembering those happy times like a *monkey for bananas*, following the popular Brazilian expression. In addition to this, he is a member or correspondent of the Grand Lodge of France under the mask of the Institute. This is sufficient that I can swear on the Holy Saints that M. Bonpland, for whom M. Grandsire went to such extremes, is an archmason and from the highest and most terrible grades of that shady association. He has it in mind to travel as a botanist in Brazil, above all through Minas [Gerais] and Mato Grosso. I believe the imperial government will have all the right to deny him permission, in spite of any treaty or convention.[78]

This note was written on 15 May 1829. On 8 June, Francia wrote the ultimatum that the Brazilian diplomatic representative Correa da Câmara himself should leave the country. The diplomat abandoned Itapúa after a stay there of twenty-one months, arriving at Rio de Janeiro on 4 February 1830.[79]

But Bonpland would not cross the Paraná before February 1831. Twenty months elapsed between the order to release him and his actual removal from Paraguayan territory. The motives for the timing of Francia's initial order were never made clear. Bonpland himself said nothing about this in the various letters he sent outlining the news of his release. However, by 1840, he offered the opinion in a letter he wrote to the French countess Victorine de Chastenay that "irreproachable conduct and the high consideration with which the inhabitants honored me" were stronger motives for the expulsion than any requests coming from the exterior.[80] The only explicit reason Francia gave for freeing Bonpland was the knowledge that his captive was married. This, however, was hardly news; it was a fact Francia had known for years. He ordered that Bonpland could take his material possessions out of Paraguay, thus avoiding a pretext for return or the seeking of damages, but he would not allow Paraguayans associated with him to leave their country. Ten days later, Francia amplified his instructions for the frontier commander. Bonpland could take his livestock out of Paraguay, after paying the export taxes. An alternative was to sell them to the Brazilian merchants who did trade in Paraguay, considered the only people inclined to buy the animals.[81] It is probable that sale of cattle to a Brazilian was what gave Bonpland an initial toehold on Riograndense soil. Little concrete is known about the nature of the realization of Bonpland's assets in Paraguay, or about the consequences of his removal for his private life. Writing to a creditor at Buenos Aires in 1832, he reckoned that he had reached such a state of prosperity that he raised hope not only of settling his former debts but even of remaining with a small fortune and a fine property. He claimed, however, that Francia only accorded him two full days to liquidate his assets, with the result that he left the country much poorer than he entered it.[82]

Word of Bonpland's impending release made its way down to Buenos Aires long before the event took place. Bonpland found the means to send a small note from Paraguay to Buenos Aires through Brazilian intermediaries. The French merchant Roguin received the news of release from two Brazilian travelers, who encountered Bonpland at Itapúa, waiting for his passport to cross the river to freedom. It was to be a long wait. Expecting that Bonpland would already be in Brazil, Roguin wrote him a letter addressed to São Borja on 8 November 1829. It is most unlikely that Bonpland found the chance to read his friend's letter before reaching São Borja in 1831; his reply came from that town on 25 February of that year.

The fragments of remaining correspondence reveal that Bonpland had a difficult life while based at Itapúa, never sure if or when the arrangements to leave Paraguay were to become concrete. He would later describe his errant life from May 1829 to February 1831 as "a true chastisement."[83] Export taxes for livestock were one issue, another was the cost for the maintenance of the *"animalada"* (troop of animals). In April 1830, Itapúa's frontier commander Ramírez informed Francia that Bonpland had made repeated verbal requests for permission to establish a *chacra* where he could look after his animals.[84] They were currently held a half-league beyond the town, at the side of the public road leading to Asunción. Since arriving at Itapúa, Bonpland struggled to meet the costs of sustaining his livestock and his workforce, according to his labor force records. In November 1827, Bonpland had thirteen people in his employ. By October 1830, he was down to nine, and in January 1831 there were but five.[85]

One concrete description of activities in this period occurs for the period 25 to 29 November 1830 for which Bonpland provided a careful accounting of the consequences of a snakebite on one of his workers.[86] The individual, never named, was an Indian originally from Itapúa who was bitten on a hand around the middle of the day at Bonpland's country home about one league from the frontier town. At first, Bonpland used his own blend of local knowledge to apply remedies, including garlic leaves and *icipo* (varieties of climbing vines, some of them holding medicinal properties). Within four hours, he recognized the limitations of his resources. Thus he took his desperately sick peon in his cart to Itapúa, where he called upon the services of an Indian *curuzuya,* or healer. The latter prescribed a different set of remedies, from the familiar cooking salt to the more exotic lizard grease, in order to cleanse the blood. While the patient's outlook seemed very negative for several days (with much pain and alternate experience of hot and cold), by 28 November his urine had lost its red tinge, pain was disappearing, and the road to recovery seemed set. Neither the name of the patient nor the kind of snake are specified. Still, the scientific account of the symptoms readily conveys something of the challenges of Paraguayan frontier life.

Bonpland was subjected to a new interrogation about his motives on 6 December 1830. Francia continued to press for information on Bonpland's associations with other governments and with foreign individuals, including Grandsire, Robert de Connaut, and Rengger. Had the government of France sent him as a spy? Was he an emissary of the government of Buenos Aires? On 17 December, the news was brought to him that he could cross the river. In addition, he would only need to pay the costs for transport across the Paraná. Francia had spared him the export taxes.[87]

Bonpland kept a brief diary of his exit from Paraguay. The manuscript is still legible, but the paper is in poor condition. Written in a kind of shorthand, this document is rich in empirical detail. It shows how he tried to provide an accurate description of the topography, with brief commentary on the rock formations and the main types of vegetation. Several references to vestiges of the South American jaguar also appear. Bonpland crossed the Paraná on 2 February 1831. It was a long and difficult passage, complicated by a strong wind from the southeast and by the fact that the river was in flood. It had rained daily for several weeks either locally or in the mountains. Bonpland praised the skill and courage of the ten Indians who navigated the canoe, made from a single piece of *timbo* (timber). Once on the Misiones bank, it took time to load and prepare his eight carts. He left the banks of the

Paraná to cross Misiones around four o'clock in the afternoon of 8 February, spending the first evening under way around the chapel of Santo Tomás (an Arroyo Tomás appears on modern maps of Misiones), a place he seems to have recognized, perhaps because the road from Corrientes to Candelaria passed through it. It was beyond Santo Tomás, Bonpland claimed, that the traveler began to find forests. The vegetation offered a different aspect; it began to be "majestic." During this first evening on the move, "vagabond Indians" adroitly removed four of his best horses, offering an early contrast to the settled conditions he had long experienced in Paraguay.

From Santo Tomás a traveler could still see the ruins of the village of San Carlos, whose location was marked by a Chile pine, which rose majestically above all the remaining vegetation. When Bonpland entered San Carlos, his predominant impression was of ruin. This is hardly surprising, since this former mission was the site of a battle in 1817 between the Brazilians and the Guaraní regional leader Andresito Artigas, linked with the latter's bold but futile efforts to recover the territory of the seven missions in Rio Grande do Sul.[88] Bonpland found all the houses destroyed, save for a single room where some wooden saints had been gathered. On the wall of this room, somebody had written in block letters "vive Napoleon," an effort he ascribed to Grandsire. As usual, Bonpland was interested in the vegetation surrounding the Jesuit mission. He found it so overgrown that to walk required axes and knives in hand. Without a guide on hand, he was unable to examine the yerba said to be growing there.

On approaching the banks of the Uruguay River, Bonpland was again using the services of an Indian guide. And the passage across the Uruguay River was again made by canoe, this time a very small one. Bonpland arrived at the former mission São Borja on the evening of 14 February 1831. His carts containing his belongings arrived two days later. The town had been described in detail by his compatriot Saint-Hilaire in 1821, when circumstances for the resident Guaraní were already difficult.[89] The 1820s had accelerated population decline.[90] However, as the military and ecclesiastical administrative center of Missões, the mission district of Rio Grande do Sul, São Borja held a strategic significance that far outstripped its modest population. It formed a crucial node in external trade links with Paraguay. Given Bonpland's earlier pattern of experiences, it is not surprising that he chose to make his subsequent base for many years around this town.

Even if Bonpland had the means to receive Roguin and Parchappe's 1829 letters while still at Itapúa, he would have digested their contents more readily from the freedom of São Borja. So much had happened since 1821, the merchant Roguin wrote, that it would take volumes to describe the changes. Nevertheless, he managed in a single letter to summarize much of practical value to his old friend, about family, business, and broadscale social and economic changes. For example, he brought news of Bonpland's wife Adeline and her moving residence patterns. Roguin knew nothing in detail about Emma's fate. The next theme he raised was the status of collections. At the time he was dragged into Paraguay, Bonpland had deposited extensive materials in both Buenos Aires and Corrientes. The latter materials were in the hands of Breard, one of the associates in the French commercial venture of the early 1820s. Roguin warned Bonpland not to expect too much of their condition, thinking that the collections were either "entirely lost, or at least strongly damaged."[91] Voulquin had remained at Caacatí from the moment when Bonpland was taken prisoner; Roguin had nothing positive to say about the state of his activities there. Galup, Bonpland's legal executor at Buenos Aires, had been dead for around a year, which also had obvious bearing for the state of Bonpland's effects. Roguin held letters for Bonpland; they included, presumably, material from Bosc, from Poinsett, from Raffeneau-Delile, and possibly from others. He informed Bonpland of the current prices for Paraguayan tobacco and for yerba in the Buenos Aires market. Paper money had arrived. Revolution and war had been bad for Buenos Aires merchant houses. Many that Bonpland knew in flourishing condition had ceased to exist. Roguin & Meyer, earlier the leading French merchants at Buenos Aires, had broken their partnership two years back. If Bonpland were to arrive in Buenos Aires suddenly, Roguin informed him, accommodation would not be a problem. Three rooms were at his disposition in Roguin's home at no. 19, Chacabuco, in the heart of the city. Roguin's letter accompanied one from Parchappe, another of the French commercial adventurers.[92] The unexpected news that Bonpland was placed in liberty came as a source of joy to all his old friends. Parchappe felt that Bonpland had been dealt a rough deal in the Americas. Presuming that Bonpland would be crossing the Atlantic as soon as possible, he hoped they might be able to travel together.

Subsequent to his long confinement in Paraguay, Bonpland made many references to Paraguay, mainly detailing the stresses of the experience and his efforts to advance the scientific work: "When I came out of Paraguay, I found myself alone and bereft of everything."[93] Relative age was also a repeated theme, as became evident in correspondence with Humboldt.

Writing to him in July 1836, Bonpland did not know Humboldt's exact date of birth at the time of his letter (to which the recipient charmingly replied "14 September 1769, I am an antediluvian!"), although he knew that Humboldt was sixty-six, which, he said, was no cause for concern: "Dr. Francia is in his 85th year. He is strong, active, vigorous, and rides a horse almost every day." Humboldt noted in the margin, "it is a lot when one is bothered that tyrants have a long life."[94] Francia was, in fact, around seventy. The theme of exaggeration of the dictator's age continued in a letter to the famous biogeographer Augustin Pyrame de Candolle: "Francia the doctor, the abominable tyrant Francia, who all his neighbors and the European powers leave in peace despite the repeated insults he directs at everybody, Francia, I say, is 92 and is well. I confess to you that I have the wish to live an equally long time and that I hope to enjoy the benefit of my work in South America."[95] In poor health, and probably aware of his impending death, de Candolle claimed himself moved by this ambition for longevity, seeing it as concrete proof of Bonpland's present state in 1840 and a tribute to the benefits of his "errant and active life."[96] When Francia died in 1840, Bonpland informed Humboldt of this, forecasting the gradual emancipation of the Paraguayans from his system. Were it possible to make a scientific journey there, he said, he would not hesitate for a moment, conscious that in the nine years of captivity he had seen only "a very small extent of territory."[97] This ambition would be realized in 1857, but again involving only very limited terrain.

Bonpland received considerable stimulus to publish his Paraguayan experiences. Writing from Glasgow University in 1835, William Jackson Hooker noted: "I have read with peculiar interest the brief notices I have seen in the papers respecting your adventures in Paraguay. I have seen with pleasure the statements that you have spent many a leisure hour in collecting the vegetable treasures of the country you have visited."[98] Wondering whether Bonpland had yet published his Paraguayan "adventures," Hooker returned to the same theme in 1842, now from the Royal Botanic Gardens at Kew: "I know not whether you have published any account of your very prolonged stay in Paraguay."[99] Writing from the closer vantage of South America, the French medical doctor Adolphe Brunel also made the point that Bonpland had all the necessary skills and experiences to write a superb book on Paraguay.[100] Brunel was almost certainly in error here, ignoring the fact that his friend Bonpland had led a highly circumscribed life in the country. Unlike Rengger, for example, Bonpland never found any chance to interact with

Francia in person. There can be no doubt that the experiences in Paraguay left their deep psychological scars. Some of the best evidence supporting this comes not in a letter but in a much later reference to plant work undertaken while in captivity. In a discussion of pumpkins and gourds, Bonpland commented on how the Paraguayan population made use of starchy tubers to replace bread in the diet, even leading people to forget the existence of this last. He maintained that during the nine years of captivity, "I never ate bread, I was never able to drink wine, and I was able to speak French only once."[101] These were very specific forms of torment for a Frenchman.

CHAPTER THREE

From Paraguay to Pago Largo

> One who has traveled through diverse parts of the Americas is astonished and saddened by the landscapes of the Buenos Aires pampas. As much as nature has been lavish in almost all parts of the New World, it has been equally parsimonious in this part here. The Buenos Aires countryside presents a picture of the greatest sterility, destitute as it is of trees and bushes. . . . It is truly shameful to see that the European Spanish, in the space of three centuries, have left this land so short of trees.
>
> FROM BONPLAND'S PLANS FOR AN INTEGRATED AGRICULTURAL PROJECT, 1832[1]

> At last I can breathe freely about our old business projects. If I could have predicted that the enormous lists of books Messrs. Belgrano, Sarratea and Rivadavia [leading figures in the independence of Argentina] demanded of me for the Buenos Aires library would not have been accepted, we would not have had such lovely dreams. Beyond that, there are a multitude of misunderstandings too long and too painful to remember.
>
> LETTER FROM BONPLAND TO BARROIS L'AÎNÉ, A PARIS BOOK DEALER AND PUBLISHER, 1838[2]

Following his sudden and unexplained release from Paraguay in 1831, Bonpland faced the challenges of setting up a new life, the considerable task of adjusting to freedom. While educated Europeans took for granted his imminent return to that continent, the long experience of Paraguay and the friendships developed there anchored him in the subtropics. He came to divide his residence between the former Jesuit missions of Rio Grande do Sul (including São Borja) and the grasslands of southeastern Corrientes. He would make extended descriptions of the geography of both these regions. During the first year of freedom, his correspondents were almost wholly American, testimony to the immediate challenges of subsistence. Soon after began a flurry of correspondence with European intellectuals, mainly botanists, which included discussions of plans to publish his South American materials.

Coming out of Paraguay, Bonpland was still pursued by financial problems stemming from his earlier career at Buenos Aires. These are central to understanding his work patterns. Scientific materials deposited before the journey to Paraguay remained to be recovered. Offers of employment from politicians sympathetic to Bonpland's plight all needed to be weighed and called for diplomatic answers. Trips to Buenos Aires in 1832 and 1836–37 provided rare opportunities for sustained library-based studies of published materials, including of some of Humboldt's writings about the equinoctial journey. Scientific journals compiled while at Buenos Aires provide an important window into Bonpland's major preoccupations. While he was written up earlier exclusively in relation to French metropolitan scientific institutions, there is evidence from this period of broader links, with Britain and with Italy.

As financial obstacles cleared for Bonpland (he received part of the arrears of his French state pension in 1837, for example), he paid closer attention to describing Corrientes, a part of Argentina famous for its degree of geographical variety. His manuscripts are an important source on the greater degree of rural organization of this period. Part of his concern for making regional surveys was practical. He filed a land claim in the 1830s for a ranch at Santa Ana, the place where he would die in 1858. The gathering promise of this period (for example, he sent very extensive collections to the Jardin des Plantes in Paris) was undercut by the battle at Pago Largo in 1839. In the long struggle to design a workable political and economic framework for Argentina, Bonpland had identified with the interests of the interior, in this instance the losing side.

Adjusting to Freedom

Bonpland arrived at São Borja on the evening of 14 February 1831. It was the first secure place on the route out of Paraguay. The town presumably appealed also because it was on the line of communication with Paraguay, where he had left behind friends, and possibly also family. Even so, Bonpland did not acquire a fixed home at São Borja for several years. Given the circumstances of his sudden removal from Paraguay, he was doubtless short of resources. But he worked with energy to pick up the threads of his life, quickly throwing himself into research. He used São Borja as the base for various expeditions, making new travels in districts around the valley of the Uruguay River and to the former missions in the interior of Rio Grande do Sul.[3]

Bonpland also spent some of his time in newly found freedom communicating with the broader world. His first letter aimed at a distant correspondent appears to be that to Dominique Roguin of 25 February, bringing knowledge to the world that he was now free.[4] This picked up the threads from 1821, when Roguin himself had narrowly escaped capture by Francia's troops. Bonpland had more grounds to trust Roguin's reliability in connection with seeking his release from Paraguay than that of Consul Mendeville at Buenos Aires. However, he also wrote to Mendeville on the same date.[5] He had known Mendeville socially during his early sojourn at Buenos Aires; his wife Mariquita held an important salon that the Bonplands attended.[6] Arriving out of Paraguay only a few days earlier, Bonpland claimed not to know that Mendeville served as French consul general at Buenos Aires. He had learned this through the 1829 letter Roguin sent to him in Paraguay. Bonpland regretted that he could not travel immediately to Buenos Aires. He needed to stay around São Borja for some time to work on his collections and to settle pressing business affairs. Bonpland informed the consul about the state of some of the French still resident in Paraguay, including a M. Montenegro at Asunción "who passes for a Frenchman." He also sent him concrete news of some of Mendeville's in-laws, who were still living prosperously in Paraguay from "all the cattle and hidden treasures." These included Evarista Thompson, based at Santiago. After giving the news of Mendeville's family, he sought some about his own, but not, we note, about his wife Adeline. Roguin had already clarified something of that situation. Bonpland wanted to know whether his brother still lived at La Rochelle: "He is a medical doctor and very well known under the name of Goujaud-Bonpland."[7]

There were also important bridges to build with the political leaders of the broader region. Bonpland wrote to Pedro Ferré, the governor of Corrientes, from São Borja in March 1831, telling him that he had crossed the Paraná during the previous month "by disposition of the Supreme Dictator of the Republic of Paraguay."[8] As soon as he had placed his collections in order and had the chance to visit the former Jesuit missions located on

Brazilian soil, he wanted to visit Corrientes and see Ferré in person. In part, his motive must have been to recover books and materials left on the soil of Corrientes in 1821. This trip was projected for early May, but it did not take place until near the end of the year on account of a quickly growing workload in Missões. Ferré responded to the news of freedom on 25 April 1831, through a letter full of support. Bonpland's reply to this was slow, probably because he was away from São Borja, engaged on field visits in the interior of Rio Grande do Sul.

The positive overtures came not only from Ferré. Bonpland also received support from Fructuoso Rivera, the first president of independent Uruguay. In specific, Bernabé Magariños, Rivera's nephew, and the political chief of northwestern Uruguay, offered him a home in the colony at Bella Unión (the borderland settlement where many of the Riograndense Guaraní were congregated following Rivera's brief occupation of Missões).[9] Bonpland replied that he would like to follow the impulse of his heart. Still, he rejected the idea of going to Uruguay immediately, arguing that he wished to follow a plan established since leaving Paraguay.[10] While he never laid out explicitly what he meant by his plan, no doubt it involved revisiting the places where he had left books and materials prior to his enforced stay in Paraguay, in part in an effort to recover lost money. In the following year, while visiting Buenos Aires, he would also reject, in respectful language, an offer made by Alejandro Heredia, the governor of Tucumán, of a work base there.[11]

In September 1831, Bonpland was already drawing together some of the results of his recent work. He wrote to the frontier commander Lieutenant-Colonel José Boaventura Soares da Silva about medical plants he had found in the region.[12] He also reflected on what other intellectuals had made of his surroundings, interested particularly in the work of Auguste de Saint-Hilaire and of Friedrich Sellow.

Bonpland replied at last to Ferré's April letter, inviting him to settle in Corrientes, in October. The delay has its value today because it encouraged Bonpland to explain his actions to the governor. He had planned to leave for Corrientes when a smallpox epidemic broke out at São Borja. As he phrased it, he was obliged to delay in order to vaccinate the frontier commander's family, a person from whom he had received many favors. One session of vaccination of the local population quickly led to considerably more. Then Bonpland took ill himself and spent six weeks in bed, a period during which other people saw the benefits of the treatment. The pest was now coming to an end, he reported, noting with his characteristic optimism that "only the class which refused vaccination has suffered." Bonpland appreciated the offer of official help to make his journey but noted that he would use this only with moderation, taking his own peons as far as La Cruz (a former Jesuit mission and a frontier post with Corrientes). He also intended to use his own horses as much as possible. Based on what he had learned in Paraguay, and what he was now hearing from São Borja, Bonpland evinced the opinion that the province of Corrientes was "the happiest, richest, and freest of South America."[13] This was flattery for sure, but it also provides some reflection of Ferré's reputation for good government.

Bonpland wrote Ferré a letter acknowledging a passport on 14 December. He said he had been with his "foot in the stirrup" since the end of October, making it difficult to predict his exact day of departure, but he was now planning to leave São Borja for sure on 20 December.[14] He met this objective, taking several weeks to reach the city of Corrientes.[15] This journey was one made under escort, with soldiers supplied by the government. It was a time of very hot weather, which evidently rendered much of the journey uncomfortable. Bonpland noted that he was traveling with only fourteen of the sixteen horses that he brought out of Paraguay. He began the journey with fourteen horses, a mare, and a colt, but exchanged these for government horses at Curuzú Cuatiá.

Crossing the Uruguay River at a point near Itaqui, the main feature of interest was a *puesto* (military station) established by Chamorro, the former commander of the Correntino frontier near La Cruz, in order to engage in contraband trafficking more easily with Brazil. Contraband was always an important theme of life in the valley of the Uruguay River, and Bonpland would later gain direct experience of its consequences from his Estancia de Santa Ana. He commented on a striking feature on the Corrientes bank of the river, the putrid remains of mules that had drowned when a Brazilian tried to make them cross the river at an inappropriate time. Bonpland was not allowed to take his servant into Corrientes. The first place encountered in Corrientes was La Cruz, one of the southernmost of the former Jesuit missions, described as essentially depopulated, a reflection of the raids made from Brazil earlier in the century. At the end of 1831, the tiny population of La Cruz was heavily slanted toward military authority. A picket of ten soldiers guarded the place, headed by a corporal "with the pompous title of commandant."[16] The remainder of the population was almost exclusively Indian, including Colonel Cabañas, a well-known figure. Although Ferré's recommendations speeded the bureaucracy at La Cruz, Bonpland still found time to visit the ruins of the former mission. The remains of the imposing former mission church had been used to erect a low structure, but one long enough to hold two hundred people. He slept outside of La Cruz, near the "dismal hut" of an old Paraguayan. Neither time nor the revolutions, he said, had budged this man from his elevated location looking out over the two banks of the river.

During the journey across the plains of easternmost Corrientes, Bonpland was always interested in the geography of the soils and of where specific types of vegetation began and finished. Using vegetation to establish settlement patterns, he noted the presence of orange woods and signs of former inhabitance in the form of *taperas*. The trajectory from São Borja to the Miriñay River included immense *bañados* (marshy areas), where the vegetation was mainly the famous tall-grass cortadera (*Panicum giganteum*) of Paraguay, used to roof houses. Like any other traveler, Bonpland was always keen to spend the night in places that offered some comfort. Expecting on the night of 26 December to be a guest at the Estancia Ombú, belonging to the Acosta family of the city of Corrientes, the absence of the *capataz* led to other plans. When one of the Barañados, a scion of another ranching family, met up with Bonpland for the pleasure of his company and to offer his services, the latter noted somewhat sarcastically that he was forced "to make a detour of four leagues and to sleep at a wretched sheep *puesto*. I dined outdoors on lamb and I also slept outdoors, on a hide." But not all met with criticism in this corner of Corrientes. In the margin of the manuscript, Bonpland added the following: "It is in Doctor Acosta's estancia that I first saw some signs of civilization since my exit from Paraguay. The house, its layout, and its furniture are reminiscent of Europe. In addition, a small library containing some law books gave me a happy moment. For the last ten years, I had not seen a single book."[17]

At first Bonpland lived under the impression that the sun-burned prairies around Curuzú Cuatiá were sterile and bad. He later corrected this. He came to recognize that the pastures on the plains of Curuzú Cuatiá, at La Esquina, and at all intermediate points were the best in the province. They rivaled those farther south around the Paraná and in Uruguay. The cause of the high-quality pasture was ascribed to the presence of the grass known as *flechilla*. The animals of these pastures were reminiscent of Europe on account of their size and overall fatness. In Curuzú Cuatiá, Bonpland's list of the people he encountered includes members of the regional elite, such as Antonio Díaz de Vivar and Joaquín Madariaga, later a governor of the province.

At Curuzú Cuatiá, Bonpland exchanged his own horses for government horses. He began to write about the state of poverty in parts of Corrientes. Crossing the Corrientes and Batel Rivers on New Year's Day 1832, he noted these would be dangerous to cross in the winter. Around the Batel, the forests of Yatay palms began: "The palm forests are found in very sandy and mobile terrain. They offer a great abundance of vegetation, which is found only there, and they are worthy of being visited at greater leisure and with the greatest care."[18] He spent a fair amount of time at San Roque, mainly to give the commander Romero news of his relatives in Paraguay.[19] The environs of San Roque did not appeal. It was a flat country burned by the sun, with what he termed a "dismal vegetation."[20]

Approaching the Paraná, Bonpland was aware of a greater level of economic development. He could already sense the influence of the city of Corrientes in the landscape. Dwellings were more frequent and more land was in cultivation. Near Empedrado, he noted observing sugarcane very small in stature, fields of sweet potatoes, and a little manioc. The journey ended on 5 January 1832 at Corrientes, where he spent around a month.

On 20 February 1832, Bonpland left brief notes on a visit he made to the estancia of José Santos Maciel, located to the south along the Paraná River in Santa Fe. He made this journey specifically to examine the plant known as Guaicurú root, first identified on the Maciel estancia. Travel by canoe did not prove easy, on account of the islands and shifting channels in the river.[21] Presumably long known to the Indians of this name, the raíz del Guaicurú was a considerable novelty in the medicine of the remainder of the population. Bonpland sent samples of it to the Jardin des Plantes in January 1837. Although sold by all the pharmacists at Buenos Aires, he had no confidence in its claimed efficacy as a medical remedy.[22] Bonpland left Santa Fe for Buenos Aires on 5 March 1832.

Work at Buenos Aires, 1832

Given the circumstances of his life since leaving Buenos Aires over a decade earlier, and the personality of his adversary, Bonpland's return to this city took on the character of a "fantastic phenomenon," becoming something of a public spectacle.[23] According to Juan Domínguez, shortly after arriving, he had an extended interview with Juan Manuel de Rosas, presumably covering the state of politics in Paraguay.[24] A huge proportion of Bonpland's time while in the city was spent in reconnecting with the world beyond

South America, most importantly in connection with issues relating to his French state pension. Only a fraction of Bonpland's work at Buenos Aires in 1832 has thus far been published. For example, the only correspondence published by Hamy coming out of this extended visit to the city relates to Humboldt and to Raffeneau-Delile at Montpellier, admittedly both figures of the first importance for Bonpland's scheme of work. But records in his surviving notes attest to other letters sent from Buenos Aires to Europe, specifically to Dupuytren, Alibert, Barrois, and Bosc at Paris.[25] Although Bonpland had received an invitation in 1829 from the merchant Roguin to reside with him, in fact, he stayed with Pedro de Angelis and his wife at Buenos Aires. De Angelis was a major intellectual of the Río de la Plata, who in 1854 would later author the first biography of Bonpland.[26]

Part of the reason for going to Buenos Aires was to settle old business. In particular, Bonpland was keen to discuss a debt he contracted before 1821 with George Frederick Dickson, a British merchant, then based at Buenos Aires. Approaching Buenos Aires in March, Bonpland claimed that he was looking forward to meeting again with Dickson and his family—he read of Dickson's name frequently in the official newspapers—but found that he had returned to England. He was, in fact, living in Regent's Park, London, representing Argentina's consular interests in Britain for a spell.[27] Bonpland presented himself before Dickson's associate at his Buenos Aires merchant house. This individual, left unnamed, reminded him of a debt. Bonpland's concern was not to squeeze out of the debt owed, neither the capital nor any interest, but he understandably wanted to learn the fate of 299 original drawings given to Dickson as a guarantee against the money borrowed.[28] Before 1821, Bonpland must have felt some ground for optimism about his finances; otherwise, he would never have risked original materials as a loan guarantee. Dickson's associate at Buenos Aires knew nothing about these, which helps to explain why Bonpland wrote to London. Although he presumed the drawings were in safe hands with Dickson, questions about them remain unanswered today. Presumably, this work came from the initial stages of Bonpland's independent career in South America, and it related to subjects drawn to order for him by Pierre Benoit, his assistant at Buenos Aires. Colored drawings of insects and butterflies today found in the Bonpland archive at Buenos Aires could possibly be this material—or could it be something else, such as drawings of plants prepared for the projected flora of the United Provinces (Argentina)? A few years later, Bonpland would also maintain to Humboldt that his "little herbarium," deposited at Buenos

Aires in 1820, had also found its way to England.[29] In his letter to London, Bonpland made several references to the stars, claiming a good one had followed him up until 1816 and a poor one since. If fortune had been even a little bit propitious, he claimed, he would have been back in Europe, concerning himself with publications and living "in the midst of civilization." Bonpland told Dickson he could write to him either through his agents at Buenos Aires, the French merchant company Blanc & Constantin at Calle de la Paz, no. 11, or "directly to São Borja in the Portuguese missions."

Whatever disappointments Bonpland must have experienced about the loss of material, the intellectual resources available at Buenos Aires stimulated him to new work. In March, he began the first of a series of scientific journals at Buenos Aires, designed to record the results of his reading on technical matters. We do not know for sure where he did his reading, but there was probably no better candidate for orientation around the libraries and archives at Buenos Aires than his host de Angelis.[30] The first of the diaries is a manuscript of ten double-sided folios. Its contents are certainly evidence of a broad-ranging curiosity, mainly with regard to South American resources. It begins with notes on tanning taken from baron Louis Jacques Thénard's text on chemistry.[31] Bonpland was interested in the chemical analysis of tobacco, taking as one of his authorities Louis Nicolas Vauquelin, with whom he had worked in Paris before leaving for South America. Some of the books he consulted were marked as candidates for purchase, despite the errors he found in them. Augustin Pierre Dubrunfaut's 1824 study of the methods of distillation offered a prime example of this.[32] Another concern was the falling consumption levels of maté in Chile and Peru. This was explained through the fact that tea and coffee drinking had become almost universal within the upper classes. In addition, the quality of the Brazilian maté exported through the port of Paranaguá was viewed as a truly inferior product. Much of the diary's content concerned medical questions. Bonpland was interested in learning how long a human could live without eating and drinking. Here he took Pliny and the records of the French Academy of Sciences as authorities. The latter contained the details of a case from 1700, where a young earthquake victim at Naples lived for two weeks without food and water. Bonpland was not convinced: "The examples which are daily presented to us do not offer examples of such a long abstinence." Just where and when he was experiencing cases of starvation in the interior of South America he left unremarked. Birds being a major theme of his current collecting, it is no surprise that they receive some attention in the notes. He noted to himself to consult Alexander Wilson's ornithology of the United States, said to be a work of fine quality.[33] Another concern was how to make arsenic soap, indispensable for the preservation of bird specimens.

In April, Bonpland received surgical instruments from his brother Michel-Simon Goujaud-Bonpland at La Rochelle.[34] These were no doubt of vital importance for the generation of income. Indeed, there are notes of a medical journey made to the banks of the Paraná River in May, to Capilla del Señor (in Buenos Aires Province), to San Lorenzo, Santa Fe, and possibly to Rosario.

On 7 May 1832, Bonpland paid a visit to Santa Catalina, the site of the former Scottish colony Monte Grande developed by the Scottish merchants John Parish and William Parish Robertson in the 1820s with Rivadavia's encouragement.[35] Today, the trees planted there by the Scottish immigrants form part of a protected ecosystem distinctive in the whole of South America, on the grounds of an agronomy school. Although the colony was presumed a casualty of politics after 1829, some activity was still visible in 1832.[36] We have no direct testimony beyond a plant description, but it may be that Santa Catalina stimulated Bonpland to think once more about the prospects for extending cultivation in and around the city of Buenos Aires.[37]

Through the agency of his Neapolitan-born host de Angelis, Bonpland opened communication in June 1832 with Michel Tenore, the director of the botanical garden at Naples.[38] Bonpland sent thirty-two species of plants to Tenore, with very specific comments about the properties of indigenous plants. He also made clear that he had selected a subset of what he sent on to Paris, by choosing items particularly suitable to the climate of Naples. In return, Bonpland requested herbaceous cotton. It is on record that Tenore sent this to South America, but the fate of the cotton is not known.[39] It was probably a casualty of the recipient's inability to revisit Buenos Aires before a five-year interval.

June also offered more scope for reading and writing. Using de Angelis's library, Bonpland was able to read extensively from earlier travel accounts dealing with the Upper Plata. He also consulted more recent published works, including those of Humboldt, and made scientific notes on a wide range of topics. The contents of these notes are too extensive to report in their totality, but the following brief examples will serve to demonstrate their diversity.[40] Reading a report about Peruvian cotton made by the South Carolina Agricultural Society, Bonpland speculated whether this would resemble the cotton grown in Paraguay that he had seen. In the newspaper *El Lucero*, no doubt an organ of ready access, since it was published by de Angelis from 1829 to 1833, he read about the Chaco region. Elsewhere, Bonpland consulted newspaper reports made by the British consul Joseph Barclay Pentland at Arequipa, Peru, about the measurement of the highest peaks in the Andes, learning for the first time that Chimborazo was not the tallest peak in the cordilleras. Bonpland had not accompanied the highest climb in the world after all.[41] In addition, there are records on subjects as diverse as cholera and paleontology. On a topic such as the transport of woody plants from and to the Rio de Janeiro botanical garden, the level of detail is especially rich. In Buenos Aires, Bonpland could also finally read some of the key publications that had emerged during his long period of captivity in Paraguay. Devouring the fifth volume of Humboldt's travel account of their shared journey to the Americas and his *Tableaux de la nature*, this reader's interests mainly concerned crops and the subject of how easily authors rendered indigenous names incorrectly.[42] Criticism of Humboldt's errors was mild in comparison with those supposedly made by Saint-Hilaire in his books on Brazil. Bonpland reckoned what Saint-Hilaire had to say about the cultivation of cotton and tobacco was useless, presumably in the sense of anybody seeking to follow the written advice.[43]

In the same month, Bonpland completed a manuscript on a scheme for the agricultural improvement of the area around Buenos Aires.[44] It is unclear today what stimulated him to write this, but his recent visit to Santa Catalina may have had some bearing. The document provides an important window into Bonpland's preoccupations. His paper begins by singing the praises of the tropics for cultivation, of which he had gained direct experience in the Upper Plata, including Paraguay. He then says he will pass in silence over the colder regions, in order to see what could be done in a temperate climate, such as Buenos Aires.

An implicit understanding of the concept of land rent is present in Bonpland's paper. This concept is set out as a series of three interlocking types of rural establishment, where the intensity of land use was at its highest close to the city. Zone three was to be a carefully managed estancia. No doubt impressed by the growth of the city since leaving it over a decade before, Bonpland comments on the already immense daily consumption of the city, observing that "the population of Buenos Aires is already very large and susceptible to increase in a progression that nobody can calculate." In James Scobie's study of urban change at Buenos Aires, he noted how it was still a *gran aldea* (large village) in 1870; we need to remember that Bonpland's most immediate residence patterns before sounding so optimistic about Buenos Aires hinged around a series of former Jesuit mission settlements, whose small populations were but a fraction of what they had been in the first half of the eighteenth century.[45] He clearly saw potential for doing much more to furnish the growing domestic market, maintaining nearly from the beginning that profit from fruits and vegetables was viable. Crops such as maize, wheat, tobacco, and sweet potatoes were seen as better cultivated in fields than in gardens. Pumpkins in particular would yield a quick income. Planting trees for firewood was a less easy economic proposition; they needed more time to render a stream of income. At the time, Buenos Aires drew only on peach trees for firewood. Bonpland seemed keen to work with a managed forest of these, from which could be drawn a "true Kirschwasser drink." Distillation was another echo of his period of captivity in Paraguay. Beyond working with plants already in Argentina, Bonpland stressed the importance of making further introductions. Once a model property was established, he said, it would be easy to make direct contacts with various parts of France and with England, the United States, Mexico, and Brazil in the search for further useful vegetable material. These were precisely the main countries where Bonpland had correspondents.

Phase two of the scheme involved milk cows and merinos. With work and perseverance, Bonpland thought that the wool of Buenos Aires could conquer the markets of Europe, in the way that Saxony wools were sought to a greater degree in 1832 than those from Spain. Here, his optimism had some concrete foundation. He noted that the value of crossbreeding could be seen in the beauty of the wool produced by Peter Sheridan, the famous sheep pioneer on the pampas, whose animals were supposedly not treated with any greater care than the creole flocks. Bonpland was something of an authority on merinos, having managed an important flock for Joséphine at Malmaison.[46] He also knew Sheridan personally; Sheridan supplied Bonpland with merino breeding stock for his experiments in southeastern Corrientes during the later 1830s.[47]

According to Bonpland, the only forage plant cultivated around Buenos Aires in 1832 was some alfalfa. He called for research into forage grasses, concerned mainly about the winter feeding of his projected large flocks of merino sheep. Alfalfa would not serve here. He had seen entire flocks of merinos perish when inflated by gas. Whether this was on the grasslands of Argentina or in Napoleonic France is not specified.

Other crops worthy of closer attention included cotton. When Levant cotton arrived from Naples (a hidden reference to Michel Tenore and the botanical garden he headed), it needed to be sown with great care. In an age still dependent on candles, Bonpland saw potential great economy in using cotton in the manufacture of candlewicks. Tobacco was also destined to become important with time. He based this judgment on the success of his own planting experiments at Buenos Aires in 1819. In addition, tobacco was in cultivation on Governor Rosas's ranches; in 1832, it was supposed that "everybody" knew of the success of this venture. Ornamental flowers deserved to be encouraged for pharmaceutical purposes.

There is a particularly revealing passage in the manuscript where Bonpland made clear his displeasure with what he saw as the sterility of the landscape around Buenos Aires, showing his continuing enthusiasm for tropical vegetation. In his words, nature had been miserly, and human initiative on the part of the Spanish during the colonial era had been lacking. The *ombú* (*Phytolacca dioica*), one of the world's largest trees, and the *tala* (*Celtis tala*) were almost the only native species. He saw little economic potential for either. While he thought that the *tala* could serve only as firewood, its modern uses are broader. Today, it is a focus for conservation efforts on the pampas.

The agricultural manuscript provides details of a series of desirable exotic tree species, some of which are viewed as pests today in Argentina. Bonpland was also an enthusiast for bringing trees from the interior into Buenos Aires, but he did not specify what he held in mind. The first exotic species he recommended was the carob tree (*Ceratonia siliqua*), whose fruits, known as St. John's Bread, could serve as seasonal food for livestock. By the early twentieth century, the carob tree was described as covering "immense stretches" of the northern pampas.[48] After reviewing different types of willows and poplars, Bonpland said he had seen two examples of European oaks in the Barracas district of Buenos Aires. These had grown fairly large, he noticed, and he claimed that they would have grown bigger if they had not been maltreated by animals. He took these oaks as a certain index that it was worth trying all the variant species at Buenos Aires, whether from Europe, the United States, or Mexico. The common ash was seen as providing wood of the first rank for Buenos Aires, as in Europe. Brought from France in 1817, very probably by Bonpland himself, the species was doing well in 1832, which encouraged further introductions. This was not the only tree for which Bonpland seems to have been responsible. All the examples of the

Honeylocust (*Gleditsia triacanthos*) present at Buenos Aires were obtained from seeding done in 1817. It is interesting to see how far the many types of tree mentioned had come into use by the 1908 census.

In summary, a present-day reader of Bonpland's manuscript on agricultural development around Buenos Aires will be struck by his energy for change and by his extraordinary level of empirical knowledge about the regional vegetation systems. He never questioned for a moment the wisdom of trying exotic introductions. The optimism in his report reminds us of why Bonpland was almost always regarded as good company in South America, but his idealism is rarely solidly grounded. For example, when he proposed the planting of "immense artificial prairies," or planted pastures, who did he have in mind to pay for the cultivation? Bonpland was no more capable of seeing the future than anyone else, but it is interesting to reflect that Argentina by around 1920 devoted a greater area to alfalfa than any other nation on earth.[49] His idealism contrasts with the cautious experimentation of Rosas, such as the latter's cultivation of alfalfa along the river banks.[50] Diversification of land use was not yet a major consideration at Buenos Aires in the 1830s. The few persons mentioned by name in Bonpland's paper represent an avant-garde. Apart from a buried reference to Michel Tenore at Naples, four other individuals are mentioned by name. Three of these are British pioneers in Argentina's agriculture, whose activities in the first half of the nineteenth century are worthy of more research. The final example is Rosas himself. Domingo F. Sarmiento's famous barb that all Rosas cared for was land has perhaps obscured his practical concerns for its management. Rosas had also authored a guidebook for the effective management of estancias.

Beyond his study and writing, a great deal of Bonpland's time during this long visit to Buenos Aires was presumably spent in the preparation of the twenty-five cases of material that he sent to the Jardin des Plantes. There was, however, still some time for social themes. In July, he took up with Henry Stephen Fox, the British minister, who was interested in botany. According to Bonpland, Fox was very reclusive, a judgment borne out by others, including when he later served as minister to the government of the United States. He had taken the view that it was better to live alone than in society, showing himself to nobody and "roaming the sterile plains of the environs night and day."[51] After a long struggle to gain Fox's company, the two appear to have derived much enjoyment from each other's conversation. Bonpland made him a gift of plants.[52]

On 29 July 1832, a banquet was held at Buenos Aires to celebrate the revolutionary events in Paris of two years earlier, which saw the end of ultra-royalist policies. Roguin was on the organizing committee of this event, attended by 106 members of the French community, and Bonpland was the guest of honor. He was offered the president's chair, but desisted. He did give the toast to Rosas, and listened to speeches and poetry in his honor.[53]

The Return to São Borja and Subsequent Work

Concerned that growing political instability in Uruguay could cut his route of return to São Borja, Bonpland's departure from his first return visit to Buenos Aires was somewhat precipitate.[54] This had important consequences. For example, he sent his cases of materials across the Atlantic before he had found the chance to complete their extensive descriptive catalog. This would soon become a leading source of misunderstandings with the administrators at the Jardin des Plantes. Bonpland also left the city of Buenos Aires only shortly before Charles Darwin was to arrive there; given the latter's well-known appreciation for the Humboldt-Bonpland journey to tropical America, it seems regrettable these two figures never found the chance to meet in person.[55]

Bonpland left a detailed account of his departure from Buenos Aires on 13 October 1832 and his journey by schooner up the Uruguay River as far as the falls at Salto Grande. Leaving the city, he noted his objectives for the coming period of work.[56] These included the immediate objective of ascending the Uruguay River as far as its source, continuing the work in natural history and agriculture, and collecting medicinal plants. He took three young Frenchmen with him to help in this varied work. Auguste Banville was one of the two assistants Bonpland brought with him from France in 1816. Jean Lacour was contracted at Buenos Aires to help with the work of preparing bird specimens. The third assistant was a Pierre Besse.

Parts of the descriptions of Uruguay are usefully detailed accounts of the changing vegetation. Their substance provides much clear evidence of Bonpland's affirmative view of tropical environments. Around Colonia (Colônia do Sacramento), the economy struck him as marginal. There was not a single tree or bush. Still, Bonpland was impressed by the nature of the physical environment, noting "this part of the Banda Oriental is susceptible to a productive agricultural system."[57] He later described this portion of southern Uruguay as "an enchanting district."[58] Martín García offered a different kind of interest. Here, the main theme was not the Europeanization of the vegetation on the island, but plants washed down the rivers from Paraguay and Corrientes. Martín García Chico point was the first place where the traveler saw large trees on the Uruguayan coast, and where the vegetation began to vaguely resemble that of the tropics. Bonpland particularly liked the situation of Rincón de las Gallinas, attracted to both its resources and to the landscape scene. He was not alone in this; a later Uruguayan gazetteer remarked on the place's "absolute tranquility," and how it was much earlier the favored place of residence of the Bohane Indians.[59] Bonpland was much more interested in the physical than the human geography, although he did pay very close attention to describing Purificación, the earlier habitual residence and fortified camp of the great caudillo Artigas. Descriptions of the major towns along the river were left very sketchy. While Salto was an active commerce center, it was for Bonpland perhaps richer for its plant geography curiosities.[60] He found there hedges of *Rosa multiflora*, a plant he claimed to have introduced to Buenos Aires in 1817. He also averred that the stony soils around this town were very suitable for viticulture, an accurate prediction of an economic activity that would follow long after his demise.

Back from Buenos Aires, Bonpland turned to the work of the descriptive catalog to accompany the many cases of materials he had sent to Paris from Buenos Aires. In 1833, the main focus of any descriptions concerns the area around São Borja. He moved extensively around the Jesuit missions of Rio Grande do Sul, engaged in research and making medical trips. A leading focus of his work was the mission São João Mini (always rendered in the Spanish form in Bonpland's writings), where he made several visits during the year and where he organized planting. He made an agreement there on 15 June about the terms under which two people would work for him. By November, a leading theme was the damage caused to the crops by animals. In December 1833, he was visited at São João Mini by the French traveler Arsène Isabelle, who described him living a solitary life at the mission somewhat like the "consoler of Chactas."[61] Bonpland also appears to have put the medical instruments brought from Buenos Aires to good use, in part for the generation of income. For example, he agreed to treat a Lucien Machado, badly affected by syphilis, for the sum of 200$000, agreeing to take his fee half in money and the remainder in livestock.[62] He also left an account of his work during the difficult birthing of a mulatta slave and an examination of an eleven-day-old Tape Indian baby boy.

A general theme of the year 1833 was an effort to rebuild resources. In February 1834, Bonpland attempted to set down roots, buying a small farm outside the town of São Borja for 76$800. He does not appear to have remained there long enough to develop the property, because much of 1834 saw him traveling in different parts of Corrientes. His work involved private research and medical consultations, including with one of Governor Ferré's daughters. His preoccupations along the year could hardly be more various. As he started his travels in southeastern Corrientes, a leading interest was in gathering oral testimony about the relative qualities of the pastures. Revisiting Caacatí, where he had last been in 1821, he made extremely detailed notes on the local methods of cultivating and making sugar. Beyond the usual botany, there are notes from September 1834 about a type of armadillo, whose remains he examined at Corrientes. The following month he described the problems posed by Nuazo snakes in the country around Bella Vista. Piecing together the various writings, there is a sense of great energy but no single theme preoccupying his South American life at this time. Also in 1834 Bonpland read in a Buenos Aires newspaper about the work Alcide d'Orbigny had undertaken in South America, surmising that, if that work were published, it would make an interesting addition to the journeys of Humboldt, of Saint-Hilaire, and of Spix and Martius.[63]

By traveling extensively around Corrientes, Bonpland became increasingly aware of the economic potential of ranching in parts of the province. He seems to have become interested in this as soon as 1835, when he met up at São Borja with Henry [Henrique] Symonds, a British immigrant to Corrientes tied with Liverpool mercantile interests. They appear to have discussed the possibility of working land together. The plan was undoubtedly to petition the Correntino authorities for a land grant. In March 1835, Symonds sent Bonpland brief details from Curuzú Cuatiá of the several estancias currently available for development in southeastern Corrientes.[64] He started with a ranch bordering that of his former business partner, considered by one local authority (probably Mariano Araújo) as the best in the entire province. Currently occupied by a blind man, the advantages of this ranch included the security of its river and arroyo boundaries. It possessed appreciable amount of woodland, yet it was sparse, and the trees were large and old. The pasture was formed of *flechilla* grass. Boundaries and water supplies were the other major factors under consideration. There is a sense in the descriptions that they were looking for cohesive communities. Ranches exposed to political boundaries, such as with Uruguay and Entre Ríos, lost some favor, as did property known to be part of a "very bad neighborhood." Symonds was also advising that they seek a property for their agricultural projects where they could proceed with the least interruption by the military authorities. Location mattered.

Symonds appears to have been very keen to work alongside Bonpland, both for the pleasure of his society and the utility of what they could accomplish. His "most ardent desire" was to realize the plans discussed earlier at São Borja. Nevertheless, these changed in under a week, motivated by the shifting external context.[65] According to Symonds, so many people came looking for land that he felt compelled to settle on a property immediately. Without the necessary capital, Bonpland was not yet ready to settle on an estancia. The project of working with Symonds thus became merely one of a series of ephemeral schemes. The latter went on to lose considerable resources in Corrientes, as he related in a letter written from Montevideo in 1849, on the point of leaving South America for good.[66]

A Second Sojourn in Buenos Aires, 1836–1837

After a fruitful spell of collecting materials in the Upper Plata, Bonpland traveled south again in 1836. Somewhere in the background motives of this second visit to the leading South American metropolis of the era was money. It was time to renew the formalities in connection with his French pension. In addition, he had materials he was anxious to forward to the museum in Paris.[67] In August 1836, Aimé Roger, the interim French consul at Buenos Aires, told the authorities at Paris that Bonpland was expected to show up there very soon.[68] He did not, in fact, arrive in the city before November, but he does not appear to have wasted a minute while present there, working at his usual wide range of preoccupations.

At some point in the early part of his visit, Bonpland met with the Polish traveler Paul Edmond de Strzelecki (1797–1873), later knighted by Queen Victoria for his contributions to the exploration of Australia.[69] The subjects of their discussions are today unknown, but both had considerable American experiences to compare. On 28 November, Bonpland provided a report for Pedro Ferré on a dismantled French industrial saw, offered in exchange for Correntino timber.[70] Originally supplied to a Paris-based furniture-making business in 1825, Bonpland presumed the machine was designed for use with steam or water power. He recommended that Corrientes buy new equipment from Europe rather than rely on machinery of unproven efficiency from Buenos Aires.

At the beginning of December, Bonpland signed a receipt in connection with the final portion of his share of the parental estate; this gave him a sum of over 19,000 francs, more than six years the value of his French state pension.[71] Although he was still working at this time on retrieving unpaid pension money (the sum of 14,700 francs of that came through the following year), he already had firmer grounds for financial optimism, to the point that he could make plans.[72] Before the year ended, he sketched out in writing the plans for a company for the improvement of livestock in Corrientes, the so-called Sociedad Rural de Mejoramiento, which would trade under the name of Bonpland & Company. The administrators were to be Bonpland himself, the French diplomat Alphonse Petitjean, and Frédéric Desbrosses, a merchant and the son-in-law of Petitjean. Most of any visible capital promised for the scheme by the end of 1836 came from Desbrosses.[73] Sheep were very much on the agenda at Buenos Aires in this period, as the province began to benefit from the first concrete results following the introduction of Saxony merinos. Brought in at great expense, the French consul claimed, the breed had acclimatized easily to the pampas. In the export statistics compiled by the French consulate at Buenos Aires for the year 1836, wool exports were already gaining some prominence on the schedule, worth more than half of the long-established salt-beef shipments. Some of the richest rural proprietors were seriously pushing the business of crossbreeding sheep, leading to its considerable expansion.[74]

Although Bonpland lodged with interim Consul Roger, he certainly appears to have maintained his close link with his earlier host de Angelis.[75] Notes in a journal made in November 1836 point to a good deal of reading and to the use of the latter's rich library resources.[76] It is difficult to tell whether he was working with manuscripts, works in progress, or material already in print, but he was certainly interested in de Angelis's work. Since the previous visit to Buenos Aires, this prolific author had launched what became his main work, the enormous *Colección de obras y documentos relativos a la historia antigua y moderna de las provincias del Río de la Plata*.[77] The multiple volumes were very much underway at the time of Bonpland's visit; the project would soon be cut off abruptly with the French blockade, however, on account of shortage of paper on which to print. The topics noted by Bonpland include the history of Buenos Aires, of the Jesuit missions, and of the boundary area between Paraguay and Mato Grosso. He was plainly interested in learning more about the formal history of the places he knew, noting, for example, that the mission Santa Ana was founded in 1633. Bonpland read about the past with a mind to how it could inform his present. Reviewing the history of settlement in northeastern Paraguay, he reminded himself to look on old maps for the pueblo of Mbaracayú, located at the foot of the "mountain" (in fact, a range of hills) carrying the same name: "In the environs of this pueblo, there are immense forests of the maté tree."[78] When the Jesuits moved south from São Paulo in the seventeenth century, they and their charges experienced a dysentery epidemic that took as much as a sixth of their population.[79] Bonpland noted they had used to good medicinal effect a plant found on the banks of the Yabebiri: "This plant is doubtless the wild celery of the missions, which the native doctors are still using against dysentery and a multitude of other illnesses."[80] Reading some of the work of the Spanish boundary commissioner José María Cabrer, he commented especially on the sometimes dangerous violent swellings of the Uruguay River, which was useful and practical information for any resident of the valley considering navigation by canoe.[81] Bonpland himself had witnessed such an event at Santo Tomé in June 1836. He also made interesting reflections on what the Jesuit priest Pedro Lozano had to say about the settlement of the Chaco (de Angelis produced his bibliography of this important region around this period) and the state of the Indians there.[82] Reflecting on the current state of poverty of the Indians on the streets of Corrientes, Bonpland could only blame the Spanish colonial administrations for their fate.

But life at Buenos Aires involved a good deal of writing in addition to reading. Consul Roger drew heavily on Bonpland, "the renowned prisoner of Paraguay," for an analytical report he was asked to compile on the tobacco cultivation of Paraguay and its adjacent regions. The request for the report came from the Régie du Tabac (Tobacco Excise Department) at Paris and was communicated to Buenos Aires in May 1836, a time when the Marquis de Vins de Peysac was still the chief French authority in the city. The plan was to expand on an analytical report on tobacco this last had written from Havana in 1829, a copy of which was in the French consular archives at Buenos Aires to serve as a guide.[83] On 19 December, Roger informed the French government that he had recently finished synthesizing the detailed notes furnished to him in large part by Bonpland; he admitted there were still errors to rectify, but that his informant held the ambition of publishing a work on tobacco cultivation, and any errors could be dealt with in that work. Bonpland had also sent seeds of a tobacco indigenous to Paraguay to the Jardin des Plantes.[84]

The report on Paraguayan tobacco compiled by Roger with Bonpland's help is a tour-de-force in the spirit of trying to convey the manner of cultivation as exactly as possible.[85] In the colonial period, tobacco cultivation in Paraguay was under tight control. As Thomas Whigham has shown, it was hardly the subject of free commerce under the administration of Francia, but the individual cultivators did have somewhat more room to maneuver. Bonpland maintained that two types of tobacco were cultivated in Paraguay after 1812. The first was the colloquially known red tobacco (*Nicotiana tabacum*), drawn initially from Havana. He also maintained that another species, *Pety pucu,* or long tobacco, was cultivated by the Guana Indians, presumably since pre-Columbian times. In the document, a reader understandably gains the direct sense of most developments occurring in the 1820s, the decade when Bonpland was living in Paraguay. Paraguayan tobacco cultivators faced the conundrum that long tobacco produced a greater yield than red tobacco, yet it was recognized to be of inferior quality. Bonpland maintained that the opening of a market to Brazil through Misiones in 1824 brought changes in the patterns of Paraguayan production. He argued that Brazilians cared more about the size of the product than its quality. When samples of long tobacco showed up at Itapúa, a new market opened for the neglected product in Brazil. The conclusion of the tobacco report is bold. It argued that if France was interested in gaining leaves of Paraguayan tobacco, the best approach was probably to direct a request to the dictator himself. Roger knew the risks implied by this approach. But he maintained that some São Borja merchants had been doing business directly with Francia for the past three years and that the latter was susceptible to flattery. Here again in the report, the hand of Bonpland seems clearly evident.

The second return visit to Buenos Aires provided an occasion in which Bonpland's portrait was drawn by Carlos Pellegrini, in a three-hour sitting of 9 January 1837. This image, important for being the earliest along his long southern South American career, was not published until 1854, when some of its viewers confused it with contemporary work.[86] Bonpland's correspondence written during his second return to Buenos Aires runs to twenty-seven pages in Hamy's biography, making it the most heavily documented section of his South American life from any single period or place.[87] Many of the letters are compressed into a portion of the Buenos Aires visit, probably reflecting the most efficient way of handling the work. While Bonpland was working on the tobacco manuscript, his correspondence seems to have been mainly concerned with renewing contacts with friends and family in France. These letters reveal what he liked about residence in South

America, with emphasis on the quality of the climate and excellent friendship. He informed his old friend Gigaux at La Rochelle that the town São Borja had more than tripled in population during the past four years, a level of economic development in singular contrast to what he had learned about the place of his birth.[88] In a letter to his sister, very detailed memories of specific landscape geography related to family property; he maintained that he experienced no wish to die in the Americas.[89] The new year of 1837 brought a huge and concentrated effort in relation to collections for the Jardin des Plantes. Bonpland revisited the contents of the twenty-five cases of materials sent from Buenos Aires to Paris in 1832, adding in addition three new ones. These last paid special emphasis to the description of birds, an explicit effort to add to the work of Félix de Azara.[90] He sent his geology catalog to Humboldt, something of very close concern to Bonpland. In addition, he gave instructions to the botanist Adrien de Jussieu (1797–1853) at the herbarium of the Jardin des Plantes about how his material should be handled there, noting that he still held to the ambition of publishing the flora of the Upper Plata.[91] A letter to the zoologist Constant Duméril (1774–1860) mainly concerned the giant fossil remains to be found in South America. Bonpland had read an 1825 edition of Duméril's work; this, from the date of publication in itself, shows that he was trying to keep current in his reading.[92] One of the strongest themes of this group of scientific letters is that he was clearly looking for support from the metropolis, but not always finding it.

After so much visible activity, it seems strange to find nothing in Bonpland's records relating to February 1837. Invisibility induced through relaxation was not a likely theme with him. It may be that he was out on the pampas selecting sheep. There is certainly some evidence that he visited Peter Sheridan's ranch. On 1 March, Bonpland received news from John Hannah, another of the famous pioneers on the pampas, that Hannah was sending a consignment of sheep.[93] It comprised thirty rams of a quality similar to those indicated in person by the recipient. Hannah also sent a young ram and a lamb as a present. Weather delayed the transport of the sheep; even then, they were moved to Buenos Aires by cart rather than on foot. Once Bonpland had the animals he needed, he could leave the city. He asked for his passport to leave Buenos Aires on 2 March 1837.[94]

Sheep were very much on the agenda. Bonpland wrote on the day following Hannah's letter to the Delessert merchant bankers at Paris about the wool business in the Plata. Merino flocks, pure and crossbred, he said,

Figure 3.1 Portrait by Carlos Pelligrini of Bonpland at Buenos Aires, 1837.
SOURCE: Reproduced from Bonpland, *Bonplandia: Zeitschrift für die gesammte Botanik* (Hannover). This image appears at the head of the January 1856 issue (vol. 4). By permission of the Archives of the Gray Herbarium, Harvard University.

were the topic of the moment at Buenos Aires, partly because "one called Sheridan" had made a large fortune from them. Bonpland claimed in this letter that his earlier experience with large agricultural projects, presumably meaning his work for Joséphine at Malmaison and Navarre, had led to offers of employment. He had rejected these, but found himself drawn into a project whose viability was under consideration by the Blanc & Constantin merchant company.[95] The plan involved a search for ten to twelve square leagues of land in either Entre Ríos or Corrientes. The partners, probably led by Bonpland, had the idea of perhaps drawing capital from the Delesserts at Paris to the order of 300,000 francs, an amount described as a minor consideration for this imposing French merchant house.[96] In writing to the Delesserts, Bonpland did not mention his potential partners, but it is certain some of these were drawn from the French diplomatic and merchant communities based at Buenos Aires.

The above letter to the Paris bankers was written on the same day as one to Humboldt, which is also full of enthusiasm about the sheep project and the possibility of involving the Delesserts in it. But Bonpland's letter to Humboldt holds an even more important key to his thinking. It treats several themes, including an overview of the work recently undertaken at Buenos Aires. It also draws out the author's preoccupations near the moment of pushing back into the interior for another effort at economic development. On leaving Buenos Aires for the second time, finances were still a major preoccupation, and in Bonpland's mind, they stood in the way of publication. He told Humboldt that he had written letters about issues of materia medica to Jean Louis Alibert and to Achille Richard, both leading medical authorities at Paris. But life at Buenos Aires was not solely about work. Bonpland provided a brief account of the British diplomat Henry Mandeville, who had supposedly seen a lot of Humboldt at Paris: "He is an excellent man; he gives fine dinners and has, like all the wealthy English, excellent wines."[97] Here is a clear signal that Bonpland had not gone entirely native.

A Further Return to the Upper Plata

Bonpland's receipt in December 1836 of over 19,000 francs for his share of the settlement of the parental estate meant that he could return to the interior with financial resources, even while he was still waiting for the arrears of his French state pension. His journey along the Uruguay River to the Upper Plata began on 10 March 1837, starting from the Riachuelo south of the city.[98] Even while waiting for the departure, his curiosity never let up. He speculated that the sand around the mole, and in the estuary of the Riachuelo, resembled rock in the Jesuit missions. Central to his baggage for the journey stood thirty crossbred merino rams and a ewe. He traveled with other people drawn from his circle of close acquaintances at São Borja. Bonpland soon found that he was not the only person diffusing crossbred merinos into the interior. At Diamante, he met up with two Britons who were driving merino crossbred sheep to Concordia with the aim of establishing a flock. One of these, William Wilson, was a medical doctor "obliged to abandon his clientele" at Buenos Aires on account of differences with Dr. Cosme Argerich.[99] Bonpland moved his own sheep from ship to land near Concordia, Entre Ríos. On 23 March he was at Yuquerí, close to Concordia, from where he described the extreme challenges of driving his flock overland.[100]

Shortly before entering Corrientes, Bonpland left a description of the pastures at Mandisoví, in the northern part of Entre Ríos. He compared the tough stems and leaves of the grasses with those of the missions, arguing that the prairies had nothing of interest to offer for fattening livestock unless they were burned frequently.[101] It was around here also, when moving north, that the stands of *espinillos* (spiny hardwoods) began. Bonpland also made an interesting description of a *quilombo*, a community of escaped slaves, which he recognized in the light of day. He theorized that this community contained a fugitive slave from São Borja who belonged to the political leader of that town: "The daylight made me notice several *ranchos* and some fields of corn. These huts are inhabited by some Portuguese blacks who have fled from Brazil and established themselves here, where the government tolerates them. The mulatto who is charged with conducting my sheep is associated here with a companion, a fugitive black Brazilian."[102] Traveling up the Uruguay River gave Bonpland a chance to observe the ranches in southeastern Corrientes, of which he left a generally favorable account. His flock of merino sheep was deposited temporarily on the land of Valentín Virasoro, a family with which he later developed business connections. The Virasoros sat at the apex of the regional elite, supplying several governors to the province.[103]

Once at Curuzú Cuatiá, Bonpland took the opportunity to write on 10 April 1837 with his news to his friend José Ingres at São Borja. Ingres, a brother of the famous French painter of the first half of the nineteenth century Jean-Auguste-Dominique Ingres (1780–1867), was a merchant based in the Brazilian frontier town.[104] He made his living trading across the frontier of southern Brazil, including in contraband. Ingres's reply from São Borja provides an especially interesting window into Bonpland's economic plans.[105] The letter begins with the writer commenting he was pleased to see that age was not diminishing Bonpland's energies. Ingres wrote that he hoped very much that his friend would secure land for his sheep-breeding speculation in Corrientes, a region he considered a superior option for this than Missões, the Jesuit mission area of Rio Grande do Sul. As for yerba, Bonpland seems to have considered opening a road from Santo Ângelo, in the Riograndense missions, to the Uruguay River, transporting the yerba southward from some point on the river above São Borja. Ingres considered this project to be a chimera that would lead to unnecessary expense and loss of time, neither of which the French merchant recommended in South America. Much of his objection lay with the poor navigability of the Uruguay above São Borja; the many falls there rendered the river dangerous and much more difficult to navigate than the stretch from São Borja downstream to the major falls at Salto, Uruguay. If Bonpland insisted on developing the resources at Santo Ângelo, it would be better in Ingres's view to use the land-based transport of carts, including those of established haulers. Understanding something of Bonpland's character, however, he knew his correspondent would not find this to his taste, "since you like to have plenty of people under your orders." Ingres added that he would not back down from his advice because it was based on years of experience of the country. The letter ended with commentary on the politics of the São Borja region ("nothing is more miserable than the political affairs of the province"), where there were now two rival frontier commanders.[106]

Bonpland then crossed the territory of Corrientes to the city of that name. Along the journey, he paid a visit (10, 11, 12 April 1837) to the ranch of Henry Symonds, described as "the young Englishman." His house at this stage was no more than a "sad hut." Bonpland noted the severity with which this landowner treated his staff. His journey provided the chance to cross all of Symonds's land. Bonpland was struck at the quantity of *espinillo* trees, thinking that their quantity would impede the successful grazing of cattle.[107] This was certainly the view of the neighboring Araújo family, who had sold some of their land to Symonds. When Bonpland next viewed this ranch, on 12 July 1838, he opined that the Englishman had been right and the locals wrong.[108] The greater part of the woods were so sparse that they were easily and inexpensively cleared. *Renovales*, or regrowth forests, were not dealt with so easily. Bonpland now took a positive view of this ranch. Like all others between the Miriñay and the Corrientes rivers, it comprised pastures of high quality with abundant *flechilla*. Witnessing the rapid development of this and other ranches no doubt stimulated Bonpland to hasten the realization of his own ranching ambitions.

Bonpland arrived in the city of Corrientes on 18 April 1837 and he stayed there for three weeks. His recent trip to the south had stimulated people to write to him. For example, Henry Hoker sent him a letter from Paraná. Hoker, present in the subscription list to the Robertsons' book on Paraguay, and a correspondent of Darwin, wrote asking for seeds for a colony of mission Indians established at Punta Gorda.[109] According to their *alcalde* (administrator), the items most in demand were a few tobacco seeds and some manioc roots. Hoker also informed Bonpland that he had begun a collection of fossils, partly with the remains of a very large animal of which "Charles Darwin, the naturalist of the English discovery vessel *Beagle*" had recently found a large shell.[110] On 29 April, Bonpland was present at Pedro Ferré's *chacra*; while there, he made notes on the giant water lily.[111] Based on the contents of a letter made in reply by the French merchant Frédéric Desbrosses, Bonpland received offers of land during this relatively brief stay in the Correntino capital.[112] He left the city on 8 May, carrying the particular regret that he would not be able to accompany the commander of the port there on a journey into the Chaco, whose motive was to seek a wood to be found only there, which was appropriate for the fabrication of lances:

> This wood, which the indigenes of the Chaco call *Curundey* and the Spanish call *Palo de lanza*, is furnished by a large tree. Its timber, of a deep violet color in its fresh state, takes with time a shade of black. This wood is heavy and flexible. All the lances of the Indians from the Chaco, as well as their bows and the points of their arrows, are made from the wood of the *Curundey*.[113]

While his informants reckoned this species of tree did not have leaves, Bonpland claimed that it definitely did. He gave a sack to the port commander, asking him to bring back the fruits of the tree, which he still intended to study later in detail in the Chaco.

Bonpland was unable to travel in the Chaco in person in May 1837 on account of more pressing plans. He needed to survey the southeastern portions of Corrientes, taking the opportunity to accompany the rancher Justo Díaz de Vivar. Among the places he planned to examine stood Tupantua and Curuzú Cuatiá, plus the lands of the Paso de Santa Ana, close by the famous and much-frequented pass across the Uruguay River into Brazil. Díaz de Vivar and Bonpland began their journey out of the city by carriage. The latter's main preoccupation during the early parts of the journey appears to have been the treatment of syphilis cases in both men and women. At San Roque, he met with his friend Estebán Périchon, returning from his estancia to the capital. Bonpland commented on the poor condition of Périchon's face, "covered with numerous small ulcerous buttons! This religious man will no doubt have been much tormented by the cancerous virus."[114] He and Périchon left the carriage behind at San Roque, "in order to travel by horse, as is the custom in the country."[115]

The journey to the Uruguay River took Bonpland past some affluent landowners. Based on his descriptions, these were clearly doing very well in 1837. For example, he visited Pedro Cabral, one of the richest landowners in the whole of Corrientes; he had sold eight to ten thousand head of cattle from his properties during recent years. This was a huge operation, with a large number of mares and sheep of ordinary quality in addition to the cattle.[116] Individuals such as Cabral sat at the apex of rural wealth in Corrientes. The party then crossed the Yuquerí River in a boat made from a hide, in order to visit the property Tupantua, formerly belonging to the Atienza family (the father of Rafael de Atienza, a governor of Corrientes) but now under the control of Díaz de Vivar, who wanted Bonpland to examine the best part of his land. The latter provided a detailed account of the rural property, beginning with a fine description of the plain of the Miriñay River with its seasonally flooded pastures and short-grass prairies. After outlining some of the specific grasses present, he noted there was not a single anthill across the plain of the Miriñay. In summary, it presented a level of physical uniformity Bonpland reckoned he had seen nowhere else in South America. The fat state of the animals was a sure indicator of the high quality of the pastures. The owner had begun to build up this ranch only in 1832, with very few livestock. Five years onward, the situation was already very different, with large instances of cattle, sheep, and mule breeding all taking place. Among other things, Díaz de Vivar was attempting the development of merino breeding, with a flock of some six to seven hundred of these.[117]

Continuing in the direction of Curuzú Cuatiá, Bonpland found the pastures were not of the same degree of quality. He ascribed this to overgrazing. The richer ranchers did not show much concern for ranching ecology: "The richer ranchers have their estancias more heavily stocked with animals and they do not observe the desirable ratio between the given area of land and the number of animals that this can easily feed."[118] He provided an interesting account of a ranch belonging to a Mr. Noguera, in business with a partner for only three years, but already described as "the most modern of all the ranchers in this province." Modernity was reflected in the condition of the house and the kitchen, but also the sense that Noguera and his partner were running their operation as a business. Here the people were housed with all the material comforts contemporaries could expect to find in South America's larger cities. In the Curuzú Cuatiá district at least, raising livestock outstripped any other business in its margin of profit.[119] After the intensive work of estancia examination, the party moved to the town of Curuzú Cuatiá, where it celebrated the national holiday of 25 May. As the evening wore on, the inhabitants abandoned the formal European dances in favor of the local ones, which, Bonpland opined, they danced better, perhaps because the women were not ordinarily in the custom of wearing shoes.[120]

On 8 June 1837, Bonpland made an initial description of the Santa Ana ranch, the place where he would soon settle.[121] The popular view held that its land, a mix of hills and *bañados*, was good—an assessment Bonpland quickly shared. In several directions, the property was cut by streams and small lakes, securing it from the worst effects of drought. Santa Ana forms part of a considerable drainage basin emptying into the Uruguay River, thus providing a privileged location within Corrientes. In addition, the land had good natural boundaries, always a prime consideration for successful South American ranching before the fencing of the range. It was bounded in the east by the Uruguay River, in the north by the Santa Ana River, to the west by the Arroyo Cardoso, and in the southeast by the lands of the Abalos family. The work of assessing property was briefly interrupted by the provision of an immediate medical description of one of the people present. Mr. Santos Maciel, the son-in-law of Luís Araújo, the proprietor of Santa Ana, was suffering from a bad case of syphilis.[122] Bonpland described the syphilitic ulcers on his legs and thighs, reminiscent to him of the symptoms on an Indian woman at San Nicolás and on the legs of an Italian at São Borja. Maciel appears to have died in fairly short order from a cerebral phlegmasy; Bonpland later added the note to his manuscript that this man had "confided his health to charlatans." On the same day that he visited Santa Ana, Bonpland wrote to de Atienza, the governor of Corrientes, noting he was waiting to hear what had been decided in connection with the land requested there. In the spirit of reciprocal favors, his letter also supplied de

Atienza with a good deal of political intelligence about developments in parts of Corrientes, western Rio Grande do Sul, and Paraguay.[123]

Nearby Santa Ana, Bonpland was soon presenting an interesting portrait of a ranch under development by the Marques family. The land they controlled was good and recently stocked with animals. It boasted a herd of six thousand cattle, mule and horse breeding, and a sheep flock. This last was composed of six hundred animals of ordinary quality; in addition, however, the rancher had three young, but not very pure, merino rams, which he placed in a flock of 160 young sheep, "the whiteness of whose wool resembled the albatross." Based on such a beginning, Bonpland predicted, the Marques family would soon be very rich. Marques the elder was described as an educated and very liberal individual, one with a fine library. He evidently enjoyed acting as the host to visitors. Bonpland profited in their hut from samples of mustard, very fine beet sugar, and delicious champagne. He seems to have enjoyed the conversation there so much that he forgot to take his customary distance measurements for this part of the journey. The presence of iron wheels, a cast-iron fireplace, and large sections of sheet iron for covering buildings was taken as further evidence of Marques's curiosity. In a few years, it was presumable that the current huts would be transformed into good, comfortable houses.[124] Descriptions such as the above provide a concrete sense of the optimism for Corrientes in the period before armed struggle with Rosas.

After such careful observation of some of the most advanced ranches in Corrientes, Bonpland continued his travels by making his fourth visit to the former Jesuit mission of Yapeyú, the birthplace, as he phrased it, of the famous General San Martín. He joined a young rancher, who was going to Yapeyú in search of orange trees, figs, peaches, and olives. Bonpland's description provides an interesting account of the degree of organization in this part of the province during the past years. Three years earlier, all the roads, the square, and the streets were closed. Now the traveler saw pathways opened in various directions. In the midst of the ruins, the considerable remains of earlier houses were to be found hidden in the vegetation. But the mission church scarcely offered traces of its former existence. Its tiles, bricks, and olive trees had all been removed to other locations, leaving little more than the quarry stones. All the saddle stones had been taken away, so that from La Cruz to the Miriñay River every house bore some souvenirs of the former Yapeyú mission. Between the mission and the river, a lane formed of olive trees had once stood; now Bonpland saw for the first time the only three remaining trees, commenting that there was something majestic about the descent from the mission to the Uruguay River. On the right-hand side of the path, he saw a large, ancient tree deposited there by a strong flood. This mimosa trunk, known as *timbo*, was surely older, he argued, than the mission itself.[125]

After the mission visit, Bonpland headed for his home in Brazil, arriving at São Borja on the night of 15 June.[126] Within weeks, that town became the scene of considerable instability connected with the Farroupilha Revolt (1835–1845), a regional struggle from Rio Grande do Sul against inept central authority. Bonpland recorded the impending arrival of a considerable Farrapo force commanded by the Brazilian General Lima, but drawing much of its strength in the officer cadres from Spanish-speaking soldiers linked to Fructuoso Rivera. The troops themselves were mainly from Indian backgrounds. In fact, Lima's explicit motives for invading the São Borja region appear to have included the search for both additional horses, always indispensable, and for Indians to press into the ranks of the soldiery. Bonpland kept a detailed diary of the events as they unfolded, which is strong on conveying the atmosphere of rumors in the civil war. Given the prospect of conflict, most inhabitants of São Borja with means had chosen to leave the town. General Lima entered at daybreak on 7 July, accompanied by only thirty-two soldiers, although he controlled many more outside. Bonpland found himself involved in the political developments:

> At General Lima's demand, Mr. Serny [a French merchant], myself, and several other individuals, accompanied him to the Paso de São Borja. Lima was about to pass to the other bank in order to reassure the emigré families, and to invite them to return to their houses, offering them a guarantee. But on reflecting that the opposite side was not Brazilian property, he abandoned the idea of going there, and personally designated Mr. Serny and me to fulfill his intentions.[127]

They had little success in meeting Lima's designs. Bonpland later argued that the composition of the latter's forces was unhelpful: "If Lima had come here with Brazilians, everybody would have gone home."[128] Although he made no strong comment of support for the Farrapos in his diary, he was clearly sympathetic. On 15 July, Bonpland wrote a letter to Juan Francisco Gramajo, the interim governor of Corrientes. Its gist was that the Republicans had restored good order at São Borja but they were also sending an emissary to Corrientes to communicate their wishes for "union and friendship" between the Riograndense Republic and the province of Corrientes.[129]

In June 1837, Frédéric Desbrosses, described by the French consul at Buenos Aires as "one of the most commendable French merchants of this residence," wrote Bonpland a letter full of news, but also airing his considerable degree of frustration.[130] Keen to see Bonpland conclude his dealings over land with de Atienza, the governor of Corrientes, the message Desbrosses wished to deliver was clear: it was essential to have something decided, and, now using double underlining, "as promptly as possible." In Buenos Aires, Bonpland was informed, the population dreamed of nothing but estancias to the point that land was seeming to be scarce there. Since the quality of the lands in Corrientes was viewed as good, it could not be long before capital from Buenos Aires turned its vision northward, thereby closing opportunities for Bonpland and for his partners. Desbrosses kept his own flock of merino rams at Santa Catalina on the fringes of Buenos Aires. He planned to move at least some of these animals to Corrientes as soon as Bonpland cleared the way. No doubt the exasperation he showed was linked in part to the fact he was the largest shareholder in Bonpland's projected scheme, as the subscriber for a half of the shares.

Bonpland's correspondence with de Atienza shows that he was already actively seeking land without any push from his colleagues at Buenos Aires. A letter written from São Borja to the Correntino governor, only days after Desbrosses had written his appeal to Bonpland, served in part to relay news of the conduct of the civil war both in and around São Borja. But Bonpland then followed his account of public affairs with his private interest in gaining the land at Santa Ana. He described two *rincónes,* or sections, close to the Uruguay River in his letter. The one with more elevated land was described as propitious for sheep, but not for cattle. Another, formed mainly of *bañados,* was fit for cattle only and not for sheep. Both of these *rincónes*, he claimed, offered land suitable for the cultivation of yerba, which points to ambitions beyond ranching alone. Clearly Bonpland wanted a property with varying types of land. He described the segments of land in his letter as suitable for forming an *hermosissima,* or lovely, estancia, which could be developed to both public and private profit.[131]

Bonpland's lobbying of the government of Corrientes came at a time when his finances were on the upswing. In July 1837, the Delesserts wrote from Paris announcing that five years of back pension had come through. Less commissions, this left him with 14,700 francs on account. The Paris merchant bank paid him 3 percent interest but recommended investment in French national debt at 5 percent, which to the bankers no doubt looked much more solid than any South American undertakings. The Parisians reminded him of the bureaucratic steps necessary to keep the pension valid. After three years of nonpayment, state pensions were presumed extinct.[132]

These pension requirements were probably part of the reason why Bonpland seems to have schemed for a third visit to Buenos Aires. This project comes up in a letter, without date or address, to the merino breeder Pedro (Peter) Sheridan, to whom Bonpland owed money for the supply of thirty crossbred merino rams. He told Sheridan that a trip to Buenos Aires in September 1837 had proven impossible and that he could not visit the capital of the Argentine Republic before September 1838. Given the delay, and the impossibility of selling fine-wooled rams in Corrientes, Bonpland wanted to pay for the animals supplied by Sheridan, drawing on his account with his agents Blanc & Constantin at Buenos Aires. Interestingly, he claimed to have written three times already about the state of the sheep business since leaving Buenos Aires in March 1837. He also informed Sheridan of his plan to ascend the Uruguay River to San Xavier and maybe higher.[133]

Bonpland finally made his formal request for land from Corrientes on 11 September 1837, when de Atienza was still governor. He made the claim to land at Santa Ana through his compatriot Périchon, backed by the powerful support of Ferré. The wording of the claim reveals Bonpland's appreciation of the dynamism surrounding the lands of Corrientes in this period. Praising the state of administration, and knowing the presence of fertile land in Corrientes, he formed the project of moving there. The land he would need was destined not only for agriculture and ranching but also for the cultivation of medicinal and exotic plants. This was what Bonpland used to strengthen his argument for a grant of land in public hands. He also used his age as a factor in trying to sway the government: "On account of my advanced age, I have already sought to find a place where I can finish my days peacefully. I chose the territory of the province for this, but I am living in a vacillating way."[134] The reason for the instability was that any properties identified as suitable for his objectives were either already occupied or had a land claim registered with the government. The decree supporting this land claim came on 13 February 1838 under the government of Genaro Berón de Astrada. The government recognized the value of Bonpland's work assessing the region's resources and used this as a possible justification for granting a coveted piece of rural property to him. The title in emphyteusis for the land at Santa Ana came during Ferré's government in June 1841. Definitive ownership of this land came only very late in his life, during the government of Juan Pujol, an individual who valued the various types of work undertaken by Bonpland. However, the key point is that Bonpland had the right to develop the land at Santa Ana from February 1838 onward.

Communication between Corrientes and Buenos Aires clearly had its problems. No doubt frustrated at the lack of concrete news from Bonpland, Desbrosses traveled in person from Buenos Aires to the Upper Plata in an effort to speed negotiations. Catching up with Bonpland presented serious challenges. Writing from Goya in September 1837, Desbrosses was under the impression that Bonpland had left São Borja for the interior of Rio Grande do Sul. He politely noted that this caused him infinite regrets, since he had "left everything at Buenos Aires, in order to devote myself entirely to our enterprise."[135] He informed Bonpland that Petitjean was working from Buenos Aires to find more subscribers for their scheme. In addition, a cloth manufacturer from Amiens had supplied current prices for wool drawn from Buenos Aires considerably superior to those the partners had used in their calculations. By November, Desbrosses had moved eastward across the territory of Corrientes to Curuzú Cuatiá. After a stay of already fifty-seven days in the province—twenty-four of them expecting to see Bonpland from one moment to the next, and nineteen during which supposedly only a canoe was lacking in order to travel down the Uruguay River—he was still waiting to meet up with his projected business partner.[136] After proceeding to São Borja (Desbrosses was there by 26 November), the plan to examine rural properties together in detail did not work out. Bonpland was suddenly called from Brazil to attend de Atienza, taken desperately ill in southeastern Corrientes.[137] He traveled with Desbrosses down the Uruguay River in a large canoe built from a single piece of *timbo*, bought by Bonpland several years earlier. The places described along this journey include Itaqui, Yapeyú, and the Paso de Santa Ana, where they transferred from river to land. Desbrosses was left alone to make his examination of several estancias in eastern Corrientes, including the land at Santa Ana. Bonpland noted that it was painful to separate himself from his colleague but that it was "necessary in virtue of our agricultural plans." He left his colleague under the guidance of a local rancher in order to make a reconnaissance of several properties.[138] Pulled away by urgent medical work, this appears to have been the last direct link Bonpland had with Desbrosses.[139] In December 1837, Bonpland was at Corrientes to attend the funeral of the late governor. According to a note in his journal, he arrived there on 6 December and left on 29 June 1838.

The land decree for Santa Ana in early 1838 probably boosted Bonpland's confidence. In March, he wrote to the Delesserts from the city of Corrientes about his plans to build "a new Malmaison" in this part of Argentina.[140] He also sent them authorization to clear, at long last, the debt for 5,045 francs he incurred in 1816 with the Paris book dealer and publisher Barrois.[141] In late March and early April, his correspondence with Mirbel and Humboldt from the same city was mainly about science.[142] Bonpland kept a copy of a letter written in May 1838 by the expatriate ranchers Diego and Roberto Davison to the government of Corrientes, seeking tax relief on their wool operation.[143] He marked at the head of this, "Sociedad del Río Corrientes" (Río Corrientes Company). The Davisons' letter is interesting because it speaks of the efforts to develop the region at this time. They argued that Corrientes could follow the same path to wealth of France, Holland, Saxony, and Germany, whose sheep flocks had already outstripped those of Spain in quality. However, this would take prolonged effort. Buenos Aires was setting the standard in crossbreeding. Corrientes could try to replicate this, but it confronted particular obstacles. For example, the province faced the problem of transport costs, both for the raw materials of expensive breeding stock and for wool. In addition, the physical environment of Corrientes posed its own issues; sheep were afflicted with worms for much of the year. These sheep entrepreneurs argued that they could not compete; unless granted government help, they would need to pull out, which was not in the strategic interest. They sought tax relief for all those working to cross creole sheep with merino rams. No wonder this was interesting to Bonpland. Even well-financed operations appear to have been struggling in this interior location.

In June 1838, Bonpland was still in the city of Corrientes, treating medical patients. He also sent a small collection of cactus seeds to Mandeville, the British minister at Buenos Aires, as "a present made for your rich English gardens."[144] Treating patients was typically a full occupation while also making the preparations for his journey to the Uruguay River. Legal permission to take horses east of the Aguapey River was conceded on 19 May.[145] He also worked to secure a supply of oxen with which to undertake the journey. The journey to the banks of the Uruguay began on 29 June.[146] He traveled in the company of five Guayana Indians, designed to form the core of his labor supply for the development of Santa Ana. A few days out of Corrientes, he noted that the Guayanas were still well disposed and he hoped to continue their management, despite the very negative reputation the general public held of them.[147]

Bonpland made a detour along the journey in order to see the merinos of the Estancia del Río Corrientes. Managed by Pablo Bernal, a young *porteño*, this ranching company was an atypical property for the region because it stood in the vanguard of money coming from Buenos Aires.[148] Mariano de Sarratea was also present there, son of the same, and nephew of Manuel de Sarratea, then serving as the minister for Argentina to the Brazilian Empire. The Sarrateas had long been known to Bonpland, since before he emigrated to the Río de la Plata. During the journey to meet Bernal, Bonpland traced out the geography of the vegetation. Near the Batel River, he saw extensive ground covered by the Yatay palm. He took the opportunity to make comparisons in the ethnobotany of this palm species with that of the agave in Mexico. After an elbow in this river, however, the trees disappeared, to be replaced by an undulating plain covered in pasture.[149]

Pablo Bernal's physiognomy reminded Bonpland of his elder brother Michel-Simon. He made a detailed description of an establishment busily engaged in sheep breeding at an incipient stage. For example, purebred merinos and English sheep had arrived from Europe only weeks earlier, the latter bought through the agency of the famous breeder Pedro Sheridan. All this provided a good chance for Bonpland to catch up on empirical experience with sheep breeding, a business he had left behind in Europe decades earlier. He was especially interested in seeing the results of crossing the pure merinos with the animals from an English breed, noting that the latter were larger in stature. As always, he made close empirical observations about how breeding was proceeding on the Bernal property in comparison with the patterns he understood from earlier work in Napoleonic France. The crops on the estancia were suffering extensive damage from "an enormous multitude" of capybaras.[150]

Once east of the Corrientes River, the largest in the interior of the province, the journey took Bonpland through the land of Henrique [Henry] Symonds once more. The main interest there was how this British rancher had rendered land once covered with *espinillos* suitable for ranching. He had proven the viability of working with this specific type of environment.

When Bonpland arrived in the town of Curuzú Cuatiá, he took the chance to break the news of his successful claim to the land at Santa Ana. This was not received with universal acclaim. He noted the disapproval on the face of a Francisco Lopez, probably, he recorded, one of the competing contenders to the property.[151] The brief stay in this town was also much devoted to medical business. The few days spent at Curuzú Cuatiá provide a fine example of Bonpland's broad interests. On 16 July, he recorded the difficulty presented by the fact that some local residents were so slow to embrace western medicine. The following day was spent entirely in making iron heads for the arrows of his Indian laborers.[152] From Curuzú Cuatiá, he then doubled back into the interior, in order to meet with Thomas Dulgeon, a young British surveyor engaged in attempting to measure the Laguna Yberá. Given the scale of this huge zone of seasonally changing swamps and marshes, parts of which are still little known to science even today, it is unsurprising that he was not having much success with his mission to determine the limits of the lagoon.[153]

The travel journals then record Bonpland's important detailed description of his first effort to survey the Santa Ana property in detail. He arrived at the Río Santa Ana on 27 July 1838. Given the quantity of water in the river, he decided to cross in his canoe, a craft delivered to him in an extremely dilapidated state.[154] The next four days were partly spent in making a reconnaissance of a portion of the land of the Santa Ana ranch. The main item of note was a large number of horses. All of these were in the temporary possession of intruders, who held them on the land prior to sending them across the Uruguay River as contraband: "Amongst all these individuals, there is not one who has some plantings, sowings, or animals to provide for their food needs. They occupy themselves only by gambling and contraband."[155] Santa Ana held a strategic location, on account of the river, and it served as a gateway to Brazil. However, the river was passable for livestock only during parts of the year, especially the months of December and January. Floods took place mainly in June, July, and October. Those of October were generally the strongest and were useful for the property because they covered the fields with enormous cedars and other species of tree. Bonpland spent some time thinking about where exactly within the large property he should begin to settle, opting to begin on land close to the river, occupied at the time by Angelo Vais. In many places, the banks of the Uruguay were hindered for port development by a curtain of vegetation. Bonpland showed particular interest in the banks of the Uruguay close to the junction of a small river on his property, where the near-perpendicular *barrancas* (deep clefts) seemed ideal for a firm anchorage. Not far away was a small sandy hill covered with Yatay palms. While of modest elevation, this site was still high enough to be secure from the seasonal floodings presented by the main river. He proposed to test planting there, beginning with manioc, sweet potatoes, peanuts, and chickpeas. A neighbor argued that this was not the place to develop the estancia, but Bonpland held firm to the location currently occupied by Vais. The elevation there was such that he could discern the entire length of the section of the Uruguay bathing his pastures, and all the places on the river where it was convenient to pass livestock from one bank to the other.

In the new month of August, Bonpland began to plant. He started with a "still very rare" sweet Chinese orange obtained from Pedro Ferré.[156] A huge amount of effort went into planting. The labor came from the multicultural mix of Guayana Indians, an unnamed settler on the property, a German, and others drawn from Bonpland's domestic staff.[157] Carrots, cabbages, and various types of cherries were itemized. The materials planted came from a wide variety of regional locations. For example, the seed for the planting of Valencian red peppers was drawn from São Borja, Corrientes, and Montevideo. Last in this first phase of planting were some alfalfa seeds. There was also the work of fencing the planted area, where the trunks of willows formed the main material used. After the plantings of vegetables and fruits, the next theme was trees. The wide variety of types planted included mimosas, the spina de corona, almonds, peach trees, and the *algarrobilla*. While the workers took the Sabbath as their day of rest, Bonpland continued his work. On 5 August, his journal records the following: "Today, Sunday, the laborers have not worked. I occupied myself in preparing several remedies, in separating my seeds, in putting the rams to the sheep. In addition, I killed three hawks; my Guayana Indians need their wing feathers to arrange their arrows."[158] The following day he was called to the Paso de Santa Ana to treat a seven-year-old boy pricked on the foot several days earlier by the rowel of a spur. Whatever treatment Bonpland supplied came too late; the boy died from tetanus during the following morning.

The work of surveying the resources of the estancia continued. A visit to the Santa Ana *tapera* left Bonpland firm in the conviction this was not the place to establish an estancia, in part because the best part of the land there formed the property of his neighbor Cardoso. The former settlement was suitable only for locating a *puesto*. On the other hand, he took a positive view of the *espinillo* woods on this part of the property as an excellent place to pasture sheep. Although the woods were not very thick, they would provide excellent shade. In addition, this section of the estancia was large and good for horses.

In this initial work of setting up the Santa Ana property, a range of contacts provided some evidence of the interest of this frontier location. The repair of Bonpland's canoe was confided to a locally resident Englishman. Most of his contacts were with his Correntino neighbors, but people also came through from farther afield. A man with the Brazilian name of Maciel, based at Montevideo, arrived from the interior of Brazil with fourteen carts loaded with hides, yerba, and other commodities. Bonpland also received a visit from Severino Ribeiro, a Farrapo from a ranching family based at Alegrete in the western interior of Rio Grande do Sul. The motive for this visit was left unspecified, but it probably related to moving livestock into Corrientes out of the civil war in southern Brazil. Bonpland already had some earlier knowledge of Severino's brother Sebastião:

> Don Severino Ribeiro has all the manners and style of conversation of his brother Sebastião. This one is in all more civilized, more educated, and more reserved. Don Severino aspires to obtain the hand of a young rich girl from his country, whose father is a passionate Legalist. On these grounds, Don Severino plays the Legalist, but he is positively a Republican and he works for the Republic. Like all the members of his family, he is miserly. However, he is frank and prompt in his business dealings, fulfilling them with exactitude, which, in general, the Brazilians do not do.[159]

In this brief portrait of a Riograndense, something of Bonpland's future skepticism about Brazilians already comes through.

The attractions of developing Santa Ana did not hold Bonpland there for long. By the end of the month, he was already in the former Jesuit mission of La Cruz, from where he wrote to Governor Berón de Astrada, full of concern about the depredations being made in the *yerbales* of the former pueblos. He named the specific missions he had in mind (San Carlos, San José, Mártires, Santa María la Mayor, Concepción, and San Xavier), along with the sources of his oral evidence. Although Bonpland's thoughts had recently been on the state of ranching in eastern Corrientes, before arriving in La Cruz he was clearly spending much time gaining oral evidence about the state of exploitation of the *yerbales*. His main point was that the government was throwing public resources away. In Bonpland's view, if Corrientes took prompt steps to regulate economic activity in the *yerbales*, it could cut the "scandalous disorders" that damaged public order. In a marginal comment on his draft letter, he commented interestingly at some point that Francia by contrast had provided numerous examples of "*yerbal* conservation." Bonpland argued that any measure the government of Corrientes took in the direction of conservation would be approved in Paraguay. All the people working clandestinely in the *yerbales* knew that these constituted public property.[160]

He picked up the same theme again within six months, this time writing to Ferré, the new governor. His letter was written along a journey aimed at reaching San Xavier, the northernmost Jesuit mission in the valley of the Uruguay River. This was a survey mission in search of maté plants. Bonpland also wanted to examine the *yerbales* around this former mission, so that he could propose the measures needed to take maximum profit through good management. He had been telling Ferré about the importance of managing the mission *yerbales* since shortly after emerging from Paraguay. There followed a microhistory of what was taking place. In the previous summer, between fifty and one hundred men had worked with the mission resources. They had successively devastated a series of *yerbales*, but especially that of San Xavier. Who was responsible for this damage? Bonpland exempted the inhabitants of San Nicolás (São Nicolau, in Rio Grande do Sul), whose impact was at a small scale. Ultimately, the main suspect was the frontier commander Chamorro from La Cruz. In Bonpland's view, he supported the illegal activities of three key individuals. These were a Paraguayan called Lorenzo, Barroso, a Brazilian from around Itaqui, and Pedro, an African American. All had been active for more than a year, drawing off considerable quantities of yerba. These three opened the way for many others, something that became known to a broader public through the activities of a Genovese river trader who bought the yerba they produced. This person bought the yerba from Misiones, paid the import duties to bring it across the territory of Corrientes to the customhouse at Paso de São Borja, then planned to market it down the Paraná River. The Genovese had recently traded five hundred arrobas or more of yerba. An Indian named Cornelio, who earlier worked for Bonpland at São João Mini, was also active in the business. This person had recently introduced one hundred arrobas of Correntino yerba in São Borja and Itaqui; earlier, he had robbed Bonpland of horses when working for him in Missões. The outcome was that Bonpland wished to put an end to these depredations of natural resources, and he urged the government of Corrientes to set a good example.[161]

By 1838, Bonpland had land and some capital. He remained active in his medical work, which included supplying other medical doctors with remedies, some of them of his own preparation. For example, he supplied extensive supplies of medicines to João Lindau, a doctor in the western rural interior of Rio Grande do Sul. Lindau seems to have had difficulty in paying for the materials provided; thus in a letter from 1838 Bonpland noted that he "speaks again of paying in steers."[162] The missing element was livestock for Bonpland's ranch. One option he appears to have considered was using Santa Ana as accommodation land for animals caught within the theater of Rio Grande do Sul's civil war. Sometime in December 1838 and January 1839, he explored the idea at São Borja of taking animals from Luís Nascimbene, a rancher resident in southern Brazil.

With matters falling gradually into place at Santa Ana, Bonpland felt able to act on some of his other ambitions. He had long been active gathering extensive information about the state of the *yerbales*, and keen especially to see those in the vicinity of the former mission San Xavier.[163] In January 1839, he left São Borja, a place where he would not reside again before 1843, in order to ascend into the Alto Uruguay. The main purpose of the journey was to gather maté plants that he would transplant elsewhere (at a destination left unspecified). This trip required considerable help for the navigation of the canoe through the falls of the Uruguay River and to manage the boxes and other equipment necessary to his plant mission. Thus he traveled with no less than eight men, of whom five were his Guayana Indian helpers and two were Correntino servants. Made at a time of civil war in Rio Grande do Sul, the consequences of which sometimes spilled across the river frontier into Corrientes, it was to be a journey with ill omens.

The retinue had barely left São Borja before Bonpland "recognized the corpse of Mr. Nuñez, who was assassinated at a quarter past midnight. He had ten wounds, of which three were made with a cutting instrument (saber) and seven with the point of a knife, or, rather, a dagger."[164] Across the river at Santo Tomé, he was interested in how the local population was making use of the infrastructure left in abeyance by the expulsion of the Jesuits. He left a description of how a new settler there was doing extensive agricultural work in the former mission, using slave labor. But in Bonpland's view, the scheme showed no plan, with the result that Santo Tomé was losing much of its formerly magnificent and imposing aspect.[165] In the sparsely settled territory around the Uruguay River above São Borja, Bonpland left several descriptions of how people were trying to live in isolation, in order to remove themselves from party struggles. At the Mercedes falls, he noted more than twenty-five huts on the Correntino side, belonging to Brazilian emigrés.[166] The strong currents of the major falls at Garruchos posed a major challenge; the rocks and tree trunks in the water injured his sailors (this same Paso de Garruchos was used by the Paraguayan soldiers as an invasion point during the 1864–1870 Triple Alliance War).[167] Near the Ilhas das Taquaras, Bonpland met up again with Auguste Banville, one of the French assistants he had brought from Europe in 1816.[168] Already well into the territory of important *yerbales*, the project quickly began to founder on political grounds around Santa María la Mayor. Here he met up with a party of Legalists and claimed that he was almost killed in a planned assassination.[169] The Legalists maintained that Bonpland was a Farrapo. After receiving a written warning, he learned from Brazilian emigrés in Santa María that the plan was to assassinate Bonpland, to steal his goods, and to incorporate his staff into the Legalist troops. Given the strongest recommendations to abandon his plans by Francisco Pinto de Queros, son-in-law of Colonel Silva, the commander of Missões, Bonpland reluctantly agreed. He left the boxes for the collection of maté at Santa María la Mayor until a later date, one that would never come. Almost all his helpers were sent downriver in the canoe, while Bonpland, accompanied by Pinto de Queros, undertook a very difficult journey southward by land. On 2 February, they dined and supped frugally on a morsel of roasted cheese. For a cup, they used an untanned hide, which, Bonpland said, did nothing to improve the taste of the water.[170]

A narrow escape from being killed by a party of Brazilian Legalists was only the beginning of political complications for Bonpland in 1839. By identifying his interests with Corrientes, he placed himself in a position where the evolving political stances of the province had direct implications for him, even though he seems to have done his best to stand outside the immediate issues of the day in South America. Bonpland was in no position to ignore the political swaying of Corrientes, at least while he remained on South American soil. As Nicolas Shumway has argued, a basic dividing fault underlying Argentina's society and history had been visible from around the time Bonpland arrived on the shores of the Río de la Plata—one between liberals, mainly Unitarians, closer to European notions of political economy and the Federalists, readier to draw upon American roots.[171] The problems between Buenos Aires and the interior intensified especially when the authority of Rosas solidified in Buenos Aires after 1835. Even before this time, Bonpland's patron Ferré had been a leading critic of Argentina's polity, with the lack of free navigation of the rivers among the key issues. Such geopolitical matters were of limited import to Buenos Aires province, but they were critical for the development plans of the riverine regions of the Upper Plata. Standing against any policies of economic absorption promoted by the Rosas government, the governments of Corrientes moved toward a hostile position with regard to the south. A treaty linking Uruguay with Corrientes against Rosas, one fomented in part by French diplomatic representation in the Plata, urged on by French merchants resident at Montevideo, was signed at the very end of 1838 and pointed toward heightened tension. Following a declaration of war against Rosas in late February 1839 on the part of President Rivera in Uruguay, Corrientes very quickly followed suit, leading to the formation of the first of several Correntino armies designed to dislodge Rosas from power.

While Bonpland had been engaged for most of the 1830s in the inevitably slow business of regional and resource appraisal, the politics around him had moved much more quickly. On 8 March 1839, he arrived at the Correntino military headquarters in Curuzú Cuatiá, where his medical services were in demand for the care of sick soldiers. He described the army of five thousand as being in a state of disorganization.[172] At the end of the month, this force would lose the famous battle of Pago Largo, which in turn ushered in a long phase of instability for Corrientes. Bonpland was close enough to these events that Governor Berón de Astrada, finding himself "almost in front of the enemy," wrote him a brief letter from what would soon be the field of battle where he would lose his life.[173] The recipient marked on this letter, "the final signature of Governor Berón."

. . .

In the years since leaving Paraguay, Bonpland had worked extremely hard to reconnect with a broader world. The abrupt manner in which his business affairs were broken in 1821 left consequences that took years to repair. But through his visits to Buenos Aires, contact with Europe eventually brought a marked improvement in his financial resources. These visits to the city were also critical for the preparation of shipments of scientific materials to Europe, notably to France. Most of Bonpland's scientific heritage from South America extant today in European collections results from this period. Bonpland first established a modest home on Brazilian soil in the former mission of São Borja. However, he was also drawn to the province of Corrientes, where he joined the contemporary fashion of lobbying for land. By 1838, he was poised with land, labor, and capital to improve his fortune quickly. Such plans were quickly undone with the battle of Pago Largo, which cast him back into shadow.

CHAPTER FOUR

Somber Years of Civil War

> All the Brazilians here assure me that Francia is always watching my steps. But since I have not been at Santa Ana since October, and he knows nothing for certain about where I have been staying, he has sent a young Brazilian merchant with the express purpose of finding out. Well, that merchant, whom I have seen here, is an old friend from São Borja. I can assure you he will report the following to Francia, and nothing more - that God has designated General Rivera to be the Liberator of the South American peoples.
>
> LETTER FROM BONPLAND TO FRUCTUOSO RIVERA, FIRST PRESIDENT OF THE URUGUAYAN NATION, 1840[1]

> You can see that I am far from aspiring, like you, to the years of your kind doctor Francia. I am delighted to see this sound hope in you, which proves your good current state better than any words, and I desire with all my heart to see your wish fulfilled.
>
> LETTER FROM A. P. DE CANDOLLE TO BONPLAND, 1840[2]

Bonpland's interest in subtropical resources had drawn him into regions of growing political instability, expressed mainly as a struggle between the interests of Buenos Aires and the remainder of the Plata. As Shumway has noted, individual areas showed a cultural uniqueness that political leaders often ignored.[3] Geography mattered, especially while trade along the rivers frequently remained extremely slow. The issue of regional expression was not one easily resolved while power lay concentrated in the hands of Rosas. Although the Rosas government talked about federation, it was firmly against allowing free navigation of the rivers, wishing to keep customhouse revenues for the entire region concentrated at Buenos Aires. By the late 1830s, a new level of nastiness in political discourse between Federalists and

Unitarians was achieved.[4] As the main alternative port to Buenos Aires, it is no surprise Montevideo became the main focus for Argentine Unitarians in exile. French and Italian immigrants in Uruguay were strong supporters of the Unitarian cause and key contributors of propaganda against Rosas and his system.

Although nobody in high office at Paris saw the Plata as a key issue, the French were drawn into the war between the Argentine Confederation and Uruguay. Much of this involvement was linked with the perceived need to protect the rights of French immigrants around Buenos Aires and in Uruguay. As Iwan Morgan has argued, the French came to feel they were being picked on.[5] Slow channels of official communication between the Plata and Paris left French diplomats on the ground with more latitude than their British counterparts. Some of these local agents also held rigid expectations of the region's major politicians, greatly exaggerating, for example, Rosas's animus against foreigners, and also holding idealistic notions of the potential success of Rivadavian types of schemes for such issues as northwest European colonization.[6] Henri Buchet de Martigny's creation in November 1838 of the Argentine Commission at Montevideo formed a definite landmark in French policy, as it involved subsidy of the Unitarians in exile.[7] In the long civil war in Uruguay between Manuel Oribe and the Blancos, and Fructuoso Rivera and his Colorados (the Guerra Grande of 1839–1851), the former was backed by Rosas, while the latter drew critical financial support from the French. Rivera's campaigns were totally dependent on French naval assistance. France also backed the controversial Argentinean Juan Lavalle in his unsuccessful efforts after 1839 to unseat Rosas. This ended for Lavalle, once described by Bolívar as "a lion to be kept in a cage and loosed only on the day of battle," in a particularly grisly death in September 1841.[8] In idealistic thoughts about future commercial expansion, French diplomats sometimes considered alternative political geographies for the broad region, contemplating, for example, the notion of bringing Paraguay, Entre Ríos, and Corrientes together as a political unit.[9] In any such schemes, Bonpland's regional experiences served potentially to make bridges between a range of politicians in the Upper Plata.

Like every other resident of the Río de la Plata, Bonpland found his life heavily affected by the political struggles between Rosas and his shifting opposition. As already seen, he identified firmly with Corrientes in its struggle against the hegemony of Buenos Aires. The fact that the Plata had assumed a key place in French foreign policy after 1838, and that the country of his birth had lent extensive support for the Unitarian cause, gave Bonpland considerable scope for political action for a spell. When France declared its blockade of the river in 1838, French national claims concentrated on the dossiers of two individuals rich in experiences of imputed humiliation by Rosas. Bonpland had direct links with both. He had stayed, and worked, at Buenos Aires with Aimé Roger, the consular official who engineered the diplomatic rupture between France and the Rosas government.[10] And he had been in contact with the lithographer and printer César-Hippolyte Bacle (1794–1838), imprisoned by Rosas for political intrigue; he subsequently died, it was claimed, from broken health resulting from his prison treatment. Beyond all his considerable importance as a printing pioneer in the Plata, Bacle shared Bonpland's interest in the natural history of the Plata and of southern Brazil.[11]

Scientific interests, medical work, and French state pension paperwork, among other themes, gave Bonpland some grounds to justify continuing mobility. Whether he was truly a spy is not readily determined from his laconic commentaries, but after Pago Largo he certainly became an important intermediary between Correntino political interests, especially those of Ferré, and the sources of opposition to Rosas elsewhere in Argentina, in Uruguay, and in Rio Grande do Sul, itself still torn by civil war for the first half of the decade. Given the contradictory nature of French policy toward the Plata, Bonpland was well placed to lobby French naval officers in the region to act in concert with Ferré's plans. The window of political opportunity for Bonpland closed as French geopolitical ambitions for the Plata moderated, partly on account of British pressure, and Ferré fell from political power (following the battle of Arroyo Grande in 1842).

Bonpland's writings are greatly fragmented for the period of the civil wars. Reconstruction of his movement patterns alone poses a major challenge. When Hamy published his 1906 biography, he could scarcely trace his subject's career in the 1840s for the basic reason that few of Bonpland's letters reached Europe from the interior of southern South America. In fact, only a short series of letters written from Montevideo in 1840 appear to have made it through. As the struggle between Unitarians and Federalists intensified, journeys between Bonpland's homes and the Atlantic coast of South America became too dangerous to contemplate, especially after Uruguayan forces loyal to Rosas began a nine-year siege of Montevideo in 1843 (often rendered more expressively by the defenders as 3,201 days). Politics, including the civil war in Rio Grande do Sul, were very clearly an obstacle to resource development. Juan Domínguez made the point that this period of Bonpland's life shows parallels with the period of confinement in Paraguay; it in no way lent itself to the development of scientific work.[12] The regional geographical pattern of any botanical work he achieved in this period reflected the whims of politics more than a purely scientific agenda. At different stages in this period, Bonpland found himself under threat, and protracted residence in either of his homes was too dangerous to contemplate. His writings are a record of survival, showing directly how political instability hampered economic development, including on his own rural properties.

The battle of Pago Largo stood as a seminal event in Bonpland's life. It was a notably bloody affair. In addition to the heavy losses of life during the battle itself, the troops loyal to Rosas then proceeded to massacre more than 800 of the 1,300 prisoners. Given his close links with opposition leader Berón de Astrada, it seems surprising that Bonpland himself escaped the violence, at least in his person, if not in his property. The answer is speculative, but lies perhaps in the social capital he had built up during his earlier visits to Buenos Aires. Juan Domínguez even suggests that Bonpland was under Rosas's protection while in the South American interior, an argument that remains to be proven.[13]

Following Pago Largo, Bonpland remained for some time at Santa Ana, where the victor Pascual de Echagüe had given him the *buenos consejos* (good advice) to remain, concentrating on the business of his estancia. Despite the fighting, he continued his work of botanical description, though he had to be preoccupied with the loss of livestock in the disorder, especially of his pedigree sheep. According to Bonpland himself, he lost 5,000 crossbred merinos, 500 cattle, 400 mares ready to bear mules, and 200 horses, a respectable complement of animals on any estancia.[14] A potential solution to the shortage of livestock appeared in the idea of taking animals into refuge from war-torn Rio Grande do Sul, something Bonpland had contemplated even before the battle of Pago Largo, when he set terms at São Borja with Luís Nascimbene for receiving animals.[15]

A letter written by Nascimbene from Caçapava (in the interior of Rio Grande do Sul) to Bonpland on 26 April 1839 more than anything appears to show interest in what political information the recipient could forward from Corrientes. Bonpland deflected all interest in this in his answer on 9 June, claiming that he wished only to restock his estancia, following an interview he had held with Echagüe. Santa Ana could receive animals, Bonpland informed Nascimbene, but he warned him of the risk that any division or troop that showed up would need to *carnear*, or, literally, "feed on meat." Depending on how long such troops stayed on a given property, this could become a massive source of the loss of livestock resources on individual ranches. Huge losses were something that many Brazilian ranchers soon incurred on the properties they held in northern Uruguay during that country's long civil war. Bonpland claimed that the estancias between the Miriñay and the Aguapey Rivers, in the Misiones department, still had all their cattle. He thought that things had been carefully managed, arguing that it was in the government's interest to treat the inhabitants well. And he emphasized a key point: both Bonpland and Nascimbene were foreigners. The fact that "We do not take part in the dissensions," in Bonpland's view, made them both worthy of government respect. This was very much an idealistic and impractical argument, given the political circumstances. He asked Nascimbene to move quickly if he wanted to send animals, thinking, no doubt, about the seasonal navigability of the Uruguay River. Bonpland himself could supply the horses and men for their conduct: "Every head that arrives safely on the western side is secure, since the pastures are excellent and very conducive to fattening."[16] He then wrote to Echagüe as the chief military commander, making sure that military authorities would expedite the passage of any livestock that Nascimbene chose to send across the river. This letter was also an occasion for expression of the need to maintain order in the Paso de Santa Ana, always a lively point of social, political, and economic interaction between Corrientes and southern Brazil.[17] This activity, coupled with the population disruptions occasioned by wars, would soon give rise to new towns in the international borderland—Restauración (today, Paso de los Libres) in Corrientes and Uruguaiana across the river in Rio Grande do Sul, both founded in 1843. A few years later, the small town of Federación emerged in Entre Ríos, again based on similar origins.

At the end of June, Bonpland wrote to Nascimbene again, pointing out that his slowness to act had become a problem. While the Uruguay River had been passable during the first half of June, this was no longer the case. Bonpland saw little hope of sending a large number of cattle through the Paso de Santa Ana before January 1840. As for labor, he recommended Correntino cowboys as both cheaper and more convenient for the bulk of any staff.[18]

Despite Bonpland's protestation of neutrality before Nascimbene, he had many links to the Farrapo cause in Rio Grande do Sul. In early 1840, he informed the Farrapo leader Bento Gonçalves da Silva that politics in Corrientes had pulled him away from Santo Ângelo, presumably referring to the project of developing the *yerbales* there: "I also believe that Your Excellency is not in a position to realize your just desires."[19] The wording points to some earlier connection between the two regarding the economic resources of Rio Grande do Sul.

By late 1839, the political context in Corrientes had already shifted, with the arrival there of Unitarian forces under the command of General Lavalle.[20] Bonpland felt the need to keep abreast of political intelligence, so by 5 November he was on the move from Santa Ana. He left there noting that all his seedings and plantings were in good condition, save from some minor effects from drought. His destination was Lavalle's military camp close to Curuzú Cuatiá, visited as an ancillary enterprise to some medical work undertaken in the town. The topics of an interview with the soldiers Lavalle and Martiniano Chilavert (1804–1852) included "Frutos [Fructuoso Rivera], Rosas, and the Brazilian Republicans [the Farrapos]."[21] Recent news from Buenos Aires was around three weeks old by the time it reached southeastern Corrientes, but by 23 November Bonpland already had seen news of the rebellion made by the large landowners in the south of Buenos Aires province against Rosas, and he had seen a copy of the manifesto prepared by Pedro Castelli, the leader of the movement.[22] He was assiduously copying any reference to recent battles and political movements. In early December, this included the fact that French warships were patrolling the Paraná River, where they had already accomplished the destruction of the battery at Rosario.[23]

Following his earlier connections, Bonpland was closely involved with Pedro Ferré in this period, to the point that they often traveled together. When not in each other's company, they exchanged an intensive correspondence during the years 1840 and 1841, especially when Bonpland was away in Uruguay and elsewhere. January 1840 found Bonpland at San Roque, treating there 109 sick soldiers from the armies of both General Lavalle and of Corrientes. He maintained that the leading problems were either syphilis or feigned illness on the part of men wishing to avoid any military service.[24] While at Santa Lucía in the same month, Bonpland made an overt political move. He wrote to José María Paz, an important Unitarian general, reviewing his earlier services to the cause of Spanish American independence and his own ambitions when starting out in Buenos Aires. By offering help, he showed confidence that the campaign against Rosas would succeed. He told Paz that he pinned his hopes for a new era on General Lavalle.[25] Any new era was not to be long lasting. This major figure in opposition to Rosas would be killed the following year while on his way to Bolivia.

Ferré and Bonpland spent a considerable spell in early 1840 based at Santa Lucía, where they awaited the arrival of French ships patrolling the Paraná. The temporary stability gave Bonpland his opportunity to make a detailed description of the Indian village of Santa Lucía, which, he noted, was originally a Jesuit foundation.[26] Repeated incursions by Chaco Indians had obliged the Jesuits to seek another location, thus the present settlement and church, the only one built of stone in the province of Corrientes, was not their work. A popular view claimed that the fine church was built with the priest's own money, but Bonpland held "it will be above all with that of his parishioners and with the sweat of the Indians."[27] The sacristy to the church contained rooms used by the governors when traveling. Two spacious rooms recently finished under the de Atienza government Bonpland described as "more spacious than comfortable."[28] While most people praised the situation of Santa Lucía, Bonpland did not share the general view: "You do not see a single wood, not a sole tree; one discerns nothing more than an undulating plain offering here and there some hills covered in white sand."[29] He noted the place was formerly settled by Tobas Indians (Guaycuruans), described as "very numerous." By 1840, the population was much more modest, composed mainly of a small number of families drawn from destroyed chapels on the right bank of the Paraná.

Beyond a general description of this settlement not far removed from the Paraná, Bonpland interested himself in making observations on its economy, clearly fascinated above all in the Indian crafts:

> These Indians are not very hard working but they are good warriors. Like all the Indian tribes they only work at agriculture to feed themselves for several months. The women, on the contrary, are very diligent. You see them all the time occupied at spinning, whether of wool or of cotton, making various fabrics which they sell or use for their domestic needs. They make fine ponchos from a single piece of cloth, very carefully dyed, which find buyers everywhere.[30]

The pottery from Santa Lucia enjoyed a greater demand than that of Paraguay or Itatí. Bonpland thought that the Indian women should be encouraged through some government investment in their facilities. He noted how the indigenous people had found the specific local soil resources to tint their pots red or yellow, clearly impressed by their knowledge: "How did people without any kind of instruction come to make a discovery that alone would have made the reputation of one of our chemists?"[31] This stimulated him to examine the local beds of earth from where they drew their resources.

Reports on what was happening at Santa Ana in Bonpland's absence came in a series of letters written by José Mariano Cardoso, his *capataz*. They are full of the massive challenges of managing the property during the war. Cardoso had worked with Bonpland earlier at São Borja; the latter's marginal comments on letters he received from Cardoso consist of rather waspish comments on unkept promises to keep costs under control. In the midst of other work, Cardoso had to deal with demands for vegetables from General Lavalle's camp.[32] Cardoso also monitored the local political happenings, perceptively describing the revolutionaries in neighboring Rio Grande do Sul: "The Farrapos are as you know them. Their manner is like that of the English, one day they are with one and another with another."[33] By this, he inferred that the Farrapos made tactical alliances, keeping their politics fluid.

Captain Lalande de Calan of the French warship *Bordelaise* arrived at Santa Lucía on 8 March 1840. Bonpland spent the evening discussing politics with him. Based on the captain's oral account, Bonpland wrote a detailed secondhand account of the ship's passage through the Rosario battery.[34] He later departed with Ferré's party and French naval personnel for Corrientes, where a major preoccupation of his work for March and April was medical work.

At Corrientes discussions not recorded in Bonpland's travel journey presumably took place that focused on how to coordinate the opposition to Rosas. Ferré and Bonpland both decided to use the French naval vessels in the Paraná to promote their own agendas. The French ships were accompanying a mercantile convoy with more than fifty sails destined for Montevideo. Ferré took this route to La Bajada (Paraná), in the hope of meeting there with General Lavalle and Fructuoso Rivera. Bonpland then traveled on to Montevideo to attend to his pension issues. He had written in February to the French botanist Mirbel, claiming that for the past two years he had wished to go to either Buenos Aires or Montevideo in order to deal with pension matters; the reason he held back from doing so was the "state of convulsion" of the Plata.[35] While Bonpland had dealt with pension issues from Buenos Aires in 1836, he had no chance to follow up before reaching Montevideo in 1840.[36] A commercial aspect also influenced his planned visit to the Uruguayan capital. He helped his friend Ingres, the São Borja merchant, to market Paraguayan yerba and tobacco embargoed in a warehouse at Goya. This was an atypical pattern, as Brazilian merchants in general had little to do with the trade along the Paraná, but it perhaps reflected the opportunism of foreigners during war.

Bonpland's Initial Visit to Montevideo

The journey began at Corrientes on 1 May on the schooner *Luisamaria*, where the governor with his retinue (including Bonpland) were escorted on board accompanied by music and the sound of cannon.[37] At Goya, Bonpland learned the unsuccessful fate of the Guaicurú Indian military expedition against Santa Fé. This was a venture formed of two hundred Indians and one hundred whites, led by one of the latter. Bonpland opined there would have been a greater chance of success had the advice of the Indian cacique José Largo been followed. While in this town, he arranged for the transfer of the Paraguayan products "so long deposited in the province of Corrientes."[38]

On 5 May Bonpland went on board the French warship *Bordelaise*, which clearly impressed him with its size and sleek condition, making from there a listing of the French ships and their officers. Other vessels mentioned included the frigate *Atalante*, the *Atrevido*, and the brig *Vedette*. After Paraná, Bonpland transferred to the *Atrevido*, in order to continue to Montevideo. At some point during the journey descending the Paraná, his skills came in useful: "We stopped to cut grass for our mounts. The sailors, little skilled in this type of work, went to cut the famous Polygonum, *Caa-tay*, but following my observations, they abandoned their project and made an ample harvest of a type of Paspalum very common hereabouts, whose tall stems filled with a medullary substance offer an excellent pasture."[39] On 9 May, his vessel was close to San Nicolás, heading for the island of Martín García. On the brig *Vedette* was a party of around a dozen Argentineans, including Dr. Alsina (presumably the jurist and politician Valentín Alsina) and a Colonel Pueyrredón.[40] Bonpland described the nature of his conversation with these individuals. He belonged to the school of thought favoring a more forceful coordination by Lavalle in his opposition to Rosas. He also made an unequivocal statement here that "all the people of judgment" wanted to see the end of Rosas and his bloody regime.[41] He offered no recognition that Rosas's government enjoyed popular support.

In May 1840, Bonpland formed part of a considerable party of French nationals present on Martín García, occupied by French marines since October 1838 as part of their blockade strategy. The island was a significant place for Bonpland, as the site where he began his fieldwork in subtropical southern South America in 1818. It was here, on his return visit, that he made his own ink from seeds of the shrub *algarrobilla*, or carob bean.[42] The product has thus far stood the test of time. After lunch, "where only good wine was lacking," the party made a random excursion by horseback across the island: "They assure me that the two stands of the plant that bears maté still exist here. We searched for them without finding them. Mr. Roland [a medical doctor] took on the task of having the Portuguese black [presumably a Brazilian] show them to me. I recognized with pleasure all the plants I had described in 1818."[43]

While off Montevideo, Bonpland had the chance to visit powerful figures in the French naval presence in the Plata. Part of his motive for the visits was surely politics, but this was kept veiled in a commentary that focused heavily on social matters. Bonpland, like many French residents, presumably wished to keep French naval opposition to Rosas alive, at a time when steps had already been taken toward lifting the blockade of the rivers, mainly the Araña-Dupotet conference of 29 February 1840.[44] It has been claimed that Bonpland also used this visit to relay a proposal for the annexation of the Riograndense Republic by France, but there is no comment on this idea in his journal, making it difficult to establish whether he was truly engaged on a clandestine mission.[45] He began by visiting the French frigate *Atalante*, a vessel then commanded by August Nicolas Vaillant (1793–1858), who a few years earlier had led the circumnavigation of the globe on the *Bonite*. Vaillant, whose manners Bonpland found "polite but affected," pressed him for information about Lavalle. Bonpland was particularly interested in the portrait of Admiral Duperré (1775–1846) hanging in Vaillant's cabin. Although Bonpland did not record the reason for his interest in his travel journal, Duperré was his near contemporary and they shared the common origin of La Rochelle.[46] Duperré had a brilliant career, rising to become the minister in charge of the French navy and the colonies. Bonpland then had an extended interview with Admiral Dupotet, in which the admiral showed himself friendly toward Rosas and Rivera, but the enemy of Lavalle.[47] They also spoke of Paris, but above all about Admiral Duperré and the countess Victorine de Chastenay. Known to Bonpland from Paris before he left France, the countess had spoken at length about him to Dupotet.[48]

Madame de Chastenay and Dupotet shared the link of Burgundian roots; the former mentioned the latter in her important memoirs of French life.

After a lunch on board the ship, marked mainly by a visible hostility between Dupotet and Vaillant, Bonpland descended to shore in the afternoon on what was to form his first visit to Montevideo. The city was especially flush with French influence in this period; between 1835 and 1842 slightly more than a half of the immigrants arriving in the port of Montevideo were of French origin, most of them Basques.[49] Bonpland arrived in style, conducted to land in the admiral's launch:

> I am astonished to see the enormous group of houses Montevideo presents, and above all the immense quantity of new buildings. The port contains at least 159 ships of all sizes; these vessels assembled in the harbor offer a forest of dry wood decorated with ropes and sails. I arrive on the mole, where I find myself in the middle of an immense crowd and soon I find several people known to me.[50]

Dressed in what he termed his traveling clothes, presumably some version of rustic gaucho dress, he was aware that he must have cut a strange figure in the city.[51] At Montevideo, Bonpland found many old friends in exile

Figure 4.1 The landing place at Montevideo, 1836.
SOURCE: Reproduced from Vaillant, *Voyage autour du monde, 1836–37*, Atlas, plate 10. General Research Division, The New York Public Library, Astor, Lenox and Tilden Foundations.

from Buenos Aires. They included the French merchant Roguin and Mariquita Sánchez. His political intelligence was also clearly in demand with the French agents in the Plata. Raymond Baradère, the French consul, invited Bonpland to stay in his house, following the manner in which Bonpland had earlier stayed with Aimé Roger while at Buenos Aires. Bonpland accepted the invitation, asking only to stay several days in the French hotel where he had already reserved a room. It was during those days that he found the necessary quiet to write a series of letters to Europe, all of them to botanists; they were directed to François Delessert and to Mirbel at Paris, and to de Candolle at Geneva. Even while in the thick of politics, the fate of his scientific work was clearly on Bonpland's mind.

Writing to François Delessert, his key intermediary at Paris on pension issues, Bonpland conveyed some of the extreme challenges he faced in preparing the paperwork to meet the needs of French bureaucracy. In order to journey to Montevideo, he had crossed 160 leagues of country that for the last three years had become "the theater of the bloodiest war."[52] A major theme of the letter to Delessert is that Bonpland was consumed by his efforts to recover from his economic losses. He cataloged the locations of these, beginning with Paraguay and ending with the massive losses of livestock following the battle of Pago Largo. Despite such crippling reverses, Bonpland was still full of hope about the future, telling Delessert of his plans to publish his southern South American material, confident that no one else could assume this task in a satisfactory way. The continuing ambition to publish also appeared in the letters to Mirbel and to de Candolle.

A letter to Mirbel was stimulated in part by Bonpland's having recently received (somewhere on the Paraná River) a box of seeds from him, expedited through the means of the French navy. Mirbel had sent various specimens to Bonpland by request, including seeds from Australia. Bonpland wrote of the quick success in multiplying the horsetail tree or Australian pine (*Casuarina equisetifolia*) at Corrientes. He was very critical of the vacillating actions of French political agents in the Plata, wanting France to take a stronger position on Rosas. Bonpland's most interesting comments by far, however, are about changing theories and methods in botany, in response to information from Mirbel about the work of Schleiden, the German pioneer in classifying plant material from its cells, using the microscope.[53] Bonpland was aware of the advantages of this method, but he revealed his continuing faith in what today we call economic botany. The properties of plant materials, in his view, had been too much neglected. The Chinese had found the very useful properties of tea; the indigenous people of Paraguay, those of yerba maté; and the Peruvians, those of cinchona, all without the use of any microscopes—an instrument in decidedly short supply in the interior regions of South America.[54] Mirbel was the key pioneer in microscopy in French botany, yet Bonpland was energetically defending his own corner of intellectual advance.

In 1840, Delessert and Mirbel were already established correspondents for Bonpland from South America. A letter in a different mold is the one he wrote in this brief spate of intellectual activity to A. P. de Candolle (1778–1841), a close associate during the period when Bonpland had worked for Joséphine at Malmaison. He had been trying to ascertain de Candolle's whereabouts for almost a decade, ultimately learning from a young officer in the French navy that the great botanist was resident at Geneva. Bonpland began his letter by referring to shared experiences near the beginning of the century, including a journey in the Swiss Alps. He was especially interested to learn what de Candolle had published, correctly presuming that he may have embarked on a new system of plant classification. Such was the measure of Bonpland's esteem that he could not envisage anybody else in the French-speaking world capable of such a work. He accounted for his own scientific activity and the will to publish not just the botany but the geology and the descriptions of fauna. Reviewing, as so often, his trials with Francia, Bonpland evinced the ambition to live as long as the dictator and to draw the fruit from his southern South American researches. The financial losses of the past three years (30,000 francs) were an obstacle. But he then laid out his current publishing plans. The ideal would be to publish all his manuscripts, if a backer could be found to extend the finance. Otherwise, he could begin with a flora in two volumes, which he foresaw as a sequel to the *Plantes équinoxiales*. And as he had earlier done for Humboldt, Bonpland made explicit his philosophy of publication, extending his view that only direct field experience led to satisfactory botanical publications. Working in the field was not only a matter of what was written down but also of "a mass of circumstances . . . that stay deeply etched in the memory."[55] Bonpland requested de Candolle's input on the current publication costs of a botanical work along the lines of those earlier works prepared for Humboldt that carried his name. While reflecting back to this earlier model, Bonpland showed some clear awareness of changes in taste, noting that everything had turned into commerce.

De Candolle wrote an interesting response to Bonpland's letter, which the latter presumably first saw on a subsequent visit to Montevideo.[56] He told Bonpland that his reply had been delayed by ill health. Indeed, the beginning of the letter mainly concerns de Candolle's considerable health challenges. He wrote it on what he claimed was his first good day in three months, reckoning the sedentary work of the past two decades had ruined his health, which stood in contrast to the benefits Bonpland appeared to have drawn from an errant life. Unlike Bonpland, de Candolle saw himself as unlikely to compete successfully with the dictator Francia for long life. After reviewing de Candolle's professional history, here Bonpland learned that his main occupation was indeed the systematic description of plants, through the work *Prodromus systematis universalis*. De Candolle had already described forty thousand species in seven volumes. His herbarium contained more than eighty thousand species of plants. Whether he could achieve the description of all of these was doubtful, he knew. De Candolle made clear the collaborative nature of his venture. He had counted on travelers and botanists resident overseas to send him much of his raw material for description in a work that now dominated science. Perhaps this was an avenue to publication with advantages for Bonpland?

De Candolle did tell Bonpland the main trends in botanical publication in Europe: "Since your departure from Europe, botanical works in luxurious format have become rarer." One problem was that the number of plants known to science had expanded vastly since the time of the French empire. Any works still appearing in a luxury format (mainly meaning with colored plates) were usually supported by a government subvention, such as Karl Friedrich Philip von Martius's study of palms prepared in Bavaria. Reading habits had also changed. Books containing political debates were more in fashion than those of botany. Based on the information provided by an unspecified botanical illustrator ("intelligent painter") at Geneva, de Candolle told Bonpland that to publish a folio volume of a hundred plates with the corresponding text would cost between 12,000 and 20,000 francs, depending on the degree of quality in the preparation. On receipt of this news, Bonpland seems to have used the publication budget estimates to work out roughly in the margins what de Candolle's own works must have cost to bring into print. We sense from this a degree of competition.

De Candolle also issued the warning to Bonpland that he would probably find many of his plants already described in the publications produced during the past twenty years. The authorities given specific mention comprised Martius (1794–1868), Friedrich Sellow (1789–1831), and Auguste de Saint-Hilaire (1779–1853). The quality ranged in de Candolle's view from a low of "around 1,200 mediocre plates of Brazilian plants" in José Mariano da Conceição Veloso's *Flora fluminensis*, to work of very high quality on Brazil conducted by Martius, based on his travels there with Spix during 1817–1820. Beyond major works such as those authored above, de Candolle cautioned, Bonpland would also need to watch out for further specialized work published in dissertations and monographs, often contained in scientific journals and the serials produced by learned academies: "It seems impossible to me to describe objects already described under other names." De Candolle offered Bonpland the clearest of advice about how to deal with his publishing project. The best course would be for Bonpland to establish himself at either Paris, London, Berlin, Vienna, Munich, or Geneva, with a marked preference for the first of these cities: "Your reputation as a botanist, the strangeness of your adventures, all of that will make your arrival in Europe an event."

Following his intensive work of correspondence about botanical matters, Bonpland moved his lodging on 19 May to the house of Consul Baradère, where he was drawn more intimately into the region's politics, receiving, for example, a visit from General Vidal, the Uruguayan minister of war. On the following evening, Baradère took him to a political meeting held in the house of Santiago Vázquez, then a former minister of Rivera. It was an assembly, held daily, "in which they speak loudly against the conduct of the president."[57] Noting the core members of this salon, Bonpland said he would not be returning to further meetings. Since he gave no reason, we can only speculate that such a strongly Unitarian gathering would have compromised Bonpland's own sense of himself as a neutral. In addition, the political slant present at Montevideo represented a slice of Europeanized urbanity already at some distance from Bonpland's accumulated sense of the political realities of the South American interior, notably of Corrientes. Shumway has noted how civil discourse in this period was becoming particularly intense. Despite their brilliance, the leaders of the Unitarian movement were viewed as condescending by the population at large.[58] Bonpland appears to have picked up on their limited appeal.

Perhaps more to Bonpland's taste was a visit made to examine merinos in the environs of Montevideo. Brought from Europe, this important flock of two hundred sheep and fifty rams was originally destined for Buenos Aires. Its detour provides a good example of economic disruption during war. Since the animals arrived shortly after the beginning of the French blockade, however, their owner Tresserra (very probably the Catalán merchant Juan Antonio Tresserra, a partner in an important Barcelona merchant house with a branch at Montevideo, and married to one of the daughters of Bonpland's friend Mariquita Sánchez), was forced to find accommodation land for his animals near the port of Montevideo. Bonpland described how the owner of this land used the political circumstances to squeeze very unfavorable terms from Tresserra, seeking to retain all the product from the first two annual lambing cycles.[59] Just when the French blockade would be lifted was a matter of speculation.

On 2 June 1840, Bonpland took lunch on board the frigate *Atalante*, in the company of Admiral Dupotet. Guindet, the captain of this vessel, immediately became a major focus of interest for Bonpland because he had seen Bonpland's sister Olive Gallocheau toward the end of 1839. This was far from the sole occasion when the French navy bridged the Atlantic in relaying Bonpland family news. The focus of Bonpland's letter written the same day to Olive was understandably directed more toward domestic affairs than his other letters written from Montevideo.[60] He sought to reassure his sister about his quality of life in South America, pointing out that he had something resembling a substitute family in the Périchons of Corrientes. He noted he had always lodged at Corrientes with the Périchons since 1820, where he maintained rooms of his own in their house. As a family with six daughters, the Périchons' home must have contained considerable domestic space. The only reasons Bonpland avoided Corrientes as a place to live were that he found the climate to be too hot and the local pastures to be of inferior quality. In discussing the climate, he pointed out the errors of a crude environmental determinism. While most people in Europe still felt that the American climate led to premature death (precipitating the "fear of the tropics"), Bonpland explained that this was certainly not true for the parts of South America where he resided. He gave several examples of longevity in the region, including of "that bad beggar" Francia. Bonpland was clearly concerned about Francia's life expectancy.

Return to the Interior

Bonpland conveyed his sense of frustration about loss of time while based at Montevideo. He had arrived there on 14 May with business he reckoned he could accomplish in a week. Several times he contemplated a return journey overland, but the onset of a rigorous cold snap of winter weather and the dangers of the Uruguayan interior ruled against this. On 23 June, he noted he had been ready to leave Montevideo for thirty-two days, yet he had still not been able to embark on account of the lack of favorable winds.[61] As soon as the sailing conditions permitted, he returned on the French warship *Fortune*, which was accompanying a commercial convoy of around forty vessels ascending the Uruguay River. Writing to Consul Baradère from Salto on 10 July 1840, he complained that his journey was proving difficult for many reasons, including contrary winds. The extensive shoals on the river just above the town hindered navigation except during the rainy season. During the journey, he had met briefly with the Unitarian soldier Chilavert at Paysandú. Part of his motive for writing to Baradère at Montevideo was to expedite the movement of three thousand arrobas of yerba belonging to his friend Ingres from the Uruguay River to the Paraná. This was sought by General Lavalle.[62]

Bonpland also used the stay in Salto as an opportunity to inform Rivera about developments in Paraguay. His knowledge of affairs there was broad enough that it points to a wide network of contacts. Bonpland's long letter began by observing that Francia was following the same system of government as earlier, although he had supposedly become less cruel, ordering fewer executions than earlier. In an interesting reversal of fortune, José León Ramírez, the official who had emotionally seen Bonpland off from Itapúa back in 1831, was now in prison.[63] Trade along the route from Itapúa to southern Brazil had been in a state of stagnation for more than six months. Part of the explanation for this lay with the spread of the cattle tick, which two years earlier had "desolated" the southern portions of Rio Grande do Sul. Under these circumstances, Francia suspended supplies of yerba and tobacco to Brazil. Bonpland seemed to think that Francia had reaped what he deserved. After Pago Largo, he noted, bands of Correntinos had raided livestock in both their home province and in Rio Grande do Sul. The malevolents, as Bonpland termed them, presented themselves at Itapúa, seeking asylum in Paraguay, a request that Francia conceded: "It is clear that if Francia had not declared himself the protector of robbers, he probably would not have had so many *garrapatas* (cattle ticks)."[64] Other themes of the letter included a progress report on Francia's construction of a defensive wall made from dry stones opposite Itapúa, what became known as the Trinchera de los Paraguayos (the site of present-day Posadas). There is a clear sense in Bonpland's letter that intelligence brought into Paraguay by Brazilian merchants was a mixed blessing for Francia. For example, contact between the indigenous peoples around Itapúa and the Brazilians hastened the desire in the former to be free. Francia had taken the initiative to remove some of the indigenous people from around Itapúa, leaving a number far inferior to that when Bonpland lived near the town for nineteen months. The Brazilian merchant who brought news of the "memorable victory of Cagancha" (Rivera's remarkable victory of 29 December 1839 over Argentine forces) to Paraguay had been treated as a liar. And Francia viewed the political movements in Corrientes "positively with disgust." The year 1840 had seen an uprising of the indigenous people in part of Corrientes, headed by Carabí.[65] Francia tried to use this revolt for his own geopolitical purposes, claiming that La Cruz was part of Paraguayan territory. A party of 330 Indians (80 men in arms, 50 women, and 200 children of all ages) moved on account of the rebellion toward Francia's protection in Misiones. When General Lavalle sent troops seeking horses to that region, notably around Itapúa, it understandably had a very negative effect; Bonpland viewed this as "bad politics." It led to Francia presenting a paper to the government of Corrientes claiming the territory of the missions as far as the Miriñay River: "During my sojourn in Paraguay, every year we had a fine comedy with similar bluffs."[66]

The final part of Bonpland's long account of affairs in Paraguay moved from the general to the particular. Francia was interested to learn what Bonpland had been doing in relation to the French squadron in the Plata and with Rivera at Montevideo, sending a young Brazilian merchant to monitor his movements. According to Bonpland, Francia's spy was an old friend of his, thus a double agent. By feeding lines back to Paraguay, the spy reported that Bonpland had met with Rivera in person, finding him to be "a friend of the liberty of the people." In particular, he wanted the authorities and his "many friends" in Itapúa to learn that "God has designated General Rivera to be the Liberator of the South American peoples."[67]

In September 1840, the month of Francia's death, Bonpland made an interesting short journey into the Chaco accompanying Ferré, one of Ferré's daughters, and a minister in his government. The purpose of Ferré's mission was political intelligence; he needed to communicate with the political chiefs of such places as Salta and Tucumán, where opposition to Rosas coalesced as the short-lived Coalition of the North.[68] Bonpland made specific mention of General Aráoz de La Madrid, the military commander of the northern opposition. The Correntino messenger was to travel accompanied by a powerful escort of Chaco Indians and an interpreter "who speaks perfect Spanish and all the languages of the Chaco," no mean qualifications.[69]

Based on his earlier experience, the interpreter promised Ferré he would not take more than ten days to travel from the banks of the Paraná to Salta.

On account of his trip with Ferré, Bonpland left an interesting description of the Indian *tolderia* (encampment) headed by the cacique José Largo and the material circumstances of some of the people living there. He estimated the population at around five hundred. He was not romantic about the way of Indian life here: "Everything is of a filth without parallel."[70] Like his compatriot Saint-Hilaire, Bonpland seems to have been somewhat taken aback by the limited amount of clothing worn by many of the South American Indians, observing that "the few rags that cover them have never been washed but by water from the sky."[71] He observed what happened when Ferré's daughter arrived with presents for the Indians:

> They were distributed with all the grace of youth, but the Indians received them with that indifference which characterizes them. Nevertheless, one must render justice to the Indians. They are appreciative and know how to prove their gratitude through their actions. It is by this means that the Chaco Indians have become good friends of the Correntinos since they made a peace treaty with Governor Ferré, whom they call their father.[72]

The village presented a striking example of longevity, in the form of an Indian woman claiming an age of not less than 140 years:

> This woman has all her hair; it is white but straight in the Indian manner. For several years she has lived crouched on an old calf skin. She takes no more exercise than that of sitting on her bottom and of reclining on her back or side. She is thin. Her skin is flaccid. She has no more teeth and the lower jaw is extended and falling. She speaks little but everything she does say is full of sense. As soon as the old Indian woman saw the governor, she asked him for the benediction and everybody observed that she made the sign of the cross with the left hand, using her right hand to eat some roast fish. All the onlookers asked themselves if it was through inadvertence that she made the sign with the left hand or whether she did not wish to disturb her meal.[73]

The government of Corrientes drew on the fighting resources of the Guaicurú Indians. At the time Bonpland made his visit, 28 of them went off to join the army of General Paz. He noted that if Paz wanted more of these "semi-civilized Indians," Ferré could send as many as five hundred.

In a marginal note to his travel diaries on 2 October 1840, Bonpland recorded that Echagüe of Entre Ríos had withdrawn his army from La Esquina.[74] This cleared the way for a second visit to Montevideo, which began on 16 October. Traveling initially by launch gave Bonpland the chance to read the newspaper *El Nacional* from Montevideo. Numbers 533–35 and 541 were deemed worthy of a close rereading because they contained phrasing of interest to the government of Corrientes. General Paz wrote to Bonpland on 20 October, aware that he was on a mission to Uruguay.[75] It is clear from the content of the general's letters that he held Bonpland in high regard. They met up on 26 October, when Bonpland received his dispatches and other documents, described as "a multitude of letters and innumerable commissions."[76]

Before the definitive departure to Montevideo, Bonpland was back at Santa Ana for a spell. He wrote to Ferré telling him of the extraordinary rains that had left small lakes throughout the grasslands of his property. Given the swells in the rivers at such a time, travel was extremely hazardous. Prior to leaving for the south, Bonpland had prepared medical remedies for the Correntino army and to send for the inhabitants of the capital. Trouble was brewing in Rio Grande do Sul, where Rivera had supplied arms and munitions to the Farrapos. Bonpland needed to repair his *chalana* (barge) in order to depart for Salto, and presumably then seek a ship to Montevideo. He promised Ferré a report on the Paso de Santa Ana, one describing the conditions on both sides of the river.[77]

On 5 November 1840, Paz informed Bonpland of the death of Francia in Paraguay, an extraordinary piece of news in any event, and certainly for the recipient. Paz believed that this development could lead to new political combinations, and he saw Bonpland as an extremely useful figure for establishing closer relations with Paraguay—whether of a political or of a purely commercial nature. The correspondence with Paz provides clear evidence of how closely Bonpland was bound up with the political affairs of Corrientes and the surrounding regions. He delivered the promised report on the state of affairs at Santa Ana to Ferré on 10 November. The impending battle between Farrapos and Legales he reported on ten days earlier had not happened. Instead, all sorts of negotiations were taking place, with soldiers crossing the battle lines. He felt concerned about the growing state of disorder at Santa Ana: "There is a large gathering of individuals and families. All remain here, hopeful of the profits from a clandestine commerce. They damage the state and would be more useful in their own homes and away from the banks of the Uruguay."[78]

The journey south to Montevideo proved extremely difficult. At Las Higueritas (Nueva Palmira), the military commander confronted Bonpland with two published letters that spoke of his relations with Ferré and with Paz.[79] This publicity was an unwelcome development because it compromised still further any sense of neutrality that he may have felt. He continued his journey by land through Uruguay, touching Las Vacas and Colonia. Along this journey, he was shown the portion of the Arroyo de las Vacas that had been sketched by his compatriot, painter and lithographer Adolphe d'Hastrel. He spent the night in this region with Juan Francisco Nollet, a doctor of French origin. Nollet's horses and people were of little practical use to Bonpland, thus he continued on alone with his "little Indian" and a guide he took on at Las Vacas, described as "old, lame, and not very brisk."[80] He spent the day traveling in very picturesque, hilly country, arriving at an estancia where four Basques were in the process of shearing a flock of three thousand sheep. Around Colonia, he noted that the fine landscape reminded him of Europe. The military commander at Colonia offered Bonpland an overland escort to Montevideo. Based on local information, however, Bonpland chose not to pursue by land, given the high risk to life posed by the *blanquillos*, or bands of robbers. Thus he continued the journey to Montevideo by ship, arriving there on the morning of 1 December. He wrote Ferré that he met that day with Admiral Dupotet and dined alone with the president, presumably meaning the civilian in charge of Uruguay's administration while Rivera was in the field attending to military affairs.[81]

Although he had sought to meet with Rivera, Bonpland instead set out in writing just what governor Ferré and the government of Corrientes needed from him.[82] When visiting Rivera's wife Bernardina, in the house they had occupied since 1834 (today Uruguay's Museo Histórico Nacional), Bonpland was able to view a portrait of the general very recently begun (presumably the oil by Baldassare Verazzi). He then moved on by carriage to the Miguelete district, the place in Uruguay where Rivera was born. The driver of the carriage lost his way, so that they spent the night trying to find the correct route. Bonpland and Rivera ultimately met up and together visited Canelones and Santa Lucia. He described the latter as an elite space in the interior of Uruguay, perhaps struck by its differences from the Indian village of the same name in Corrientes: "Santa Lucia is the Versailles, the Meudon, the Montmorency of Montevideo. It is the favored place for taking baths and for the outings of the rich."[83] He ushered in the new year listening to Rivera talk about the anniversary of Cagancha (29 December 1839) and his other successful battles. In the distance, he saw the Estancia Azotea, the closest of Rivera's properties to Montevideo and supposedly the first house in the countryside installed with a roof terrace. He mentioned the sheep there; the greater part of the flock was crossbred and poorly managed. After some days of travel, Bonpland finally settled to his discussions with Rivera on behalf of Corrientes, seeking the supply of the arms and cannon promised earlier. It was not an easy mission. Bonpland found himself in the position of defending the conduct of General Paz before Rivera, who viewed Paz as a traitor. Leaving Rivera's company on 4 January to continue his journey across Uruguayan soil, he noted the following in his travel diary: "I had naturally been very serious and very cold with the president."[84] Ultimately, his negotiations with Rivera brought some success for Corrientes.

On 20 January 1841, Bonpland wrote to Rivera from Salto. While there were no new significant developments in Paraguay, considerable political movements had taken place in the western interior of Rio Grande do Sul on account of the civil war. The only thing known for sure at Salto was that considerable migration had flowed into Corrientes from São Borja and Itaquí.[85] He also wrote on the same day to Roguin, whose newsy reply read almost like a diary of the major political happenings at Montevideo. The merchant clearly counted on Bonpland for news of happenings in Corrientes. Politics, not surprisingly, were having a very negative impact on commercial affairs there. Roguin told Bonpland that many Argentineans were disposed to leave Uruguay. He also made a list of some of the French people heading back to France, including the French consul Baradère, who had recently "sold everything it is possible to sell to a curious public," including his wife's jewels and dresses.[86]

In early February 1841, Paz informed Bonpland that the Rosista forces had assembled to invade Corrientes. He had turned to Bonpland for help with the supply of troops, uniforms, and munitions from Rivera. While these things had still to arrive, the item of "absolute necessity" was gunpowder.[87] In March, Bonpland served as the agent for the transfer of 5,000 *patacones* (the prevailing currency) from Rivera to the government of Corrientes.[88] Arriving back at Santa Ana in the same month, Bonpland described his property as lying "in a deplorable state of abandon."[89] Part of the problem was the location of the ranch, sitting in the midst of a zone of "clandestine commerce." As so often in his South American career, his return brought a rash of activity on the property.

In April, Bonpland visited San Marcos on the eastern bank of the Uruguay River. Close to the former Jesuit mission of Yapeyú, San Marcos was a former settlement established by the Theatins. He carefully traced the geography of the timber resources. With the help of two carpenters from the town of Corrientes, Bonpland ferried considerable timber to Santa Ana, where he proceeded to construct a series of barges out of cedar and black laurel. He did not specify his motive for doing this, but troop transport seems the most probable objective. A sustained bout of activity in May breathed new life into Santa Ana and restored it as a useful economic enterprise. The work involved in part cleaning up the garden, planting garlic and onions, and roofing buildings. Throughout all this, there were always local medical trips to undertake.

News from Montevideo came in July from Juan Andrés Gelly, an urbane Paraguayan diplomat who had long lived outside his homeland. He would soon play an important role in the political opening of Paraguay. In 1846, for example, he was sent from Asunción to Rio de Janeiro, laying some of the groundwork for an eventual treaty of alliance between Paraguay and Brazil. Having been associated with the earlier government of General Lavalle at Buenos Aires, Gelly then went into exile at Montevideo, forming part of the opposition to Rosas. Gelly wanted Bonpland to funnel political intelligence to Paraguay through Ferré's hands. He maintained that a British effort to seek a commercial treaty with Paraguay following Francia's death included hidden motives on the part of Rosas and his relatives the Anchorenas, a family of extremely wealthy ranchers.[90] Gelly believed the Paraguayans would prevail "but perhaps they do not know all the arteries, power, and dissimulation with which the ambitious pursue their projects. The citizens who compose the government of Paraguay are honorable and sincere; men of this character are often victims of the swindles of the wicked." This was a highly optimistic view of a government then formed of illiterate militiamen. His was not a glowing view of British actions in South America: "You know everything that England has done in America under the pretext of commercial treaties." Pedro Sheridan, described as Rosas's secret agent, was somebody known to Bonpland, having supplied him with pedigree sheep before the battle of Pago Largo.[91]

Increasingly in this period Bonpland was a conduit for the transfer of political intelligence across Corrientes, Entre Ríos, Rio Grande do Sul, and Uruguay, and he continued to make considerable journeys. But it was also sometime around this period that he became seriously involved with Victoriana Cristaldo, the woman who would bear three children carrying the Bonpland name.[92] A property report from Santa Ana in January 1842 revealed that Dona Victoriana was personally engaged in shearing the sheep.[93] In

May, Bonpland forwarded José Pinheiro de Ulhoa Cintra's request to Ferré that Corrientes supply three hundred horses for the Riograndense Republic.[94] Later in the year, he journeyed to Uruguay, where his diary noted many political meetings with Rivera, Paz, and other political leaders, including the famous Garibaldi. It also contains interesting reflection on how the Blancos were working well in Uruguay, pulling together in a concerted campaign.

On 15 October 1842, Bonpland showed his awareness of impending political changes. He saw a grand battle brewing between General Oribe, Rivera, and Paz. It appeared that Rivera's troops were about to cross the Uruguay River in order to take the offensive in Entre Ríos. Bonpland claimed that he happened to be in Paysandú by chance at the moment of a major political meeting between Bento Gonçalves da Silva, other Farrapo leaders, and Rivera. The meetings were broader in significance than this, however, since they harbored discussions about the formation of a new federation that would link Entre Ríos, Corrientes, and Santa Fe with Uruguay. They also addressed lesser subjects. Rivera entered one meeting for discussions at a time when Bonpland and the Farrapo leader were discussing the latter's rheumatism.[95] The following month Bonpland placed his resources directly into the logistical preparations for the combat. On 6 November, he noted that his barge was used at the Paso del Higo to transfer the escort of the governor (presumably Ferré) and his horses. In the afternoon, it was the turn of Giuseppe Garibaldi, who used the vessel to transport his sailors into Uruguay: "At 1 p.m., Mr. Garibaldi arrived with his sailors and an hour later he crossed to Uruguay in my barge, along with his troops. Mr. Garibaldi is a likeable and well-educated man. He speaks all the living languages well and besides he shows an extreme bravery. One could say he is intrepid and he keeps his sang-froid in the greatest of dangers."[96]

During the rest of the month, Bonpland's leading preoccupations were medical visits, and working on the garden, the *chacra*, and the livestock, above all the merino flock. The breeding results failed to equal those of the previous year. He found explanations. First, a number of young rams of ordinary quality had been introduced into the flock, presumably inadvertently. A further problem lay in a recent wet winter. The terrain had remained very humid with parts of the land often standing in water. The sheep had lost weight and many suffered from gangrene.[97]

While Bonpland was traveling, somebody needed to maintain his establishment at Santa Ana. The problem was presumably that domestic-born staff were liable for military conscription. This may help to explain why in September 1842 the Salto-based French homeopathic doctor Apollon de Mirbel was in charge of affairs on this property. He gave Bonpland a full report of events at Santa Ana. Among other things, the wool had been washed "and we are about to make the mattresses."[98] The letter also revealed something very rare, brief details of the life of Bonpland's new wife. When Mirbel received a letter from Bonpland to Victoriana, he passed along its contents; she replied verbally (it is likely that she was illiterate) that everything would be accomplished in the manner her husband desired. She was engaged in drying rose petals to make essence, even though the harvest had not been so abundant as during the previous year.

Corrientes was often the main staging ground for opposition to Rosas. Despite the failure of General Lavalle's invasion of Buenos Aires in 1840, the spirit of revolt remained very much alive. The seesaw of political events deeply affected life in the province. The battle of Arroyo Grande on 6 December 1842 in Entre Ríos, which involved as many as eighteen thousand soldiers in the field, dealt a severe blow to Correntino ambitions. Since the province's elites were divided on the subject of Rosas, Corrientes endured a high degree of instability—no less than five different governments held power between 1841 and 1845.[99] Arroyo Grande also marked the end of Rivera's territorial ambitions beyond Uruguay. Governor Ferré went into exile, first in Paraguay, but then in Rio Grande do Sul. He would eventually write his memoirs from São Borja, where Bonpland was living. Under these difficult political circumstances, life in Corrientes became temporarily untenable.

Retreat into Brazil

In April 1843, Bonpland moved back to his *chacra* at São Borja, where he had not resided since January 1839. The decision to cross the river to Brazil may have been motivated in part by the recent arrival of his daughter Carmen, born at Santa Ana on 15 February. São Borja was a place to lie low until politics permitted his return to Santa Ana with security. In fact, Bonpland developed a closer attachment with the town, spending much of his time there for over a decade, where his family grew to include two sons.

The physical condition of the São Borja property cannot have been pleasing. In January 1839, Bonpland claimed that he left the *chacra* and house in the best state possible: "Today I find a field open to all passersby, with no vestige of the solid fences I had left. All the ground I had left covered in seeds and useful plants offers no more than a third of the orange trees I had planted."[100] Even the four doors and six windows of the house had been taken away. Fortunately, in the subtropics crops did not take long to mature, thus he was soon self-sufficient in his basic food needs. Toward the end of October, he noted he had long been harvesting sufficient cabbages, parsley, onions, garlic, and lettuces for his consumption. He would have liked to replant large numbers of orange trees, but a lack of workers stood in the way.[101] On 1 January 1844, Bonpland received a box of seeds from his old friend Raffeneau-Delile (professor at the medical school in Montpellier), which he found disappointing, since it contained "few seeds for the kitchen-garden and not a single useful plant for forage."[102] Bonpland conducted all kinds of medical work at São Borja, presumably to support the family, some of which can be reconstructed from unpaid medical bills. On 4 January he treated a small black belonging to Gregorio Maciel, presumably a slave, for spina bifida.[103] From January to April 1844, Bonpland was busy at São Borja with smallpox vaccinations. In total, he vaccinated 162 people in this period. He maintained that the smallpox arrived in the town in the last days of December 1843, carried from Alegrete, then the capital of the Riograndense Republic, by an Indian woman. He treated this woman in the first days of January 1844, then used her as the source of his vaccine in order to inject children. Most of the people Bonpland treated were blacks and Indians, especially the latter. This probably reflected the significant indigenous presence in the demographic profile of Missões. On 19 January, the patients he vaccinated in Ferré's house included "a 24-year-old Guaicurú Indian woman, strong and robust."[104]

While based at São Borja, Bonpland worked to maintain his economic interests in southeastern Corrientes. By Bastille Day of 1844, he was traveling from Santa Ana to Paso del Higo (in the northwest corner of Uruguay, very close to Rio Grande do Sul), where his barge was deposited after being used for passing Farrapo troops from Corrientes into Uruguay. It was the second effort to salvage the vessel. During this mission, he also recovered sheep bearing the Bonpland mark from Augustín Miller's estancia (422 in total). In August, there was a great deal of activity at Santa Ana of erecting fences and repairing roofs, using timber drawn from the property itself or the immediate region. Always hard at work, Bonpland had little use for Sabbath celebrations in his corner of the interior of South America, as he noted on Sunday, 4 August: "Today it is Sunday, the day of the slothful, the gamblers, and the drinkers."[105] By 10 August, he had finished his arrangement of the quinta, leaving him ready to return to São Borja.

It was not an easy journey. Arriving at Restauración (Paso de los Libres) on 11 August, illness had taken hold during the night, but Bonpland found the will to note his circumstances: "I find myself suffering greatly from a very strong dysentery that attacked me during the previous night. Very strong fever all night, accompanied by a continual delirium. I found myself too ill to disembark, so I spent a dreadful night in my barge."[106] Neither at Restauración nor at São Marcos could he find anywhere suitable to stop and take remedies. The only relief provided in the latter place was finding his flock of crossbred sheep in good condition. After a stop made for medical reasons at Itaqui (where he stayed with the Swiss merchant Thédy), he arrived at São Borja on the morning of 19 August, finding his friends impatient to see him. For once, he could describe the garden at São Borja as in good condition, noting particularly the more than ten thousand onion plants. Joaquin, a black man, and Roque, a mulatto, had worked together "passably well," high praise coming from Bonpland. Only a square of flax, seeded before Bonpland's departure for Santa Ana, had failed to prosper; the explanation, he thought, was failure to hoe it at the appropriate time.[107]

Bonpland arrived back at Santa Ana on 27 March 1845, when he approved the work his Indian servant Tomás had performed on the trees. The main motive of this particular visit to his Correntino property was to reinforce the quality of his sheep-breeding operations. He traveled to Curuzú Cuatiá in order to inspect some sheep brought from the south following the invasion of Entre Ríos and Salto by the Madariaga brothers, Correntino political leaders.[108] The sheep originally formed part of a substantial flock belonging to Campbell, a British rancher, but they were now in the hands of a Sergeant José Silvero. Bonpland's company along the journey to Curuzú Cuatiá included the soldier Nicanor Cáceres, later a famous general in the defense of Corrientes against the 1865 Paraguayan invasion.[109] While the sheep in Silvero's flock seemed in good condition, Bonpland did not rush to buy them, as he already owned sheep a great deal finer. Part of the motive for traveling to the Curuzú Cuatiá region was to inventory the work of other breeders holding crossbred sheep drawn from the same origin. While the breeding of fine-wooled sheep was usually something associated with elites and immigrants, especially those of northwest European origin, war may have opened opportunities for others. Of three other improved sheep breeders Bonpland became aware of on this trip, one, Clemente, was a black, while another came from Paraguay.

One positive consequence of Bonpland's longish spell of residence in the Brazilian missions was that his relatively fixed address attracted a series of people, some to visit, others to settle, who provided stimulus in the small mission town.[110] As already seen from the period when Bonpland was released from Paraguay, São Borja was no ordinary small place because of the trade route between Brazil and Itapúa. Any traveler on the way to Asunción from the coastal cities of Brazil usually approached Paraguay via São Borja. However small the town, it sometimes brought Bonpland the novelty of visitors. And these in turn provided some brief account of how he was living there. One French travel account, the work of the pseudonymous Armand de B. (Just-Jean-Étienne Roy), traveling with a Dr. Philips, was structured entirely around a visit made in the 1840s from the mouth of the Plata ascending the Uruguay River to Bonpland's home at São Borja. They planned to use Bonpland's knowledge of the region as the basis for attempting a journey into Paraguay, one that does not seem to have taken place.[111] Roy found little of originality to report in his book. He did comment on Bonpland's vast garden planted with oranges and European trees. His material circumstances were described as highly modest, in that the only items of note were portraits of Napoleon and Joséphine in a small reception room.[112]

Figure 4.2 Bonpland's home at São Borja, c. 1845. Drawn on site by Alfred Demersay.
SOURCE: Reproduced from Demersay, *Histoire physique du Paraguay*. Atlas, n.p. Courtesy of the University of Arizona Library Special Collections.

A far more important French visitor was Alfred Demersay, later a key figure in the Société de Géographie at Paris, who gained a French government mission to visit South America in 1844. Demersay had a number of points in common with Bonpland. First, he was a medical doctor, trained at Paris. He traveled to South America with the specific aim of reporting on Paraguay, part of the international interest in gathering intelligence on that country that followed Francia's demise. In the 1860s Demersay published a major work on the historical geography of Paraguay, the major foci of which were physical description and accounting for the country's current resources; he never finished a planned volume dealing with the history and archaeology of the Jesuit missions. Demersay approached Paraguay through Brazil. He traveled south from Rio de Janeiro accompanying the royal party that visited Rio Grande do Sul as part of a celebration of the end of the Farroupilha Revolt. In fact, it was Brazil's emperor Dom Pedro II who guided Demersay toward Bonpland at São Borja.[113] Bonpland and Demersay spent considerable time together. The former guided the latter's research, something Demersay readily acknowledged and that is also apparent in his publications. The important illustrations from the atlas that accompanies Demersay's study of the historical geography of Paraguay had their origins in encouragement from Bonpland.[114] Demersay, in turn, played an important role in carrying news of Bonpland to various places, both when arriving and departing from South America.

Figure 4.3 The ruined mission at São Miguel, c. 1845. Drawn on site by Alfred Demersay.
SOURCE: Reproduced from Demersay, *Histoire physique du Paraguay*. Atlas, n.p. General Research Division, The New York Public Library, Astor, Lenox and Tilden Foundations.

Demersay reopened Bonpland's link with Paraguayan authorities through José Antônio Pimenta Bueno, later the marquês de São Vicente, the Brazilian minister to Paraguay. Bonpland received a letter in November 1846 from Pimenta Bueno.[115] We can infer from its contents that Bonpland had sent message of his interest in coming to Paraguay through Demersay. Pimenta Bueno advised against this, since the present circumstances did not appear favorable. The Brazilian also gave Bonpland the mission to find smallpox vaccine with which to treat the inhabitants of the Paraguayan capital. Antivariolic campaigns were in vogue, although the British commercial agent sent to Asunción in 1842, George J. R. Gordon, had been expelled for distributing smallpox vaccine without permission. Bonpland's reply announced that he planned to go to Montevideo soon, described as his main point for contacts with Europe on account of the intensity of shipping touching its port. His letter treated the vaccine issue as a footnote. Most of its content reviewed his interest in sheep breeding stretching back to Malmaison and Paraguay's position on this subject. He explained two frustrated wishes to the Brazilian minister. One was his desire to introduce the merino to the grasslands of the Paraguayan missions. He explained how this could be a potential source of wealth for that country. In return, he also sought to bring the long-wooled sheep he had seen around San Miguel, Paraguay into Corrientes.[116]

Still within November, Bonpland forwarded a flask of smallpox vaccine prepared by the Jennerian Society in London, obtained with the help of the president of the medical society at Montevideo. He emphasized his estimate that the vaccine could not be more than six months old, maintaining that he had used a similar vaccine with success on three occasions at São Borja, including on a virus that was eighteen months in age.[117] In Pimenta Bueno's letter of thanks, he advised Bonpland against making a journey to Montevideo on the grounds of political instability. On the other hand, the prospects for a visit to Paraguay looked better. Pimenta Bueno had relayed Bonpland's ideas about sheep breeding in Paraguay to President Carlos Antonio López. Nobody doubted the unquestionable advantages of spreading sheep across the grasslands of the Paraguayan republic, but it would take an industrious individual to provide the way through example. President López told the Brazilian minister he would be pleased to see Bonpland set himself up again in Paraguay.[118] While López gained the reputation as the "Great Builder" for his efforts on behalf of Paraguay, drawing considerably on foreign help, he did not manage to attract Bonpland back.[119] The memory of this failure was still alive when the two of them met in person at Asunción in 1857.[120]

Returning from Paraguay to France, Demersay also talked about Bonpland's work at Rio de Janeiro, obtaining contacts for him with Brazilian national institutions. It was partly through Demersay that Bonpland gained links to the leading medical practitioners in Brazil around the middle of the nineteenth century. For example, a letter Bonpland wrote to the French-educated Dr. José Martins da Cruz Jobim, who came from a wealthy Riograndense ranching family, was read before the full medical academy at Rio de Janeiro. By 1849, and possibly earlier, he was also in contact with the French-born José Francisco Xavier Sigaud (1796–1856), who published a very important work on medical topography, *Du climat et des maladies du Brésil*.[121] Sigaud was also interested in the medical properties of plants. Not surprisingly, he thought Bonpland represented a potential mine of knowledge on this subject and that he should be consulted while he was based on Brazilian soil. Sigaud asked Bonpland, if his health permitted it, to send "detailed notions about the medicines of São Borja and adjoining places, and to present other works concerning the medical topography of the province [of Rio Grande do Sul]."[122] He tried to set up a system in which Bonpland would send written contributions in return for recent French publications that the Rio de Janeiro–based intellectuals had privileged access to.[123] It is still uncertain what response, if any, Bonpland made to this publishing opportunity. A second letter from Sigaud was motivated in part by the fact that he was delegated in 1854 to convey the Legion of Honor to Bonpland. This was Bonpland's second occasion to receive it, and both times it was forwarded through the network of French medical influence in South America.[124]

Sigaud was clearly interested in Bonpland. At this time, short biographies of Bonpland were beginning to appear widely, but Sigaud warned him that they were often replete with errors or inaccuracies, most notably in the accounts appearing in the newspapers of the United States. He reminded Bonpland how he was working to popularize botanical knowledge about Brazilian plants, confident that a public demand now existed for this field in Brazil. The scientific basis for Sigaud's project was contained in the "immortal works" of such authors as Bonpland, Humboldt, Kunth, Martius, and Saint-Hilaire. Yet the problem with these sources was their use of Latin, and a language that was "less overloaded with technology" was needed.[125] Sigaud told Bonpland that Auguste de Saint-Hilaire was not a supporter of Sigaud's project for the Brazilian public. While Sigaud was clearly enthusiastic to gain Bonpland's support, it is not clear whether

Bonpland sent any material from São Borja to aid with his work. José Praxedes Pereira Pacheco wrote from Rio de Janeiro in 1851, sending an honorary membership of the Imperial Nucleo Horticolo Brasiliense (Imperial Brazilian Horticultural Nucleus); as its name implies, this body enjoyed the patronage of the imperial family. In his reply, Bonpland noted he had lived now for years "in an almost forced isolation." He listed his preoccupations as mainly agriculture, medicine, mineralogy, and botany, and he reviewed the history of his natural history collections since leaving Paraguay in 1831. Seeking to meet the objectives of the horticultural society at Rio de Janeiro, he was already organizing his first shipment of specimens of dried plants destined for this organization.[126]

A further solace for Bonpland during his life at São Borja was the French-born priest Jean-Pierre (João Pedro) Gay (1815–1891). Gay, who shared Bonpland's intellectual leanings, is most remembered today for his account of the invasion of Rio Grande do Sul by Paraguayan troops in 1865.[127] His extensive writings also included an unpublished biographical account of Bonpland. Gay was to become extremely close to Bonpland during the final decade of his life. He served as his proxy for business with Brazil (receiving letters, for example) during Bonpland's many periods of absence. He also served as the executor for Bonpland's Brazilian estate, which soon led to the unjustified claim in some French diplomatic quarters that he was blocking the deceased's manuscripts. The working relationship between Bonpland and Gay began in 1847, when the latter, then serving in southern Rio Grande do Sul as the curate at Alegrete in the Campanha, paid a visit to São Borja.[128] It is clear from Gay's letters to Bonpland that the priest angled for the post of vicar of the former Jesuit mission at São Borja. A great part of the appeal for Gay in moving to São Borja was the possibility of sustained contact with "a notability as erudite and famous" as Bonpland.[129] Despite claims of Bonpland's fame, Gay only began to spell his family name correctly once he took up residence in São Borja in 1850. The letters Gay wrote to Bonpland before 1850 convey a sense of excitement. He had yet to grasp the heavy responsibilities he would soon assume in connection with his compatriot.

. . .

Despite the new connections opened by Demersay, Gay, and others, there is evidence that Bonpland was not fully content with life in São Borja. Just as so many of his compatriot settlers were under siege in Montevideo after 1843, life in the Brazilian Missões, where he was cut off from his state pension and from most of his international correspondence, brought its own sense of confinement. On the other hand, the peace in Rio Grande do Sul that followed the ending of the Farroupilha Revolt would have provided some scope for mental regrouping. The Battle of Vences (27 November 1847) no doubt obliged him to stay out of Corrientes for longer than he desired. In this major conflict, Urquiza, the great caudillo of Entre Ríos, destroyed the "forces of Joaquín Madariaga, the anti-Rosas governor of Corrientes, and installed a client regime," one headed by Benjamín Virasoro.[130] The Battle of Vences was followed by a degree of violence noteworthy for the period and the region. Paraguay viewed very negatively the fact that Misiones now lay in enemy hands for the first time in a long period. The disturbed politics of the 1840s appear to have affected Bonpland's psyche, leaving him unsure about where in South America to focus his energies. Months before Vences, he had written to Apollon de Mirbel, a French friend then based in the small Campanha town of Uruguaiana, seeking advice about which location in the interior he should pursue. We know the places Bonpland mentioned only from the reply. Beyond the obvious candidates of Santa Ana and São Borja, the prospects included Paraguay; this idea followed the recent contacts with the Brazilian minister there. Mirbel's response, written from a small town with what he described as a veneer of "civilization," was interesting for its sense of hierarchy in what should be attractive to a northwest European immigrant. He saw Santa Ana, Corrientes, and Paraguay as the worst prospects; in Mirbel's words, the people in these places were *semisauvages et rien de plus* (nothing more than half savage). He took the emphatic view Bonpland should settle in Montevideo and forget about agricultural speculations in the interior.[131] As usual, Bonpland chose to heed his own advice, in order to go a different way. In the final portion of his life, he would pursue rural resource development with still renewed vigor, but he would never find true stability.

CHAPTER FIVE

The Challenges of Peace

> Do you count it for nothing to be placed in the first rank of society in the countries you are visiting? These are your expressions. What is the lot of botanical workers at Paris? Cliquishness, lodging in the garrets, and penury for many.
>
> LETTER FROM ALIRE RAFFENEAU-DELILE
> TO BONPLAND, 1848[1]

> Are you back from your journey to Paraguay at last? Are you at home? Or has the need for locomotion led you again to the determination to make another excursion, another journey. With you, who has a little bit of the character of the interminable wanderer, one never knows where you are . . . and yet you cannot know just how much your friends wish to know your news; they wish in vain. I have been preaching the same sermon to you for thirty years; it would have just as much effect if I went into the middle of the pampas and gave it to the Indians living there. It is better to take your side, since you are made thus.
>
> LETTER FROM FRENCH MERCHANT DOMINIQUE
> ROGUIN TO BONPLAND, 1852[2]

> If by chance you are inclined to come to Rio de Janeiro, I shall be happy to receive you at my home, as I am convinced this rural abode will be preferable to a *philosophe* than any other in the city.
>
> SENATOR CÂNDIDO BAPTISTA DE OLIVEIRA,
> DIRECTOR OF THE RIO DE JANEIRO BOTANICAL
> GARDEN, TO BONPLAND, 1854[3]

The final decade of Bonpland's life saw a remarkable degree of activity. His discipline for the study of natural resources in subtropical South America remained intact. The fall of Rosas from power in 1852 and the opening of the major rivers to international commerce brought an increased circulation of ideas to southern South America during the 1850s. Bonpland's work became a symphony of threads, where he continued his long-standing interests but also took on new ones. The greater calls upon his time meant that no single thread was ever followed to its conclusion. He attempted to rebuild his rural properties after the long years of civil unrest. Juan Pujol (1817–1861), the governor of Corrientes, called upon him extensively for advice on colonization and on how to exploit the yerba resources more systematically, among many other themes. Bonpland threw considerable energy into gathering seeds and plants at the behest of the French government for the Algerian colony. In 1857, he even welcomed the chance to revisit Paraguay, meeting an ambition kindled for years. Contacts with Europe became more intense again, but they were still unable to be sustained. The issue of distance from the coast continued to hamper the development of his work. More important, Bonpland still had no clear patron or institutional support within the region, despite his ties to emerging scientific bodies in Montevideo and Rio de Janeiro. While his circle of professional contacts continued to grow even in late life, his most intense linkages were mainly to people who were in some sense outsiders to the regional culture.

Much of this new emergence receives at least some attention in the existing literature. What has never been satisfactorily explained is Bonpland's relationship with Brazil. In 1849 and 1850, and at his own initiative, Bonpland undertook highly detailed resource appraisals of parts of the Serra of Rio Grande do Sul. The timing is very significant. His records were made on the eve of the massive deforestation associated with German and, later, other European colonization in southern Brazil. Instead of stripping the forest cover prior to cultivation, Bonpland favored agroforestry schemes designed around the more rational use of wild yerba maté resources. He placed his ideas on this in writing for the provincial government of Rio Grande do Sul, and went so far as to file for a land grant along the *picada* (colonial trail) leading to the new colony of Santa Cruz. Had politics gone in his direction, Bonpland might have devoted the work of his latter years to Brazil. Since they did not, he turned away from this country, spending his final years in Corrientes, Argentina.

Bonpland's 1849 journey across parts of the Serra of Rio Grande do Sul represented a break with his past. This was the first trip in decades that took Bonpland away from the Plata river basins and his first trip far into the interior of Brazil. Although the botanical character of the region east of the seven missions had been kindling his curiosity for a long time, Bonpland's letters reveal clearly that, in 1849–50, he was pushed from Corrientes toward Brazil by the politics of the Plata. Rio Grande do Sul had been the theater of a decade-long civil war after 1835. By the late 1840s, unlike its neighbors, the province was at peace. As so often with Bonpland, the catalyst for the journey was a quickly developed friendship.

Bonpland's emergence from a long silence toward the end of the 1840s can be directly linked with the sale of some of his merinos. In 1847 he received a visit in São Borja from Pedro Rodrigues Fernandes Chaves (1810–1866), a judge, politician, diplomat, and landowner. A controversial figure, Pedro Chaves was characterized by some as a retrograde conservative, largely responsible for the slide of Rio Grande do Sul into civil war in 1835.[4] Whatever his temperament, Chaves brought stimulation to São Borja. He had studied in Europe and had served Brazil as a diplomat, including a brief spell as minister to the United States.[5] His experience of a broader world and his wealth likely appealed to Bonpland.

During his stay at São Borja, Pedro Chaves quickly became a patron of some of Bonpland's schemes—including merino raising and crossbreeding as well as a joint enterprise to plant maté trees on part of the Santa Cruz property.[6] But the task of working out the details of these projects fell to a son, Antônio Rodrigues Chaves, whose own family developed much closer ties with Bonpland. The merino project was slow to develop. Although Pedro Chaves had clearly raised Bonpland's expectations for an animal sale while in São Borja, he made no commitment before September 1848. As a result Bonpland has left a sheep correspondence running from August 1847 until shortly before his departure for Santa Cruz in February 1849, a period of negotiation of almost two years.[7]

The main purpose of a stream of letters was to build up Antônio Rodrigues Chaves's confidence in the idea of breeding merinos for their fine wool, an enterprise Bonpland repeatedly encouraged as profitable. The themes covered by letters to Chaves were not confined to sheep; they reflected the wide variety of his interests, including politics, maté, and European society. As soon as the business of the merinos was concluded, Bonpland showed that he was anxious to begin a joint project of producing maté on a large scale at Santa Cruz.

Bonpland's early letters to Chaves are preoccupied with politics and with the rescuing of animals from war-torn Corrientes. Rio Grande do Sul formed a refuge for Bonpland from the chronic instability of Corrientes in this period; this can be inferred from his references to the prudence of lying low in the woods.[8] A comment that he might settle at Santa Cruz should be interpreted in the same light.[9]

After March 1848, Bonpland's correspondence with Chaves became regular (a letter each month from March to July), a sign that he was increasing the pressure to sell animals. A visit to Corrientes in April to verify new losses caused by different political raids surely stiffened Bonpland's resolve to do something in Brazil.[10] As confidence in the future of his flock grew, Bonpland started to make more requests of Chaves; in June 1848 he asked for not less than ten *quadras* (17.4 hectares) of virgin land. Admitting no knowledge of the local climate or land quality at Santa Cruz, Bonpland suggested a list of crops to try, including manioc, sweet and English potatoes, maize, pumpkins, grains, and legumes. This list would have occasioned little surprise for the recipient; most of the items were familiar staples of Indian cultivation in the missions. Bonpland's interest in forage plants proved much more innovative. He told Chaves that Angola grass (*Panicum purpurascens*) was successfully being cultivated at São Borja and suggested experiments at Santa Cruz with all the forage plants that were recognized, indigenous as well as exotic.[11]

Bonpland needed the money that this sale to Chaves would bring. As winter began to give way to spring, lack of word from Chaves had dampened even Bonpland's extraordinarily resilient spirits.[12] In fact, Chaves had already sent confirmation in a letter of 20 September 1848.[13] There may be significance in this timing, since Rio Grande do Sul had recently passed legislation (law 131 of 12 July 1848) designed to encourage improved breeds of animals in the province by subsidizing a breeding station. This law was part of the modernizing effort of General Andréa (provincial president from 10 April 1848 to 6 March 1850).[14] We do not know what bearing the breeding law had on Chaves's thinking, but it certainly encouraged Bonpland, who read reports about it at São Borja drawn from the Porto Alegre newspapers. He urged Chaves to do his utmost to ensure the fame of the Santa Cruz flock, already planning that it would serve as the seed stock for the *estancieiros*, or ranchers of Rio Grande do Sul.[15]

Bonpland's early letters from São Borja are dominated by concerns about political stability and his flock. Later ones are mainly requests for information, some of which seem genuine, others thinly disguised efforts at boosterism. Anxious to plot a route, Bonpland turned to the best map of Rio Grande do Sul available at the time but found that this offered only blank space ("a sad wasteland") where he intended to travel.[16] Reading in the Porto Alegre newspapers that the provincial government sought to improve the animal breeds offered him more encouragement.[17] Bonpland began his journey on 11 February 1849, starting a travel account on the same day with a matter-of-fact description of its motives:

> This trip has several objects: the first is to drive to Mr. Antonio Rodrigues Chaves the two hundred fine-wooled sheep that he asked me for . . . ; the second to see the woods of the *erva-mate* shrub or the maté trees and to judge if they are rich enough to be cultivated and to see also if his land is suitable for planting maté trees in order to establish a profitable plantation, such as the Jesuits did in all the mission settlements. The third [is] to go to Porto Alegre and see if it suits me and whether I can send a *certificat de vie* (proof of life) to France in order to recover the past semesters of my pension.[18]

Moving a caravan of 562 sheep, horses, and mules nearly five hundred kilometers to Santa Cruz was an act of geographical exploration in its own right. The journey lasted twenty-five days; it took Bonpland and his peons through a territory very sparsely occupied even by regional standards.[19] The main obstacle along the journey was the crossing of the Jacuí River, which the merinos traversed in canoes. During the trip to and around Santa Cruz, Bonpland identified plant species more rapidly than at any other part of his southern South American residence.

If Europeans often presume a high degree of physical uniformity over vast areas in Brazil, Santa Cruz ran against this assumption. Located at the edge of the Serra, it offered variety, a strong contrast to the rather monotonous rolling grasslands of the Campanha. The relief around Santa Cruz ranges from eighty to six hundred meters, and most of the district is hilly.[20] At midcentury most of this land was still covered with a dense band of subtropical forest, which hindered communication between the temperate Campanha grasslands of southern Rio Grande do Sul (the economic core of the province) and the grasslands of the plateau or Planalto. Above five hundred meters the subtropical forest began to give way to the distinctive pine (*Araucaria angustifolia*) of the southern Brazil plateau.

When Bonpland arrived at Santa Cruz, the area already constituted one of the most dynamic margins of settled Rio Grande do Sul. Santa Cruz formed part of the developing hinterland of Rio Pardo, an important garrison town of the colonial period. In 1849 Rio Pardo still stood as a clear boundary; it was the place where a traveler coming from the Atlantic was forced to substitute travel by steamboat for the much slower horse. Efforts

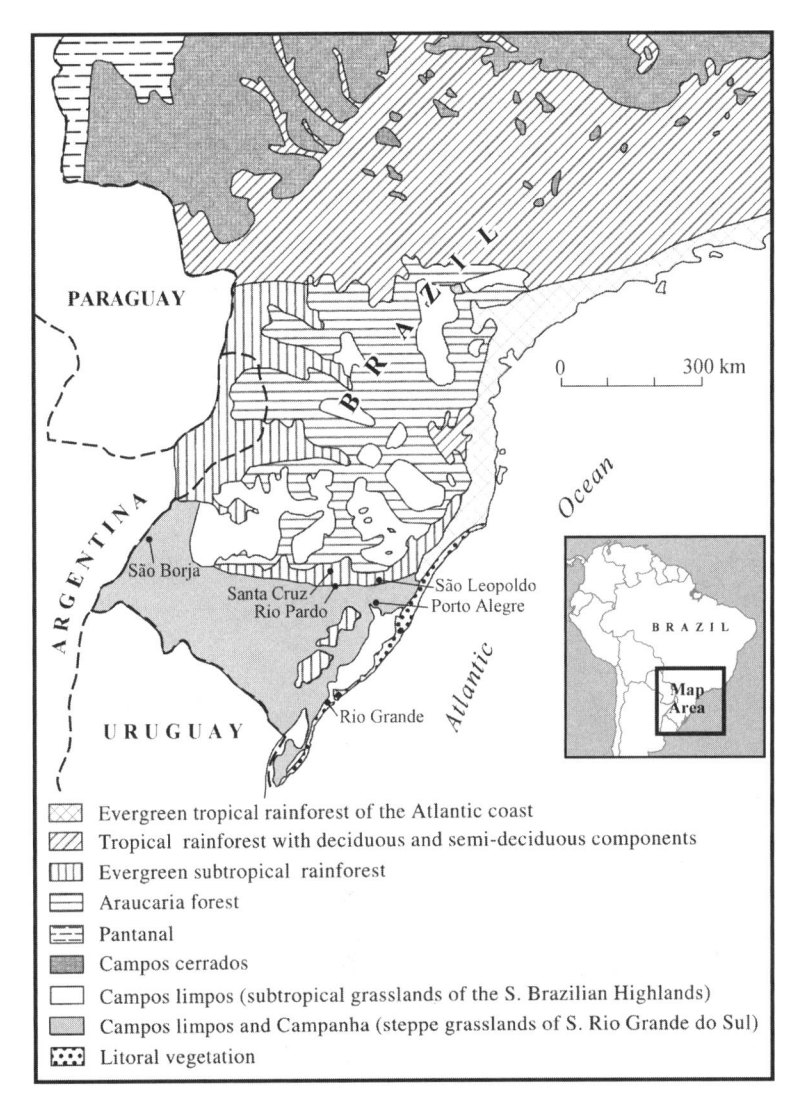

Figure 5.1 The natural vegetation regions of southern Brazil.
SOURCE: Prepared by Chase Langford, Department of Geography, UCLA.

to open roads from Rio Pardo toward the Serra since about 1820 had been quickly followed by Luso-Brazilian land speculation.

Brazilian public policies surrounding land were very dynamic in these years around midcentury, fueled largely by the impending abolition of the international slave traffic. At the national level, the central government wished to substitute smallholdings for latifundia.[21] By the general law 514 of 28 October 1848, each province received thirty-six square leagues of land for colonization. The provincial government of Rio Grande do Sul responded to this stimulus from the imperial government by planning a strategic belt of colonies where the grasslands gave way to forest at the edge of the Planalto. These colonies helped to justify the expense of building roads linking the central depression of the Jacuí valley and the Planalto.[22]

The groundwork for a colony at Santa Cruz had been laid in 1847, in legislation preparing for road construction.[23] Santa Cruz, established in 1849, was the first in a series of new German colonies that would fill up the Serra by around 1870. The foundation of a new colony in an isolated location, about 150 kilometers west of the flourishing German settlement at São Leopoldo, was deliberate.

After the extensive speculation in his letters about what could be achieved at Santa Cruz, a physical environment of which Bonpland had no previous knowledge, his arrival at this place on the edge of the Serra witnessed the intrusion of reality. The farm itself was relatively undistinguished in appearance, save for a line of magnificent palm trees. Barren hill slopes surrounding the primitive buildings of the ranch seemed to offer little promise for

Figure 5.2 A Riograndense rural property, c. 1852. While the exact location of this property is unknown, it is clearly somewhere on the edge of the Serra—note the summit clearly visible in the middle background.
SOURCE: Wendroth, *Album de aquarelas e desenhos*, fig. 144.

successful sheep breeding.[24] Later, Bonpland journeyed thirteen kilometers to the *puesto*, the animal-gathering point of the *fazenda*, or landed estate, where he began to evince very different impressions. The pastures were superior, the soils were better for cultivation, and above all there were rich pine forests, some of which contained maté trees. Bonpland regained his optimism.

Assuming that Chaves might proceed, Bonpland was forced to consider what a project combining merino breeding with tea planting would require, and he hesitated over the potential difficulties of labor. He calculated that the scheme would require fifteen to twenty-five peons but recognized that the labor supply was insufficient; in any case, wages would be prohibitive. Labor would have to be brought from outside, preferably blacks or Indians. Based on his earlier experiences, Bonpland was a great enthusiast for Indian labor: "We should obtain some Indians above all else. The indigenes are the most useful class for agricultural work. They are also the least ambitious. All you need to know is how to treat them and guide them."[25] Any plans to contemplate slaves on even a reduced scale showed his ignorance of Brazil's evolving land policies; law 514 of 1848 expressly forbade the use of slave labor on the lands of the colonies.[26]

Based on his trips around Santa Cruz, Bonpland started to develop the idea of clearing the woods of undergrowth to exploit the stands of maté, partly to test his theory that more exposure to sunlight would lead to a higher-quality product. Further field reconnaissance led him to think about opening trails into the forests, in order to assess the sizes and qualities of the maté stands. He found that the extent of the resources was great enough to lead him to question his long-held ambition of planting "a *yerbal* in the open fields."[27] This judgment was based in part on climatic risk; Bonpland was aware from floristic observations that the seasons came later at Santa Cruz than in any of the Jesuit missions where these had planted maté.

Bonpland had long been aware of the growing economic potential of maté in southern Brazil as a competitor to the expensive traditional Paraguayan product. In March 1832 at Buenos Aires, he compiled notes on the emergence of the maté trade through the port of Paranaguá (in what is today the state of Paraná). By the 1830s, traders achieved considerable success in marketing their maté from the Paraná region as far as Chile and Peru, despite its poor reputation for taste and quality.[28] Considerable experimentation was taking place with maté in the Serra before Bonpland arrived. He found that local producers prepared it with more than the *hierba legitima* (genuine yerba), also using plants broadly described as *cauna* as well as others. Some of these plants produced a bitter maté, thus producers tended to mix in leaves of aromatic plants to improve the taste—falsifications that Bonpland considered "excusable and very commendable."[29] Bonpland was soon making simple experiments with the different species claimed by the local population. These field experiences heightened his inclination to work with blends of the different types of plants.[30] Detailed field observations around Santa Cruz later led Bonpland to claim five new species of maté.[31]

Bonpland's scientific research at Santa Cruz was mainly achieved on account of delay, while waiting for Chaves to settle their animal business. It is clear that Bonpland could not have continued to Porto Alegre without a sale. Chaves returned on 19 April from a trip to Passo Fundo and a few days later bought 103 horses and mules from Bonpland, making in addition a commitment to form a joint business for breeding merinos. By the time Bonpland arrived in Porto Alegre in May, he was seriously ill (with a failure of the gastric system), thus his travel diary fades for a spell.

Even so, there are signs of life from Porto Alegre. A visit to the capital of Rio Grande do Sul provided important opportunities for renewed contacts with France. On arriving there, Bonpland received two long and very de-

Figure 5.3 Porto Alegre, c. 1852. The population of the capital of Rio Grande do Sul was still under twenty thousand at this time. This provincialism explains in part why the city would have held limited attractions for Bonpland. At the time of Wendroth's watercolor, the German influence on the built fabric, of considerable importance in the later nineteenth century, was still barely visible.
SOURCE: Wendroth, *Album de aquarelas e desenhos*, fig. 98.

tailed letters written from Montpellier during the previous year by his old friend the botanist Raffeneau-Delile. The latter clearly envied Bonpland his American residence and painted a rather negative image of life in France since 1815. Commenting on the changing fortunes of botanists and of botanical illustrators, he argued that their standard of living had slipped. As for the promise of the 1848 revolution, this was seen thus far as poisoned fruit: "There are neither Jeffersons nor Madisons in France, such as you knew them in the United States," a reference to Bonpland's return to France with Humboldt in 1804.[32] Raffeneau-Delile also conveyed the important news that Bonpland's patron Benjamin Delessert had died. Bonpland wrote a series of letters to France on 10 June. The main point reported to Raffeneau-Delile was that his collections and manuscripts were in such good order that he held to the ambition of publishing them.[33] This letter also conveyed some sense of the stimulus of the recent plant descriptions made while crossing the Serra: "I will not speak to you about species or genera I consider new. Lacking books and objects for comparison, I would seem a boaster."[34] Three drafts exist of letters to the Delesserts. The first two dealt with the changing logistics of his French state pension. At the time of writing, it was seven years in arrears. Bonpland noted that the reason for this was well known in France, namely the wars in the Río de la Plata. Marooned at São Borja for six years, he had been deprived of all the European news. This is something of an exaggeration, as visitors from Europe would have brought him at least some indirect information on current developments. The third draft mourned the loss of Benjamin.[35] In addition, Bonpland summarized the news of his crossing of Rio Grande do Sul for Alfred Demersay. In this, he repeated his pleasure at the richness of the botanical findings along the journey. On a practical front, he described his budding scheme with the Chaves family. He had reached the conclusion that sufficient maté was lacking on the Chaves property for the partners to work the land on an economical basis. He felt it was essential to survey the resources along the *picada* of the provincial government's new project. The letter is especially interesting for its specific ambition of forest conservation. Bonpland held a high opinion of the value of his own economic schemes in Rio Grande do Sul.[36]

Bonpland made a request for land along the new road to Santa Cruz on 3 August 1849, assuming this would be conceded in areal units of a quarter of a league (1,089 hectares), sometimes called *sesmarias de mato*. Bonpland petitioned for the conservation of 6.75 leagues of land along the road from Faxinal toward the summit of the Serra (presumably the location where the maté bushes were concentrated).[37] This petition was unlikely to meet success without assiduous lobbying, yet he did not wait in Porto Alegre to press his case, moving on instead to Montevideo, where he stayed from 29 August to 7 October.

Still under siege, Montevideo had evolved a distinctive society at this time, one heavily marked by French influence. While in the city, Bonpland supplied information about Rio Grande do Sul to Arsène Isabelle, a compatriot preparing a study that promoted colonization in the region. Isabelle was quick to mention the success of Bonpland's São Borja merino flock in his work.[38] Apart from some interesting society, the more Europeanized urban milieu of Montevideo also gave Bonpland the opportunity to stock up on supplies. Buried away in his accounts, along with such purchases as gloves and visiting cards, appear eleven pamphlets on merinos, bought for distribution to ranchers interested in establishing flocks of the fine-wooled sheep in Rio Grande do Sul.[39] Additional work at Montevideo included the sending to the physicist François Arago, another great collaborator of Humboldt, of temperature reports that Bonpland had compiled at São Borja. In his letter summarizing the results, Bonpland also provided a generally optimistic report of the physical environment in and around that small Brazilian town.[40] As was now usual, Bonpland's appearance in the coastal cities was also sought as an opportunity to glean political information about the South American interior. Thus Carlos Creus, the Spanish diplomatic representative at Montevideo, reported to his government the gist of his extended conversations with "the famous naturalist Bonpland," which focused on the brewing trouble between Argentina and Paraguay, a vague reference to the latter country's unease with having a current Corrientes government that was sympathetic to Rosas (around this time, there was, in fact, a major Paraguayan incursion into the Correntino Misiones, with troops under the command of the Hungarian-born Franz Wisner von Morgenstern).[41] His informant had noted that the Paraguayans were in the position to place twenty thousand soldiers in the field "but they are so brutally docile and disciplined that they seem more like Russians or Prussians than soldiers hailing from a southern nation."[42]

Leaving Montevideo, Bonpland set out to retrace his course to his home in São Borja, a journey that brought further opportunities for visits to Porto Alegre, Rio Pardo, and the Santa Cruz district. In the provincial capital, Bonpland set out the gist of his agricultural scheme in *un petit travail* (a short work) sent to General Andréa.[43] The recipient answered that he was not authorized to grant land to individuals, recommending Bonpland should form an association with a view to forming a demonstration property.[44] Around the same time, the provincial engineer Philip von Normann was trying to move this debate beyond the provincial confines of Rio Grande do Sul. He talked with Conselheiro Cândido Baptista de Oliveira, the director of the Rio de Janeiro Botanical Garden, sometime around the beginning of November 1849 about Bonpland's project to form a company designed to process yerba on a large scale. Baptista de Oliveira expressed support for an agricultural school with a botanical garden attached and inquired whether Bonpland would be prepared to direct such an establishment.[45] It is clear from Bonpland's records that he did follow the provincial president's official advice. A list of his petitioners included Andréa himself, members of the Chaves family, and a Corrêa da Camara. The only non-Portuguese names in the list are the provincial engineer von Normann and Bonpland himself.[46] It is hard to imagine a more interesting mix of talents in the Rio Grande do Sul of the period.

Bonpland appears still to have had little or no sense of evolving Brazilian public policy on land. From Porto Alegre, he revisited Santa Cruz via Rio Pardo, enthusiastically accompanying Frederico de Vasconcellos, a recently arrived provincial engineer, who had been charged with surveying land and preparing several dozen lots for the first colonists. The engineers had a natural appeal to Bonpland. They were mainly educated to a high level and like Bonpland himself they were usually outsiders, subject to the vagaries of regional elites. Watching Vasconcellos direct his German laborers in clearing a new forest trail, Bonpland gained visible evidence that the lots of seventy-seven hectares each were going to be much smaller than what he needed.[47]

Bonpland's journey across the Serra in 1849–50 led to a flurry of communications with those of the provincial engineers involved with the project of opening the new *picada*. In the estimation of Vasconcellos, Andréa went from being a potential hero, who was trying to develop the *picada* as a sustainable project, to an obstacle. He changed his view of Andréa when he learned that the provincial president had just refused Bonpland "a miserable *data* [a small portion of land] of a quarter league square," while giving the same area of land to Peter Kleudgen (the first director of the Santa Cruz colony), who was also a foreigner.[48]

Around the same time that the first colonists were arriving at Santa Cruz, Bonpland wrote to Andréa from São Borja asking how the land was going to be divided and whether a *ferme model* (demonstration farm) would be located along the edges of the *picada* or elsewhere. Bonpland emphasized the integrated character of his plans, stressing their public as well as private value. Not only did he seek to improve the southern Brazilian maté industry, but "one ought to engage with the types of agriculture best suited to the climate, to the place and to the terrain." The letter ended with a plea for the conservation of natural resources. Bonpland maintained that the forest workers' "old custom" killed the maté trees, and he sought a regulation to keep these workers out of the lands that the provincial government might concede as a model farm.[49] He had plenty of empirical evidence to back his claim, as his travel observations reveal.[50]

In March 1850, Philip von Normann forwarded the news from the coast that Andréa had been dismissed from his post as president of Rio Grande do Sul. He saw Pimenta Bueno, the new provincial president, as an opportunity for Bonpland (presumably, he was aware of Bonpland's links with this politician over Paraguayan affairs) and argued that they should register their land titles along the Santa Cruz trail there and then. The signs of impatience on von Normann's part were reminiscent of the French diplomats who tried to work with Bonpland in land projects during the 1830s. The plan was for Bonpland and von Normann to work at maté together as neighbors. Unlike Vasconcellos, who wrote to Bonpland in French, von Normann used Portuguese. He sent extensive printed material for Bonpland's reading benefit from the coast to the missions.[51] Later in the same month, Vasconcellos covered some of the same issues, this time writing from the Picada de Santa Cruz, where some thirty-eight German colonists were already established along the initial parts of the colonial trail. He relayed his opinion that he did not think Bonpland's land project would work. The reasons given were veiled political opposition and a feared lack of persistence on the part of Andréa. Vasconcellos wrote interestingly about problems in connection with the survey work of establishing the colonial trail to the summit of the Serra, maintaining that the work had been poorly conducted at unnecessarily high expense. He then moved to politics, telling his friend there had been an "atrocious war" in the press against Andréa. Vasconcellos knew Bonpland had close links with Pimenta Bueno. He thought, however, that any apparent reluctance on Pimenta Bueno's part to draw upon Bonpland's expertise would be a reflection of the latter's foreign status. He did predict that Pimenta Bueno would offer singular help to any agricultural project Bonpland conceived, but that it would be necessary to call upon the president's patronage.[52]

Bonpland's private view of the land negotiations came in a letter to Vasconcellos from São Borja in April 1850. He had clearly enjoyed his time in the company of this provincial engineer. After the time they spent together at Porto Alegre, Rio Pardo, and along "that magnificent *picada* that I like so much," a typical positive comment about the appeal of the subtropics, it had become extremely difficult to part. Bonpland had no doubt appreciated the intellectual qualities of his correspondent. However, he thought that the prospect of living in closer proximity was hardly realistic. Provincial engineering was run out of Porto Alegre, he observed, while his own pharmaceutical and medical preoccupations were based in São Borja. Nevertheless, if a large-scale project presented itself to work on agricultural projects together, he claimed to be ready. Beyond the problems with his personal interests, especially collecting payment for his medical services, Bonpland was disappointed with Brazil, partly on account of the political intrigue against General Andréa:

> In addition to all my private interests, I am angry for Brazil and for the inhabitants of São Pedro [Rio Grande do Sul] about what happened to Mr. Andréa. Men are not gods. I have always been of the view that you need to consider their qualities as well as their defects, and establish some just equilibrium. I have had the honor here of getting to know personally His Excellency Pimenta Bueno [José Antônio Pimenta Bueno, marquês de São Vicente, a politician-intellectual]. He is an agreeable man, educated, filled with excellent manners, and fully capable of carrying out the elevated position just confided to him [the presidency of the province Rio Grande do Sul]. But tomorrow the ambitious and the jealous will shout out against him, and we will have the pain of seeing him withdraw.[53]

Andréa had been an especially farsighted provincial president, one willing to contemplate structural reforms in Rio Grande do Sul's main economic activity of ranching, including in the patterns of landholding.[54] This guaranteed him stiff opposition from the regional elites. Bonpland was fed up with Brazil. If he had the heart, he said, there were a thousand forest trails, a thousand locations where they could prepare yerba on a large scale. Yet the chances of achieving anything serious in Brazil had slipped away for him.

Santa Cruz developed in a manner very different from anything Bonpland had envisaged. Provincial law 229 of 4 December 1851 further reduced the size of the colonial lots, splitting them into units of forty-eight hectares each. In the same year, the province signed a contract for the introduction of colonists to the colony. When the Prussian traveler Robert Avé-Lallemant passed through the district in March 1858, the oral memory of Bonpland's research there was still alive.[55] Avé-Lallemant echoed Bonpland's impressions about the sense of solitude in the sea of forest. Taking a high vantage point along the *picada*, however, the vista was now punctuated by the smoke rising at isolated points, where colonists were clearing land for their farming.[56] Santa Cruz soon became one of the few successful commercial agricultural zones of Rio Grande do Sul of the period.[57]

The opening of roads connecting the Planalto with the rest of the province appears to have had a dramatic impact on the production of Riograndense maté. Following the success of Paraná, the Serra of Rio Grande do Sul became an important new periphery of Brazil in maté production. Exports from the province rose steeply after 1851, peaking in 1864 for the imperial period at almost five thousand metric tons, nearly five times greater than 1850 levels.[58] Tea-gathering remained almost exclusively in Luso-Brazilian hands and was regarded as marginal to the society of the German colonies.[59]

In 1850 Bonpland journeyed to Montevideo again, this time traveling down the Uruguay River. After his negative experiences in Brazil, he now found the opportunity to experience a part of South America of growing economic power. The journey gave an opportunity to examine the sheep flocks of Entre Ríos, then in rapid development under the protection of the great caudillo Urquiza, the leading landowner and political chief.[60] By mid-century there were about two million sheep in Entre Ríos, almost 30 percent of Argentina's national flock.[61] The river journey also gave Bonpland the opportunity to visit merino flocks belonging to ranchers in the vicinity of Concordia, where a British enclave economy was already developing. Taking detailed notes on what he saw of their work, Bonpland recorded that one British rancher alone kept a flock of twenty-seven thousand merinos in various states of purity, not far behind the largest flocks of Buenos Aires in the same era.[62]

Along this journey, he undertook a two-day visit to Urquiza in person at his estancia near Concepción del Uruguay, recording a positive description of the general's character.[63] Later in the year, this already powerful politician joined Brazil and Paraguay in breaking with Rosas, an act that would soon lead the politics of the region in a new direction, including a first genuine effort to build a national government in Argentina.[64] Urquiza soon put Bonpland's capacities to use, calling upon him to resolve a dysentery epidemic in the army then under formation. This was important work. When Urquiza's army met that of Rosas at Caseros in 1852, it comprised no less than twenty-four thousand soldiers, a huge number by the standards of the region's battles. Bonpland's answer was to draw on knowledge from Paraguay and Corrientes about the uses of the plant granadilla, taking as his raw material a related species growing in Entre Ríos in the valley of the Uruguay River. He later told Urquiza's representative that he used granadilla in his own medical practice. While used widely against dysenteries in Corrientes and Paraguay, he maintained that the method of use there was insufficiently specific and that there was a tendency to prescribe overly strong doses.[65]

Bonpland made the journey from São Borja to Montevideo accompanied by three daguerreotype artists, part of the first wave of photographers to pass through the region recording the faces of the elites. The most important of these was the New York–born Charles DeForest Fredricks (1823–1894), most remembered today in South America for his early images of the city of Buenos Aires.[66] Bonpland found a rare companion in Fredricks, sharing in common the experience of having journeyed along the Orinoco.[67] The photographer was quick to send a brief account of Bonpland's circumstances to the Société de Géographie in Paris. Listening to Bonpland at the age of seventy-eight planning for the future, Fredricks commented, one might think that he was still *à la fleur de son âge* (in the prime of life).[68]

The visit to Entre Ríos boosted Bonpland's spirits, as is clearly revealed in his summary of the journey sent to the Chaves family at Porto Alegre. Claiming to have examined ninety thousand merino or merino crossbred sheep during the journey, the euphoria engendered by this experience shone through in the comment, "more than ever I am following this speculation, for which, as you know, I have always had the greatest affection." Even so, there was room for improvement. "Although the province of Entre Ríos has the benefit of peace, the flocks are not controlled as they ought to be or could be. In general the management is bad and this branch of agriculture that is already producing prodigiously could offer more profit."[69] Bonpland may have been right, but the settlers he observed could afford to make some mistakes; they held the incalculable advantage of access to capital.

Bonpland spent a little more than three months at Montevideo in 1850, where the full range of his activities remains obscure. Although he tended to complain about city residence by this stage, the more diverse society than his usual one provided stimulus. He certainly furthered his links with both British and French diplomatic personnel and used residence in the city to catch up on some of his correspondence with France. His correspondents included François Delessert of the French banking family; the Delesserts had long provided valuable financial services to Bonpland from their base in Paris. Following the death of Benjamin, the senior member of the family, they passed their interests along to the merchant house Desmarest & Ducoing. Bonpland transferred his business to this last from Montevideo, using the occasion to inquire about the prospects for developing a Paraguayan tobacco trade with France. He wanted the French merchant house to inquire of the Régie du Tabac how much they would pay for an arroba of tobacco: "In a country where there are no outlets, where the people are of an indolent disposition and often live without working, it is necessary that they see some advantages in order to emerge from their extreme apathy."[70] Bonpland was always keen to put people to work; hedonism, a feature of some of his own earlier life in France, found very limited support from him in South America.

The Desmarest & Ducoing house followed up. They told Bonpland that the Paris tobacco administrators were interested in receiving Paraguayan tobacco, asking him to send several tons of the product as samples.[71] It is not clear whether he obliged. Stimulated by reading about the giant water lily in British publications, Bonpland sent the Paris botanist Mirbel recently collected mature seeds of this plant, hoping that France could compete with the English and the Viennese in its cultivation.[72] Following an interrupted conversation about Paraguayan tea, Bonpland wrote a brief account of its significance for the Chevalier Gavrelle, which stressed the importance of this plant in Guaraní culture.[73] The name the Guaranís gave for this plant (*caa guazú*), Bonpland said, was "pronounced with a holy respect. Thus one could say, perhaps with reason, that the Guaraní regard the maté plant as the most useful of all."[74] Noting that the Paraguayan product was considerably superior in quality to that produced in Corrientes and in Brazil, Bonpland nevertheless regretted that nowhere had the methods of production advanced. In writing to Gavrelle, he was probably doing his best to encourage some French investment. A visit on board one of the vessels in the French squadron, the frigate *Zénobie*, seems to have brought especially great stimulation. Dr. Liautaud, the surgeon attached to this ship, shared Bonpland's interest in natural history. He had earlier studied the cultivation of tea in China, leading to further interest in expanding the cultivation of tea to Algeria and to southern Brazil. Bonpland made very extensive notes on material provided to him by Liautaud. His findings from China had some bearing on the development of his own ideas about the prospects for tea cultivation in southern Brazil and even for the development of the maté resources in the Serra of Rio Grande do Sul. Bonpland's comments are also revealing, however, on where his own philosophy differed with that of Liautaud:

> He seems to reject the practical knowledge of the Chinese. I am far from sharing Mr. Liautaud's opinion. I am of the strong belief that we should follow throughout the long-standing routines that have offered useful results for a very long time. Aided then through studies enlightened by chemistry and physiology, we can perhaps improve the products of the past producers, or we can at least generalize their condition.[75]

In October, Bonpland made comments on 135 species of plants described in an illustrated Jesuit study lent to him by Dr. Bartolomé Odicini, soon to be a fellow member of the Sociedad de Medicina Montevideana (Montevideo Medical Society). This clearly dealt mainly with plants indigenous to America. He did not identify the author, but he was unimpressed with the quality of the illustrations, commenting, "all the figures in this work are of a remarkable inexactitude."[76]

On 15 November 1850 Bonpland left Montevideo to return to São Borja. He traveled the Uruguay River route on a vessel that touched land at Concepción del Uruguay. There is a hint in his travel notes that he was kept here longer than he desired. It was the anniversary of the battle of Vences (27 November 1847), in which Urquiza smashed the Correntino army. Bonpland spent a week in the general's company, which afforded obvious scope for the discussion of politics as well as a forced holiday for Bonpland.[77]

While the politics of the Plata remained so unsettled, Bonpland made his main focus São Borja. He continued his habit of planting anything that came to hand there. It is in this period that he developed his links with the Brazilian horticultural society in Rio de Janeiro. Seeds sent by Vilmorin from France included Dutch tulips. He also wrote of success with a particular type of potato. The letters Bonpland wrote to Europe during this period convey a sense of both dissatisfaction and imminent change. In a letter to François Delessert, a key idea was that Bonpland felt paralyzed by the politics of the Plata. Writing in October 1851 to Alfred Demersay, Bonpland showed some of his pessimism and realism about politics. He saw the region as far from attaining a lasting peace, regretting that France had not acted with greater direction and firmness. What he termed the "inaction" of Paraguay was a problem, as was the geopolitical ambition of the Brazilians. He then set out his personal view of what was needed in politics, including the need for more French *colons* (colonists) in the Río de la Plata—something his South American contemporaries might have easily disputed. Other wishes, such as the need for more transparency in politics and for the definition of frontiers, make more sense. Bonpland also provided a sense of what had happened to São Borja since Demersay took his leave in 1847, stressing what seems to have mattered the most to him: "This place conserves its admirable climate and its multitude of orange trees in the midst of political troubles."[78] The town had grown since Demersay left, with a good number of new houses both in the town itself and at the Paso de São Borja. But in 1851 São Borja was now suffering from inaction, with widespread poverty: "In the middle of all disasters, I keep your lodging on the square; the *chacra* is my adopted home."[79] An incursion by Paraguayans into Misiones in 1849 had done nothing good for the São Borja trade.[80] Here he referred to Paraguay's effort to assure its sovereignty over Misiones. López had sent more than 1,600 troops southward into disputed territory, causing considerable economic disruption on the opposite bank of the Uruguay River from Bonpland's home.

The Prospect of a Real Patron

Despite his links to some major figures, Brazilian patronage had proved elusive. The reason Bonpland was living at São Borja in the early 1850s was connected with political instability in the province of Corrientes. Things began to change there after the fall of Rosas, with the ascension to power of Juan Pujol. Pujol had a reforming agenda for Corrientes, one in which he knew Bonpland could play an important role. In this vein, he wrote to Bonpland in São Borja from Restauración on 18 November 1852 expressing his high opinion of Bonpland and announcing his own political successes. Pujol expressed an interest in courting Bonpland's support for his economic plans, specifically the wish to develop agricultural resources in Corrientes. The idea was already present in Pujol's mind that Bonpland could head up a natural history museum and an agricultural establishment designed for the diffusion of new crops across the province. While Pujol's leading prospect was the cultivation of cotton, the expression of interest in agricultural resources gave Bonpland his opening to promote other areas, notably tobacco and yerba. In his reply to the Correntino governor, the start of an extensive correspondence that would run until shortly before his death, Bonpland expressed his approval for the idea of promoting cotton cultivation, but also sent his opinion that the development and management of tobacco and yerba would bring no less revenue to the province.[81] He also used his reply to lay out briefly his interest in rural development in a series of southern South American locations: "I have always been guided by interest in working usefully for the public good and I have never taken care of my private interests."[82]

Pujol's patronage was undoubtedly of great importance in stimulating Bonpland to return to Corrientes. Pujol served as a protector in many important ways, including helping with land issues at Santa Ana. Bonpland's high degree of mobility served to provide the governor with a stream of political and commercial intelligence on a wide series of themes. But the most important single theme in Bonpland's many letters to Pujol was the lack of management of the *yerbales* in the Alto Uruguay. During the 1850s, Bonpland showed a consistent interest in gathering information about the state of the *yerbales* around San Xavier. The main importance of this place was that it stood as the gateway to a huge area of poorly understood resources.[83] His ideas seem to have found some modest practical impact; as Thomas Whigham observes, "by the late 1850s, the eastern *yerbales* abounded with Corrientes-based workers," not least around San Xavier.[84] Bonpland was deeply suspicious about Brazilian efforts to work these resources, viewing the environmental destruction wrought by working the *yerbales* at inappropriate times as "a true crime." Beyond his own field observations, he relied heavily on the oral testimonies provided by others, which included interviewing three *yerbateros* (yerba workers or collectors) in the prison at Restauración, the place where he provided medical help to the prisoners of the barracks. Bonpland argued consistently that Corrientes made a grave mistake in not securing the yerba resources of Misiones.[85]

Bonpland fell ill a few days after his 30 November 1852 reply to Pujol. He had not completely recovered when he next wrote to the governor on 14 January 1853. Although planning a trip to Montevideo, his illness stood in the way of travel. In this second letter to Pujol, Bonpland reviewed his ideas about what was needed for the constructive development of the Correntino *yerbales*. It all made sense, but it called upon a government with a grander set of resources than that headed by Pujol. Bonpland wanted Corrientes to compete effectively with the yerba producers of Paraguay and Brazil; in his view, yerba was "one of the richest mines of the province." He also used the occasion to summarize the gist of his recent Brazilian experiences for Pujol, beginning with reminiscence of a visit to the *picada* connecting Rio Pardo with Cruz Alta and Passo Fundo. The *yerbal* there was eight leagues in length, but whatever vantage point was chosen along the route, an observer never saw fewer than eighty to one hundred stands of yerba of different heights. Bonpland told Pujol how he tried to persuade General Andréa at Porto Alegre of the need to conserve these resources. When this president of Rio Grande do Sul asked him to write down his management proposals in French, Bonpland did this the same afternoon of their meeting. While Andréa's reply was flattering, Bonpland remembered the substance as nothing more than "offers and promises." The basis for Bonpland's ideas for the *yerbales* had already been laid out for the government of Corrientes as early as 1832.[86]

The developing link with the new governor meant that Bonpland could now venture to return his main residence to his Estancia Santa Ana. In preparation for this, he needed to clarify his business affairs at São Borja. In the letter he wrote in April to Gay, making him responsible for his effects in Brazil, a considerable amount was revealed about his possessions and about his material circumstances. The *chacra*, or small farm, was clearly a simple affair that could be managed in his absence by Maria Michi (an Indian servant) and a gardener. Its main feature was several hundred orange trees. Bonpland wrote out detailed provisions of the pay and supplies (from meat to candles) that Gay should provide the caretakers on a weekly basis. In the case of his death, the priest was to direct all of Bonpland's natural history collections and his manuscripts to the Minister of the Interior in Paris, using the agency of the French diplomatic personnel based in South America. The *chacra* outside São Borja, the house, the pharmacy, the furniture, and other properties in the town itself or on the Estancia Santa Ana—then still held in emphyteusis with the government of Corrientes—should go to his two small children, Carmen (1843) and Amado (1845). Why he refrained in his written directions from including Anastasio, born at São Borja in 1847, we shall probably never know. The boy was certainly still in his family at the end of Bonpland's life. Nor was there any mention of Victoriana at this stage; nothing in Bonpland's records mentions her following the brief glimpses of her activities at Santa Ana in the 1840s. By Bonpland's own admission, he was owed "numerous sums" for his medical work in and around São Borja. He asked Gay to act as he saw fit on debts in the interests of Bonpland and his children. His detailed requests ended by asking Gay to translate into Portuguese his letter granting him power of attorney, which the latter did in his neat hand.[87]

In the following month, Bonpland was recommended at the age of eighty to be a member of the local Masonic lodge Cordialidade no Oriente, which practiced the Scottish rite.[88] The rationale for the invitation at a time when Bonpland was already planning to leave the town was perhaps to keep afloat a web of local contacts. The leading citizens of São Borja could plan to count on Bonpland for the accomplishment of missions in Corrientes and elsewhere. But he may not have become a full member before a later visit to São Borja in 1856, when Gay was urging him by letter to try to attend one of the Mason's regular Saturday sessions.[89] Whatever the appeal of freemasonry to Bonpland, he was probably too busy to devote much time to it.

Bonpland's departure from São Borja on 1 June 1853 was doubtlessly traumatic for Gay. They had built an interesting working relationship along the past years, bringing different skills to the international frontier. One of Bonpland's key strengths was his connections with the Correntino authorities, while Gay was of great help to his friend through his fluent command of Portuguese. Gay received considerable stimulation from Bonpland, who did not find so much scope to write when busy with his growing obligations. Moreover, in keeping with his usual circumspect pattern, Bonpland never revealed his immediate plans to the priest, one way of silencing any potential objections. When he asked Gay to assume the responsibility for his effects in Brazil, the latter was under the impression that it was for the duration of a two-month journey to Montevideo. When Bonpland left São Borja, his initial destination became not the Uruguayan capital, in fact, but Santa Ana. While Gay's early letters to Bonpland from the 1840s reveal an excitement, once he accepted power of attorney in 1853 their character changed to one of mild complaint. By the last month of the same year, Gay was unsure whether Bonpland was in Restauración, Corrientes, or even France, since the oral reports current in Missões varied.[90] All indications are that he missed Bonpland acutely. Bonpland's absence changed the tenor of life at São Borja. He did not return to the town before August 1856, which placed Gay in a position of considerable responsibility. The house at the Paso was nothing more than a mud hut with a straw roof. It suffered in the owner's absence, and Gay had the house rebuilt. It is clear that Gay was justified in arguing in 1859 that he had exercised his legal responsibilities carefully in the period 1853 to 1856 (he was still being accused of stealing the fruit of Bonpland's research in a Porto Alegre newspaper in the early 1880s).[91] That Gay remained subsequently in Bonpland's confidence is shown by a letter the latter wrote from Restauración on 8 November 1856, which gave the priest the authority to open and to read mail addressed to Bonpland in the Brazilian frontier town.

After the battle of Vences, Bonpland maintained that he was forced to abandon Estancia Santa Ana in 1848. The changed politics following the fall of Rosas in 1852 provided the opportunity for a return to the ranch. However, major work was required there in connection with the recovery of assets. Before Vences, he reckoned he had a numerous flock of crossbred merinos (around seven thousand in some mentions, the greater number being pure merinos). Like many Correntino ranchers, his interests suffered greatly from the raiding parties that followed the conflict. A partial solution appears to have arrived by associating yet again with powerful contacts. He received an offer from Colonel José Antonio Virasoro (a relative of the recent governor of Corrientes and nominal Rosista, Benjamín Virasoro) to work in conjunction. This project originated through discussion along a journey made in the company of Ferré and Virasoro from Santo Tomé to Restauración, when Bonpland accepted the plan to concentrate his remaining animals on Virasoro's estancia.[92] For some reason left unclear, the deal went sour, with Virasoro subsequently denying the presence of any of Bonpland's horses or sheep on his property.[93] It took legal action supported by Pujol to authorize an inspection of the Virasoro ranch on 19 July 1853. This turned up no horses bearing Bonpland's mark, but the judge and witnesses did find three hundred sheep.[94] Once he had recovered some animals, Bonpland wrote to Pujol thanking him for the decree of 13 July that enabled him to recover sheep from the Virasoro estancias. These livestock provided the raw material for him to advance his sheep-breeding operations once more. He used his letter to reiterate that wool improvement was something of great potential benefit to Corrientes.[95] In an animal count from June and July of 1853, Bonpland concluded he owned 521 head of sheep, less some eaten along a journey.[96] He now had the basis, with selective additional purchases, to begin his sheep business anew.[97] In October 1853, Bonpland took on livestock belonging to an Ambrose Lange. These comprised more than five hundred cows, mares, and donkeys (both male and female, the former presumably present for use in mule breeding). These were to be kept in the corral every night, and Lange arranged to pay Bonpland for the use of his land on a monthly basis.[98] With the beginnings of recovery at Santa Ana under way, Bonpland then took off to Montevideo for an extended spell, partly to deal with back pension issues. When the French geographer Victor Martin de Moussy passed through Santa Ana, he told Pujol that he missed seeing his "very good friend for many years."[99]

Bonpland at Montevideo, 1853–1854

By early December 1853, Bonpland was at Montevideo, where he stayed until early February 1854.[100] This has long been one of the best documented periods of his South American life, which surely reflects the recent freedom of travel. Hamy was able to publish no less than six letters about Bonpland's affairs from this Montevideo stay, half of these directed to Humboldt.[101] Bonpland's sense of the volatility of Correntino politics and his approval of Pujol both came through in a letter he wrote to the Brazilian former engineer Vasconcellos; this predicted that the reelection of Pujol would bring for Corrientes a long period of peace, and thus the chance to realize the project in the *yerbales*.[102] A long letter to François Delessert mainly summarized Bonpland's considerable experience of studying the giant water lily and yerba, and traced the geographical distribution of these plants.[103] In a letter to his Paris agents, Bonpland ordered books, including such important botanical works as Endlicher's *Genera plantarum* and the thirteen volumes of de Candolle's *Prodromus*.[104] This book order was a sure sign of ongoing intellectual activity; once they arrived in South America, these studies supplemented older published works in helping Bonpland to make his plant classifications in his manuscripts.[105]

During this visit to Montevideo Bonpland happened upon a project that suited his talents. Since leaving Paraguay, he had shown considerable interest in the French colony of Algeria, a place he perceived as opening to development. The 1848 French Constitution declared Algeria "an integral part of France," so that it could eventually be absorbed into the metropolitan administrative structure.[106] By November 1853 the needs of the French metropolitan government were communicated to South America in a document dealing with general concerns of French commerce in the Plata, which also included "an enumerative note of a number of plants native to Uruguay and to Paraguay, [but] unknown for the greater part in our latitudes."[107] The acclimatization of these plants in Algiers was seen as offering potentially great advantages, by building up that colony's economy, and eventually saving the metropolis from importing specific items from beyond French colonial possessions. The minister of war sought seeds from Montevideo and Buenos Aires in order to foster the agricultural development of Algeria. Paris wanted to know the geography of where the seeds were drawn from, including some account of geological and climatic conditions. The costs of plant transfer were to be assumed by the ministry. France's policies of economic expansion in South America during this period created new opportunities for expatriates such as Bonpland, and they brought something vital: the possibilities of sustained support.

Demonstrating the importance of contingencies, these specific requests for help from Paris arrived at Montevideo at one of those infrequent times when Bonpland was visiting there. As soon as he gained wind of the seed transfer project, probably from the French consul Maillefer, he wrote to Napoleon III offering his services. His letter to the emperor carries an even earlier date than Consul Maillefer's official reply to Paris about the scheme.[108]

In writing to Napoleon III, Bonpland began by referring to thirty-six years of forced residence in South America, where he reckoned he had done nothing to jeopardize his nationality. What he meant by "forced residence" is not easily determined. In any legal sense, he was free to return to France except during the period of his detainment in Paraguay. Any sense of force was probably psychological; he felt he had work to complete in South America. As late as 1856, at his birthday celebration in São Borja, he was calling for four more years to complete his South American studies.[109] After referring to the brilliant reign of Napoleon I, Bonpland reminded the new emperor that he had seen employment at the "incomparable" Malmaison and Navarre for nine years. The experiences of what he termed "that short phase" working with Joséphine had left their mark for life. Although now eighty-two, "the new order of things" left Bonpland wishing to revisit Paris. He would be happy to find an opportunity to present his South American researches to the emperor, in the same way he presented to Napoleon I those made in the equinoctial regions "in concert with [Humboldt], the most famous of travelers."[110] There was perhaps some reason for sentiment when seeking imperial preference, since Bonpland had held the new emperor as a baby.[111]

On the same day he wrote the piece of flattery above, Bonpland returned to Consul Maillefer his additions to the "nomenclature" of the trees of Paraguay and Uruguay, sent by the ministry of war in the search for seeds for the experimental botanical garden at Algiers, as part of its efforts at colonial development: "It is unfortunately very common to find foreign names, and above all those of plants poorly described, even in published works. The naming system that we have on hand provides a very striking example of this." Thus Bonpland had seen fit to revise the list. He repeated the names sent from France but also included other names under consideration, the botanical names, "whether using the Linnean or natural systems," and a series of practical observations directed toward issues of acclimatization: "I imagine I have been too prolix in my explication of the indigenous names and in the observations that I made about each plant. My firm desire is to be useful to science and to my country."[112] Shortly after his release from Paraguay, he pointed out, the materials sent to the Paris museum included a collection of seeds supposed useful for Algeria, a place, as he phrased it, that had always fixed his regards. The difficulty of communicating with France from the South American interior had suspended all his plans for Algeria. We know Bonpland had sent materials for Algeria to Paris in the 1830s at his own initiative; he told Humboldt that he never received a response about these.[113] Thus the minister of war's project, with its clear mechanisms for transfer, held much appeal for him. He promised to work at this scheme, gathering both seeds from species in the plant catalog and others he considered potentially useful in North Africa. In his properties at Santa Ana and São Borja, Bonpland told the consul he constantly sowed seeds as fast as they came to him. He also pointed out that he was in the long-standing habit of taking all the necessary precautions for their germination and growth. Part of a request for catalogs from the experimental garden at Algiers was to avoid duplication. In addition, by knowing what species grew in Algiers, it could be useful to work by analogy, so that shipments could be more complete and useful.[114]

In response to this offer of help, Consul Maillefer was able to send by the return mail boat to France "a valuable work by Mr. Aimé Bonpland, the most competent man in South America" in the matter of seed exchanges.[115] No doubt the offer of practical help was a boon to an overburdened French consul. The services of the consulate were provided to draw up the seed table sent to France, where the minister was alerted he would find "corrected indigenous names, botanical names, the places of origin, and a good number of observations even more practical than academic."[116] Maillefer forwarded the request for catalogs, both from Paris and Algiers, so that Bonpland would be able to better direct his operations. He also pointed out that Bonpland was working without self-interest. Enriching his request with flattering words from the imperial government, Consul Maillefer showed his understanding of how to use the French government apparatus in order to stimulate Bonpland's work.

The first shipment came from Concordia, Entre Ríos, in March.[117] It comprised two boxes filled with fully ripe fruits of the Yatay palm (*Butia yatay*), a species Bonpland considered valuable. In the 1850s, he observed, the palm still formed extensive woods in Entre Ríos and Corrientes, growing in sandy terrain almost invariably formed of hills that followed no constant direction. While common on the western bank of the Uruguay River, the species was scarcely present on the eastern side.[118]

The character of the leaves of the Yatay meant that it served better than any other grass to make the roofs of houses and huts. The numerous bittersweet fruits were also of use. When the fruits were mature, the inhabitants made daily visits to the Yatay forests. Oxen, cows, and pigs, whether feral or domesticated, fattened promptly on this fruit. As for the seeds, people laid in ample provisions of these for the winter, feeding themselves on the hard and oily perisperms. As of yet, nobody had tried to make oil from the almonds, even though these were rich in the substance. From the young and undeveloped shoots of this palm, people made eau-de-vie. Bonpland deplored this habit because it destroyed the forests. He advised instead the fermenting of the ripe fruits as an alternative method.

After giving this palm's potential economic uses, Bonpland explained how to conserve the seeds. He wanted them stratified in new earth in Montevideo, suggesting that Margat, a French-born gardener resident there, was the person who could best achieve this.[119] In Algiers, since the number of samples was large, he suggested that local authorities should find some sandy terrain to plant a palm forest (very specific planting instructions were given). In closing, he lamented that the excessive dryness of the summer had limited his first shipment to a single species.

When Maillefer wrote to the minister of foreign affairs from Montevideo in July 1854, his themes were many, including French diplomatic representation about to be established in Paraguay. After observing that it was hard to find Uruguayan official newspapers of the kind sought by the Ministry of Agriculture and Commerce in France, he continued: "On the other hand, I have the satisfaction of sending . . . a third case of seeds for our Algerian colony. Gathered with care by the celebrated Mr. Bonpland, who sent them to me from Entre Ríos, these seeds of useful vegetables have been packed under my supervision by Mr. Margat, [Uruguay's] leading horticulturalist."[120]

Catalogs arrived from France in September 1854. The consul forwarded them to Bonpland by a sure route, accompanied by a letter of thanks outlining the high opinion the departments of war and of foreign affairs held of his "learned and useful researches."[121] The official stimulus for greater things was clear. Shipments of plant materials from Montevideo to Algiers via France turned regular, despite the frequent difficulties of transport between the Upper Plata and the coast, and the problem of finding appropriate material in season. In later asking the French government to send some new words of satisfaction and encouragement for "Humboldt's companion," Maillefer noted that earlier such encouragement had fed Bonpland's ardor and seemed to knock a half-century from his age.[122]

Bonpland returned to the interior full of ambitions to continue his planting. Benjamin Poucel, a compatriot, wished him "happiness in the magnificence of your wilderness, which has so many allurements for you," a comment catching much of the spirit of what moved Bonpland.[123] Poucel was a well-connected member of the French community in the Plata. Like Bonpland, he showed a strong interest in merino breeding. The disruptions to his model project in southern Uruguay caused by war turned Poucel into one of the spokesmen in France who urged stronger political intervention in South America.[124]

Bonpland arrived back at Santa Ana a few weeks later, specifically on the early afternoon of 22 March 1854.[125] He hurried to visit his garden and farm, an experience that brought a mixture of pain and pleasure. His major complaint was the usual one that the workers had accomplished far less than he considered they should. The only crop described as doing very well was the manioc, while the sweet potatoes had been devoured by deer. The fence around the quinta had been destroyed by an "inexcusable negligence," possibly for use as firewood.[126] He set to work to make the necessary repairs, but he also began new activities on the estancia, notably by planting Chinese tea drawn from Brazil. In this, Bonpland was a true pioneer. Based on his fieldwork nearly a century later, on the then–northern fringes of Corrientes (bordering Misiones), the German geographer Herbert Wilhelmy described tea planting as something "quite new."[127]

By the 1850s, Brazil had already accumulated an interesting history with regard to tea cultivation. Tea was brought by the Portuguese to Rio de Janeiro from Macau in 1812, the first successful transfer of the crop outside of East Asia. Initially using Chinese labor, the Botanical Garden at Rio de Janeiro became an important locus of experimentation in attempts to acclimatize tea. While the plant grew well in parts of Brazil, commercial success was harder to reach. Even so, considerable interest was shown in the commodity during the first half of the nineteenth century by the planters of south-central Brazil, especially by those of São Paulo. Although Bonpland's efforts to acclimatize tea much farther south have escaped previous notice, these would still fall under Warren Dean's rubric of "desultory experiments" of the 1850s in his discussion of the crop.[128]

The planting of Chinese tea would no doubt have seemed a logical outgrowth for Bonpland from his interest in maté. Even while captive in Paraguay during the 1820s, he unsuccessfully sought tea seeds from Rio de Janeiro through the Brazilian diplomatic agent Correa da Câmara, who treated this request as providing nothing more than a cover for spying on him.[129] Bonpland had also written from São Borja in January 1853 to Cândido Baptista de Oliveira, the director of the Botanical Garden at Rio de Janeiro, seeking seeds. They had met in person at Porto Alegre when Bonpland visited the Riograndense capital. Bonpland was pleased to intercept his first consignment of tea seeds, destined originally for São Borja, in the Brazilian ministry at Montevideo.[130] In April 1854, he made his first experiment, by planting three hundred plants at Santa Ana.[131] After a promising start, these suffered very badly from an extended drought during a period of Bonpland's absence in November and December. By 1855, the sample was reduced to only two living tea plants. When Bonpland told the Brazilian senator that these "two little cherished organisms" were the focus of all his care, we can be convinced.[132] A subsequent shipment of seeds was composed of seeds from Brazilian tea grown in São Paulo. Bonpland considered this less aromatic than the Chinese and slightly bitter in taste, but he still considered it susceptible to improvement. He later gave Baptista de Oliveira a detailed accounting of what he had done with the tea samples by way of experiment. Some went to various friends at a series of locations in the valley of the Uruguay River, including to General Urquiza at his palace of San José, later described by Bonpland as his "incomparable establishment."[133] The massive stone-built house reflected the immense wealth of Urquiza's estancias. He also sent seeds to São Borja. But in these cases the scope for management was limited. Santa Ana remained the key locus for experiment, but Bonpland also had plans—never realized—to try planting it farther north at San Xavier, where the rainfall was more reliable in January and February.[134]

In May 1854, Bonpland told governor Pujol that he was anxious to make the trip to Corrientes, preferably by horse. There, he wanted to deal with Pujol in person about the business of improving the state of the *yerbales* in the province.[135] In early June, Bonpland returned to Santa Ana with Pierre Reboul, a relative of Padre Gay.[136] Reboul arrived at the ranch in the hope of developing a viticulture project as a joint venture with Bonpland and of undertaking "pork butchery on a large scale." This instance of working with a European was something very rare. As explained to Pujol, the viticulture project followed the established theme of wishing to bring a new branch of useful agriculture to the province.[137] At the same time that all this activity was under way at Santa Ana, somehow a different ambition had diffused to France, where, in the Gironde, a woman informed her son that a "savant" with the name of Bonpland had two properties in South America that he wished to sell in order to return to Europe. According to his letter, the son was interested in combining farming with the daguerreotype business.[138] He would have found limited scope for the latter in either Santa Ana or São Borja.

The immense work based at Santa Ana meant delay for Bonpland's travel to Corrientes. Writing from Restauración on 30 September, he explained why he had not yet been able to visit the governor. The "new and obscure happenings" had left him without peons and horses. Shortage of labor remained a particularly acute problem because it was the time to plant many of the staple crops, such as manioc, potatoes, and maize.[139] Bonpland used this same occasion to write his detailed comments on the state of the *yerbales*—perhaps the idea was to brief Pujol more fully prior to any meeting they would have in person. Building from work achieved decades earlier with Humboldt in the Andes, Bonpland stressed the point that yerba, like cinchona, had a very distinctive geography: "Take a ruler and place one of its ends on the Rio Grande bar, which takes its waters to the [Atlantic] ocean, and the other upon Villa Rica in Paraguay; along this entire line, natural *yerbales* are to be found; all the lands to the northeast of it offer *yerbales* with different degrees of remoteness, while to the southwest of this same line you find only some scattered bushes, whether on the edge of the woods or in the interior of them."[140] A huge amount of direct field experience lay behind this comment. Bonpland seems to have been satisfied with the state of his agriculture around this time, telling Pujol he was flattered that "no other inhabitant to the east of the Corrientes River would be able to offer a property so rich in productive plants and so useful, with time, to the country."[141]

In October, Bonpland's extensive writing to Pujol began to pay him some dividends. The governor announced his intention to visit southeastern Corrientes. He also nominated Bonpland to head up the permanent exposition of the province, based in the capital. The dispositions for what Pujol intended with this make interesting reading. Designed as a utilitarian project, it was also clearly part of a program of modernization. Pujol's government wanted to create a place where the prizes and applause should go not to those "who know how to brandish a lance, but to those who know how better to guide a plough, to plant a vine and collect its fruits. And to direct and preside over this great work of humanity and civilization the government is hoping for the powerful contribution of your talent, so devoted to the practical sciences."[142] The exposition was designed to hold all the products of Corrientes, whether reflecting "savage, semibarbarous, or civilized" states of development. Pujol chose Bonpland as the director for his fame, "in the interest of linking a great name to our pygmy of an institution."[143] In accepting the post of director in chief of the Corrientes museum or permanent exposition, Bonpland reviewed the places where he had accumulated his knowledge, including before 1817, and he provided a clear statement of his guiding philosophy: "The greatest wealth known down to the present consists of the vegetable kingdom."[144] On the same date that Bonpland accepted this directorship, he wrote a further letter from Santa Ana about the need to improve the methods of exploiting yerba. He had read with the "greatest jubilation" the news that the governor would soon take the steps to put in motion his *gran proyecto* (large project). For Bonpland, the first step was to survey the extent of the *yerbales*, whether wild or planted, located between the Paraná and Uruguay Rivers. The area concerned was not then known, but Bonpland estimated it could not be less than nine hundred square leagues. At the present, the region's resources were exploited not by the Correntinos but by Brazilians.[145] Ten days later, Bonpland summarized at length his yerba experiences in South America from 1817 onward. These included comments on the yerba planting he accomplished while a captive in Paraguay. It is particularly interesting to read about what happened to the yerba plantation in the former mission at Yapeyú in Corrientes. This once produced thousands of arrobas of yerba per annum, but when Bonpland visited it, all he found was one bush formed from some roots that had not yet been completely removed.[146] In his final surviving letter of the year, Bonpland gave concrete details of *yerbal* destruction accomplished by the Brazilians in San Xavier, Santo Ângelo, and Santo Cristo. He termed working in *yerbales* at that time of year a "crime."[147]

Bonpland met with Pujol in person sometime in early 1855 in southeastern Corrientes. He wrote to Gay from Santa Ana on 4 January, announcing the governor's arrival at Curuzú Cuatiá. Bonpland's more general plans hinged on what he achieved in his discussions with the Correntino governor.[148] Pujol had traveled across his province in the company of Lieutenant William Henry Murdaugh, an officer in Thomas Jefferson Page's U.S. expedition to investigate the rivers of the Río de la Plata. Murdaugh went on to visit Bonpland at Santa Ana, leaving a generally sympathetic description of his circumstances there by stressing his continuing energy, his "exceedingly interesting conversation," and his interest in developing the agricultural resources of Corrientes.[149]

In January 1855 Bonpland wrote the gist of a recent conversation held with the governor about the *yerbales*. The plan took San Xavier as its central point for the work. Bonpland's most interesting point related to the idea of reconcentrating indigenous labor around San Xavier. Bonpland opined that the Guanás Indians, in particular, would be happy to return to the yerba forests where they were raised. He showed a high opinion of their qualities as workers in the *yerbales*.[150]

While dealing with Pujol over the general management of resources, there were still immediate practical problems to confront. In April 1855, Bonpland learned that he had a serious land dispute with the neighboring Abalos family. General Abalos held land in emphyteusis with the government of Corrientes that he set out to buy but died before any payment was made. Remígio Abalos, the brother of the dead general, then asserted the same pretensions over the land. According to Bonpland, Abalos made his proposition to buy the estancia, making no mention of the fact that Bonpland had stocked it with animals following the guidance of José Virasoro, the frontier commander. In addition, Bonpland had planted crops on a large scale there, partly for his own utility, but also for what he saw as the good of the country, hoping to set an example his neighbors would be stimulated to follow. He objected that the Abalos family had ignored his legal rights to buy the disputed property, claiming that he had been in effective possession of the land for seven years and had given value to it through his agricultural work. Learning on 3 April 1855 from justice of the peace José Ledesma that Remígio Abalos had gained this land by a decree of 3 December 1854, Bonpland noted the following: "If I must be expelled from the land . . . , this will serve as a sad example to hard-working men, and agriculture will not prosper as desired by His Excellency Pujol and all those fond of order and of the public good." He followed this summary of developments with a list of the many types of fruit trees on the disputed land, including 467 orange trees in a tree nursery.[151] While the outcome of this dispute remains unclear, there seems little doubt Bonpland would have turned to Pujol for help.

Bonpland continued his intense correspondence with the governor about his favorite themes, including crop planting, how to raise funds for the museum, the state of the sick soldiers he treated in the barracks at Restauración, and of course the *yerbales*. With respect to this latter, he wrote with classic understatement: "I am perhaps more anxious than the governor to see the *yerbales* worked according to my wishes."[152] Bonpland told Pujol that he was surprised to see his earlier correspondence with Humboldt being published in the Corrientes newspaper *El Comercio*. Since he claimed not to have duplicates of his own letters, he could not understand the source of this newspaper's raw material. He decided that his old friend Roguin had probably reported his conversations about Humboldt to Pedro de Angelis: "The substance of these letters is truthful, but they contain a rare mixture and notable errors of places and names."[153] From these reminiscences about the past, Bonpland moved to the news of the present, congratulating Pujol on the recent arrival of French colonists (a reference to the province's first agricultural colony at San Juan). It interested him that the French were working to bring in a complete community, something that stood in contrast with the usual patterns of French immigration in the Río de la Plata. The prospect of building a cultural enclave reminded Bonpland of an earlier conversation with General Andréa at Porto Alegre. When the German director of the already noteworthy São Leopoldo colony proposed to expand that settlement, the provincial president had replied that he "did not want to make a Germany within Brazil, and if more colonists came, he already knew where to place them." This was a veiled reference to the early development of the German colony at Santa Cruz. Bonpland also held in mind drawing some specialized help from within the French immigrant community, although his recent effort to work with a compatriot had failed. Pierre Reboul had renounced his residence at Santa Ana; Bonpland noted that "his education, his character and his conduct did not agree well with my habits." What lay behind this rather vague comment remains unknown, but the general labor pattern for Bonpland was to seek people dependent on him, something less easily achieved with Europeans than with others. He wondered whether anyone among the new French colonists was prepared to undertake the work of viticulture at Santa Ana. Once his vine shoots were planted on a more extensive scale, he was even thinking of bringing a good *vigneron* (a vine grower or wine specialist) out from Europe. The general report on the state of the viticulture at Santa Ana was positive. His news ended with criticism about the poor state of the local barracks. Bonpland maintained that soldiers in such a dangerous occupation deserved better lodging. Part of his argument here involved the need for the physical reform of the medical services he himself had developed.[154]

Whether with or without a compatriot resident at Santa Ana, there are signs things were not always easy there. Returning from a week's absence in September 1855, Bonpland regretted the lack of harmony in the people working for him.[155] In October, he told Pujol the winter weather had bothered him for the first time in his life. He also announced his ambition to plant yerba at Santa Ana, a further sign of his obsession with this plant. Bonpland had recently spoken with three *yerbateros* who were prisoners in the jail, "said to have discovered a large *yerbal*." In this way, he sought oral information about the state of the *yerbales* in the Alto Uruguay. In the catalog of the Rio de Janeiro Botanical Garden, received days earlier, he noted there were many fruit trees that would prosper in Corrientes. And he alerted the governor to the considerable environmental destruction then happening in southeastern Corrientes, mainly motivated by the commercial supply of fuel wood to Restauración, an interesting observation considering that at the time the town could still only boast a population of around five hundred people.[156]

The Final Visit to Montevideo

On 13 October 1855, Bonpland left Santa Ana to go to Federación and onward to Montevideo, taking his young servant José Maria with him.[157] Near the beginning of this journey, he received at Uruguaiana a packet of letters stuck in the French consulate at Porto Alegre since 1851. They were forwarded by the Baron d'Ornano, the recently arrived French vice consul in that town, who tried to elicit Bonpland's help in the writing of a report for the government of France.[158] Bonpland pointed out that the consular official had much better access to any printed sources than he did. He recommended that d'Ornano send him a list of the specific points he needed to cover, in order to avoid any duplication of effort. Since Bonpland no longer resided permanently at São Borja, he suggested that the vice consul should communicate with him there through the cover of Padre Gay.[159] It became clear from a subsequent letter that the French vice consul had no taste for conducting archival research.[160]

The journey to Montevideo was a slow one, reflecting the usual challenges of the Uruguay River. Bonpland regretted the lack of steamships on the river to take him south from Santa Ana. He later claimed to have spent twenty-two days stuck off the coast of Colonia, where his ship braved daily storms coming from the south.[161] But if getting around was far from easy, slow travel expanded some research opportunities, notably the chance to gather more current information about yerba supplies. Bonpland synthesized his findings from the various places that he had landed in a letter to Pujol from Montevideo, claiming that the yerba he had found was invariably "scarce, generally bad, and sold at a high price."[162] At Montevideo, he took place as an honored guest in the festivities of 26 November to mark the fall of Sebastopol.[163] As was usual with his city visits, Bonpland must have devoted considerable time to his correspondence. He told Humboldt that he missed the pure air of his property at Santa Ana, while that of Montevideo was thick with dust.[164] A new correspondent from this period was William Gore Ouseley (1797–1866), who had earlier served as the British minister in the Plata and was extremely hostile to Rosas.[165] Ouseley had just accompanied the Paraguayan soldier Francisco Solano López to Asunción on board the British-built war steamer *Tacuarí*, during the latter's return from his European tour of 1853–54.[166] Sir William Hooker had urged Ouseley to visit Bonpland, in one of his periodic efforts to encourage the latter to contribute material to the Royal Botanic Gardens at Kew; in Hooker's mind, Bonpland's reputation remained strongly connected with Paraguay. Ouseley had written to Bonpland from Encarnación in April 1855, telling Bonpland he had long wished to meet him in person.[167] In making his reply, Bonpland noted that he had not yet found the chance to visit Asunción, an ambition he had held several years. His motives for wishing to travel there included the wish to revisit several old friends and to offer his respects to President López and his family, especially General Solano López, "of whom I have heard spoken by Mr. Pimenta Bueno, General Paz and several other distinguished people."[168]

Bonpland completed a considerable correspondence on Christmas Day 1855. The letters included a reply to Gontier at Paris, who had been looking for word from his old friend since 1816. The naturalist d'Orbigny had not been able to inform Gontier about Bonpland's whereabouts, but he had finally met success with Demersay.[169] Bonpland's letter to Demersay was mainly a reprise of his projects; he also evinced the strong will to visit France but claimed that his obligations for Pujol stood in the way.[170] He also wrote at length to Senator Baptista de Oliveira at Rio de Janeiro, outlining the progress of his tea-planting experiments.[171] During this visit to Montevideo, Bonpland first encountered *Bonplandia*, the German-language botanical journal that carried his name, receiving his copies through the hands of Friedrich von Gülich, the Prussian minister to the Plata. He wrote at once to the publishers, telling them that his immediate research collaboration was slowed only by his poor command of German and his lack of manuscripts and collections, which were then conserved at São Borja.[172]

The visit to Montevideo lasted longer than Bonpland desired. Ships leaving the port there for the Uruguay River route were in short supply.[173] On the return journey he spent a few days visiting Urquiza, later informing Pujol: "On two occasions in my conversations with General Urquiza, I have tried to persuade him that your pen is worth more than the best lance."[174] Following Urquiza's encouragement, he had also written to friends in Montevideo, informing them of the caudillo's success in maintaining his power in Entre Ríos. Traveling in the upper reaches of the Uruguay River appears to have been demanding. On leaving Urquiza, Bonpland had found it necessary to swim on horseback across the Arroyo Grande in order to reach Concordia, from where he told the caudillo: "This afternoon I am thinking of continuing my journey by land, on account of the complete lack of water in the San Gregorio falls. The *tordillo* [a black and white dappled horse, whose coat turned increasingly white with age] will be my faithful companion and as soon as we arrive at Santa Ana we shall both rest from our fatigues. It will take ample enjoyment from the excellent pastures and I from the fruits and vegetables of my garden."[175]

In July 1856, Bonpland was not finding it easy to pay the property taxes on the Estancia Santa Ana. He counted on either incoming French state pension money or the collecting of a debt in order to deal with this. Bonpland and Pujol had earlier discussed the former's designs to gain full ownership of the property. He wrote to the governor about the losses of livestock he had suffered at Santa Ana after the battle of Vences.[176] As a foreign national, he could presumably have made a claim against the government.

Arrival at São Borja in late July provided the opportunity for sending news to Pujol. He found his property and collections there in poor condition but still hoped to depart for Restauración within around a week. He did not enjoy being stuck at São Borja, at least from what he told Pujol. In fact, the work of recuperation took much longer. While it was under way, Bonpland resided with his friend, Padre Gay. The rural economy around São Borja appears to have improved since Bonpland's previous residence there. Some of the *estancieiros* were now showing interest in stocking Misiones with their animals. Bonpland performed the role of advertising the superior quality of Pujol's government. Seeing the value of drawing new capital into Corrientes, he informed the governor he was prepared to act as a proxy for "well known" Brazilians seeking land in that province. The lands of Misiones needed to be surveyed, establishing which lands were best suited to estancias and which to small farms.

If the recent developments in ranching proved positive, the Correntino management of yerba resources left less room for satisfaction. Using as his example the recent export statistics for yerba shipped through the Brazilian port of Itaqui, gained from field observation along the recent journey to Rio Grande do Sul, Bonpland argued that this should lead Pujol into making serious reflections about the management of the immense *yerbales* of Corrientes. He maintained that he held daily conversation with men who worked in the Correntino *yerbales*, drawing the unfortunate conclusion that these were being quickly destroyed.[177]

The extended visit to São Borja became an important platform to Bonpland for gauging changes in the yerba industry. This led him to make interesting comments on the *yerbales* of Santo Ângelo, which Bonpland had seen in a very rich state in 1831. The Brazilians were working their *yerbales*. Bonpland argued that Pujol should be showing more commitment to the Correntino resources, so that Argentina could compete with Brazil and Paraguay. He did his best to foster this plan while at São Borja. Thus he crossed the river to São Tomé, seeking to help a reconnaissance mission to São Xavier that was in the hands of Francisco Suárez. Beyond communicating his oral knowledge of the *yerbales* in the upper reaches of the valley of the Uruguay River, Bonpland went further by giving Suárez a copy of his map of the *yerbales* to the northeast of the geographical line that he imputed to run from San Xavier to Corpus. In Bonpland's view, the key issue was to visit the Ñuguazú district.[178] Despite his enthusiasm and insistence, Suárez and his party managed to gain much less direct experience of the *yerbales* than Bonpland desired, partly on account of heavy rains but also because they lacked the necessary degree of organization for serious field research.[179] Bonpland held firm to his view that the *yerbateros* beyond any official control were ravaging the natural resources of Corrientes.

Bonpland wrote to the Prussian minister Friedrich von Gülich while at São Borja, telling him he was in the town in order to remove the remainder of his possessions. He planned to make Santa Ana what he called his "general headquarters."[180] The phrase seems especially apposite for his lifestyle. Roguin would soon write from Montevideo, wishing Bonpland well in his project of setting up Santa Ana on a definitive basis after a vagabond life: "I think, my old friend, there are few travelers as keen as you have been, still are today, and who have traveled with as much good luck as you have."[181] Bonpland began the work of pulling all his moveable goods out of Brazil at the beginning of September 1856. His house there was subsequently occupied by the family of Manuel Luís Osório, then the military commander of the frontier in Missões, later a key Brazilian figure in the Paraguayan War and in the politics of his native country.[182] As Bonpland prepared to leave São Borja, not even Gay had any sure sense of his future plans. Encouraged by Gay, the idea of a visit to Paris certainly continued to hold a strong appeal. But Gay told the French consular representative at Porto Alegre that he thought this unlikely. Bonpland was still pushing the governor of Corrientes to accept "his propositions for the new model establishments which he still projects in his head."[183] He stressed the point that his octogenarian compatriot was still very active. Bonpland left Gay a duplicate copy of his notes on the advantages of cultivating maté and of his correspondence with General Andréa.[184]

Bonpland left São Borja at five thirty on the morning of 4 September 1856 to go to Corrientes, traveling on a raft formed of three canoes. Given problems of lack of wind and of water, he seems to have encountered major difficulties in transporting southward a portion of his extensive collections, including plants, minerals, and manuscripts. Despite seeking it, he had found no landward alternative to the river route. The obvious challenge was to protect his boxes from the water, given that he had been unable to procure a tarpaulin at São Borja. At Restauración, he had the use of two rooms in the old custom house for storage.

Once back at Santa Ana, Bonpland described his garden there as *propre* (in decent condition). But the *capataz* and the gardener had been in dispute. Bonpland sided with the gardener, whom he viewed as trying to defend the property against the manager's petty thefts.[185] One thing that gave pleasure was a fine crop of roses; Bonpland regretted that he did not have the equipment on hand for the distillation of the petals.[186] He was also excited to try rice cultivation, using seed obtained during his recent visit to São Borja.[187] On 12 October 1856, Bonpland left Restauración in order to make the journey to Corrientes, moving at least parts of his collections from southeastern Corrientes to the capital. It was a time of very hot weather. Pujol lent logistical support to the journey by sending a *galera* (covered wagon) for Bonpland's use, in addition to a military escort. When it rained at night, Bonpland took refuge in the vehicle, but he later stretched out on the grass, an act he described as refreshing his body: "It is truly a necessity to sleep on the grass and in the open when you travel in hot countries," a clear sign of adaptation to local mores.[188]

A spell of residence at Corrientes was no doubt in part designed to advance the business of the museum located there. In November, Bonpland wrote his instructions about how to preserve the vegetative properties of maté seeds, part of his long-standing project to move seedlings southward from the more isolated *yerbales*.[189] More important, the issue of land at Santa Ana finally approached settlement. Bonpland gained sure title to the ranch through a decree made by his friend Pujol on 25 November 1856. The declaration made by the provincial congress in his support makes interesting reading. It took the theme that Bonpland had made concrete contributions to Correntino development, through such areas as his scientific work and his disinterested practice of medicine.[190] Santa Ana was also held as important for demonstrating some of the potential of cultivation, as seen in the wording "now numerous gardens and vineyards are to be found in these towns or villages, formerly so uncongenial to any type of cultivation." In another passage, the decree described Santa Ana as "a true botanical garden."[191] The cart bringing part of Bonpland's collections had still not arrived in early December.[192]

Bonpland finally took up an offer to make a return trip to Paraguay, but this time to the capital. He made his journey from the comfort of a French warship, the *Bisson*. The travel diary from this journey stands apart from the remainder of Bonpland's work because part of it was written by an amanuensis.[193] Never much given to accuracy when recording names, especially non-Latin ones, his diary leaves much that is difficult to interpret. Despite the brevity of the visit to Asunción, Bonpland continued the pattern of his earlier visits to urban centers by exploring a wide web of social contacts, including politicians, diplomats, engineers, and scientists. He scrupulously noted the presence of people he had known during the time of his captivity, refraining from any negative comments about the Franciata. Much of his emphasis was on botanical collecting, drawing on local help wherever possible. The diary reveals a man still with a high level of intellectual energy. When he learned that a railroad was under construction in the environs of Asunción, Bonpland wisely sought out plant specimens from the engineer along the transect of the line. Most of the themes in the diary are Bonpland's usual ones. Beyond botany, he was interested in geology and mining issues. He wanted Paraguay to develop its agriculture by opening the economy. And as at Corrientes and Porto Alegre, he saw the practical potential for a museum displaying natural products. As always, seed transfer possibilities were explored, with Bonpland seeking red and white rice, probably to sow on his ranch at Santa Ana. His reception from the president was relatively cold. López chastised Bonpland for not accepting his earlier invitation to settle in Paraguay. Perhaps trying to keep a brave face, Bonpland later wrote to Humboldt more positively about this event, and he wrote with great enthusiasm about the quality of his botanical work around the city.[194] The journey to Paraguay also provided a chance to further the work in connection with Algeria. Once returned to Corrientes, Bonpland informed Consul Maillefer that he was sending seeds down the river with Ernest Mouchez, the commander of the *Bisson*. At Asunción, he made a botanical excursion with Mouchez, "and we used all possible means to procure useful plants for Algeria. I am working without pause to gather new useful seeds."[195] These would accompany the new shipments of seeds of the Yatay and date palms that Bonpland planned to send very soon.

On the same day he sent this account, he wrote in a separate letter that he would not be able to visit the consul in Montevideo for around a year. During this time, he planned to mark animals at Santa Ana and would make new plantings on his property there. In addition, he would gather seeds for Algeria and work in governor Pujol's museum of natural history. Perhaps he would find the time to return to Asunción once more, he speculated (although this would never happen, in late 1857 he did receive an invitation to make a second journey from Corrientes to Asunción, when the *Bisson* was conveying the Comte de Brossard, France's diplomatic representative, to Paraguay).[196] Then he referred to Maillefer's own trip on the *Bisson* along the lower reaches of the Uruguay River, making comments that reveal his continuing wonderment at subtropical vegetation. He regretted the consul's short journey had not been extensive enough to let him appreciate "the beauty of the South American vegetation." On the Uruguay, it was necessary to ascend as far as the Piratini River in Rio Grande do Sul to find exciting vegetation. On the Paraná, vistas grew interesting beginning at Candelaria. A better idea still was to ascend the Paraguay River to Asunción, "the Chamonix [near the foot of Mont Blanc, France, and visited by Bonpland in 1805] of tropical vegetation."[197] Maillefer had baptized the small towns of Paysandú and Arroyo da la China [Concepción del Uruguay] in the Uruguay valley as a budding Venice and an Amsterdam. Bonpland was impressed by neither of these places, which he viewed as sad and backward. His judgment stemmed foremost from the vegetation. The towns

Figure 5.4 A daguerreotype image of Bonpland from the 1850s. This image of Bonpland at an advanced age is drawn from the collections of Asa Gray (1810–1888), the leading botanist of the nineteenth-century United States. It carries the inscription "taken in Paraguay, South America, 1850." If the stated location is accurate, the year should read 1857. It is worth remembering, however, that Bonpland traveled from São Borja to Montevideo during 1850 in the company of daguerreotype photographers. There is also reference to his having his photograph taken at São Borja in 1856.
SOURCE: By permission of the Archives of the Gray Herbarium, Harvard University.

were surrounded by nothing but "very small trees," of which people made nothing more than "a savage use."[198] Here was yet another clear example of his preference for subtropical areas over temperate ones.

Bonpland was also interesting for Maillefer on the subject of the European colonization taking place in Corrientes, where Auguste Brougnes, a French doctor, had signed a contract in 1853 with governor Pujol for the introduction of immigrants.[199] Although little practical good ever came of this scheme, it nevertheless provided an important landmark in the history of Argentine colonization, providing a basis that would soon be followed with much more success farther south in the temperate parts of the country. Brougnes had gained direct experience of the Río de la Plata before launching into this venture, and his initial interest appears to have focused on Uruguay, so heavily marked by French immigration during parts of the 1840s. The basic theory of taking impoverished rural dwellers from overpopulated parts of Europe, in his case especially southwestern France, in order to establish them as independent commercial farmers on the underpopulated public lands of the interior of Argentina, had much merit.[200] But the execution of the French colony at San Juan was weak from the outset. When Brougnes delivered his first consignment of colonists to Corrientes in late January 1855, nothing was ready for their reception, whether in terms of initial food needs, housing, land survey or agricultural planning. But not all the soon rapidly growing difficulties at San Juan stemmed from the provincial government of Corrientes. As Bonpland noted, some of the settlers were bringing servants out from Europe and trying to live off them. He saw the root problem of difficulties in the venality of the entrepreneur responsible for the colony, whose thirst for money was making "slaves of white men at a time when we are giving liberty to all the Africans."[201] Bonpland had given his ideas about how to reorganize the French colonization to Pujol, but coming after several cycles of insignificant crop harvests it was already too late to bring any success to San Juan.

This interesting account of life was followed a month later by a further missive from Corrientes, documenting a new shipment of seeds "for our Algerian colony."[202] When yet more material arrived at Montevideo in September, Maillefer showed signs that he was emotionally affected by the shipments and their results. He pointed out to the minister of foreign affairs that should the minister survey Bonpland's accompanying notes in detail, he could not help but be struck by the efforts this octogenarian was making on behalf of France. Despite the matters of expense, fatigue (and sometimes personal dangers), correspondence, and requests too often unanswered, plus trips in the primitive forests and the Chaco desert, Bonpland spared nothing to enrich the "vegetable treasure" of France's Algerian colony.[203] He was also working for science in a different direction around this time, sending specimens of eight types of maté, five of them claimed as new, to the British engineer and botanist John Miers. These specimens, accompanied by brief notes on where they were drawn from Bonpland's botanical manuscripts, were sent to England through the agency of the Botanical Garden of Rio de Janeiro.[204] This was an important instance in which his work found eventual publication through the work of another scholar.

Back from Paraguay, the work relating to the Corrientes museum remained. Bonpland wrote to von Normann at Porto Alegre seeking mineral specimens from Rio Grande do Sul and offering to send material in return from his own collections. The idea of a natural history exhibit at Porto Alegre was a topic Bonpland had discussed at length with General Andréa. He was pleased to learn that something concrete was happening at last, "as a modest proof of my patriotic affection for Brazil."[205] Part of the appeal of a natural history collection was his desire that young people have a means for studying the resources of the region with an eye to their further development. At Corrientes, an obstacle to the museum's progress was waiting for the completion of cupboards in which to place materials.

While at Corrientes, Bonpland was using his influence with Pujol in June 1857 to argue petitions for land and other rights for the inhabitants of São Borja, such as ecclesiastical rights for Gay in Santo Tomé on the other side of the Uruguay River from Brazil. In terms of Gay's own request for land, the property involved was an island. His main problem was that he could not obtain good data about the topography of the banks of the Uruguay River. Meanwhile, Gay translated Correntino newspaper stories about Bonpland and Pujol for the *Correio do Sul* at Porto Alegre. This material included Bonpland's notes on how to revitalize the economies of the former Jesuit missions of Rio Grande do Sul. In March 1857, the *Correio do Sul* took up the theme of the need to reform public education in Rio Grande do Sul and the advantages of taking hold of Bonpland's stimulus.[206] Gay informed Bonpland that São Borja had changed little; he seems to have craved novelty—which was presumably part of the reason that he moved from Alegrete in the heart of the Campanha region to the frontier garrison town.[207] In July 1857 the great issue at São Borja was one close to Bonpland's heart. It involved the discovery (presumably a rediscovery, Gay admitted, since it would have been known to the

Jesuits) of pastureland and of a *yerbal* closer to São Xavier than those currently exploited. The provincial government took this finding seriously, making a reconnaissance along the lines Bonpland had suggested some years earlier. It sent an expedition of more than forty men, headed by Captain Tristão de Araújo Nóbrega, a resident of São Borja, to examine the resources and secure them for commerce. The caravan included a surveyor brought expressly from the capital at Porto Alegre and nine Indians from Nonoai, the government colony in the extreme north of Rio Grande do Sul.[208] Bonpland had promised Gay a visit to São Borja in August 1857, possibly in part to celebrate his birthday there. The priest was looking forward to extended conversation, and he advised Bonpland that a visit to his small farm would be useful.[209]

. . .

Despite his considerable age, Bonpland showed little sign of letting up in the scale of his activity, although he had given up working late at night—in contrast to Humboldt. Yet frequent movement hindered completion of any single portion of his work. Pujol would have preferred to keep him based at Corrientes, but Bonpland was still thinking of further visits to other urban centers. No single place in the broader region appeared to offer him sufficient stimulation, not even Montevideo where he stood as the sole honorary member of the Sociedad de Medicina Montevideana.[210] In addition, he remained keenly interested in the management of his rural properties. The letter he sent to Humboldt from Corrientes in June 1857 is filled with the sense of action. It is also replete with sentimentality, notably on the theme of their shared early encounters with tropical vegetation. Bonpland reminded Humboldt how much the latter was moved by the sight of the palms and the orange trees during their journey along the southern coast of Spain at the very end of the eighteenth century: "Today I have both of these on my farm at Santa Ana, and I prefer the orange trees to the palms for their appearance, above all for their permanent foliage of a fine deep green and their exquisite fruits, similar to Havana oranges."[211] Bonpland still held forth the prospect of making a quick trip to Paris, in order to deliver his collections there, but when death came, he wanted it to happen in the shade of the trees he planted at Santa Ana. No closer identification with the subtropical landscapes of the Americas was possible than that. The work of the Estancia Santa Ana was calling him.

CHAPTER SIX

Journey's End

> Let Death Die
>
> His sore body is aching to mix itself with the American earth. Aimé Bonpland knew this was where he would end up and linger on, ever since that distant day when he landed with Humboldt on the Caribbean coast.
>
> Bonpland dies of his death, in a mud and straw hut, serenely, knowing that stars do not die; that ants and people will not stop being born; that there will be new cloverleaves, and new oranges or suns on the branches.
>
> EDUARDO GALEANO, *Faces and Masks*, p. 182

Bonpland's journey back from Corrientes was one with delays on account of heavy rains and medical obligations. Wherever he traveled, patients needed his services, which slowed his progress. Bonpland carried news about the state of Corrientes's politics across the province and even into Brazil at Uruguaiana, arriving at Restauración on 10 July.[1] On 29 July, he journeyed from Restauración to Santa Ana in his canoe. Returning to the Estancia Santa Ana after an absence of eight months, he was accompanied by four workers and by his children Carmen and Anastasio. They reached the port on his property around two thirty in the afternoon. Following the unloading of the canoe, the party arrived by cart at Santa Ana (described as "my humble cottage") around sunset.[2] Although it was almost night, he could not resist a visit to the garden, which he found in a "truly sad state."[3] Everything around the hut and its environs showed signs of poor management. One exception was the sheep flock, although even here he regretted that the *capataz* had not followed his orders to shear the fleeces. While this latter had left important tasks undone, Bonpland leveled the main blame for the poor state of affairs at the black worker Antonio. Sometimes described as "the Portuguese," he was presumably a Brazilian. Specific complaints were recorded, such as not hoeing the paths, leaving the vines and young fruit trees unsupported, and failing to maintain the fences in a good state. Following Bonpland's departure from Santa Ana, Antonio had followed the same procedure as two years earlier. He forbade Bonpland's *capataz* entry to the garden, refused him vegetables and fruits, and disposed of everything according to his own will. Bonpland described Antonio as having rendered himself "absolute master of my quinta."[4] The general picture was one of general neglect while Bonpland was away, followed by tremendous bursts of activity when he returned. The next project was to plant vine-shoots, a task finished on the evening of 13 August 1857, when Bonpland recorded he had 2,493 vines.[5]

Back from Corrientes, Bonpland gained an interesting source of news from there in the form of Louis Marceaux, the French teacher in charge of his son Amadito's education, whose letters begin in August 1857. Marceaux was providing an education for the most notable families at Corrientes and served as conduit for news from the capital, passing on news about the state of progress with the provincial museum, for example. With Bonpland absent, work on the preparation of the physical equipment of the museum had slowed: "You know His Excellency; he has the finest of intentions, but he is short on memory."[6] Marceaux also provided brief details about what was happening in the colony of San Juan, where Swiss colonists were now arriving. Schisms in the administration and an assassination there had become the talk of Corrientes. Bonpland had tried to recruit one of the colonists to Santa Ana, but he was unsuccessful in this ambition. As Marceaux explained, "they are all heads of families full of children, who do not wish to undertake the journey by land."[7] They would have regarded this as too dangerous. Irritated by the fact that most parents did not pay him, Marceaux took over the direction of the public school in Goya in mid-December. Failing instructions from Bonpland, he did not take Amadito with him, but left the boy behind in the town of Corrientes, presumably with the Périchon family. Amadito appears to have made his way back to his father's home.

After Bonpland left Corrientes in mid-1857, he would never find the chance to return to that seat of regional political power. Yet Pujol continued to draw on his expertise. He wrote to the Frenchman telling him he was thinking of repopulating the mission region with European immigrants. Pujol offered Bonpland the job of general director and administrator of the colonies, seeking out his views about how to direct the European colonization.[8] In his prompt reply, Bonpland began by congratulating Pujol on his efforts to keep the peace with Paraguay and to settle differences "without the noise of the cannons." Bonpland for his own part was not optimistic about the international politics of the region, saying prophetically "I see the horizon as very dark and I fear an uprising, whatever that may be." He then set out his views on colonization, as requested by the governor, beginning by stressing the variability of the physical environments, and setting out the specific regions the government needed to consider.

The first step was that Paraguay must recognize the Paraná River as its frontier. Then Bonpland would proceed to settle the east bank of that river. His methods would begin with an assessment of the physical resources, building on local agricultural knowledge in order to produce a resource map: "The need for preparing an accurate map of all the lands of Misiones has always been manifest." The land would be divided into units suited to farms and to estancias, both large and small: "There are large *bañados* (marshy areas), and it is necessary to divide these in such a way that they do not form a single estancia or chacra." As was now long the case, he argued that San Xavier should be the "central settlement of the *yerbales*," as it would provide a suitable point for the congregation of the Indians. He was influenced here yet again by the geographical line he saw as running between San Xavier and Corpus, stressing that the *yerbales* lay to the northeast of this. His idea was clearly that San Xavier could serve as a model for the Indians dispersed in the woods to the northeast of that point. Bonpland thought that the Indians deserved good compensation for their work: "Of all the classes of people, the natives are those who work the most assiduously and those who suffer the most arduous tasks."[9]

The *Journal d'agriculture* that Bonpland kept during the final portion of his life contains notes about agriculture at Santa Ana, but it records more than farming alone.[10] By this stage, it contains numerous references to the merchant Karl Wilhelm Kasten, a sure sign that the recent friendship of the well-educated young German based at Uruguaiana was important to Bonpland.[11] In November 1857, he was still moving his furniture by cart from Restauración to the Estancia Santa Ana. These objects were presumably his property from São Borja. In the same month, his property suffered heavy damage from locusts, a specific documented instance of what would become a massive, if occasional, problem for the farmers of Argentina during the second half of the nineteenth century.[12] On 13 November, he recorded that his plantings were all covered with young locusts, newly born. Five days later, they had left the property, but not before causing great damage to the beans, tomatoes, peppers, and other crops. Another highlight of late 1857 was the visit that Bonpland arranged for Fortunato Francisco da Silva, an Uruguaiana rancher interested in breeding mules at Santa Ana in a partnership. The plan called for Bonpland to provide the land and for Silva to provide the animals from Rio Grande do Sul. In his initial proposal, Silva expressed that Bonpland's land was "very appropriate for mule breeding."[13] On 26 November, they spent the morning surveying the land of Santa Ana close by the river, looking for the most appropriate place to establish a post for mule breeding.

The town of Restauración and the presence of Kasten there were important in Bonpland's late life. On a trip there of 11 February 1858, he bought from Kasten six silk handkerchiefs and a pair of enameled gold earrings for his daughter Carmen. Two weeks later, his main purpose in visiting Restauración seems to have been the delivery of his *declaración* (statement) to da Silva that he could not join the Brazilian mule-breeding enterprise. He spent the afternoon in Restauración "without being able to do anything of use."[14] His mention of this inactivity leads to the suspicion that he found the experience trying.

The locust damage was more serious than earlier reported. In February 1858, Bonpland told Pujol that these had occupied his property for three months and seven days, describing their impact on his crops. Santa Ana was experiencing a severe patch of drought, which took a heavy toll on Bonpland's plantings.[15] On 20 March, Bonpland wrote what would be his final letter to Pujol. Given the long history of his struggles surrounding South American lands, it seems appropriate and poignant that its leading theme was disorder surrounding land. The provincial decree from the previous year had not put an end to this issue. When he took possession of the Estancia Santa Ana in the 1830s, Bonpland noted, there were *mojones* (boundary tiles) marking the margins of the property. Two decades later, these had disappeared entirely. When the neighboring property belonging to Remígio Abalos was sold, the new owner took possession of a considerable area that Bonpland considered his. The property maps from the 1830s and the present were no longer in unison. The answer, claimed Bonpland, was to compare property maps in the city of Corrientes, then measure the estancias once more, using more than one surveyor. A further motive for accurate measurement was the growing pressure on land used for ranching coming especially from Brazil, meaning from Rio Grande do Sul.[16] While many in Corrientes held the view that no more vacant land existed, Bonpland did not share this opinion; the answer for him was to map all the unused lands. General Abalos had supposedly sold his land without the consent of the remainder of his family. While he had still to pass along any money, this was not, in Bonpland's view, what his relatives sought. They were not seeking money but "a piece of land to live on," a comment that reflected the deep commitment to the ranching culture in this part of the province.[17]

Another regular correspondent from this final portion of life was the teacher Marceaux, now based at Goya. He used his link with Amadito Bonpland, described as his favorite pupil, to reflect more generally on matters concerning Corrientes. The boy, then aged thirteen, had returned to Santa Ana for the summer holidays. Marceaux was clearly angling to draw him back as one of his boarding pupils. When Bonpland had reported Amadito was enjoying country life, this brought a critical response:

> I see from what you tell me that my dear Amadito is playing in the countryside a lot, making near continually his little hunting parties on horseback, and dressed *en gauchito* [as a little gaucho]. You should not spoil him so much, my dear Mr. Bonpland, and you should not give him so much liberty. He has already reached an age where he needs to use his time usefully, dedicated to study.[18]

The character of the entries in the agricultural journals provide clear testimony of Bonpland's declining forces. By March of 1858, he was definitely slowing down, although he was still assiduous about taking his meteorological readings. Beyond brief notes on the state of the pastures and on nocturnal theft of horses, the leading theme is the continuing novelty of visitors. On 18 March, he made a marginal reference to the American Thomas Jefferson Page, the commander of the *Water Witch*. On 17 and 18 April, the key matter was the important visit by the German medical doctor and traveler Robert Avé-Lallemant.

In what would become his final letter to Humboldt, written in June 1857 from the town of Corrientes, Bonpland expressed the thought that it would make him happy to speak with somebody who had seen Humboldt recently. This wish was met, though not through any explicit design on Humboldt's part, in the form of Avé-Lallemant. In December 1856, this last consulted Humboldt at his Berlin home, seeking there his help in joining the coming Austrian circumnavigation of the globe on the *Novara* (1857–1859). Avé-Lallemant subsequently joined this expedition, but left it upon reaching Rio de Janeiro, a city in which he had earlier resided. He went on, instead,

Figure 6.1 Bonpland's rustic home, the Estancia Santa Ana, Corrientes, 1858. After a sketch made on site by Robert Avé-Lallemant.

SOURCE: Reproduced from the title page of Avé-Lallemant, *Reise durch Süd-Brasilien*. General Research Division, The New York Public Library, Astor, Lenox and Tilden Foundations.

to make an extensive journey through parts of Brazil. The visit to Bonpland forms an important segment of the text in the first volume of his two-part travel account *Reise durch Süd-Brasilien*. Indeed, the trip was important enough that the frontispiece of his book ostensibly about southern Brazil was illustrated not by an image from that country but by a drawing of Bonpland's rustic home at Santa Ana.[19] Avé-Lallemant would eventually also be responsible for writing parts of Humboldt's biography, especially those portions relating to Bonpland.

Along his southern Brazilian journey, Avé-Lallemant kept Humboldt informed as to his progress. Writing from the former Jesuit mission of São Borja, he told him that Bonpland's supposed presence there was the reason he took the particular direction he followed across Rio Grande do Sul.[20] When he learned that Bonpland was no longer present in the town, he then resolved to move beyond Brazilian soil; he traveled into Corrientes "in order to send to Europe the most accurate news of the traveling companion of my worthy patron Alexander von Humboldt." Avé-Lallemant left Humboldt with a detailed picture of the degree of abandon of Bonpland's former home at São Borja, but noted evidence that the hand of an expert gardener was still present. He seems to have been especially keen to find some kind of "dear and precious relic" of Bonpland.

In the travel account published by Avé-Lallemant, his visit to Bonpland in Corrientes is presented in dramatic form. He crossed the Uruguay River into Argentina from Uruguaiana, using the logistical support of the German merchant Kasten, one of Bonpland's closest friends at this stage in his life. Avé-Lallemant spent an evening at Santa Ana, which allowed time for several extended interviews and prompted him to describe Bonpland's material surroundings. His image of Bonpland was one of a broken man. Prior to recrossing the Uruguay River back to Brazil, he sought a souvenir:

> I begged him to give me his autograph as a remembrance, and he wrote upon the back of an old letter: "Aimé Bonpland." "That is badly written," he remarked, and wrote his name a second time, but even less successfully. "Ah," he exclaimed, "I have no longer the power to write"; and it seemed to me as if a tear stole down his cheek. Probably this was the last time that he ever wrote his name.[21]

Avé-Lallemant left Santa Ana to cross back to Uruguaiana on 18 April. He maintained that Bonpland was full of a deluded optimism about the prospects for a more prosperous future: "And as if to begin at once with arrangements for the latter, he commissioned me to ask Herr Kasten to send him a dozen knives and forks."[22]

Avé-Lallemant summarized his journey for Humboldt at once upon regaining Brazilian territory, writing on 19 April a description of his "useless visit" to Bonpland. He claimed that oral reports had prepared him for the miserable condition in which he found his subject. As at São Borja, he gave Humboldt a detailed account of the extreme modesty of the house, furniture, and garden. Avé-Lallemant showed no understanding of Bonpland's attachment to the Americas. His short visit was also hardly conducive to gaining an understanding of the constraints Bonpland faced in the management of his rural property. He did stress the independence of the aged Bonpland: "How much I would have liked to save him, to lead him to the civilized world!"[23] For Avé-Lallemant, science was nothing unless linked to what he termed an able hand in the crown of European civilization. He saw Bonpland as lost, anchored in the past, and maintained that he had traveled thousands of kilometers in order to offer a mark of esteem to Bonpland in the name of science. Avé-Lallemant failed in his romantic mission. When writing a portion of Humboldt's biography, he described Bonpland as "the cynic of La Plata, for whom Europe had ceased to possess any attraction."[24] This comment missed the way Bonpland had for many years worked to straddle the tension between the demands of European science and his engagement with the Americas.

Avé-Lallemant was also in error about his subject's writing capacity. Although confined to field notes, Bonpland recorded his own impressions of the emissary from Humboldt, in spite of his weak health. Thus his difficulty with writing that Avé-Lallemant recorded appears to have stemmed from temporary exhaustion, if not from pure fiction written for dramatic effect. In Bonpland's agricultural diary, a late entry contains a generally accurate description, flawed mainly by rendering the visitor's name incompletely, a common trait with the author:

> 17 April 1858. Saturday. Today I have received a very curious visit. Dr. Robert L'allemant, a Prussian, has come here to see me and to get to know me. He is a doctor of medicine, which he practiced at Rio for seventeen years. A year and two months ago, he saw Humboldt at Berlin. Returned to Brazil, Mr. L'allemant has come here expressly to see me and he is going back to Brazil to undertake a large journey. . . . Mr. L'allemant is an educated man, he speaks all the living languages well, and he shows an extraordinary liveliness of spirit.[25]

And on the very same day that Avé-Lallemant was writing from Uruguaiana to Humboldt, Bonpland sent a brief written account of his recent German visitor across the river to Kasten. He asked Kasten to forgive him for not replying to an earlier letter sent through Avé-Lallemant:

> He is without doubt a truly extraordinary man, for his wide and deep knowledge, and for the great journey he is going to undertake [through Brazil]. In the few hours he was with me, we were able to discuss Humboldt, his earlier life, his learned works, etc. I was already suffering greatly, but the 24 hours of interview with this intellectual increased my pains to such a point that I was unable to take up the pen to write you a word.[26]

A key feature of Avé-Lallemant's efforts to render Bonpland native was his argument that the latter could no longer use a knife and fork, an element in treatments of Bonpland that is much repeated down to the present. As with the writing issue, the facts of this small matter were different. Since the time one of his former servants had robbed him of his table knives, Bonpland claimed that he had found it impossible to find serviceable replacements. He asked Kasten to send him a dozen good ones, such as those he used on his own table at Uruguaiana. And he assured him that his health was on the mend.

Conscious that it had a wide European circulation, Humboldt sent Avé-Lallemant's account of Bonpland for publication in the botanical journal *Bonplandia* at some point in 1858. He judged the account of Bonpland's lifestyle to be *"la description si exacte de la manière de vivre tout-à-fait indienne"* (a wholly accurate description of his completely native way of life). This was something Humboldt himself claimed to have seen during the journey along the Orinoco. Perhaps he was in part remembering how Bonpland had dried his plants within the huts of the indigenous people. Nevertheless, Humboldt also seems to have held some doubts about the veracity of Avé-Lallemant's account. Thus he directed the editors of *Bonplandia* to print his former traveling companion's most recent letter to him intact in its original French, so that the readership would also gain a recent sign of Bonpland's active spirit. It was a letter full of the desire to live, not to die.[27] Still, Avé-Lallemant's published judgments fixed our impressions of Bonpland for the remainder of the nineteenth century and down to the present. The distinguished historian of science George Sarton called Avé-Lallemant's description "a vivid picture" in 1943, but argued that his "pathetic account of [Bonpland] should be discounted."[28] Subsequent English-language biographers of Humboldt have not heeded this valuable advice.[29]

Following Avé-Lallemant's important brief sojourn at Santa Ana, Bonpland's agricultural diary entries become very brief, indeed, mainly concerning weather. The final entry came on 30 April.[30] According to the priest Gay, Bonpland gave up his ordinary preoccupations on 3 May but had written near continually for almost a week more.[31] If the subject of his writing concerned his scientific heritage, it was regrettably already too late.

Bonpland died on 11 May 1858. Living close to the oral sources, the German merchant Kasten probably gave the most accurate account that we have of Bonpland's demise.[32] It has long remained in manuscript form in Humboldt's papers. Kasten was away on business when Bonpland's condition deteriorated. Otherwise, he affirmed he would have hurried to Santa Ana so that Bonpland could have had at least one European friend by his deathbed. The details of his death came from the oral testimony of Bonpland's daughter Carmen, then aged fourteen or fifteen. Bonpland took to his bed on 3 May and talked and wrote from his bed occasionally until 9 May. Kasten's main concern seems to have been the future of Bonpland's scientific manuscripts. He seems to have held only the vaguest sense of their value, but he wanted the European diplomats in the Plata to act quickly, thus ensuring that material of value would "not be destroyed through brutal hands," an unflattering but probably realistic appraisal of the capabilities of the local authorities.[33]

Still unaware of his collaborator's death, Humboldt's final letter to Bonpland was written on 10 June, when the intended recipient was already a month in his tomb. He noted that Bonpland's scientific reputation grew from year to year, but even more in Germany and England than in France. A possible explanation for this apparent anomaly is the impact patterns of the journal *Bonplandia*. Bonpland's letters to Humboldt printed there subsequently made their way first through the German, then through the British newspapers. This was helped in the latter case, no doubt, by the fact that the publisher, Berthold Seemann, was based in the botanical gardens at Kew.[34] The explanation for any increasing indifference shown toward Bonpland coming from France is also probably linked to the success of d'Orbigny's work, a competitor not only of Bonpland in the field of South American natural history but also, famously, of Darwin.[35] Referring to plant exchanges between the University of Greifswald (which conferred an honorary doctorate on Bonpland in 1856) and Corrientes, Humboldt urged Bonpland not to leave his American plants in America. What would perpetuate the true glory of Bonpland's name, he claimed, would be to combine all his collections in the "vast and stable" Jardin des Plantes: "You can distribute some duplicates, but the bulk of the work of an illustrious traveler such as you should stay intact in a single establishment, the largest, the most stable, and the most open to the public in scholarly Europe."[36] There was no sentiment here about the need to build up scholarly establishments in the periphery. The conclusion to Humboldt's letter reads movingly: "There is nobody on this earth more given to you in heart and soul than me."[37]

Still unaware of Bonpland's death in July, Humboldt wrote to François Delessert at Paris, passing along the sad picture conveyed in Avé-Lallemant's letter.[38] The Delesserts, who combined interests in banking and natural science, had served as key figures in the Humboldt-Bonpland relationship for decades.[39] Both men were close to this family, even Bonpland from the distance of South America. Humboldt later took steps quickly to secure Bonpland's collections and manuscripts for the Jardin des Plantes. He was clear that he did not wish to see his friend's scientific legacy confined in the Upper Plata: "I fear a little the museum forming under M. Bonpland's auspices at Corrientes."[40] Humboldt claimed that Bonpland was disorganized, and that because Bonpland held a singular confidence in his own longevity, it was to be feared that his scientific papers would suffer great disorder during the remainder of his life.

Humboldt claimed to learn of Bonpland's death on 9 August 1858 through the auspices of Sir Woodbine Parish, the diplomat and scholar, in a letter written from England.[41] He then wrote to Élie de Beaumont, the perpetual secretary of the Académie des Sciences, in an effort to secure Bonpland's herbarium for the Jardin des Plantes.[42] In discussing this, the issue of what seeds and plants Bonpland had taken with him to South America in 1816 resurfaced. Humboldt maintained that the herbarium had been split into three equal portions. Elsewhere, he had frequently stated that Bonpland took the majority of the collection with him in 1816. Apart from working to save Bonpland's scientific collections, Humboldt also sought to help the three children born in South America who were recognized by Bonpland. Carmen Bonpland had written directly to Humboldt from Argentina, describing in Spanish her father's funeral. Humboldt claimed that he would take steps through the French foreign minister to seek the transfer of a part of Bonpland's French state pension to his "very needy children." He added further that "the right has foundation, but whether it will be recognized is another question."[43] There is no evidence that it was.

Requests for his work followed Bonpland beyond his demise. In April 1858 the French minister of war agreed that Bonpland should be informed of the results of his work in Algiers. A report was finally forwarded by the director of the experimental garden there, documenting the success of a large part of the material sent from South America. In addition, the French government wished to systematize exchanges of plant materials between Algeria and southern South America, with a particular focus on Paraguay. The means of communication would involve *serres de voyage*, or traveling hothouses. The first item on the list of desiderata was manioc, a staple food.[44]

By the time this report arrived at Montevideo, Bonpland was already dead. Maillefer stressed the irony that Bonpland would never see its account of the success of his shipments. France still sought material for Algiers from southern South America, above all from Paraguay. But Maillefer was unsure whether the consul there, Alfred de Brossard, "with all his taste for intellectual things," would be able to conquer the apathy Bonpland had complained about on the part of his Asunción correspondents; in April 1857, these were extensive.[45] With Bonpland's death, the project of plant exchange between Paraguay and Algeria was suspended, although not before the comte de Brossard attempted a catalog of plants indigenous to Paraguay drawn in part from the deceased's manuscripts.[46]

Conclusion

The major biography of Alexander von Humboldt edited by Karl Bruhns in 1872 drew a strong contrast between the lives of its subject and of Aimé Bonpland. While the former, from "a sense of duty," had supposedly been "detained . . . amid the cheerless surroundings of his native home," it was argued that Bonpland had been "content to spend his days in quiet inaction, in the enjoyment of a life of contemplation."[1] This clearly unfair comment stemmed directly from Avé-Lallemant and his impressions of Bonpland toward the end of his life. The notion of inactivity in the European literature left a deep legacy of misunderstanding, but it was also very far from the mark. A safe filled with Bonpland manuscripts at Buenos Aires is alone concrete testimony to that. Pharmacy, medicine, farming, ranching, advising (to governments and to other parties), species transfer, and museum development occupied so much of Bonpland's time and energies that we are bound to wonder how he maintained his commitment to research. It surely took enormous levels of discipline. Although France always remained close to Bonpland's sentiments, he threw himself wholeheartedly into the major issues of land and life in the portions of South America where he resided. Whatever new developments were present in land use—including estancia development, sheep breeding, forest resource conservation, and colonization by minorities drawn from northwest Europe—Bonpland was usually involved to some degree, and often directly. All this activity left records, many of which are of unusual value for the reconstruction of the regional environments, societies, and economies. They have formed the backbone of this study.

Bonpland maintained that, until 1816, he had lived under a lucky star. By this, he was thinking principally about the success of his researches with Humboldt and of his career working at botanical description and plant acclimatization for Empress Joséphine at Malmaison and Navarre. In both of these instances, somebody else had been paying his bills. Following his emigration to the Río de la Plata, the character of his life changed to one of numerous setbacks. His life was conflicted even during the early part of his South American residence at Buenos Aires, and to a greater degree than earlier appreciated. While plenty of evidence of the spirit of improvement seemed to be present in the revolutionary city, political instability undid the greater part of any practical impact. The failed efforts to develop a botanical garden provide a key example. Following his long period of forced confinement in Paraguay, Bonpland always seemed to be struggling to overcome the consequences of earlier actions, about finances for example. Money borrowed before imprisonment in Paraguay still needed to be repaid following release. The financial basis of his work in South America showed important variations along time, but it was rarely on a sound footing. This is surely a key to his behavior. For a brief window in the 1830s his ambitions appeared to be falling into place, with a land grant for an ecologically diverse estancia and the greater portion of his parental inheritance and recouped pension funds all coming on stream around the same time.

This temporary good fortune was soon undone by the battle of Pago Largo. Following the unfavorable outcome of that political conflict to Bonpland's interests, he spent much of the 1840s confined to the South American interior, often engaged in semiclandestine political work. The final years of his life were also on a firmer basis as he regained access to French state pension funds, as part of France's extensive and deliberate outreach toward Latin America under the Second Empire.

None of the vicissitudes of South American life seem to have irreparably dented his optimism. Despite his often expressed—and realistic—fear of drowning while crossing a river during a winter swell, and the other numerous challenges of life in the regions he inhabited, most notably the loss of life associated with civil wars, Bonpland died from natural causes and at home. He never did succeed fully, however, in building his second Malmaison, in the sense of developing a stable center somewhere in South America for plant acclimatization. Nor did he realize his ambition of transporting his collections to Europe in person.

Bonpland remained hard at work until almost the end. The many annotations in his botanical registers seem to point to a work of synthesis still under way. In 1856, he had called before friends for four more years of life to complete his scientific work. However accurate he was in this forecast was of little consequence, of course, since he died in 1858, leaving extensive manuscripts where much was advanced but nothing truly finished. With

Bonpland dead, his difficult work could not easily continue, not least because the physical condition of the specimen material in his herbarium also wore the impact of his lifestyle. His collections had been his main capital. Like most collectors, he expended a great deal of worry over them, even to the point of hiding them during the periods of most heightened political insecurity. Most of his plant descriptions have still to attract close research scrutiny, which mirrors the fate of his extensive botanical manuscripts written in the field with Humboldt between 1799 and 1804.[2] Researchers have been slow to grasp that there are striking overlaps between these collections, including references from the earlier work in the southern South American research. This is reflective, perhaps, of the fact that Bonpland truly lived "a life in shadow." Other collections, including mineral specimens and insects, were folded into the general collections of the Paris natural history museum. Timing was not especially helpful for the long-term fate of his collecting, as with much else in his life. While Bonpland was forcibly confined to Paraguay, his compatriot d'Orbigny (treated by Darwin as a rival during his South American field research) took much of the prize of what was available from the Upper Plata.[3] In Bonpland's case, lines of communication with the Paris museum were broken more than once, even before he became a prisoner in Paraguay, thus leaving a legacy of mutual misunderstandings. Today, Bonpland's scientific work seems most interesting for its comparative dimensions and for the way he was prepared to revisit his conclusions drawn from earlier material in the light of new evidence. His willingness to sometimes cross out detailed descriptions (of the circumstances of crop production, for example) presents a record begging us to reflect carefully on the supposed accuracy of the historical and geographical knowledge offered to the world by European travelers.

The ambition for the Americas was never realized. Bonpland never found another patron to compare with the empress Joséphine. He certainly tried hard to find one. But this is an area where exploration is best seen less through heroics than through vulnerability. In South America, Bonpland developed a striking range of contacts with potential patrons that included statesmen such as Rivadavia, Ferré, Rivera, Urquiza and Pujol, both British and French merchants based at Buenos Aires, the Delessert merchant banking enterprise at Paris, French diplomats based at Buenos Aires, and several members of the landed elite from southernmost Brazil. All these relationships required time-consuming negotiation.

Bonpland's life was at the core of developments through an interesting period of transition. For example, when he arrived in South America, Brazil was still a colony and Uruguay was but a part of another. Considerable political consolidation occurred along the course of his South American career. He escaped the horrors of the Paraguayan War (1864–1870), but he knew the fall of Rosas would not mark an end to South American political instability.

Bonpland crossed important temporal boundaries. But more significant was his choice of locations. In particular, his actions on Brazilian soil have been slow to receive the scrutiny they deserve. The records relating to his life around the former Jesuit mission of São Borja, for example, offer much valuable historical material on the nature of social and economic interactions along this important international frontier, and in a region of uncommon geopolitical interest. Some of the small places he wrote about in detail would soon become staging points for the Paraguayan invasion of Brazil, South America's most important war since those associated with independence. In numerous ways, Bonpland provided a key thread to connect interests in southernmost Brazil with Corrientes and sometimes even with Paraguay (regarding political intelligence, commercial developments, and even the administration of ecclesiastical affairs). He reflects the general pattern identified by Glick, in which scientists in nineteenth-century Latin America—a tiny portion of the already small, educated minority—found it hard to resist becoming drawn into politics.[4]

Bonpland was also extremely interesting in the ways he crossed social boundaries, ranging from the *tertulias* of Buenos Aires to close involvement with indigenous labor on his rural properties. Transculturation currently informs many studies, boosted to great degree by Mary Louise Pratt's widely read study *Imperial Eyes*. Bonpland's is a very interesting life in this respect because it mainly concerned transplanting knowledge systems. The fame of the Avé-Lallemant interview, especially, with its image of Bonpland's very rustic home on the Estancia de Santa Ana, helped some to claim him as an example of a disinterested European savant who went native, part of his supposed "tragic fate" that still crops up in the literature.[5] This issue needs to be approached with greater care, however. His consumption patterns during visits to Montevideo during the 1850s provide overwhelming evidence that Bonpland retained many of the habits of a French bourgeois even in advanced age. The patent-leather boots, cashmere coats, and bottles of Sauternes and of Château Margaux present in his accounts were hardly part of the repertoire of most South American creole country dwellers. It is most unlikely that Avé-Lallemant understood much of what he was seeing at the time of his 1858 interviews. Bonpland seems to have been well aware of the limitations of his property and lifestyle. His estancia reflected the usual deleterious impact of a recent prolonged absence, compounded by the effects of locust invasion and of drought.

The challenge of the subtropics seems to have seized hold of Bonpland in the most tangible way during the journey with Humboldt. Along the remainder of his life, the appeal of nature took hold of him once again. It is unfortunate that we do not have much close description, including direct testimony, of how Bonpland lived in the interior of South America. Demersay and Gay are the best sources on this, in part since their accounts are products of extended interaction. However, they relate mainly to São Borja. There is nothing of similar caliber for Santa Ana. And the city of Corrientes remains lost from view, despite the key significance of Bonpland's many sojourns there. The records relating to his business with the Périchon family at Corrientes were probably a casualty of the early-twentieth-century decision to keep Bonpland's private records from public view.

Writing at a time close to Bonpland's death, Brunel argued that his subject left deep traces in the Americas.[6] In a material sense, this was not true. For example, he left only modest property to his descendants. A statue promised by the British community at Buenos Aires never materialized, nor did one that was decreed by the provincial government at Corrientes. It is difficult to dislodge the image of the intellectually inclined Brazilian emperor, Pedro II, rooting around São Borja in search of the remains of Bonpland's former home, as he did out of curiosity less than a decade after Bonpland last occupied it. The material condition of the town in general had greatly suffered from the recent Paraguayan invasion. But even prior to the invasion, nothing remained of Bonpland's simple house, merely some of his plantings, mainly orange trees.[7] Brunel argued that Bonpland was worthy of memory because of the level of his disinterested activities. He seemed to prefigure something almost Schweitzeresque. Juan Francisco Pérez Acosta perceptively reckoned that Bonpland took on the characteristics of a "superman" in his South American residence, more admirable in the circumstances of his Paraguayan captivity than he ever would have become in France.[8] Bonpland was sorely tested by his experiences in the Americas, but seems to have never given up. Juan Domínguez argued that Bonpland lived a life of placid resignation like an ancient philosopher.[9] These observations imply an overall impression that Bonpland was able to weather the challenges of life in the interior of South America. It is certainly the case that he gave much stimulus to other European immigrants.

Despite the interest that a variety of scholars have shown in Bonpland, modern writers have been slow to give him his due. Given the extraordinary range of his interests and contacts, it seems strange that an extended treatment has been so long in coming forward. No doubt, part of the explanation lies with the challenges of an archive divided between South America and Europe. The present book by no means ends the research challenge offered by Bonpland. The emphasis here has followed traditional geographical themes of land and life, concentrating on Bonpland's struggle to evaluate and to mobilize resources. But his career did not end there. Much room still exists for closer study of other themes. Prime candidates include his medical work, mainly undertaken in the South American interior, and his various involvements in the politics of the region. Extensive records survive for both of these themes. In addition, a critical edition of his extensive correspondence, something promised from Argentina in the early twentieth century, is still much to be desired.[10]

Felix Driver has reviewed the limited attention paid to fieldwork in comparison with other aspects of the history of geography.[11] Given the importance of fieldwork for understanding the development of the discipline, this situation is changing rapidly. Where Latin America is concerned, a recent burgeoning of the literature has been seen.[12] Thus far, however, scholars have tended to concentrate heavily on European travelers whose journeys resulted in extensive published writings. Humboldt and Darwin are the leading cases in point. Almost all the European travel accounts from the nineteenth century exist in Spanish or Portuguese translations, finding their way into the curricula of a great many South American university courses. The challenge remains, however, of dealing with the research findings of those who did a great deal of work but for various reasons (often early death) never saw their findings in print. Bonpland is only one example of important figures whose South American work deserves renewed scrutiny. It seems appropriate here to begin with the Swede Eberhard Munck af Rosenschöld, who worked as a naturalist in Paraguay between 1843 and 1869. Most of his extensive collections were lost to science.[13] The work of the Bavarians Spix and Martius in Brazil (1817–1820) is often compared with that of Humboldt in Spanish America. While Martius is heavily commemorated, especially in Brazil, the contributions of the zoologist Johann Baptist von Spix, have been largely forgotten.[14] The Austrian ornithologist Johann Natterer spent eighteen years traveling in Brazil, long enough that on his return to Vienna in the autumn of 1836 he was barely recognized. Despite the signal importance of Natterer's collections to the natural history and ethnographic museums at Vienna, Gabriele Mauthe observes that few have written of his labors.[15] Given the intense cultural cooperation between Germany and Brazil, it is difficult to understand why southern Brazilian academics (not a few of whom stem from German-Brazilian backgrounds) have not done more to assess the papers at Berlin of the naturalist Friedrich Sellow. These include his drawings of indigenous people and his plans of the former Jesuit missions in Rio Grande do Sul. There are also British explorers of South America whose contributions until very recently remained more elusive than their significance deserves. Here, Henry Walter Bates provides a strong example.[16]

. . .

Through extensive journeyings, Aimé Bonpland provided a clear channel for the diffusion of ideas about new forms of land use. He was a planter of seeds in both the literal and metaphorical senses, in a region where the audience interested in economic diversification was often tiny. Despite a consistent history of economic losses in South America, even in his old age Bonpland continued dreaming and scheming about agricultural development.

Bonpland had few peers as a field-worker. He was continuously experimenting. Nobody had more experience with the character (the botanical nature and the uses) of maté plants than he. Other strengths include his ability to learn from others; he recognized the concrete agricultural achievements of the Jesuits and saw the positive qualities of the Indians. In societies marked by increasing polarization between city and country, or elites and working folk, Bonpland was at ease with both. Following his generally unsuccessful residence at Buenos Aires, however, he had an emphatic preference for country dwelling.

While he did much that can be characterized as disinterested science, Bonpland also provides a clear example of how allegedly nonpolitical professionals can be readily drawn into political projects. Working for France became a more important theme of the last years of his life than previously recognized. While Hamy summarized Bonpland's South American achievements in his important biography by viewing them as strictly technical, of interest mainly to botanical specialists, nineteenth-century French official opinion saw things differently.[17] For Consul Maillefer in Montevideo, Bonpland raised himself above what he termed "the usual vanity of science" to offer much of truly practical value. He did not confine himself to arid classifications and purely technical descriptions. Moreover, he put the results of forty years of experience and observation from different parts of South America into the notes accompanying his shipments.[18] The force of Maillefer's argument will probably strike anyone reading Bonpland's still unpublished comments today. Thus the Nestor of botany was also a utilitarian, above all (perhaps today we could say a developmentalist). In pharmacy, medicine, and cultivation, allied with domestic, rural, and industrial economy, Bonpland drew on all fields of science.

The record of Bonpland's involvement with merinos extends almost a half-century over a vast canvas.[19] But while his interest was sustained, the practical fruits hardly seem worthy of his initiative. Bonpland's midcentury timing for merino promotion was astute. The wool business increased markedly in the early 1850s, becoming the predominant form of land use for a radius of 150–200 kilometers around the city of Buenos Aires.[20] But his choice of location to push his scheme went against him. While Bonpland made a sustained endeavor to breed merinos, he did not pursue that, or any other interest, in a single-minded manner. As the successful wool enclaves of Urquiza's Entre Ríos in the 1850s demonstrate, a critical mass of pioneers of shared interests was key. A wide range of personalities, many of them foreign and some of them known to Bonpland, went into sheep-breeding partnerships with Urquiza and prospered.[21] Sheep rearing concentrated on the pampas grasslands, and Bonpland—fixed on plant gathering—showed only a limited interest in these. Throughout his South American career he faced the major issue of how to balance the appeal of differing locations. Very little of what Bonpland had seen since 1817 compared with the botanical wealth of the equinoctial regions traveled earlier with Humboldt. In relative terms, however, the Serra of Rio Grande do Sul was a region of treasures for him, far more exciting than the grasslands of the Campanha. In all the years that Bonpland resided around São Borja, there is record of only a single instance of his botanizing in the Campanha proper. Botanical interests may well have deflected him from the very part of Rio Grande do Sul with economic potential for sheep, although even here, that potential only began to be realized toward the end of the century.[22]

Working with only intermittent access to European publications set limitations, which Bonpland recognized. A migratory life diffused his energies and reduced his potential impact. It is clear that politics more frequently hindered than helped his ambitions, but also that Bonpland's gift for detailed natural resource appraisal was not matched by an equal appreciation of the constraints of public policy. The ever-larger circle of acquaintanceship that came from moving around reflected a restless curiosity. It was perhaps also a conscious survival strategy in the extremely unsettled political context of the region and period. Just as he had not seen the botanical publication project for Humboldt through to the end, leading many to question his capacity for discipline, his major initiatives in South America remained unfinished. Only a few of his findings reached print in his own lifetime (and then mainly through the agency of others), despite publication offers reaching South America from such distinguished colleagues as Augustin Pyrame de Candolle and William Jackson Hooker. His findings on Paraguayan tea were of sufficient importance that they eventually formed the core material for a series of nineteenth-century British, French, and German publications.[23] As with his earlier work for Humboldt, the quality of his manuscript research material was usually extremely high.

Bonpland was ahead of his time in his pioneering of agricultural practices and plans. His interest in cultivating maté in plantations was replicated only in the 1890s, but then on a major scale in Argentina, Paraguay, and southern Brazil. Bonpland's attitudes to forest resources were even more farsighted, coming close to the core of the current notion of sustainable development. A strong emphasis on the local development of natural resources in a sustainable way was always present in his writing. Bonpland's concern for the protection of natural resources was an innovation in itself in the southern South America of the middle nineteenth century. Although his pleas fell on mainly deaf ears, they would receive a wider hearing today. In this way, Bonpland was a prophet and a visionary.

Reference Matter

Abbreviations

AAB	Archivo Aimé Bonpland, Buenos Aires
AHRGS	Arquivo Histórico do Rio Grande do Sul
AN	Archives Nationales de France
ANA	Archivo Nacional de Asunción
AvHF	Alexander-von-Humboldt-Forschungsstelle
BBAW	Berlin-Brandenburgische Akademie der Wissenschaften
BMLR	Bibliothèque Municipale de La Rochelle
BN	Biblioteca Nacional, Rio de Janeiro (*seção de manuscritos*)
DHRE	*Documentos para la historia de la República Entrerriana*
LCGE	*Londres, cuartel general europeo de la emancipación americana*
MFJAD	Museo de Farmacobotánica "Juan Aníbal Domínguez," Facultad de Farmacia y Bioquímica, Universidad de Buenos Aires
MHN	Muséum d'Histoire Naturelle, Paris
MRE	Ministère des Relations Extérieures, Paris
NYBG	LuEsther T. Mertz Library of the New York Botanical Garden, Bronx, New York
PRO	Public Record Office, London

Notes

Introduction

1. Sarton, "Aimé Bonpland (1773–1858)," pp. 394, 395–96.
2. Stoddart, *On Geography*, p. 143.
3. Barreto, *Bibliografia sul-riograndense*, 1:176.
4. Pratt developed this concept in her 1992 book *Imperial Eyes: Studies in Travel Writing and Transculturation*.
5. Captain Allègre, Bonpland's nephew, told Bonpland in 1851 that his name was still inscribed on the registers of the naval medical school at Rochefort, where it was conserved with considerable pride. Allègre was trying to persuade Bonpland, the inheritor of his elder brother's herbarium, books, and manuscripts, to leave these to the natural history section of that institution. He was not successful. Bonpland preferred to leave them to a young relative (Camille Marquet) who was studying medicine, leaving room for Bonpland to make further dispositions in the probable case that he visited France. His reply is interesting:

> Bonpland's herbarium [meaning the property of Michel-Simon Goujaud-Bonpland] is not composed solely of plants from our country [France] but also from others. Before my departure for America under the Directory, after my return, and at several other times, I sent my brother a good number of plants that were supposed to serve us usefully someday. These plants were also accompanied by some books from my library along with a lot of papers, composed for the most of extracts I had made during my classes at Paris. I should say something more to you. After my exit from Paraguay, [Goujaud-] Bonpland and I thought of reuniting at Paris and of occupying ourselves seriously with publications in common. It is true, however, that [he] did not reply to a very detailed letter I wrote him on this subject.

The material stemming from both the Bonpland brothers appears to have eventually found its way into the collections of the Muséum d'Histoire Naturelle de La Rochelle. See the letters from Captain Allègre to Bonpland, Chauvins, 29 May 1851, and Bonpland to Allègre, Montevideo, 10 Sept. 1853; AAB, *carpeta* [docket] 6, MFJAD.

6. Two copies of surviving family letters from Bonpland to his sister Olive are written from Rochefort on 30 July and 20 Oct. 1794; AJ^{15}, 570, AN.
7. See Brunel, *Biographie d'Aimé Bonpland* (1871), pp. 17–18. Brunel is in error on the timing when Bonpland left Paris for La Rochelle.

8. Ibid., p. 5 of the 1859 edition.
9. Sarton, "Aimé Bonpland (1773–1858)," p. 387.
10. This is readily established from examination of the manuscripts at the Muséum d'Histoire Naturelle at Paris. See Margot Faak's edition of a portion of Humboldt's diaries (Humboldt, *Reise durch Venezuela*), p. 473n189. The proportion of the botanical work Humboldt claimed for himself varies considerably in his American correspondence.
11. See Botting, *Humboldt and the Cosmos*, p. 67.
12. See Wilson's introduction to Humboldt, *Personal Narrative*, p. li.
13. See Margot Faak and Christian Suckow's interesting comments on how the style of Humboldt's diaries varies from his published travel accounts in their introduction to Humboldt, *Reise durch Venezuela*, pp. 21–22. Accounts of the near-accident include ibid., p. 258, where Bonpland's original French words appear in the transcription of Humboldt's German diary, and Humboldt, *Personal Narrative*, p. 192.
14. Sarton, "Aimé Bonpland (1773–1858)," p. 388.
15. See, for example, the discussions of Bonpland in Humboldt to the French chemist Antoine François Fourcroy, La Guaira, 25 Jan. 1800; to his brother Wilhelm, Cumaná, 17 Oct. 1800; and to Thomas Jefferson, Philadelphia, 24 May 1804, printed in Humboldt, *Briefe aus Amerika*, pp. 76, 106–7, 292. This edition of Humboldt's letters from the Americas, edited by Ulrike Moheit, is a painstaking piece of research. It supersedes all the earlier versions.
16. See the collection of Humboldt's surviving letters to Bonpland, published in facsimile in Trabajos del Instituto de Botánica y Farmacología, *Lettres inédites de Alexandre de Humboldt*; these have been partially transcribed in German translation in Schulz, *Bonpland . . . Humboldts Begleiter*.
17. Hossard, *Humboldt et Bonpland: Correspondance*, p. 13.
18. Sarton, "Aimé Bonpland (1773–1858)," p. 395.
19. See Humboldt to Karl Ludwig Willdenow, Havana, 21 Feb. 1801, printed in Humboldt, *Briefe aus Amerika*, esp. p. 124.
20. Hossard, *Humboldt et Bonpland*, p. 60.
21. Humboldt to Willdenow, 17 June 1810, quoted in Leitner, "Botanical Results," p. 4; the same letter carries the variant date of 17 May 1810 in Fiedler and Leitner, *Alexander von Humboldts Schriften*, p. 251.
22. See Leitner, "Botanical Results," p. 6.
23. Sachs, *Humboldt Current*, p. 65; see also the section "Outing Humboldt" in Rupke, *Humboldt: A Metabiography*, pp. 196–202.
24. Arnold, *Problem of Nature*, p. 146.
25. Outram, "On Being Perseus," p. 285.
26. See the letter from Bonpland to M. and Madame Gallocheau, Paris, 12 Nov. 1804, printed in Hamy, *Aimé Bonpland, médecin et naturaliste*, esp. p. 13.
27. Along the journey from his home at São Borja to Santa Cruz, Bonpland claimed to have found two hundred plant species that were new to him, including two new varieties of yerba maté. In making his judgment about the Paraná pine

(*Araucaria brasiliensis*), he referred back to a different kind of araucaria tree bought by the Empress Joséphine in 1810. See the letters from Bonpland to Raffeneau-Delile, Porto Alegre, 10 June 1849, and Rio Pardo, 8 Nov. 1849; AJ[15], 570, AN. Hamy published only an interesting fragment from the June letter in his *Aimé Bonpland, médecin et naturaliste*, p. 149.

28. Léopold Vivielle was a retired rear admiral from the French navy. At age eighteen, he met with Bonpland at Montevideo in 1850–51. His brief reminiscences of this are in the French national archives, written from Sainte Marguerite par la Garde (Var), 10 July 1907; AJ[15], 570, AN. Part of Vivielle's mission to South America had included the ambition of leading his relative Bonpland back to France. See also Hamy, *Aimé Bonpland, médecin et naturaliste*, p. 160.

29. See the letter from the comte de Brossard to Mr. Lefebre de Bécour, Asunción, 16 Aug. 1858; F[17], 3974, fol. 31, AN. Written from a distance, Brossard's letter is full of speculation about the contents of Bonpland's papers and their whereabouts.

30. Pujol wrote to Gay on 22 June 1858, informing him that he had kept letters from Bonpland in which Bonpland ceded to the province of Corrientes "all his manuscripts, collections, and other scientific objects." See Gay's ms. "Le naturaliste Mr. Aimé Bonpland," p. 6; F[17], 3974, AN.

31. See the letter from the administrators of the Muséum d'Histoire Naturelle (the director, Michel Eugène Chevreul (1786–1889), the secretary, Joseph Decaisne (1807–1882), and the treasurer, Adolphe Théodore Brongniart (1801–1876) to the ministry of public instruction, Paris, 9 Oct. 1858; F[17], 3974, fol. 40, AN.

32. Jean-Pierre Gay to the minister of the interior, Paris, 15 Aug. 1859; F[17], 3974, fol. 48, AN. This letter is followed by Gay's ms., "Le naturaliste Mr. Aimé Bonpland"; F[17], 3974, AN. The first 16 pages were signed off on 29 Aug. 1858 from São Borja. However, the manuscript also contains a long postscript written from the same place on 3 August 1859. It is mainly concerned with the fate of Bonpland's collections.

33. Gay's ms., "Le naturaliste Mr. Aimé Bonpland," p. 7; F[17], 3974, AN.

34. The inventory of the books belonging to Bonpland is in the French archives; F[17], 3974, fol. 10, AN.

35. See the report made by the commission of inventory, for which the key figure was Jules Desnoyers, to the ministry of public instruction, Paris, 21 July 1860; F[17], 3974, fol. 6, AN.

36. See Holmberg, "Correspondencia inédita de Humboldt y Bonpland."

37. Mary Louise Pratt's brief account of Bonpland's southern South American career provides a good example of these pitfalls, partly by exaggerating the role of Paraguay in Bonpland's life (Pratt, *Imperial Eyes*, p. 240n12).

38. The reader seeking a brief account in English can do no better than to begin by reading Jason Wilson's interesting summary. He usefully punctures the myth perpetuated by historical novelists that Bonpland was murdered. While I agree with Wilson that Bonpland wrote very little about his inner life while resident in South America, it is not the case that he wrote "nothing about himself" (Wilson, "Strange Fate of Aimé Bonpland," pp. 47–48).

39. From Argentina, see, for example, Alberto Palcos, "La segunda vida de Amado Bonpland: su existencia americana," *La Prensa* (19 Jan. 1941) and "Amado Bonpland en América: centenario de su muerte," *La Prensa* (4 May 1958); Daniel Hammerly Dupuy, "Amado Bonpland, naturalista y democrata de América," *La Nación* (11 May 1958). For Brazil, see Virgilio Correa Filho, "As aventuras de Bonpland no vale platino," *Jornal do Commercio* (22 and 29 Jan. 1956).

40. García Márquez, *General in His Labyrinth*, p. 130. The portrait of Humboldt in this book is less flattering.

41. Roa Bastos, *I, the Supreme*, esp. pp. 257–69, 298–300; Wilson, *Traveller's Literary Companion to South and Central America*, p. 351.

42. Gasulla, *El solitario de Santa Ana*. I find it difficult to see Bonpland as the hermit that Gasulla's title implies. Some of the documents this author used in the preparation of his book are now in Berlin at BBAW.

43. Foucault, *Le pêcheur d'orchidées*.

44. Kehlmann, *Measuring the World*.

45. Angelis, "Noticia biográfica de Mr. Bonpland." On the publication history of this biography, including subsequent editions, see Sabor, *Pedro de Angelis*, esp. pp. 138–39, 356–60.

46. See Demersay, *Histoire physique, économique et politique du Paraguay*, esp. 1:xxi, xxv.

47. Hamy, *Lettres américaines d'Alexandre de Humboldt*. Hamy became a member of the central commission of the Société de Géographie at Paris in 1873. Anthropology was the main focus of his work for many years; however, his interests broadened along time to include what today could be understood as historical geography, at least in the forms that this is studied in the Anglophone world. In 1900, Hamy presided over the meeting of the Congrès International des Américanistes at Paris. When passing the torch at the Stuttgart meeting of 1904, he wisely could not resist the appeal of celebrating the centenary of the return of Humboldt and Bonpland to Europe (Hamy, *Centenaire du retour en Europe*), which soon led to further work on these figures. Henri Cordier, who wrote several brief pieces on Hamy following his death, made the mild complaint that his subject dispersed his research efforts too much. There was some element of competition between Hamy and Cordier: in 1882, Hamy founded the *Revue d'Ethnographie* and Cordier founded the *Revue d'Extrême-Orient*. Remembered mainly as a distinguished sinologist, there is a fine portrait of Cordier in the collections of the Musée d'Orsay, painted in 1883 by the Impressionist Gustave Caillebotte. On Hamy, see Chonchol and Martinière, *L'Amérique latine et le latino-américanisme en France*, p. 95; Cordier, "Le docteur E.-T. Hamy" and "Le Dr. Hamy: historien et géographe," pp. 143–44, 125–47.

48. A letter written by Estanislao S. Zeballos from Buenos Aires to Hamy on 28 Mar. 1905 reveals how the latter clearly struggled with some of the pitfalls of long-distance research. At the time Zeballos wrote, he claimed that knowledge of Bonpland's circumstances in Argentina was vague: "As to the monument decreed by the government of Corrientes, this has not yet been raised. I attribute this omission to the limited knowledge there is in the country about the contributions of this intel-

lectual." AJ[15], 570, fol. 130, AN. This situation would begin to change a little with the reappearance of many of his manuscripts in the following year.

49. For example, Pierre Duviols, in a 1993 publication, presents the letter from Bonpland to Humboldt written from Buenos Aires on 1 June 1832 as something new ("A propos d'une lettre d'Aimé Bonpland," esp. pp. 131, 139–42), yet Hamy had already published this in his 1906 study (*Aimé Bonpland, médecin et naturaliste*, pp. 84–87), a book readily available in France. Both Hamy and Duviols made errors in transcription, but the earlier version is greatly the more reliable.

50. Cordier, *Papiers inédits du naturaliste Bonpland*.

51. Ibid., p. 2.

52. "Unbekannte Humboldt-Briefe," *Berliner Tageblatt* (2 Mar. 1906). There is a copy of this newspaper article in the French archives; AJ[15], 570, AN.

53. Trabajos del Instituto de Botánica y Farmacología, *Lettres inédites d'Alexander von Humboldt*. In the note to the reader in this publication, Domínguez announced the ambition to publish not merely folio facsimiles, but also six volumes in smaller format dealing with scientific correspondence and politics, travels, and notes on agriculture. This project remains to be completed.

54. Ibid., *Journal de botanique*. This appeared in 1924, a decade later than the Humboldt facsimile letters. In the prologue, Juan Domínguez hinted at the imminent publication of the travel accounts "full of interesting observations as much from the medical and biological account as from the geographical and ethnographical ones."

55. Domínguez, *Urquiza y Bonpland: antecedentes historicos*.

56. Sarton, "Aimé Bonpland (1773–1858)," p. 391.

57. Ibid., p. 393.

58. Beck, *Alexander von Humboldt*, 2:62, 74.

59. Schulz, *Bonpland . . . Humboldts Begleiter*.

60. For example, Alfredo Boccia Romañach's study, *Amado Bonpland: carai arandu*, is mainly devoted to Paraguay.

61. Given the success in recent years of finding new material written by Humboldt, including in European collections, it would be foolish to rule out the prospect of the same where Bonpland is concerned. For example, an 1836 publication by the popularizing French historian Amans Alexis Monteil (1769–1850), which dealt with "De la géographie et des géographes," described a manuscript of Bonpland's accounting for the journey of 1799 across Spain in the company of Humboldt (Monteil, *Traité de matériaux des manuscrits de divers genres d'histoire*, 1:357–61). Where this resides today is unclear. When writing his account, Monteil showed his awareness that Bonpland was currently resident at Buenos Aires. He also maintained that he had a way for his manuscript account to reach the latter, in order to make him aware that he was the author of "literary monuments."

62. See the collections by Laissus, ed., *Naturalistes français en Amérique du Sud*, and Bertrand and Vidal, eds., *À la redécouverte des Amériques*. Among studies of French individuals, see Miran, *Un français au Chili*, and Thésée, *Auguste Plée*.

63. See, for example, the exhibition catalog Kunst- und Ausstellungshalle der Bundesrepublik Deutschland, *Alexander von Humboldt: Netzwerke des Wissens*. Haus der Kulturen der Welt, Berlin, 1999.

64. Sarton, "Aimé Bonpland (1773–1858)," p. 387.

65. See Galeano, *Faces and Masks*, pp. 84–85, 87–94, 135–36, 182.

66. On the involved politics of France in the Plata, see Hermann, *France en Amérique latine*; Morgan, "French Ideas of a Civilizing Mission" and "French Policy in Spanish America."

67. Morgan, "French Ideas of a Civilizing Mission," p. 389.

68. Morgan, "French Policy in Spanish America," p. 315.

69. McLean, *War, Diplomacy and Informal Empire*, p. 176.

70. Hermann, *France en Amérique latine*, pp. 228–29, 259.

71. Not many years following Bonpland's death, the new level of French imperialism in Mexico made room for science to the point that specimen material collected by Bonpland and Humboldt at the start of the century came under renewed scrutiny. Dunbar, "French Scientific Mission to Mexico," p. 237.

72. See the study by Dean, *With Broadax and Fire*.

73. Ottone, "Bonpland and Paleontology," p. 163.

Chapter One

1. Sir Joseph Banks, Soho Square, London, to Bonpland in France, 7 Apr. 1810; AAB, carpeta 2, MFJAD.

2. Bonpland to Pedro Serrano, printed in Trabajos del Instituto Nacional de Botánica y Farmacología "Julio A. Roca," Facultad de Ciencias Médicas de Buenos Aires, ser. 2, no. 2, *LCGE*, n.p.

3. Sir Joseph Banks to Bonpland, Soho Square, London, 7 Apr. 1810; AAB, carpeta 2, MFJAD.

4. Bonpland to Goujaud-Bonpland, 6 July 1814, printed in Hamy, *Aimé Bonpland, médecin et naturaliste*, p. 63.

5. Humboldt and Bonpland, *Plantes équinoxiales* and *Monographie des mélastomacées*; Bonpland, *Description des plantes rares*.

6. Bonpland to Goujaud-Bonpland, 6 July 1814, printed in Hamy, *Aimé Bonpland, médecin et naturaliste*, pp. 63–64. See also Bonpland's letter from Malmaison to his sister Olive Gallocheau on the same date, printed in ibid., pp. 64–65. Bonpland was hit hard by Joséphine's unexpected death. He was working to draw his finances into order and thought it probable that he would throw all his available resources into landownership in the Americas. There is a sense that he found his life in Europe too measured ("mon existence est toute calculée").

7. Goujaud-Bonpland to Bonpland, La Rochelle, 14 July 1814; AAB, carpeta 6, MFJAD. Is the Bastille Day date merely a coincidence? Michel-Simon Goujaud-Bonpland's letters are revealing on aspects of Aimé's life, his circumstances of work and of publication, family property issues, and longer-term plans. The fact that he signed himself off more formally is in itself indicative of his character in relation to his younger brother.

8. Bonpland to Olive Gallocheau, Paris, 6 June 1815, printed in Hamy, *Aimé Bonpland, médecin et naturaliste*, p. 69.
9. Bonpland to Pierre-Barthélémy-Amable-Honoré Gallocheau, Paris, 1 Apr. 1816, printed in ibid., p. 71. Some brief biographical details on Gallocheau also appear on p. 9.
10. Bonpland to Olive Gallocheau, Paris, 1 Apr. 1816, printed in ibid., pp. 71–73.
11. See Karen Racine's interesting study, "Community of Purpose."
12. Bonpland to Pedro Serrano about the emancipation of the Americas, printed in *LCGE*.
13. See, for example, those written in 1815 by Servando Teresa de Mier [José Servando Teresa de Mier Noriega y Guerra (1763–1827)], published in facsimile in ibid. Mier made an unsuccessful attempt to sail from Portsmouth to Buenos Aires in 1815. Among his other tasks, he promised to send notes on New Granada to Humboldt. A Dominican friar, orator, revolutionary for independence from Spain, and politician, there is an extensive literature on this polymath, especially in connection with the roots of Mexican nationalism. See, as a beginning, Mier (Noriega y Guerra), *Memoirs of Fray Servando Teresa de Mier*.
14. Vicente Pazos to Bonpland, London, 9 Sept. 1814, printed in facsimile in *LCGE*. Vicente Pazos Silva (1779–1853), more commonly known as Pazos Kanki, was of Aymara descent and came from what is today Bolivia. He had an important career editing newspapers of liberal persuasion at Buenos Aires and much more. See Bowman, *Vicente Pazos Kanki*.
15. Francisco Antonio Zea to Bonpland, London, 4 Mar. 1815, printed in facsimile in *LCGE*. There is excellent material on the fate of the Botanical Expedition around this time in Glick, "Science and Independence in Latin America," esp. p. 328.
16. See Zea to Bonpland, London, 25 Feb. and 4 Mar. 1815, letters printed in facsimile in *LCGE*.
17. Manuel Palacio to Bonpland, London, 31 Aug. 1815, in ibid. Manuel Palacio Fajardo (1784–1819) studied medicine and law at Bogotá. He was sent on a diplomatic mission to Europe, seeking help for the revolution, including from Napoleon. Palacio was close to the Bonpland family. He sent Aimé Bonpland reports on his stepdaughter Emma during the period she was living in London.
18. See Gallo, "Rivadavia y los ingleses."
19. Humphreys, *Liberation in South America*, p. 62.
20. See Piccirilli, *Rivadavia y su tiempo*, 3:92–93.
21. Bonpland told his sister that he could envisage no life better than owning a large agricultural estate in France. See Bonpland to Olive Gallocheau, Malmaison, 6 July 1814, and Paris, 1 Apr. 1816, printed in Hamy, *Aimé Bonpland, médecin et naturaliste*, pp. 65, 71.
22. Bonpland to Humboldt, Le Havre, 19 Nov. 1816, printed in ibid., p. 77.

23. Bonpland to François Delessert, Montevideo, 30 Aug. 1850; AAB, carpeta 4, MFJAD.

24. Bonpland to Goujaud-Bonpland, 6 July 1814, printed in Hamy, *Aimé Bonpland, médecin et naturaliste*, p. 63.

25. Bonpland met his wife, born Adeline-Anne-Marguerite Delahaye, through Joséphine at Malmaison. She was not a widow, as Sarton asserted ("Aimé Bonpland, 1773–1858," p. 389), but a married woman with a daughter, Emma. Rejected by Bonpland's relatives at La Rochelle, Adeline and Emma lived a semiclandestine life in London for a spell, in the midst of the South American revolutionaries there, while waiting for her divorce to become official. When Hamy prepared his study of Bonpland, knowledge of Adeline was so thin that a leading Argentine intellectual questioned whether she had ever resided in Argentina. See Estanislao S. Zeballos to Pompeyo Bonpland, Buenos Aires, 28 Mar. 1905; AJ^{15}, 570, fol. 130, AN. Knowledge of Bonpland's family circumstances has improved through Nicolas Hossard's recent study (*Bonpland . . . explorateur en Amérique du Sud*, esp. pp. 40, 45, 171–77).

26. In 1812, Aimé was told that the family investments had lost a third of their value since just before the French Revolution (their value dropped from 120,000 to 90,000 francs). At least some of the family money was invested in the Caribbean, since in 1815 Michel-Simon Bonpland noted that the settlement of at least one debt depended on revenues coming from Saint Domingue (Haiti). He also tried to ascertain Aimé's intentions with regard to property, noting, for example, that a small estate at Périgny, nearby La Rochelle, had been in family hands for over 150 years. Taking a conservative view, he recommended against selling it, thinking that his brother might one day be comfortable in finding a future home there. In the Goujaud-Bonpland correspondence, see especially the letters to Bonpland of 12 May 1812, 20 Nov. 1814, and 1 Apr. 1815; AAB, carpeta 6, MFJAD. The Bonpland family still owned the house at Périgny after Michel-Simon's death in 1850. Although unoccupied, Michel-Simon's collections were kept here. Those collections also included plants, books, and papers originating from Aimé Bonpland.

27. Goujaud-Bonpland to Bonpland, La Rochelle, 24 Apr. 1815; AAB, carpeta 6, MFJAD. Bonpland received the larger and final portion in December 1836.

28. The evidence of this discrepancy lies in the Beauharnais papers at Princeton University. See Jouanin, "Bonpland," pp. 57–58.

29. Humphreys, *Liberation in South America*, p. 60.

30. See Bonpland's review of the contents of gardens at Malmaison and Navarre made in a letter to his close friend Raffeneau-Delile, Malmaison, 7 Mar. 1814, printed in Hamy, *Aimé Bonpland, médecin et naturaliste*, pp. 60–62.

31. *La Crónica Argentina*, 1 Feb. 1817, quoted in Domínguez, *Bonpland . . . en la República Argentina*, p. 14.

32. Ibid.

33. Ibid.

34. *La Crónica Argentina*, 5 Feb. 1817, quoted in Domínguez, *Bonpland . . . en la República Argentina*, p. 15.

35. Parish, *Buenos Aires and the . . . Plata*, p. 18. By contrast, Henry Brackenridge thought that Buenos Aires wore a "gloomy aspect." Compared with Philadelphia or New York, he considered it "a vast mass of bricks piled up without taste, elegance, or variety" (Brackenridge, *Voyage to South America*, 1:277). Brackenridge provided a useful description of the city and its immediate environs.

36. Parish, *Buenos Aires and the . . . Plata*, p. 36.

37. Population taken from Kirchheimer, "Bonpland et la conspiration française," p. 124. Brackenridge gives a population of seventy thousand for the city and its vicinity (*Voyage to South America*, 1:303).

38. Among the leaders of the British community stood the Dickson family, who rented a "very pretty villa" on the northern side of Buenos Aires. When the Robertsons published their letters, George Frederick Dickson was serving as the consul general for the Río de la Plata in Britain, resident in Regent's Park (Robertson and Robertson, *Letters on South America*, 3:115, 118).

39. Ibid., p. 121.

40. Robertson and Robertson, *Francia's Reign of Terror*, 2:78. The other foreign family was that of the merchant Zimmerman, somebody else known to Bonpland.

41. María Sáenz Quesada asserts that Bonpland served as a teacher of piano and of drawing to Mariquita Sánchez's children, but his wife Adeline is a stronger candidate for this role. Mendeville arrived at Buenos Aires from France in 1818. He became the French consular agent there c. 1826 (Sáenz Quesada, *Mariquita Sánchez*, esp. pp. 75, 98–99, 263).

42. See Shumway on the type of society around Rivadavia, *Invention of Argentina*, pp. 87–88.

43. Vicente Fidel López, *Historia de la República Argentina*, 9:30. See also Shumway, *Invention of Argentina*, p. 86.

44. Un inglés, *Cinco años en Buenos Aires*, p. 71. An 1819 French report commented that there were some fairly solid French merchant houses in the Plata, but most were not well established. Corrientes was an area of particular interest to the French, where the horse oil business was at an experimental stage. Captain Drouault pointed out that the British had not yet penetrated the interior regions much. They were not liked, he claimed, in Paraguay: "I do not think they are in any part; everybody recognizes their egoistical principles." On the other hand, the report conceded that British commerce was greatly helped by the resources of the South Atlantic squadron. Captain Drouault, "Rapport sur Buenos-Ayres et la Plata, 1819" and "Mémoires et documents, Amérique," vol. 29, MRE.

45. See ms. 203, MHN. This comprises Bonpland's botanical registers for the period 1817–1821.

46. Ibid. See entry no. 23, "Cannabis sativa."

47. Ibid. See entry no. 36, "asparagus officinalis?"

48. See folder no. 27 in ms. 215, MHN.

49. Extensive records of seed exchanges survive, listing species, dates, and recipients, in ms. 214, MHN.

50. Henry Brackenridge noted Bonpland's property was "about two miles from town" (*Voyage to South America*, 2:19).

51. The matter is reviewed in Ruiz Moreno, Risolía, and d'Onofrio, *Bonpland: aportaciones . . . sobre su actividad científica*, esp. pp. 19–20.

52. Based on observations made in 1818, Brackenridge infers that instability had been the only thing stopping Bonpland from already ascending the Paraná on a research trip (*Voyage to South America*, 1:242).

53. By the early 1820s, the public library at Buenos Aires held a collection of twenty-two thousand volumes, including some particularly valuable works. Le contre amiral Rosamel, "Notes sur Buénos Ayres et la Bande Orientale de la Plata," A bord de la *Marie Thérèse* en rade de Montevideo, 3 July 1824; Mémoires et documents, Amérique du sud—1823 to 1836, vol. 32, fol. 116 verso, MRE.

54. Piccirilli, *Rivadavia y su tiempo*, 3:94.

55. Among his many intellectual contributions, Larrañaga was a pioneer in the use of Linnaean methods in the study of the botany of southern South America, using a version of Linnaeus published at Leipzig in the period 1788–1793. It seems appropriate that the Catholic University of Uruguay is today named after him.

56. See Victor Pérez Petit's essay on Larrañaga in his *En la Atenas del Plata*, p. 31. For a recent evaluation, see Anastasía, *Larrañaga: su oración inaugural de la Biblioteca Pública*. Larrañaga was involved in an anticolonial project. He took the foundation of the national library in 1816 as an affirmation of American capacity, where the indigenous, the creole, and the universal combined in a distinctive system. The library was seen as the first truly national initiative in Uruguayan culture. In his speech on the occasion of its inauguration, Larrañaga insisted the young should learn languages, including the vernacular indigenous ones. He observed that although what became Uruguay comprised a small territory, it contained no less than six indigenous languages.

57. Castellanos, "Biblioteca científica del Padre Larrañaga," pp. 607–8.

58. See Bonpland to Larrañaga, Buenos Aires, 2 Apr. 1818, quoted in ibid., pp. 609–10.

59. Ibid., p. 611.

60. Although Grigera's manual appeared in editions of 1819, 1831, 1854, and 1856, it is today a work of extreme rarity. I have not yet seen a copy.

61. Hammerly Dupuy, "Bonpland y la conspiración de Carrera," p. 90.

62. William Baldwin's background, including his supply of material for Stephen Elliott's *Sketch of the Botany of South Carolina and Georgia*, is surveyed in Rasmussen, "Diplomats and Plant Collectors," esp. pp. 24–25.

63. Rasmussen, "Diplomats and Plant Collectors," p. 22.

64. Asa Gray to Darlington, New York, 27 Apr. 1841, printed in Darlington, *Reliquiae Baldwinianae*, p. xii.

65. Baldwin to Darlington, Buenos Aires, 3 Mar. 1818, printed in ibid., p. 263.

66. Brackenridge, *Voyage to South America*, 1:299.

67. William Baldwin journals, 4 Mar. 1818; NYBG. See also Brackenridge, *Voyage to South America*, esp. 1:274.

68. Baldwin journals, 6 Mar. 1818; NYBG.

69. The situation of M. Bonpland, I understand, is not such as to enable him to devote his whole attention to botany. . . . When I saw him, he was occupied in planning a garden upon a large scale, in which it was his intention to introduce every thing useful from Europe that would be likely to prove a source of profit to himself, and a benefit to his adopted country. But, he has lost none of his zeal for botany and calculates on being so situated as to be able to devote much of his attention to it.

The number of *species* about Buenos Ayres are not so numerous as in the Brazils, but they are less known. Almost everything was new to M. Bonpland.

Baldwin to Stephen Elliott, Wilmington, Delaware, 7 Aug. 1818; Baldwin papers, NYBG.

70. Rasmussen, "Diplomats and Plant Collectors," p. 27.

71. Brackenridge, *Voyage to South America*, 2:95.

72. See Rasmussen, "Diplomats and Plant Collectors," p. 27.

73. Ibid.

74. See the postscript in the letter from Baldwin to a Mr. Atkins at Buenos Aires, 10 Apr. 1818; NYBG. This letter also reveals that Baldwin had promised Bonpland specimens from his melastomes gathered at Rio de Janeiro. He did not deliver on this earlier promise, finding them "in such a bad state of preservation that I am ashamed to send them."

75. See the Baldwin journal, 26 Apr. 1818; NYBG. This letter, the exact contents of which are unknown, is given the wrong year in Joseph and Nesta Dunn Ewans's Baldwin chronology. What reads 20 April 1815 should be 1818. See Darlington, *Reliquiae Baldwinianae*, pp. v–vi, xvii. Baldwin did not find the chance to meet with Bolívar during his return voyage to the United States.

76. See Baldwin, Wilmington, Delaware to Darlington, 9 Oct. 1818, and to Bonpland, 8 Oct. 1818. Baldwin collected potato tubers around Montevideo and Maldonado. He asked the following of Bonpland: "Be so good as to inform me whither you have ever met with this valuable plant in its wild state, in any part of South America, or north of the Equator? The tubers which I brought home were so young and so small that they all perished." These letters are printed in Darlington, *Reliquiae Baldwinianae*, pp. v–vi, 285–86.

77. Rasmussen, "Diplomats and Plant Collectors," pp. 30–31.

78. Humboldt to Bonpland, Paris, 28 Jan. 1818, quoted in Bruhns, ed., *Life of Alexander von Humboldt*, pp. 405–6 and printed in full in the original French in Hamy, *Aimé Bonpland, médecin et naturaliste*, pp. 228–30.

79. See Ruiz Moreno, Risolía, and d'Onofrio, *Bonpland: aportaciones . . . sobre su actividad científica*, p. 31.

80. In Humboldt and Bonpland, *Plantes équinoxiales*, the 144 plates were printed in black and white. The seventeen fascicles comprising this study were mainly Bonpland's work. In their *Monographie des mélastomacées*, part of which was prepared by Bonpland, the 120 engravings were prepared in color. On the complicated publishing history of the above works, see Fiedler and Leitner, *Alexander von Humboldts Schriften*, esp. pp. 250–72.

81. See Bonpland's budget for the publication project, which was presented in

French to the congress, Buenos Aires, 10 June 1818, reproduced in Furlong, "Nuevos datos sobre Bonpland en Buenos Aires," pp. 163–64.

82. Ruiz Moreno, Risolía, and d'Onofrio, *Bonpland: aportaciones . . . sobre su actividad científica*, p. 34.

83. Domínguez, *Bonpland . . . en la República Argentina*, p. 17.

84. The Frenchman Pierre Benoit arrived at Buenos Aires in 1818. He was designated to help Bonpland on official travel business on 16 July 1819. See Ruiz Moreno, Risolía, and d'Onofrio, *Bonpland: aportaciones . . . sobre su actividad científica*, p. 74. The biographical details for Benoit, who is buried in the cemetery at Recoleta in Buenos Aires, remain very sketchy. Until recently, some parties in Argentina made the case that he was Louis XVII, following the thesis that he escaped as a boy from imprisonment in Paris and took on an assumed identity. Manuel Mújica Laínez treated this theme in his historical fiction (*Misterioso Buenos Aires*, pp. 223–28). In 2000, DNA testing in France on parts of Benoit's remains ended this claim. See "Pierre Benoit, el (falso) Luis XVII que vivió en la Argentina," *Clarín* (20 Apr. 2000).

85. Bonpland to Raffeneau-Delile, Santa Ana, 1821, printed in Hamy, *Aimé Bonpland, médecin et naturaliste*, pp. 79–80. This letter to a close friend in France was written from a former Jesuit mission on the borders of Paraguay. Alire Raffeneau-Delile (1778–1850) is remembered mainly as the author of the *Flore d'Egypte* (Paris, 1824). After his travels with Napoleon's forces to Egypt, and a spell as a representative of the French government to the United States, he spent many years occupying the chair in botany in the Faculty of Medicine at Montpellier.

86. See Wilson, "Strange Fate of Aimé Bonpland," p. 40; Kirchheimer, "Bonpland et la conspiration française," p. 125.

87. Bonpland to Acard, Buenos Aires, 18 Nov. 1818. See Ruiz Moreno, Risolía, and d'Onofrio, *Bonpland: aportaciones . . . sobre su actividad científica*, p. 60. I have no biographical details about Acard and his work at Rio de Janeiro. I speculate, however, that he may have had links to the French cultural mission to Brazil of 1816. Remembered mainly in the spheres of art and architecture, this mission was designed originally to include practical components, including the study of agriculture. The members of the mission were chosen following advice received from Alexander von Humboldt. Bonpland was in contact from Buenos Aires with some of the members of the mission. See Taunay, *Missão artística de 1816*, esp. pp. 9–11.

88. See entry no. 138, "indigofera tinctoria conf." in ms. 203, MHN.

89. *El Argos* (Buenos Aires), 10 Nov. 1821.

90. The famous battle of Chacabuco was fought on 12 February 1817 between Chilean independence forces and Spanish troops. It took place just north of Santiago.

91. See entry no. 147, "Nelumbium conf. *mayz de agua*," ms. 203, MHN.

92. Bonpland made notes on experiments conducted with Vauquelin on 21 Apr. 1816. They concerned the examination of two minerals, one from Peru and another from Mexico, both containing silver; ms. 214, MHN.

93. Bonpland, "Sur la préparation des cuirs et sur le tanage," Nov. 1818; AAB, carpeta 8, legajo 9, MFJAD. The dossier contains a great deal of material on various

experiments made with bark decoctions used to cure hides. Legajo 12 has Bonpland's comments made in 1819 on the local methods of making soap at Buenos Aires.

94. Kirchheimer, "Narcisse Parchappe," p. 307.
95. See Schulz, *Bonpland . . . Humboldts Begleiter*, p. 598.
96. Bonpland to Robert at Montevideo, 28 Aug. 1818; BBAW.
97. Schulz, *Bonpland . . . Humboldts Begleiter*, p. 600.
98. Bonpland to Lebreton at Rio de Janeiro, 18 Nov. 1818, quoted in ibid., pp. 600–601.
99. Bonpland to the Chevalier Gavrelle, Montevideo, 8 Sept. 1850; AAB, carpeta 5, MFJAD. Bonpland to Juan Pujol, Restauración, 6 Nov. 1854, printed in Pujol, *Corrientes en la organización nacional*, 4:253.
100. Whigham, *Politics of River Trade*, p. 120.
101. Bonpland made extensive notes based on the local claims; AAB, carpeta 6, MFJAD. The natural distribution of yerba maté remains a topic for scientific study even today. See Giberti, "Aspectos oscuros de la corologia de *Ilex paraguariensis*," pp. 289–300.
102. Bonpland to Juan Pujol, Restauración, 6 Nov. 1854, printed in Pujol, *Corrientes*, 4:254.
103. See Giberti, "Bonpland's Manuscript Name for the Yerba Mate," p. 663.
104. Bonpland thought his project was underappreciated at Buenos Aires, seeing this as a great loss for the city. See Bonpland to Pujol, Restauración, 6 Nov. 1854, printed in Pujol, *Corrientes*, 4:254–55.
105. There is a brief discussion of the efforts made by the Carrera brothers to raise revolution in Consul B. Barrère to the minister of foreign affairs, Paris, 8 May 1823; Mémoires et documents, Amérique du sud—1823 to 1836, vol. 32, fol. 34, MRE.
106. Bonpland was subsequently in close contact with some of those expelled, including with Narcisse Parchappe and with Manuel de Sarratea. Parchappe was still in South America in 1829. See his letter to Bonpland, Buenos Aires, 9 Nov. 1829; AAB, carpeta 6, MFJAD.
107. There were, in fact, two letters sent to Pueyrredón by the French community. The first, sent on 2 Apr. 1819, was signed by no fewer than 30 individuals, headed by the merchants Roguin and Meyer, with whom Bonpland would shortly be undertaking business in the interior of South America. Bonpland was the leading civilian signature on a corrected copy of the appeal, altered to make it officially acceptable, written on 3 Apr. 1819. Mendeville also signed. Both letters are transcribed in French in Papillaud, *Journalisme français à Buenos Aires*, pp. 32–35.
108. Hammerly Dupuy, "Bonpland y la conspiración de José Carrera," p. 93.
109. See Kirchheimer, "Bonpland et la conspiration française," esp. pp. 126–30; Schulz, *Bonpland . . . Humboldts Begleiter*, pp. 598–99. Schulz points out that the "conspiracy of the French" could also meaningfully be termed "the conspiracy of the Carreras." The Carrera family played an extremely important role in the independence of Chile, especially José Miguel Carrera (1785–1821). The main individuals that the Carreras were conspiring against—Bernardo O'Higgins, San Martín,

and Pueyrredón—were all Freemasons, members of the Lautaro Lodge, founded by San Martín in 1812.

110. Bonpland to Pellier, Buenos Aires, 20 May 1819, printed in Hamy, *Aimé Bonpland, médecin et naturaliste*, pp. 78–79. Auguste Banville seems to have been remarkably loyal to his employer. He accompanied Bonpland from Buenos Aires to Rio Grande do Sul in 1832, where he appears to have ended his days living in isolation.

111. See the letter from F. Forest (Bonpland's legal representative at Paris) to Humboldt, 21 Mar. 1819; F^{17}, 3974, fol. 60, AN.

112. F. Forest to Bonpland, Paris, 19 June 1819; AAB, carpeta 3, MFJAD.

113. See the letter from Colonel Maler, French consul general to Brazil, to the baron Portal d'Albarèdes, Minister of the Navy and of the Colonies, Rio de Janeiro, 6 Oct. 1820; F^{17}, 3974, fol. 66, AN.

114. Roguin was certainly at Paris in 1819. See Bonpland to Pellier, Buenos Aires, 20 May 1819, printed in Hamy, *Aimé Bonpland, médecin et naturaliste*, pp. 78–79.

115. It is not known for sure who wrote the note, now at Buenos Aires, which claimed that Humboldt had long been unjust with Bonpland, although the prime candidate remains Dominique Roguin, a French merchant established in the Río de la Plata and a close friend of Bonpland. See Cordier, *Papiers inédits du naturaliste Aimé Bonpland*, pp. 8–9.

116. Sarton, "Aimé Bonpland (1773–1858)," p. 388n14.

117. There are extensive notes on yerba written by Bonpland in AAB, carpeta 6, MFJAD.

118. Bonpland, "Voyage dans le Guazú fait sur la sumaca de Don Francisco Belgrano," 22 Aug. 1819; AAB, carpeta 6, MFJAD.

119. Ibid., 23 Aug. 1819.

120. Ibid., 4 Sept. 1819. Bonpland was correct here. The timber resources of the marshy lands in the delta resulted later in a distinctive cultural geography, which attracted the research attention of the French geographer Pierre Deffontaines ("Colonisation des basses terres," esp. p. 158). In the twentieth century, the flower of the indigenous ceibo tree was later adopted as the national flower of both Argentina and Uruguay.

121. There was considerable interest at Buenos Aires in trading with Paraguay. In March 1820, Charles Holland, a young clerk working in an important British merchant house, told his uncle that war in the interior of Argentina during the past year had "prevented almost any communication with Paraguay." Holland relayed a very positive impression of the wealth of the latter's resources: "Paraguay is by far the richest and most populous of the provinces that have thrown off the Spanish yoke, and it exhibits the uncommon fact of a despotic Government occupied solely in promoting the happiness of the people." The merchant house at Buenos Aires belonging to Thomas Fair, for whom Holland worked, had done recent trade with Paraguay. While this was the exceptional rather than the usual pattern, the results were described as "very profitable." See the letter from Charles Holland, Buenos Aires, to Swinton Holland, Baring Brothers, London, 2 Mar. 1820, printed in Hol-

land, *Noticias de Buenos Aires*, p. 28. This book is interesting for its commentary on the characters of some of South America's leading British merchants, including William Parish Robertson.

122. "Bonpland's Useful Exertions," p. 176. This article also establishes that Bonpland sent some record of his fieldwork on the islands of the Paraná north to the United States: "Those spots of earth, never before visited by any scientific explorer, afforded him a considerable number of plants, insects, birds, and other interesting objects. In the meantime his botanical garden has not been neglected, an establishment in which he procures and combines everything that promises benefit to the country, or utility to science."

123. Ruiz Moreno, Risolía, and d'Onofrio, *Aimé Bonpland: aportaciones . . . sobre su actividad científica*, pp. 15–18.

124. Halperín-Donghi, *Politics, Economics and Society in Argentina*, esp. pp. 87–88. By 1831, five to six thousand French citizens lived in and around the city of Buenos Aires; Lynch, *Argentine Dictator*, p. 248.

125. Ruiz Moreno, Risolía, and d'Onofrio, *Aimé Bonpland: aportaciones . . . sobre su actividad científica*, p. 79.

126. The wording of the passport is printed in Hammerly Dupuy, "Humboldt y las exploraciones científicas en América," p. 7. John Hoyt Williams has the passport issued by Manuel Balcarce.

127. Lynch, *Argentine Dictator*, p. 26.

128. Bonpland, "Voyage au Paraguay, 1 Oct. 1820, fol. 1, AAB, MFJAD. This manuscript travel account runs from 1 October 1820 until 28 July 1821, although with gaps, covering parts of the journey into the interior in considerable detail. It is especially interesting for its account of the state of agriculture in parts of Corrientes and for its depiction of some of the former Jesuit missions, c. 1820; AAB, MFJAD.

129. Ibid., 5 Oct. 1820, fol. 2.

130. Ibid., 9–14 Oct. 1820, fol. 3.

131. Roguin & Meyer at Buenos Aires to Razac (and recommended to Bonpland) at San Nicolás, 14 Oct. 1820; AAB, carpeta 3, MFJAD. This letter contains interesting comments on the French commercial vessels arriving in the Plata.

132. Aguilar appears to have been a close friend of the Bonpland family at Buenos Aires. In the same letter, he commented how Emma Bonpland was very dedicated to her lessons, a comment reminiscent of when the girl was being educated at London, in the midst of the South American revolutionaries resident there. Both daughter and mother were supposedly "always sighing" at Bonpland's absence. Victoriano Aguilar, Buenos Aires, to Amado Bonpland, "in Corrientes or Paraguay," 25 Oct. 1820. In a further letter, Aguilar related the circumstances of a serious medical complaint, involving throat ulcers, that had afflicted Emma. Treatment was successful. Aguilar to Bonpland, 27 Nov. 1820; AAB, carpeta 2, MFJAD.

133. Johann Rudolf Rengger and Marceline Longchamps briefly contrasted the condition of Corrientes in 1819 with the signs of renewal they witnessed when returning from Paraguay in 1825 (*Reign of . . . Francia*, p. 195). William Parish Robertson provided a much more extensive description of the town and its social life

(Robertson and Robertson, *Letters on South America*, 1:43–44, 95–110). See also Scobie, *Secondary Cities of Argentina*, esp. pp. 20–21, 48–62.

134. Robertson and Robertson, *Letters on Paraguay*, 1:255.

135. Ibid., 1:251–55, 2:231–38. See also Rengger and Longchamps, *Reign of . . . Francia*, p. 112.

136. Bonpland to Olive Gallocheau (his sister), Montevideo, printed in Hamy, *Aimé Bonpland, médecin et naturaliste*, p. 143.

137. Bonpland's extended description of Itatí was made from 2 to 5 Jan. 1821; "Voyage au Paraguay," fols. 28–35.

138. Ibid., 3–4 Jan. 1821, fol. 28.

139. A letter from his wife of 5 Jan. 1821 (and several others carrying that date) led Bonpland to believe that the vessel had not reached Buenos Aires by that time. Bonpland at Corrientes to Razac, Breard, Roguin, Meyer et Cie. at Buenos Aires, 3 Feb. 1821; BBAW. He also sent a duplicate of this letter on 10 Feb. 1821.

140. See "Voyage au Paraguay" (no specific date is given in the manuscript, but I establish that this was written after 19 January and before 26 January 1821), fol. 25 verso.

141. See the seed record made by Bonpland at Corrientes, 15 Jan. 1821; AAB, carpeta 5, legajo 4, MFJAD.

142. Bonpland mentions this in his own letter to Razac, Breard, Roguin, Meyer et Cie. at Buenos Aires, 3 Feb. 1821; BBAW. There is more discussion of sailing difficulties in Breard at Bajada (Paraná) to Bonpland and Voulquin in Corrientes, 6 Feb. 1821; AAB, carpeta 3, MFJAD. Jerry Cooney provides an excellent discussion of navigation challenges in his "Hazards of the Carrera del Paraguay."

143. See items 15 and 16 in the Bonpland file, BBAW.

144. Bonpland to Razac, Breard, Roguin, Meyer et Cie., Corrientes, 13 Feb. 1821; BBAW.

145. Razac at Buenos Aires to Bonpland and Breard at Corrientes, 31 Jan. 1821; AAB, carpeta 3, MFJAD. The item most in demand then at Buenos Aires was wheat, on account of locust damage.

146. Roguin, Meyer et Cie., Buenos Aires, to Breard and Bonpland at Corrientes, 6 Feb. 1821; AAB, carpeta 3, MFJAD. We also learn here that Narcisse Parchappe was charged with a letter from Madame Bonpland to her husband; this reveals that he was still presumed to be in South America. This is confirmed through Parchappe, Paraná, to Bonpland, 8 May 1821; AAB, carpeta 3, MFJAD. While this letter was addressed to Corrientes, Parchappe was aware that it would not find Bonpland there, but he expected to see Bonpland again within six weeks or two months.

147. Roguin & Meyer, Buenos Aires, to Bonpland at Corrientes, 20 Mar. 1821; AAB, carpeta 3, MFJAD. Bonpland replied to this letter from Caacatí on 24 May 1821.

148. Bonpland to Araújo, Corrientes, 13 Apr. 1821, quoted in Domínguez, *Bonpland . . . en la República Argentina*, pp. 19–20. This letter is a reply to one from Buenos Aires of 25 Jan. 1821.

149. See the administrative order about the chair in materia medica, signed by Juan Manuel de Luca, Buenos Aires, 14 Feb. 1821, printed in ibid., p. 20.

150. Although somewhat older than Bonpland, Jean-Louis Marc Alibert (1768–1837) was a contemporary of his in the study of medicine at Paris. Alibert had an extremely distinguished career, notable mainly for his work on skin diseases.

151. See the report of the medical tribunal composed of the doctors Cristóbal Martín de Montufar, Juan Antonio Fernández, and Francisco Cosme Argerich, Buenos Aires, 22 Feb. 1821, printed in Domínguez, *Bonpland . . . en la República Argentina*, pp. 20–21.

152. The details are in ibid., p. 21. The earlier lobbying against his medical appointment was a theme that still preoccupied Bonpland during his return visit to Buenos Aires in 1832. He learned from Montufar on 15 June 1832 the circumstances of the intrigue against his informant and himself, which he recorded as follows. After two years, Montufar had been reinstated in his post as part of the medical faculty. The surgeon Francisco de Paula Rivero was chased from Buenos Aires; Rivero was supposedly the one who had complained most loudly about Bonpland's nomination. Fernández and Argerich, the other two doctors of the medical tribunal, were "sadly stagnating." See "Journal scientifique," no. 3, Buenos Aires, June 1832; AAB, carpeta 7, MFJAD.

153. Francisco Ramírez informed Bonpland in May that Buenos Aires had recognized Bonpland's talents by nominating him a member of the medical academy there. General Francisco Ramírez, supreme chief of the republic of Entre Ríos, to Bonpland, 24 May 1821, reproduced in facsimile in Trabajos del Instituto Nacional de Botánica y Farmacología "Julio A. Roca," *Documentos para la historia de la República Enterriana*.

154. The passport for the missions is mentioned in Bonpland's postimprisonment request to the government of Corrientes for an official letter clarifying his forced removal from Correntino soil in 1821. A letter was approved at Corrientes on 16 Sept. 1834 and witnessed on 23 and 25 September of the same year; AAB, carpeta 6, MFJAD.

155. This we learn in Bonpland to Ricardo López Jordán, the interim governor of Corrientes, 3 June 1821, in *DHRE*.

156. See Bonpland at Corrientes to Ricardo López Jordán, 3 Sept. 1821, in ibid. and published in transcription in Domínguez, *Bonpland . . . en la República Argentina*, pp. 31–32.

157. Williams, "Paraguayan Isolation under Dr. Francia," p. 110.

158. Williams, *Rise and Fall of the Paraguayan Republic*, p. 67.

159. See Maeder, *Misiones del Paraguay*, esp. pp. 252–56. José Gervasio Artigas (1764–1850) is remembered mainly as Uruguay's leading national hero. He led a rural insurrection against the Spanish after 1811 and became the chief exponent of Federalism, promoting the rights of interior provinces against the powers of Buenos Aires. He showed a distinctive trait in making efforts to include Indians in his emerging political structures. Ultimately, he underestimated the power of the forces at Buenos Aires, seeking exile in Paraguay in 1820.

160. "Voyage au Paraguay," 18 May 1821, fol. 41 verso.

161. Ibid., 19–25 May 1821, fol. 42.

162. Evaristo Carriego, Corrientes, to Bonpland, Caacatí, 30 May 1821, in *DHRE*.

163. "Voyage au Paraguay," 29–31 May 1821, fol. 44.
164. Ibid., 28 May, 1821, fol. 43 verso.
165. Letters from Bonpland to Ramírez, Caacatí, 25 May and 7 June 1821, reproduced in *DHRE*.
166. Bonpland to Ramírez, Caacatí, 25 May 1821.
167. "Voyage au Paraguay," 5 June 1821, fol. 48.
168. Bonpland to Ramírez, Caacatí, 7 June 1821.
169. "Voyage au Paraguay," 17 June 1821, fol. 51.
170. Ibid., 22 June 1821, fol. 53 verso.
171. Bonpland to Ramírez, somewhere between Candelaria and Pindapoi, 21 June 1821 (the date is subject to some minor doubt), in facsimile in *DHRE* and published in Domínguez, *Bonpland . . . en la República Argentina*, pp. 28–31. Bonpland left a note claiming that his correspondents on 22 June 1821 were Ramírez, Carriego, Périchon, and his wife Adeline; AAB, carpeta 7, MFJAD.
172. See Maeder, *Misiones del Paraguay*, pp. 160–61; Ganson, *Guaraní under Spanish Rule*, p. 64.
173. "Voyage au Paraguay," 24 June 1821, fol. 53 verso.
174. Ibid., 27 June 1821, fol. 55.
175. Ibid., fol. 55 verso. A *chiripá* is a type of loincloth, forming part of traditional gaucho clothing.
176. It is interesting to reflect that on 20 March of the same year, Bonpland's compatriot Auguste de Saint-Hilaire also interviewed an Indian caudillo, Sití, who was then based in the former Jesuit mission of São Miguel, Rio Grande do Sul, Brazil. He did not leave a flattering portrait (Saint-Hilaire, *Viagem ao Rio Grande do Sul*, pp. 153–54).
177. "Voyage au Paraguay," 29 June 1821, fols. 55 verso and 56.
178. Ibid., 4 July 1821, fols. 56 and 56 verso.
179. See note 154, this chapter.
180. See the unclassified travel notes on 13 July [1821] in AAB, carpeta 7, MFJAD.
181. "Voyage au Paraguay," 14 July 1821, fol. 58 verso.
182. Ibid., 16 July 1821, fol. 59.
183. Bonpland to Juan Nicolas Christaldo, no place, no date, reproduced in *DHRE*. Christaldo was in a camp at San Ignacio Miní.
184. "Voyage au Paraguay," 18–19 July 1821, fol. 59. A second description of this visit is found in Bonpland's manuscripts, where he noted: "We got them drunk. The captain pissed in his bed like a pig"; AAB, carpeta 7, MFJAD.
185. Bonpland and Feliberto Voulquin to Nicolás Aripí, no place, no date, reproduced in *DHRE*.
186. "Voyage au Paraguay," 22 July 1821, fol. 59 verso.
187. See the notes on 22 July 1821 in AAB, carpeta 7, MFJAD.
188. Bonpland to Ricardo López Jordán, Corrientes, 3 Sept. 1821, reproduced in *DHRE*. This is printed in Domínguez, *Bonpland . . . en la República Argentina*, pp.

31–32. The transcribed version misses the critical detail that Bonpland planned to bring his family to the Upper Plata.

189. Bonpland, Corrientes, to José Ildefonso Castro, 3 Sept. 1821, reproduced in *DHRE*. The letter is printed in Domínguez, *Bonpland . . . en la República Argentina*, pp. 32–34.

190. See Bonpland's botanical registers for 13 Oct. 1821, p. 93 verso; ms. 203, MHN.

191. Humboldt to Bonpland, Paris, 25 Nov. 1821, quoted in Schulz, *Bonpland . . . Humboldts Begleiter*, p. 606.

192. Brunel, *Biographie d'Aimé Bonpland* (1871), p. 80.

193. Robertson and Robertson, *Francia's Reign of Terror*, 2:79–80. William Parish Robertson had the opportunity to talk with Bonpland at Buenos Aires in 1832. For biographical details of the Robertson brothers and of their careers involving South America, see Humphreys, *Tradition and Revolt in Latin America*, pp. 113–17, 122–27.

194. On Isasi's relationship to Francia, see Williams, *Rise and Fall of the Paraguayan Republic*, p. 86. Isasi famously absconded from Paraguay in 1827.

195. Maeder, *Misiones del Paraguay*, p. 253.

196. See note 154, this chapter.

197. See the notes in ms. 212, MHN.

198. Robertson and Robertson, *Francia's Reign of Terror*, 2:80.

199. Francia to Norberto Ortellado, 23 Nov. 1821, S. Hist [Sección Historia], vol. 235, no. 2, ANA; printed in part in Boccia Romañach, *Amado Bonpland: caraí arandú*, pp. 147–48.

200. Later, in Paraguay, Bonpland learned that entire fields were once sown with the wild indigo plant.

201. "Francia contra todo derecho de naciones mando invadir mi suelo hageno qe. savia positivamente ser habitado por hombres solo ocupados de seus trabajos y indefensos." See Bonpland's account of the circumstances made for the government of Corrientes, 16 Sept. 1834; AAB, carpeta 6, MFJAD.

202. Robertson and Robertson, *Francia's Reign of Terror*, 2:81.

203. Ibid.

204. Brunel, *Biographie d'Aimé Bonpland* (1871), pp. 80–82. Brunel and Roguin would probably have found ample opportunity to reflect on Bonpland when they were both distinguished members of the French community at Montevideo.

205. See *El Argos de Buenos Aires*, 9 Feb. 1822, quoted in Piccirilli, *Rivadavia y su tiempo*, 3:94–95.

206. Sáenz Quesada, "La Atenas del Plata," p. 261.

207. See Piccirilli, *Rivadavia y su tiempo*, esp. 2:158–61.

Chapter Two

1. From a file of Bonpland's meteorological data, Santa María, Paraguay, 1822; AAB, MFJAD.

2. Bonpland to the Comtesse de Chastenay, Montevideo, 15 May 1840; AAB, carpeta 3, MFJAD. Bonpland came to know Madame de Chastenay while he was

in Joséphine's employ at Malmaison. She was an intellectual, the author of a study of ancient civilizations (1808) and of an important memoir covering the period from the end of the ancien régime to the first Restoration. Chastenay, *Mémoires de Madame de Chastenay*.

3. See the travel notes for 14 Aug. 1834 in AAB, carpeta 7, MFJAD.

4. See the report by Consul Barrère, Paris, 8 May 1823; Amérique du sud, 1823–1836, mémoires, tome 32, fols. 68, 69, 70, MRE. Barrère wrongly maintained that Bonpland had specialized in the cultivation of tobacco rather than the yerba that was much more the focus of his attention.

5. Le contre-amiral Rosamel, "Notes sur Buenos Ayres et la Bande Orientale de la Plata," A bord de la *Marie Thérèse* en rade de Montevideo, 3 July 1824; Amérique du sud, 1823–1836, mémoires, tome 32, fol. 122, MRE.

6. Williams, *Rise and Fall of the Paraguayan Republic*, p. 79.

7. Ibid., pp. 52–53.

8. The comparison to the 1804 killing of the Duke of Enghien in the moat of the Château de Vincennes relates in the following ways. Both cases involved seizing a person from neutral territory (both famous, albeit in distinctive ways), followed by summary justice. There is presumption that the individuals seized were innocent, thus shocking public opinion. The fact is, however, that in both cases the motives are cloudy. See Burton, *Letters from the Battle-Fields of Paraguay*, pp. 50–51.

9. Ganson, *Guaraní under Spanish Rule*, p. 162

10. See Rengger and Longchamps, *Reign of . . . Francia*, p. 174.

11. AAB, carpeta 5, MFJAD.

12. See Whigham, "Agriculture and the Upper Plata," p. 570.

13. See ms. 215, MHN.

14. See ms. 204, MHN.

15. See Williams, *Rise and Fall of the Paraguayan Republic*, pp. 95–96.

16. See also the further brief reference to this tobacco of 1822 in ms. 215, MHN.

17. See AAB, carpeta 6, MFJAD.

18. See the working notes "Dans le Paraguay"; AAB, carpeta 6, MFJAD.

19. See ms. 212, MHN. He saw the crop in cultivation in August 1829 on a *chacra* at Itapúa; see the description no. 879, "indigofera"; ms. 204, MHN.

20. Bonpland to *subdelegado* Romero, Santa María, Aug. 1822, printed in Boccia Romañach, *Amado Bonpland: caraí arandú*, pp. 148–49.

21. See the note from Francia to subdelegado Romero at Santa María, 23 Aug. 1822, printed in ibid., pp. 149–50. More on Francia's attitudes toward Bonpland, based on an interview held in late 1821, is found in Rengger and Longchamps, *Reign of . . . Francia*, pp. 80–81.

22. Williams, *Rise and Fall of the Paraguayan Republic*, p. 65.

23. Rengger and Longchamps describe how Escoffier, a native of Nice, made an unsuccessful attempt to escape from Paraguay during the middle of 1823 (*Reign of . . . Francia*, pp. 80–81).

24. Johann Rudolph Rengger to Bonpland (letter in Spanish), Asunción, 29 Jan. 1823; AAB, carpeta 6, MFJAD.

25. Williams, *Rise and Fall of the Paraguayan Republic*, p. 85.

26. On Francia's reading, see Rengger and Longchamps, *Reign of . . . Francia*, pp. 21–22.

27. See Humboldt and Bonpland, *Plantes équinoxiales*, 1. Plate 20 depicts *Bambusa guadua*. The Berkeley cultural geographer James Parsons published an intriguing paper tracing the "Guadua culture region" in Colombia and Ecuador ("Giant American Bamboo," esp. pp. 132–33, 134–36, 137, 138).

28. See the description of no. 732, "Bambusa"; ms. 204, MHN. In a later marginal entry, Bonpland noted that in Corrientes the remaining bamboos were located at a single estancia, providing the source of considerable profit to the owner.

29. Described at no. 765, ibid., and again at 846 in April 1826 from Santa María.

30. Described at no. 779 in ms. 204, ibid.

31. Description of no. 816, *urucu* (*Bixa orellana*); ms. 204, MHN. Decades earlier, Tadeo Haenke had described this little tree as abundant in the gardens throughout the Andean mountains. See his notes on the natural history of Cochabamba province, published within the 1809 French edition of Félix de Azara's South American travel account (*Voyages dans l'Amérique méridionale*, 2:524–25). Presumably, Bonpland read Azara and Haenke before journeying to the Upper Plata.

32. See the planting records in AAB, carpeta 6, MFJAD.

33. See Azara, *Voyages dans l'Amérique méridionale*, 1:125.

34. AAB, carpeta 5, MFJAD.

35. Brunel, *Biographie d'Aimé Bonpland* (1859), pp. 31–32.

36. See Grandsire to Humboldt, Itapúa, 10 Sept. 1824, printed in Hamy, *Aimé Bonpland, médecin et naturaliste*, pp. 253–55.

37. Rengger and Longchamps, *Reign of . . . Francia*, p. 82.

38. *Crónica Política y Literaria de Buenos Aires* (18 July 1827), cited in Piccirilli, *Rivadavia y su tiempo*, 3:95.

39. See Pérez Acosta, *Francia y Bonpland*, p. 41. The date varies in Hamy, *Aimé Bonpland, médecin et naturaliste*, pp. 80–82.

40. Bonpland to Raffeneau-Delile, Buenos Aires, 8 Aug. 1832, printed in Hamy, *Aimé Bonpland, médecin et naturaliste*, pp. 92–93.

41. Bolívar to Francia, Lima, 23 Oct. 1823, printed in Bolívar, *Cartas del Libertador*, tome 3 (1821–1823), pp. 486–87.

42. Bolívar to Madame Bonpland, Lima, 23 Oct. 1823 (letter in Spanish), printed in Hamy, *Aimé Bonpland, médecin et naturaliste*, 247. Humboldt appears not to have signed on to Madame Bonpland's efforts to promote her husband's release, at least as revealed in a letter he wrote on 30 April 1827 to his close friend François Arago. Sir Charles Stuart, the British ambassador to France, told Humboldt that he had learned from a Brazilian correspondent that Bonpland was in no way unhappy in Paraguay. He adds: "the *sentimental* Madame Bonpland *is a hussy*." In an 1834 newspaper article, Madame Bonpland claimed to have spent six years roaming between Europe and the Americas in an effort to free her husband. The locations of her efforts include Montevideo, Rio de Janeiro, Paris, Lima, Jamaica,

and New York. On Madame Bonpland, see ibid., pp. lxiii, lxiv. If the manuscript of her journeying still exists, it would certainly make for very interesting reading—something, perhaps, to compare with Flora Tristan's famous travel account from the same period, *Les pérégrinations d'une paria*.

43. Bolívar to Francisco de Paula Santander, vice president of Colombia, Arequipa, 20 May 1825, printed in Bierck, *Selected Writings of Bolivar*, 2:505.

> The province of Paraguay is occupied by a certain Francia, who has kept it in complete isolation these past fourteen years. It belongs to no nation, and it has no government. Its head is a tyrant who is a virtual enemy to the world at large, for he deals with no one and persecutes everyone. Those who enter never return. Thus poor Bonpland, Humboldt's companion, is kept there in captivity.

44. His full name was Jean-Baptiste-Richard Grandsire. See Hamy, *Aimé Bonpland, médecin et naturaliste*, p. lvii.

45. Humboldt's letter to Georges Cuvier, the perpetual secretary of the Académie des Sciences, and the instructions forwarded to Grandsire are printed in ibid., pp. 247–49. The document was signed by Cuvier along with the botanist academicians Antoine Laurent de Jussieu, André Thouin, and René Louiche Desfontaines.

46. See ibid., p. lix.

47. Ibid., p. lx.

48. Le contre amiral Rosamel, "Notes sur Buénos Ayres et la Bande Orientale de la Plata," A bord de la *Marie Thérèse* en rade de Montevideo, 3 July 1824; Mémoires et documents, Amérique, tome 29, fols. 115 and 115 verso, MRE. Grandsire appears to have had further difficulties with Rosamel at Rio de Janeiro in 1826. Bureaucratic difficulties explained why he left that city for Cayenne. Since no ship was taking this route, he was obliged to travel via Martinique. See Hamy, *Aimé Bonpland, médecin et naturaliste*, p. 260.

49. Grandsire to Humboldt, Itapua [Encarnación], 18 Aug. 1824 and 10 Sept. 1824, printed in Hamy, *Aimé Bonpland, médecin et naturaliste*, pp. 252–55.

50. "I suffered a lot during my journey through the almost impenetrable forests, perhaps as much as you did yourself in the forests of the Orinoco." Grandsire to Humboldt, Curitiba, 20 Nov. 1824, printed in ibid., pp. 256–57.

51. See Ramos, *Política del Brasil en el Paraguay*, p. 109; Hamy, *Aimé Bonpland, médecin et naturaliste*, p. lx.

52. Antônio Manoel Correa da Câmara (1783–1848) served as a soldier and had a distinguished diplomatic career during the early nineteenth century. Between 1845 and his death, he was in charge of collecting statistics in Rio Grande do Sul, Brazil.

53. There is a brief review of the initial success and ultimate failure of his mission in Williams, *Rise and Fall of the Paraguayan Republic*, pp. 68–69. See also Seckinger, *Brazilian Monarchy and the South American Republics*, pp. 103–8.

54. See the discussion in Ramos, *Política del Brasil en el Paraguay*, pp. 109–11.

55. See Hamy, *Aimé Bonpland, médecin et naturaliste*, pp. lx, 259.

56. Ramos, *Política del Brasil en el Paraguay*, p. 119.

57. Letter printed in Pérez Acosta, *Francia y Bonpland*, appendix, p. vi.

58. The matter is reviewed in Ramos, *Política del Brasil en el Paraguay*, pp. 135–38.

59. Ibid., p. 141. Summarizing Correa da Câmara's broad character, Ron Seckinger described him as a "paranoid reactionary" (*Brazilian Monarchy and the South American Republics*, p. 30).

60. Grandsire to Georges Cuvier, Rio de Janeiro, 30 May 1826, printed in Cordier, *Papiers inédits du naturaliste Bonpland*, pp. 21–22. Most of this letter deals with dinosaur remains recently found in the far south of Brazil.

61. See Grandsire to the baron de Damas, Martinique, 2 Sept. 1826, printed in Hamy, *Aimé Bonpland, médecin et naturaliste*, pp. 258–62.

62. The circumstances of Grandsire's demise are related in a letter from Louis-Henri Desaules, baron de Freycinet, governor of French Guiana, to André-Jean, the comte de Chabrol de Crouzol, Minister of the Navy, Cayenne, 1827, printed in ibid., pp. 264–65.

63. See the note Humboldt wrote at Paris, 28 June 1825, printed in *Hertha: Zeitschrift für Erd-, Völker- und Staatenkunde* 2 (1825): 696, reprinted in Hamy, *Aimé Bonpland, médecin et naturaliste*, p. 257. Woodbine Parish was the first British diplomat officially posted to the Río de la Plata, serving at Buenos Aires from 1824 to 1832. On return to England, he wrote a valuable historical geography of the region, *Buenos Ayres and the . . . Plata*.

64. See Hamy, *Aimé Bonpland, médecin et naturaliste*, p. 266.

65. Woodbine Parish saw himself as acting "in favour of an individual in whose fate I could justly say that all the scientific world was interested." His efforts to seek Bonpland's release are described in his travel account (*Buenos Aires and the . . . Plata*, pp. 236–37).

66. Bonpland to Woodbine Parish (letter in French), Buenos Aires, 26 Mar. 1832; FO 6/35, PRO. Bonpland argued that the source of Francia's colossal power rested in the disunity of Argentina's littoral provinces.

67. See Bonpland's diary from Buenos Aires, Nov. 1836, fols. 4 and 4 verso; AAB, carpeta 7, MFJAD. See also the letter Bonpland wrote to Francia in 1835 from São Borja on behalf of a French merchant in carpeta 6.

68. Williams, "Paraguayan Isolation under Dr. Francia," p. 117.

69. See Schneppen, *Bonpland: Humboldts vergessener Gefährte?* p. 15.

70. Bosc to Bonpland, 25 Dec. 1825; AAB, carpeta 2, MFJAD. Bosc had gained a reputation from the time of the French revolution for standing by his friends when they were "persecuted, calumnied and outlawed." Today, he is remembered mainly through the name of a common variety of pear. Bosc and Bonpland appear to have shared a number of things, foremost an interest in how botany could be applied in agriculture. They both had some direct experience of the United States (Bosc was nominated consul at New York in 1798). Rey, *Bosc, un Girondin herborisant*, esp. pp. 53, 55, 65–66.

71. Silvestre, *Notice biographique sur M. André Thouin*.

72. Bonpland to Bosc, Buenos Aires, 8 Aug. 1832; AAB, carpeta 2, MFJAD.

73. Alire Raffeneau-Delile to Bonpland, Montpellier, 22 Mar. 1826; AAB, MFJAD. He followed this with a further letter from Montpellier, 27 Nov. 1832.

74. Stewart, "South American Commission," pp. 37–38, 53.

75. Joel R. Poinsett to Bonpland (letter in French), Mexico City, 20 Nov. 1827; AAB, carpeta 6, MFJAD.
76. Robertson and Robertson, *Francia's Reign of Terror*, 2:89–90.
77. Francia to Ramírez, 10 May 1829, S. Hist., vol. 240, no. 2, ANA, printed in Pérez Acosta, *Francia y Bonpland*, appendix, p. xiii.
78. Printed in Ramos, *Política del Brasil en el Paraguay*, p. 138.
79. Ibid., 191–98.
80. Draft letter from Bonpland to Victorine de Chastenay, Montevideo, 15 May 1840; AAB, carpeta 3, MFJAD.
81. See Francia to Ramírez, 20 May 1829, S. Hist., vol. 240, no. 2, ANA, printed in Pérez Acosta, *Francia y Bonpland*, appendix, pp. xiii–xiv.
82. Draft of letter from Bonpland to George Frederick Dickson, Buenos Aires, 27 Mar. 1832; AAB, carpeta 3, MFJAD.
83. See letter to Roguin in Pérez Acosta, *Francia y Bonpland*, p. 41.
84. Ramírez to Francia, Itapúa, 30 Apr. 1830, printed in Pérez Acosta, appendix, p. xv.
85. See records in AAB, carpeta 6, MFJAD.
86. See folder no. 16 on snakes in ms. 215, MHN.
87. These details are based mainly on Bonpland's notes in ms. 212, MHN.
88. See Ganson, *Guaraní under Spanish Rule*, pp. 160–62.
89. See Saint-Hilaire, *Viagem ao Rio Grande do Sul*, pp. 125–34, 141.
90. Ernesto Maeder provides a useful summary of the fate of the Portuguese missions after their conquest in 1801 (*Misiones del Paraguay*, pp. 269–76).
91. Letter from Roguin to Bonpland, Buenos Aires, 8 Nov., 1829; AAB, carpeta 4, MFJAD. The reply, widely disseminated in print, came from São Borja in Feb. 1831.
92. Letter from Narcisse Parchappe to Bonpland, Buenos Aires, 9 Nov. 1829; AAB, carpeta 6, MFJAD. This carries the note in Bonpland's hand that he replied from São Borja, 23 Feb. 1831.
93. Bonpland to the Paris publisher Barrois, Corrientes, 28 Mar. 1838; AAB, carpeta 4, MFJAD. See also his letter to François Delessert, Montevideo, 17 May 1840, printed in Hamy, *Aimé Bonpland, médecin et naturaliste*, pp. 133–34.
94. Bonpland to Humboldt, São Borja, 14 July 1836; BBAW.
95. Bonpland to de Candolle, Montevideo, 17 May 1840, printed in Hamy, *Aimé Bonpland, médecin et naturaliste*, p. 136.
96. Augustin Pyrame de Candolle to Bonpland, Geneva, 28 Dec. 1840; AAB, carpeta 2, MFJAD.
97. Draft of letter from Bonpland to Humboldt, Montevideo, 30 Dec. 1840; AAB, carpeta 2, MFJAD.
98. William Jackson Hooker to Bonpland (letter in English), Glasgow University, 25 May 1835; AAB, carpeta 2, MFJAD.
99. Hooker to Bonpland, Royal Botanic Gardens at Kew, 25 Feb. 1842; AAB, carpeta 2, MFJAD.
100. Brunel, *Biographie d'Aimé Bonpland* (1859), p. 99.

101. In AAB, carpeta 5, MFJAD. These detailed ethnobotanical notes on pumpkins were made at Montevideo on 10 Dec. 1855 in connection with Bonpland's supply of South American seeds and living plants for the French colony in Algeria.

Chapter Three

1. Bonpland completed this manuscript at Buenos Aires, 21 June 1832; AAB, carpeta 5, MFJAD. He was clearly no admirer of the pampas grasslands.
2. Bonpland to Barrois l'aîné, Corrientes, 28 Mar. 1838; AAB, carpeta 4, MFJAD. Bonpland incurred the debt for books designed to form the basis of Argentina's national library on 14 October 1816, and this debt was cleared at Paris on 21 September 1838. No interest was offered. The senior member of the Barrois publishing dynasty had been dead for nearly a decade.
3. Domínguez, *Bonpland . . . en la República Argentina*, p. 43.
4. Bonpland to Roguin, São Borja, 25 Feb. 1831. This famous letter was widely disseminated in European newspapers.
5. Draft letter from Bonpland to Mendeville, São Borja, 25 Feb. 1831; AAB, carpeta 3, MFJAD.
6. For background on Mendeville's early career at Buenos Aires, see Sáenz Quesada, *Mariquita Sánchez*, esp. pp. 79–84.
7. Draft letter from Bonpland to Mendeville, São Borja, 25 Feb. 1831; AAB, carpeta 3, MFJAD.
8. Bonpland to Pedro Ferré, São Borja, 17 Mar. 1831; AAB, carpeta 1, MFJAD. Pedro Ferré (1788–1867), who was elected governor of Corrientes on three occasions, became the leading candidate in the Littoral's opposition to Buenos Aires. On his background and projects, see Whigham, *Politics of River Trade*, pp. 46–48.
9. Bernabé Magariños to Bonpland, Bella Unión, 12 Apr. 1831; AAB, carpeta 1, MFJAD. This letter also contained the enclosure of letters from Rivera himself and another from Colonel Carriegos. Although Magariños had never met Bonpland in person, he claimed to know him "morally." He came to know Bonpland's wife and daughter Emma, presumably when they passed through Montevideo when moving from Buenos Aires to Rio de Janeiro. The date of this letter is interesting. It is almost the same date as when Rivera suppressed a supposed uprising in the Indian population at Bella Unión. The nature of this uprising is the subject of considerable dispute. On the Guaraní exodus, see Maeder, *Misiones del Paraguay*, pp. 274–75.
10. Bonpland to Bernabé Magariños, São Borja, 20 May 1831; AAB, carpeta 1, MFJAD. There is also a letter of the same date to Rivera, in which Bonpland thanked the Uruguayan president for showing interest in the circumstances of his imprisonment in Paraguay. Bonpland and Rivera later had close dealings in connection with the opposition to Rosas's dictatorship.
11. See Domínguez, *Bonpland . . . en la República Argentina*, p. 47.
12. Bonpland to Lieutenant-Colonel Silva, São Borja, 8 Sept. 1831; ms. 215, MHN.
13. Bonpland to Ferré, São Borja, 17 Oct. 1831; AAB, carpeta 1, MFJAD.
14. Ibid., 14 Dec. 1831; AAB, carpeta 1, MFJAD.

15. See Bonpland's travel journal, "Diario de viaje de San Borja à Corrientes," 20 Dec. 1831–35 Jan. 1832; AAB, carpeta 7, MFJAD.
16. Ibid., 23 Dec. 1831, fol. 2.
17. Ibid., 26 Dec. 1831, fol. 3 verso.
18. Ibid., 1 Jan. 1832, fol. 5.
19. Bonpland to Ferré, Curuzú Cuatiá, 28 Dec. 1831; AAB, carpeta 1, MFJAD.
20. Bonpland, travel journals, "Diario de viaje de San Borja à Corrientes," 2 Jan. 1832, fol. 5 verso.
21. Ibid., "Voyage à la Stance [estancia] de Dn. José Santos Maciel dont l'objet est de voir et connôitre la plante connue à Sta. Fé sous le nom de Rayz del Guaycuru"; AAB, carpeta 7, MFJAD.
22. See Bonpland, at Buenos Aires, to Chevreul, director of the Muséum Royal d'Histoire Naturelle, 5 Jan. 1837, printed in Hamy, *Aimé Bonpland, médecin et naturaliste*, p. 112.
23. See Domínguez, *Bonpland . . . en la República Argentina*, p. 43.
24. Ibid., p. 47.
25. Dupuytren, chief surgeon at the Hotel Dieu, and Baron Jean-Louis Alibert (1768–1837) were both major medical figures. Alibert pioneered the study of skin diseases in France, borrowing from botany in his studies of their organization. Charles Barrois, a Paris publisher to whom Bonpland owed a debt, had died in 1829. Bosc, of the Jardin des Plantes, was already long dead in 1832. Raffeneau-Delile was a close colleague of Bonpland's from the period they worked together in France.
26. Josefa Emilia Sabor asserts that Bonpland and de Angelis knew each other at Paris. She argues that Bonpland's account of the appeal of the Plata may have helped to draw the latter there. This seems wrong. Bonpland had already left for the Plata before de Angelis arrived at Paris. A more convincing link between Bonpland and de Angelis is through the French merchant Roguin, who lived only a few houses away from de Angelis in Buenos Aires. Roguin appears to have passed along Bonpland's letter announcing his release from Paraguay (incorrectly dated in Sabor) to de Angelis on 5 Apr. 1831. He, in turn, forwarded this news to Georges Cuvier at Paris on 28 May 1831 (see Sabor, *Pedro de Angelis*, esp. pp. 8–9, 38, 56).
27. The Robertsons dedicated one of their works to Dickson (see Robertson and Robertson, *Letters on South America*, 1:v–vi). See also the subscription table in their *Letters on Paraguay*, 1:xiii.
28. Bonpland to George Frederick Dickson, Buenos Aires, 27 Mar. 1832 (letter in French); AAB, carpeta 3, MFJAD.
29. In reviewing the losses he encountered when emerging from Paraguay, Bonpland commented that his small herbarium, presumably work from the period 1817–1820, was entirely lost: "I assume it is in England and I dare not say in whose hands." Bonpland to Humboldt, São Borja, 14 July 1836; AAB, carpeta 2, MFJAD.
30. On de Angelis's library consultation habits, see Sabor, *Pedro de Angelis*, p. 311.
31. Thénard, *Traité de chimie élémentaire*.
32. Dubrunfaut, *Traité complet de l'art de la distillation*.
33. Wilson, *American Ornithology*.

34. See Bonpland's list of surgical instruments made at Buenos Aires, 4 Apr. 1832; AAB, carpeta 4, MFJAD.

35. See Robertson and Robertson, *Francia's Reign of Terror*, 2:91.

36. Grierson, *Colonia de Monte Grande*, p. 67. There is an interesting brief review of the Scottish colonization in Fernández-Gómez, *Argentina: gesta británica*, 1:95–100. He points out that this was the first homogeneous ethnic (in the sense of non-Spanish) settlement in the Río de la Plata and of huge importance in studying the roots of agricultural improvement in the region. The Robertson brothers sank a considerable capital into the scheme.

37. See entry no. 1215, "Yucca gloriosa conf."; ms. 205, MHN. I have established the timing of this visit through Bonpland's meteorological records; AAB, carpeta 5, MFJAD.

38. See the draft letter from Bonpland to Michel Tenore, Buenos Aires, 4 June 1832; AAB, carpeta 2, MFJAD.

39. Tenore to Bonpland, Naples, 4 Apr. 1836; AAB, carpeta 2, MFJAD.

40. The notes are taken from the scientific journal Bonpland kept for June 1832; AAB, carpeta 7, MFJAD.

41. The ascent of Chimborazo volcano took place on 23 June 1802. Humboldt provided several accounts of this dramatic event in his letters, but see especially those to his brother Wilhelm from Lima, 25 Nov. 1802, and to Thomas Jefferson, Philadelphia, 24 May 1804, printed in Humboldt, *Briefe aus Amerika*, pp. 211, 292.

42. The themes noted included Humboldt's discussions of coffee cultivation at Caracas, the vague discussion of the timing of Otaheiti cane's diffusion into South America, and cereal yields in the tropics. The page references in Bonpland's notes are to Humboldt and Bonpland, *Voyage aux régions équinoxiales*, 5:82, 94, 104, 132, 134, and to Humboldt, *Tableaux de la nature*, 1:257.

43. Bonpland took notes on Saint Hilaire's recently published *Voyage dans les provinces de Rio de Janeiro et Minas Geraes*, using a copy borrowed from Henry Stephen Fox, the British minister resident at Buenos Aires.

44. Bonpland, "Nottes pour servir à un ètablissement agricole dont les fruits doivent être consomés pour la plus part dans la Capitale de B. ayres," Buenos Aires, 21 June 1832; AAB, carpeta 5, MFJAD.

45. Scobie, *Buenos Aires*, esp. p. 14.

46. See Bell, "Aimé Bonpland and Merinomania."

47. See Peter Sheridan to Bonpland (letter in Spanish), Buenos Aires, 4 July 1841; AAB, carpeta 4, MFJAD. I was still unaware of this important connection when I published an article on Bonpland and sheep, "Aimé Bonpland and Merinomania."

48. Maudit, "Arboriculture in Argentina," p. 270.

49. Alfalfa accompanied the successful emergence of large-scale wheat cultivation. See Scobie, *Revolution on the Pampas*, esp. p. 46; Bell, *Campanha Gaúcha*, esp. p. 129.

50. On Rosas and agriculture, see Slatta, *Gauchos and the Vanishing Frontier*, pp. 151–52.

51. Bonpland to Humboldt, Buenos Aires, 12 July 1832, printed in Hamy, *Aimé Bonpland, médecin et naturaliste*, p. 90. It is interesting to compare Bonpland's appreciation of Henry Stephen Fox with one written sometime later in the year by Consul Charles Griffiths, when the British minister was about to transfer to Rio de Janeiro: "I am really sorry to lose him as my chief, for after forming some acquaintance with him, his manners in private are so polished and genteel and his abilities so very superior that one cannot help admiring him. He does turn night into day tho' or rather day into night in general, as he usually retires to rest at day break and rises of course rather latish"; private letter from Griffiths, at Buenos Aires, to John Bidwell (superintendent of the consular service); F.O. 6/35, fols. 146 and 146 verso, PRO. Fox became a correspondent of Darwin. In 1834, one of the themes he took up with the latter was the floristic appeal of southern Brazil. While Fox mentioned the earlier work of Saint-Hilaire and of Sellow in Rio Grande do Sul, there is surprisingly no mention of Bonpland's residence in the region. Darwin told his sister Caroline: "I have picked up one very odd correspondent, it is M[r] Fox the Minister at Rio (it is the M[r] Fox, who in one of Lord Byrons letters is said to be so altered after an illness that his *oldest Creditors* would not know him)." See H. S. Fox to Darwin, Rio de Janeiro, 25 July 1834, and Darwin to Caroline Darwin, Valparaiso, 13 Oct. 1834, printed in Burkhardt and Smith, eds., *Correspondence of Charles Darwin*, 1:403, 412.

52. See ms. 205, MHN.

53. In part of his speech, the president of the banquet, M. Lantin, offered a poem in homage to liberal justice. Part of it reads as follows:
Si plusieurs d'entre nous ont souffert du pouvoir
De quelques vils agents, trahissant leur devoir,
Il est dans ce pays des hommes respectables,
De parfaits libéraux, généreux, équitables,

Peut-être qu'à leurs soins nous devons le bonheur
De voir à ce Banquet inscrit sur notre liste,
Le savant distingué, le grand naturaliste,
L'illustre prisonnier de Francia, le tyran,
Qui s'assied aux côtés du modeste artisan
Compagnon de Humboldt, sa science profonde
A connu les secrets de l'un et l'autre Monde
Des chants nationaux animant les concerts,
Il ne dédaigne pas d'égayer nos desserts,
Jurons tous devant lui qu'une époque semblable
Nous trouvons tous les ans assis à cette table!

Aubouin, *Banquet patriotique . . . à Buénos-Ayres*, esp. p. 11. Isidore Aubouin was a French merchant. Like Bonpland, he knew something of the circumstances of the interior, having spent time at Bella Unión, the colony founded by Rivera in 1829 in order to gather the dispersed Indian population.

54. See Domínguez, *Bonpland . . . en la República Argentina*, p. 47.

55. Darwin made only a single specific reference to Bonpland in his travel account, in connection with his appraisal of the soil qualities along the lower portion of the Paraná River. He described Bonpland as "the best of judges" (*Journal of Researches*, p. 139).

56. Bonpland, travel journals, "Voyage de Buenos Ayres à Sn. Borja," 13 Oct. 1832, fol. 1; AAB, carpeta 7, MFJAD.
57. Ibid., fol. 2 verso.
58. Ibid., 18 Oct. 1832, fol. 4 verso.
59. Araújo, *Diccionario geográfico del Uruguay*, p. 206.
60. Bonpland, travel journals, "Voyage de Buenos Ayres à Sn. Borja," 26 Oct. 1832, fol. 3.
61. Isabelle, *Voyage a Buénos-Ayres et a Porto-Alègre*, p. 402. See also the acknowledgment of Bonpland's help on p. 31. Bonpland left an account in his manuscripts of the visit made to him by four Frenchmen, including Isabelle. This last, he claimed, had "a natural liking for natural history, and above all for the commerce in objects of this nature." Bonpland, travel journals (Oct. 1833), 12 Dec. 1833, fol. 7; AAB, carpeta 7, MFJAD.
62. Brazil's monetary unit during the period of this study was the mil-réis, written 1$000. Large sums were expressed in contos. A conto equaled 1,000 mil-réis (written 1:000$000).
63. Bonpland was following the scientific discussions at Paris of d'Orbigny's work, as reported in the *Diario Comercial, Político y Literario* on 1, 6, and 9 Aug. 1834; AAB, carpeta 7, MFJAD. He later made extensive critical notes on d'Orbigny's publications. See ms. 215, MHN.
64. Symonds to Bonpland (letter in Spanish), Curuzú Cuatiá, 30 Mar. 1835; AAB, carpeta 4, MFJAD.
65. Symonds to Bonpland, Curuzú Cuatiá, 5 Apr. 1835.
66. Ibid., Montevideo, 14 Mar. 1849.
67. See Domínguez, *Bonpland . . . en la República Argentina*, p. 48.
68. Aimé Roger was thinking of Bonpland in part, no doubt, because he was completing a long memorandum on the politics of Paraguay and hoped that Bonpland might extend his own analysis for the Quai d'Orsay, or ministry of foreign affairs. Roger was scathing on the topic of *porteño* ambitions with regard to Paraguay: "Several Argentine generals and several governors of Buenos Aires have contemplated the conquest of Paraguay, but the ambitious projects of all these pygmies have vanished with their ephemeral power." After weighing the virtues and defects of Francia's methods, Roger saw benefits at least in the policy of Paraguayan isolation. Without it, he thought, "this fine country today would be a miserable annex of the wretched Argentine provinces." Aimé Roger to the minister of foreign affairs, Buenos Aires, 10 Aug. 1836; CCC, Buenos Aires, tome 2, 1836–37, fols. 150–51 verso, MRE. The reference to Bonpland comes at the end of the document.
69. The name of the Polish count defeated Bonpland. He recorded a note from "Strelech" at Buenos Aires on 13 Nov. 1836; AAB, carpeta 4, MFJAD.
70. Bonpland to Ferré, Buenos Aires, 28 Nov. 1836; AAB, carpeta 1, MFJAD.
71. See Bonpland's receipt for the sum of 19,137.95 francs, Buenos Aires, 1 Dec. 1836; AAB, carpeta 6, MFJAD.
72. Details of the payment of the arrears of the pension are in a letter from the Delesserts to Bonpland, Paris, 17 July 1837; AAB, carpeta 4, MFJAD.

73. See the plan for a rural project in Corrientes, designed to raise cattle, sheep, and mules; "Relación de documentos," item 13, BBAW. More than one version is found in the Bonpland manuscripts, and the names of the minor shareholders are not always the same. See an alternative in AAB, carpeta 2, MFJAD.

74. See Aimé Roger's report designed to reflect the "real resources" of the United Provinces of the Río de la Plata to the minister of foreign affairs, Buenos Aires, 1 Apr. 1837; Mémoires et documents, Amérique, vol. 29, MRE.

75. Proof that Bonpland lodged with Roger at least until late January comes in the letter from Bonpland to Aimé Roger, interim French consul, Buenos Aires, 25 Jan. 1837; CCC, Buenos Aires, tome 2, 1836–37, fol. 346 verso, MRE.

76. See Bonpland's journal of notes from Buenos Aires, Nov. 1836; AAB, carpeta 7, MFJAD. The contents of this journal also include some copied correspondence. In addition, Bonpland provided an interesting description of how much the frontier town Rosario had changed for the better since 1819. When he first knew the place, it was a "truly sad and poor little village." By 1836, it had gained a population of between three thousand and five thousand people. "I admired the Rosario gardens. They abound in vegetables, in flowers and in fruit trees. Amongst the last, one sees peach and apricot trees reminiscent of Europe."

77. See the discussion in Sabor, *Pedro de Angelis*, pp. 47, 48–52.

78. Bonpland journal, Nov. 1836, fol. 3.

79. See Ganson, *Guaraní under Spanish Rule*, p. 46.

80. Bonpland journal, Nov. 1836, fol. 3.

81. José María Cabrer was a Catalan. He came with his father to South America, where he worked as a geographer and cartographer on a boundary commission, and died at Buenos Aires in 1836. De Angelis bought mss. from Cabrer's widow and wrote a biographical notice of him. Cabrer's contributions were a topical subject when Bonpland arrived at Buenos Aires. Josefa Sabor argues the following: "As is known, one of the zones that most interested de Angelis was that of the Chaco and the places where the missions were established" (Sabor, *Pedro de Angelis*, pp. 163, 164–65). The comment works equally well for Bonpland. Bonpland's comment on Cabrer is found in his journal entry of Nov. 1836, fol. 8 verso.

82. De Angelis's bibliography offered a mixture of published and unpublished works. See Sabor, *Pedro de Angelis*, pp. 207–10.

83. The original request for the report came in a letter of 10 May 1836. See Roger to the minister of foreign affairs, Buenos Aires, 19 Nov. 1836; CCC, Buenos Aires, tome 2, 1836–37, fol. 261, MRE.

84. Roger to the minister, Buenos Aires, 19 Dec. 1836, CCC, Buenos Aires, tome 2, 1836–37, fol. 264, MRE.

85. Consul Aimé Roger to the French minster of foreign affairs, Buenos Aires, 15 Dec. 1836; CCC, Buenos Aires, tome 2, 1836–37, fols. 264–78 verso, MRE.

86. A good discussion of the circumstances of the portrait is found in Sabor, *Pedro de Angelis*, p. 359. But some caveats are in order. It is not the only portrait of Bonpland, as claimed there, nor is it clear that he lodged with the de Angelis family on the second trip to Buenos Aires. The image was reproduced in *Bonplandia*, pub-

lished at Hannover, in 1856. Sabor claims that this was the first image Humboldt had seen of Bonpland since their youth. However, Humboldt had already seen a photograph of Bonpland three years earlier, forwarded from New York by John Torrey of the College of Physicians and Surgeons in that city. See the excellent brief discussion in Schneppen, *Bonpland: Humboldts vergessener Gefährte?* pp. 41–42.

87. See Hamy, *Aimé Bonpland, médecin et naturaliste*, pp. 97–124. The next most heavily documented section in Hamy is the trip to Montevideo in 1853–54. In part, this frequency of writing from the leading cities of the region is evidence of the relative ease of communication with Europe from the leading southern South American cities.

88. Bonpland to Gigaux, Buenos Aires, 1 Dec. 1836, printed in ibid., p. 100.

89. Bonpland to Olive Gallocheau, Buenos Aires, 1 Dec. 1836, printed in ibid., pp. 101–2.

90. Domínguez, *Bonpland . . . en la República Argentina*, p. 48.

91. Bonpland to Adrien de Jussieu, Buenos Aires, 25 Jan. 1837, printed in Hamy, *Aimé Bonpland, médecin et naturaliste*, p. 116.

92. Bonpland to Duméril, Buenos Aires, 25 Jan. 1837, printed in ibid., esp. p. 121. Bonpland refers specifically in his letter to the third edition of Duméril's *Élémens des sciences naturelles*.

93. Juan [John] Hannah, Estancia de los Sajones, 1 Mar. 1837 to Bonpland (letter in Spanish); AAB, carpeta 3, MFJAD. We presume these were the same 30 mestizo rams Bonpland discussed in a note from an undefined time and place to Peter Sheridan. The content of the note reveals it was written sometime between September 1837 and September 1838. Bonpland wanted Blanc & Constantin, his agents at Buenos Aires, to pay Sheridan for the sheep at the agreed "moderate price" of 50 paper pesos each. See the note from Bonpland to Peter Sheridan, without date or address; AAB, carpeta 4, MFJAD. Sheridan reflected fondly on Bonpland's visit to his ranch, making reference to Ambrosian Nights in a letter to Bonpland from Buenos Aires, 4 July 1841. The main point of this letter was to recommend the British merchant Richard Hughes to Bonpland. Hughes was about to embark on a commercial mission to Paraguay. See Whigham, "Some Reflections on Early Anglo-Paraguayan Commerce," pp. 282–83.

94. See Domínguez, *Bonpland . . . en la República Argentina*, p. 48.

95. The company hedged its bets. Constantin, of the merchant firm Blanc & Constantin, reported to Bonpland in 1840 from Montevideo, passing along the news from Paris. The view there was that the project could succeed if managed by experienced hands, but that nobody wanted to invest in such distant places. Constantin to Bonpland, Montevideo, 21 Apr. 1840; BBAW.

96. Bonpland to the Delessert family at Paris, Buenos Aires, 2 Mar. 1837; AAB, carpeta 4, MFJAD.

97. Bonpland to Humboldt, Buenos Aires, 2 Mar. 1837, printed in Hamy, *Aimé Bonpland, médecin et naturaliste*, pp. 121–23. John Henry Mandeville served as the British minister plenipotentiary at Buenos Aires between 1836 and 1845. For further details of his stylish life there, see Lynch, *Argentine Dictator*, p. 377n75.

98. Bonpland, travel journals, "Viaje de Buenos Aires à Corrientes (1837)," 10 Mar. 1837, fol. 1; AAB, carpeta 7, MFJAD.

99. Ibid., 12 Mar. 1837, fol. 1 verso. Dr. William Wilson was one of the original inhabitants of the Scottish colony at Monte Grande. See Grierson, *Colonia de Monte Grande*, p. 42. Francisco Cosme Argerich (1784–1846) belonged to the first generation of creole medical doctors educated at Buenos Aires. Like his father, he had a distinguished career in Argentina, but he died in political exile at Montevideo.

100. Bonpland, travel journals, "Viaje de Buenos Aires à Corrientes (1837)," 23 Mar. 1837, fol. 7.

101. Bonpland, travel journals, "Diario, 1837, Viaje à Corrientes," 6 Apr. 1837, fol. 1; AAB, carpeta 7, MFJAD.

102. Ibid., 7 Apr. 1837, fol. 1 verso.

103. Ibid., 8 Apr. 1837, fol. 2.

104. See Isabelle, *Voyage a Buénos-Ayres et a Porto-Alègre*, p. 32.

105. Letter from José [Joseph] Ingres to Bonpland (in French), São Borja, 19 Apr. 1837; AAB, carpeta 3, MFJAD.

106. Bonpland received Ingres's letter at Corrientes on 3 May 1837 and replied from Curuzú Cuatiá on 26 May. Understandably, the main theme in Ingres's correspondence with Bonpland was commerce. Writing from Salto, Uruguay, on 10 July 1836, he noted the negative impact of the Farroupilha War on economic development: "The growth of this province [Uruguay] is in proportion with the decadence of that of Rio Grande [do Sul]." Writing from the same town again on 14 March 1839, he announced that Serny, another of the French merchants based at São Borja, was about to leave for France, having accumulated a considerable fortune in South America. A letter from Belém, Uruguay, to Bonpland at Curuzú Cuatiá, written on 26 October 1839, asked him to propose a list of commodities to the government of Corrientes for the provisioning of its troops. The items included tobacco and American cotton, for which Ingres was prepared to accept a mix of money and hides in payment. He clearly counted on Bonpland's help for commercial ventures of this kind. Ingres's letters are in AAB, carpeta 3, MFJAD.

107. Bonpland, travel journals, "Diario, 1837, Viaje à Corrientes," 10, 11, 12 Apr. 1837, fols. 2 and 2 verso; AAB, carpeta 7, MFJAD.

108. Bonpland, travel journals, "Voyage de Corrientes à la côte de l'Uruguay (juin 1838)," 12 July 1838, fol. 12; AAB, carpeta 7, MFJAD.

109. See Robertson and Robertson, *Letters on Paraguay*, 1:xv.

110. Henry Hoker, Paraná, to Bonpland in Corrientes, 25 Apr. 1837; AAB, carpeta 3, MFJAD. Darwin visited Punta Gorda himself in 1833, leaving a brief description of the Indians there (Keynes, ed., *Charles Darwin's Beagle Diary*, pp. 196, 201). Hoker's letter contains the sole reference to Darwin that I have found in any of Bonpland's records.

111. See ms. 215, MHN.

112. See Frédéric Desbrosses to Bonpland, Buenos Aires, 26 June 1837; AAB, carpeta 2, MFJAD.

113. Bonpland, "Diario, 1837, Viaje à Corrientes," 8 May 1837, fol. xx verso; AAB,

carpeta 7, MFJAD. Bonpland used Roman numerals in a portion of this manuscript, but they do not always conform with the Roman system.

114. Ibid., 16 May 1837, fol. xxxxx.

115. Ibid., fol. vx.

116. Ibid., 19 May 1837, fol. vxxxx verso.

117. Ibid., 20 May 1837, fols. xi, xi verso, and xii.

118. Ibid., 23 May 1837, fol. xiii verso.

119. Ibid., 24 May 1837, fol. xiiii verso.

120. Ibid., 25 May 1837, fol. xi. Descriptions of the celebration of Argentina's national holiday made from the interior of the country are presumably rare.

121. Bonpland, travel journals, "Diario, Viaje de Vacá Cuá à La Cruz," 8 June 1837, fol. 1 verso; AAB, carpeta 7, MFJAD.

122. Ibid., 8 June 1837, fol. 2 verso.

123. Bonpland to Rafael de Atienza, Paso de Santa Ana, 8 June 1837; AAB, carpeta 1, MFJAD.

124. Bonpland, travel journals, "Diario, Viaje de Vacá Cuá à La Cruz," 11 June 1837, fol. 3; AAB, carpeta 7, MFJAD.

125. Ibid., 12 June 1837, fols. 4 verso and 5.

126. Draft letter from Bonpland to de Atienza, São Borja, 22 June 1837; AAB, carpeta 1, MFJAD. This letter is mainly a report on politics in Rio Grande do Sul.

127. Bonpland, "Journal, Sn. Borja, juillet 1837," 7 July 1837, fol. 3; AAB, carpeta 7, MFJAD.

128. Ibid., 9 July 1837, fol. 4 verso.

129. See the draft letter from Bonpland to Juan Francisco Gramajo, São Borja, 15 July 1837; AAB, carpeta 1, MFJAD. The Republican letters were to be carried to Corrientes by the military secretary Colonel José Victoriano Origue.

130. Consul Roger made this description when informing his government that Desbrosses had recently married Louise Petitjean, the daughter of the chancellor of the consulate. Earlier in the year, Desbrosses (described as a merchant aged 37) and Petitjean served as two of the three witnesses to a copy of the death certificate of the late French consul at Buenos Aires, the marquis de Vins de Peysac. They were said to be friends of the deceased. See Aimé Roger to the minister of foreign affairs, Buenos Aires, 23 May and 29 Dec. 1836; CCC, Buenos Aires, tome 2, 1836–37, fols. 159 and 280, MRE. Desbrosses, Buenos Aires, to Bonpland in Corrientes "or wherever he is to be found," 26 June 1837; AAB, carpeta 2, MFJAD.

131. Bonpland to de Atienza, São Borja, 29 June 1837; AAB, carpeta 1, MFJAD.

132. See the letter from the Delessert Bank, Paris, to Bonpland at Buenos Aires, 17 July 1837; AAB, carpeta 4, MFJAD.

133. Draft letter from Bonpland to Pedro Scheridan [Peter Sheridan], without date or address; AAB, carpeta 4, MFJAD.

134. Pioli de Layerenza and Artigas de Rebes, "Bonpland en el Plata," p. 59.

135. Desbrosses to Bonpland, Goya, 10 Sept. 1837; AAB, carpeta 3, MFJAD.

136. Desbrosses to Bonpland, Curuzú Cuatiá, 4 Nov. 1837. This letter was addressed to São Borja "or wherever he is to be found."

137. There is an account of the journey with Desbrosses in Bonpland's diary "Viaje de San Borja à Curuzú Cuatiá por la enfermedad del Gobernador Atienza," 26 Nov. 1837; AAB, carpeta 1, MFJAD. This manuscript also contains detailed medical notes on the governor's medical condition. Of the five doctors present, Bonpland held to a minority opinion about the preferred methods of treatment, confiding to his diary on 1 Dec. 1837 that de Atienza "will die a martyr."

138. Ibid., 29 Nov. 1837.

139. In 1839, Desbrosses was described as established in Montevideo. He worked from there to foment increased French opposition against Rosas. See Hermann, *France en Amérique latine*, pp. 228–29.

140. Draft letter from Bonpland to the Delesserts, Corrientes, 28 Mar. 1838; AAB, carpeta 4, MFJAD.

141. Bonpland eventually learned from the Delesserts that the senior member of the Barrois publishing dynasty (Charles Barrois) had been dead since 1829. The business was carried on by Barrois's eldest son, but he died in 1836. Thus Charles Barrois can never have read Bonpland's fascinating explanation for the stagnation of his capital, part of which reads as follows: "I have written in vain to Chile, in order to learn the fate of all the books I had left at Buenos Aires, including those for my personal use. I am tired of writing in this country: it is necessary to go there in person, and then I shall know where they are and whether or not they have been paid for." Bonpland to Barrois l'aîné, Corrientes, 28 Mar. 1838; AAB, carpeta 4, MFJAD.

142. See Hamy, *Aimé Bonpland, médecin et naturaliste*, pp. 124–32. Two things are especially interesting about the three letters Hamy published written from Corrientes in this period. Bonpland informed Humboldt that he lacked the requisite paper on which to prepare a geological map of the regions he had visited in southern South America. In sending 57 species of seeds to Mirbel, he provided details of the introduction of some exotics to Corrientes. An Australian casuarina brought unintentionally from Brazil around 1830 (it accompanied other plants introduced by Ferré, including coffee) now had a canopy surpassing that of all the other trees in the capital and was "an object of curiosity for all the town."

143. Petition of Diego and Roberto Davison to the government of Corrientes, Goya, May 1838; AAB, carpeta 4, MFJAD.

144. Bonpland to Mandeville, Corrientes, 18 June 1838; AAB, carpeta 4, MFJAD.

145. Berón de Astrada conceded Bonpland permission to move 60 horses and two stallions, Corrientes, 19 May 1838; see the file on legal topics in AAB, carpeta 4, MFJAD.

146. Bonpland, travel journals, "Corrientes, juin 1838," 29 June 1838, fol. 2; AAB, carpeta 7, MFJAD.

147. Ibid., 3 July 1838, fol. 4 verso.

148. On Bernal, see Whigham, *Politics of River Trade*, p. 166, and "Cattle Raising in the Argentine Northeast," pp. 327–28.

149. Bonpland, travel journals, "Corrientes, juin 1838," 10 July 1838, fols. 6 verso, 7 verso; AAB, carpeta 7, MFJAD.

150. Ibid., 11 July 1838, fols. 7 verso and 8.
151. Ibid., 15 July 1838, fol. 9 verso.
152. Bonpland, travel journals, "Voyage de Corrientes à la côte de l'Uruguay, juillet 1838," 16–17 July 1838, fol. 1 verso; AAB, carpeta 7, MFJAD.
153. Ibid., 23–24 July 1838, fols. 2 and 2 verso.
154. Ibid., 27 July 1838, fol. 3 verso.
155. Ibid., 28, 29, 30, 31 July 1838, fol. 4.
156. Bonpland, "Journal d'agriculture," 3 Aug. 1838; AAB, carpeta 5, MFJAD. The agricultural diary starts at the beginning of August 1838: "On the land designated by the name of Paso de Santa Ana, which I have obtained in emphyteusis, I have begun today to plant and to sow. According to the title and the measurement, the land at Santa Ana should have 3.75 square leagues of area, but I dare to assert that it has at least five leagues of good land." Although in fragments, the agricultural diary provides some account of developments at São Borja and Santa Ana down to Bonpland's death.
157. Ibid., 7 Aug. 1838, fol. 7.
158. Ibid., 5 Aug. 1838, fol. 5.
159. Ibid., 14 Aug. 1838, fol. 14. There is a file of letters with Sebastião Ribeiro during the period 1837–40 in AAB, carpeta 3, MFJAD.
160. Bonpland to Berón de Astrada, Pueblo de La Cruz, 28 Aug. 1838; AAB, carpeta 1, MFJAD.
161. Draft letter from Bonpland to Pedro Ferré, no place or date (but probably from January 1839); AAB, carpeta 1, MFJAD.
162. There is an extensive file of letters from João Lindau, written in Portuguese. Even though Lindau did not pay, Bonpland continued to supply him. In the period 19 May 1836 to 1844, he received goods worth 229$320, which was more than the value of Bonpland's property at São Borja. See, especially, the letter about debt from Bonpland to Lindau, São Borja, 27 June 1846; AAB, carpeta 3, MFJAD.
163. See the notes on San Xavier in ms. 215, MHN.
164. Bonpland, "Voyage dans la partie haute de l'Uruguay," 12 Jan. 1839, fol. 9; AAB, carpeta 7, MFJAD.
165. Ibid., 15 Jan. 1839, fol. 1.
166. Ibid., 21 Jan. 1839, fol. 3.
167. Ibid., 23 Jan. 1839, fol. 5.
168. Ibid., 26 Jan. 1839, fol. 6.
169. Ibid, 30 Jan. 1839, fol. 8, and "Voyage dans le haut de l'Uruguay en janvier et fevrier 1839," 1 Feb. 1839, fol. 1.
170. Bonpland, "Voyage dans le haut de l'Uruguay en janvier et fevrier 1839," 2 Feb. 1839, fol. 2.
171. See Shumway, *Invention of Argentina*, esp. pp. 44–45, 79–80.
172. Bonpland, "Journal de voyage," 8 Mar. 1839, fol. 1; AAB, carpeta 1, MFJAD.
173. Genaro Berón de Astrada to Bonpland, Pago Largo, 31 Mar. 1839; AAB, carpeta 1, MFJAD.

Chapter Four

1. Bonpland to Rivera, Salto, Uruguay, 17 July 1840; AAB, carpeta 1, MFJAD.
2. A. P. de Candolle to Bonpland, Geneva, 28 Dec. 1840; AAB, carpeta 2, MFJAD. A biogeographer and botanist of world reputation, De Candolle died the following year. Bonpland's lifespan turned out to be more than a decade longer than Francia's.
3. Shumway, *Invention of Argentina*, p. 4.
4. Ibid., p. 113.
5. Morgan, "French Policy in Spanish America," p. 315. The policies of France and Britain in the Plata are reviewed in John Cady's *Foreign Intervention*. See also McLean, *War, Diplomacy and Informal Empire*. A recent study by Jean-David Avenel, *L'affaire du Rio de la Plata*, draws usefully from the extensive records of the French naval archives.
6. Morgan, "French Ideas of a Civilizing Mission," pp. 389, 400.
7. Hermann, *France en Amérique latine*, pp. 186–87.
8. For details of Lavalle's career and the controversies it created in the historiography of Argentina, see the excellent discussion in Shumway, *Invention of Argentina*, pp. 115–17, 199–207.
9. Hermann, *France en Amérique latine*, p. 246.
10. On the closure of the French consulate at Buenos Aires, see ibid., pp. 183–84.
11. Bacle spent some time in exile from Buenos Aires collecting in Santa Catarina. Most of his collections were lost to a shipwreck when returning to Buenos Aires. See Varese, *Bacle en las costas de Montevideo*. Some portion of his botanical work survives at Geneva.
12. Domínguez, *Bonpland . . . en la República Argentina*, p. 50.
13. See Domínguez, "Urquiza y Bonpland," pp. 4–6.
14. See Bonpland to François Delessert, Montevideo, 17 May 1840, printed in Hamy, *Aimé Bonpland, médecin et naturaliste*, p. 134.
15. Bonpland had discussed the project with Nascimbene somewhere in the period from December 1838 to January 1839. See Bonpland to Pascual de Echagüe, Santa Ana, 9 June 1839; AAB, carpeta 6, MFJAD.
16. Bonpland to Luís Nascimbene, Santa Ana, 4 June 1839; AAB, carpeta 3, MFJAD.
17. Bonpland to Pascual de Echagüe, Santa Ana, 9 June 1839; AAB, carpeta 6, MFJAD. In this draft, Bonpland carefully noted the appropriate manner of address for Echagüe, drawing such model phrases as "illustrious restorer of the public peace" from the *Gazeta de Buenos Aires*, where Rivera, on the other hand, was described as "the Unitarian tyrant."
18. Bonpland to Nascimbene, Santa Ana, 30 June 1839; AAB, carpeta 3, MFJAD.
19. Bonpland to President Bento Gonçalves da Silva, Santa Ana, 16 Feb. 1840; AAB, carpeta 3, MFJAD. Bonpland wrote a letter of recommendation to the botanist Mirbel at Paris on behalf of Joaquim Gonçalves da Silva, the Farrapo leader's son. Mirbel was asked in turn to recommend the young Brazilian to Alibert, Dumeril, and Richard, distinguished authorities at the school of medicine in Paris.

See also Bento Gonçalves to Bonpland, Alegrete, 4 Jan. 1843; AAB, carpeta 4, MFJAD.

20. See Lynch, *Argentine Dictator*, p. 207.

21. Bonpland, travel journals, "Diario, Santa Ana," 4 Nov.–29 Dec. 1839, Curuzú Cuatiá, and 5–6 Nov. 1839, fols. 6 and 6 verso; AAB, carpeta 7, MFJAD. Chilavert has not been forgotten in Argentine history, partly on account of the controversial manner of his death. Later switching sides, he fought with distinction at Caseros and was subsequently shot on Urquiza's orders. See the description of four letters from Bonpland to Chilvert written from San Roque in January 1840 in Cordier, *Papiers inédits du naturaliste Aimé Bonpland*, pp. 17–18.

22. Bonpland, travel journals, "Diario, Santa Ana," 23 Nov. 1839, fol. 8. On the revolt of the landowners to the south of Buenos Aires, see Lynch, *Argentine Dictator*, pp. 50, 205–6, 226–27; Adelman, *Republic of Capital*, p. 134.

23. Bonpland, "Diario, Santa Ana," 9 Dec. 1839, fol. 9 verso.

24. Ibid., 19, 20, 21, 22 Jan. 1840, fol. 2, verso.

25. Bonpland to José María Paz, Santa Lucía, 28 Jan. 1840; AAB, carpeta 1, MFJAD.

26. James Saeger notes that the Abipones, Guaycuruans from San Jerónimo in the Chaco, had taken refuge here in 1824 (*Chaco Mission Frontier*, p. 170).

27. Bonpland, travel journals, "Diario, Santa Ana," Santa Lucía, 27 Jan. 1840, fol. 6 verso.

28. Ibid., 21 Jan. 1840, fol. 2 verso.

29. Ibid., fol. 3.

30. Ibid., fols. 3–6. On the labor patterns of female Guaycuruans, see Saeger, *Chaco Mission Frontier*, esp. pp. 52–53, 65–66, 172.

31. Bonpland, "Diario, Santa Ana," Santa Lucía, 21 Jan. 1840, fol. 4 verso.

32. José Mariano Cardoso to Bonpland, Santa Ana, 21 Jan. 1840; AAB, carpeta 4, MFJAD.

33. Cardozo to Bonpland, Santa Ana, 10 Jan. 1840.

34. Bonpland, travel journals, "Diario, Santa Ana," Santa Lucía, 8 Mar. 1840, fols. 11 verso and 12.

35. Draft letter from Bonpland to Mirbel, Paso de Santa Ana, 16 Feb. 1840; AAB, carpeta 2, MFJAD.

36. In a file of his dealings with the merchant firm Blanc & Constantin at Montevideo, there is record that Bonpland received his French state pension for the years 1840 and 1841. He was unable to present further paperwork in connection with the pension before 1849. These records are contained in the Bonpland papers now at BBAW.

37. Bonpland, travel journals, "Viaje de Corrientes à La Bajada," Corrientes, 1 May 1840, fol. 2.

38. Ibid., Goya, 3 May 1840, fol. 3 verso.

39. Ibid., fol. 7 verso.

40. Valentín Alsina (1802–1869) was then in exile from Rosas, both writing and fighting against him. After the fall of Rosas, he held several high offices in

Argentina. Twice elected to the governorship of Buenos Aires province in the 1850s, Alsina was an Autonomist, a member of a political group working to guarantee the supremacy of Buenos Aires at any cost.

41. Bonpland, travel journals, "Viaje de Corrientes à La Bajada," fol. 8.

42. The carob bean was also the primary food source for some of the Guaycuruans. See Saeger, *Chaco Mission Frontier*, p. 54.

43. Bonpland, travel journals, "Diario de viaje, Paraná," Martín García, 12 May 1840, fol. 2 verso.

44. See Hermann, *France en Amérique latine*, pp. 189–90.

45. See Aurélio Porto's discussion of these claims in Brazil, *Anais do Itamaratí*, 1:243, 566–69.

46. Guy-Victor Duperré was born into opulence at La Rochelle, the twenty-third child of the crown official in charge of the treasury there. The death of his father in 1775 and the consequences of the French Revolution diminished the family circumstances. Duperré began his career at sea with a commercial voyage to Saint-Domingue, where a brother was established. See Chassériau, *Vie de l'amiral Duperré*, esp. pp. 5, 9, 11. Bonpland's parents also had investments in the same part of the Caribbean. It is a strong possibility that Bonpland's and Duperre's paths had crossed at some point in their adolescence.

47. On Dupotet's career and the difficulties of his mission in the Plata, partly stemming from conflicting orders coming from Paris, see Avenel, *L'affaire du Rio de la Plata*, pp. 25–26.

48. Bonpland, "Diario de viaje, Paraná," on board the *Atalante* off Montevideo, 14 May 1840, fol. 4.

49. See Duprey, *Voyage aux origines françaises de l'Uruguay*, p. 160.

50. Bonpland, travel journals, "Diario de viaje, Paraná," fol. 4 verso.

51. This may have been the occasion when Bonpland was witnessed at Montevideo by the great Argentine jurist Dalmacio Vélez Sarsfield (1801–1875), who later told the Chilean historian Benjamín Vicuña Mackenna that Bonpland was a crazy Frenchman, who wandered around wearing giant spurs. What this reveals most of all is that Vélez Sarsfield, born in the Argentinean interior, had completely rejected the rural values of such places by the time he went into political exile in Uruguay. See Piccirilli, *Rivadavia y su tiempo*, 3:96.

52. Bonpland to François Delessert, Montevideo, 17 May 1840, printed in Hamy, *Aimé Bonpland, médecin et naturaliste*, p. 133.

53. Matthias Jacob Schleiden (1804–81) was a botanist and naturalist, recognized as a founder of cell theory.

54. Bonpland to Mirbel, Montevideo, 17 May 1840, printed in Hamy, *Aimé Bonpland, médecin et naturaliste*, pp. 138–41. The draft of this letter varies in the wording from the fair copy. In the draft, Bonpland also stressed the value of knowledge of plant properties as coloring agents and for their uses in medicine. See Bonpland to Mirbel, Montevideo, 17 May 1840; AAB, carpeta 2, MFJAD.

55. Bonpland to A. P. de Candolle, Montevideo, 18 May 1840, printed in Hamy, *Aimé Bonpland, médecin et naturaliste*, pp. 135–38.

56. A. P. de Candolle to Bonpland, Geneva, 28 Dec. 1840; AAB, carpeta 2, MFJAD.
57. Bonpland, travel journals, "Diario de viaje, Paraná," Montevideo, 20 May 1840, fol. 6.
58. Shumway, *Invention of Argentina*, p. 113.
59. Bonpland, travel journals, "Diario de viaje, Paraná," fol. 7 verso. On the background of Juan Antonio Tresserra, see Sáenz Quesada, *Mariquita Sánchez*, esp., p. 130.
60. Bonpland to Olive Gallocheau, Montevideo, 2 June 1840, printed in Hamy, *Aimé Bonpland, médecin et naturaliste*, pp. 141–44.
61. Bonpland, travel journals, "Diario de viaje, Montevideo al Salto," Montevideo, 23 June 1840, fol. 2 verso.
62. Bonpland to Consul Baradère, Salto, 10 July 1840; AAB, carpeta 1, MFJAD.
63. On Ramírez, see also Williams, *Rise and Fall of the Paraguayan Republic*, p. 94.
64. Bonpland to Rivera, Salto, 17 July 1840; AAB, carpeta 1, MFJAD. The consequences for the Paraguayan cattle economy were massive. See Whigham, *Politics of River Trade*, pp. 167–68, and the detailed account given in 1852 from Paraguay by the Swedish naturalist Eberhard Munck af Rosenschöld (Mörner, *Eberhard Munck . . . en el Paraguay*, pp. 23–25).
65. Later in the year, Bonpland reported to the governor of Corrientes that he had no certain news of Carabí's movements. Bonpland to Ferré, Santa Ana, 10 Nov. 1840; AAB, carpeta 1, MFJAD. On Carabí, see also Whigham, *Politics of River Trade*, p. 44.
66. Bonpland to Rivera, Salto, 17 July 1840; AAB, carpeta 1, MFJAD.
67. Ibid.
68. See Lynch, *Argentine Dictator*, pp. 207–8.
69. Bonpland, travel journals, "Diario de viaje, Corrientes" (Sept. 1840), Chaco, 26 Sept. 1840, fol. 1.
70. Ibid., fol. 1 verso.
71. Ibid.
72. Ibid. James Saeger has argued that "Guaycuruan allegiances remained largely factional, personal, local, and temporary throughout the nineteenth century" (*Chaco Mission Frontier*, p. 171).
73. Bonpland, "Diario de viaje, Corrientes" (Sept. 1840), Chaco, 26 Sept. 1840, fol. 2.
74. Bonpland, travel journals, "Diario de viaje, Corrientes" (September 1840), 4 Oct. 1840, fol. 2 verso.
75. José María Paz to Bonpland, 28 Oct. 1840, printed in Domínguez, *Bonpland . . . en la República Argentina*, p. 49.
76. Bonpland, travel journals, "Diario de viaje, Corrientes" (September 1840), 29 Oct. 1840, fol. 8 verso. At least one of the letters he carried from Paz was destined for the Paraguayan diplomat Juan Andrés Gelly, then resident at Montevideo, from where he formed part of the resistance to Rosas. Writing from Bonpland's room

at Montevideo on 15 December 1840, Gelly informed Paz that receipt of his letter expressing enduring friendship had removed a great weight from his conscience. Linked during the 1820s through war against Brazil and through their support of the Lavalle government in Argentina, for eleven years Gelly feared he had lost Paz's support. The letter carried to Montevideo by Bonpland had set his mind to rest. See Ramos, *Juan Andrés Gelly*, p. 176.

77. Bonpland to Ferré, Santa Ana, 1 Nov. 1840; AAB, carpeta 1, MFJAD.
78. Bonpland to Ferré, Santa Ana, 10 Nov. 1840; AAB, carpeta 1, MFJAD.
79. Bonpland, travel journals, "Diario de viaje de Corrientes à Montevideo," 25 Nov. 1840, fol. 2.
80. Ibid., 27 Nov. 1840, fol. 3 verso. Nollet was later one of the twenty-one titular members of the Sociedad de Medicina Montevideana.
81. See the draft letter from Bonpland to Ferré, Montevideo, 4 Dec. 1840; AAB, carpeta 1, MFJAD.
82. Bonpland to Rivera, Montevideo, 3 Dec. 1840; AAB, carpeta 1, MFJAD.
83. Bonpland, travel journals, "Diario de viaje de Corrientes à Montevideo," fol. 5 verso.
84. Ibid., 4 Jan. 1841, fol. 7.
85. Bonpland to Rivera, Salto, 20 Jan. 1841; AAB, carpeta 1, MFJAD.
86. Dominique Roguin to Bonpland, Montevideo, 16 Mar. to 11 Apr. 1841; AAB, carpeta 4, MFJAD.
87. Paz to Bonpland, Villa Nueva, 9 February 1841, cited in Domínguez, *Bonpland . . . en la República Argentina*, p. 50.
88. The receipt for 5,000 patacones, dated from Salto, 4 Mar. 1841 is at BBAW. The sum is considerable. He paid one of his workers 5 patacones a month, thus this amount would have sufficed for around eighty-three years of salary. Bonpland received the funds on behalf of the government of Corrientes from Juan Feliciano Vasquez, the receiver at Salto, following Rivera's orders; AAB, carpeta 1, MFJAD.
89. Bonpland, travel journals, "Diario de viaje, Santa Ana" (March 1841), 13 Mar. 1841, fol. 1.
90. On the theme of opening British commercial links with Paraguay, see Whigham, "Some Reflections on Early Anglo-Paraguayan Commerce." For background on Gelly, see Williams, *Rise and Fall of the Paraguayan Republic*, esp. pp. 152–53.
91. Juan Andrés Gelly to Bonpland, Montevideo, 16 July 1841; AAB, carpeta 1, MFJAD. The letter also discussed terror at Buenos Aires, namely the ill treatment of women by the Mazorca (Rosas's legendary paramilitary squads) at the church doors. Gelly had also written extensively on the same date and theme to Pedro Ferré. See Ramos, *Juan Andrés Gelly*, pp. 199–203. Although slight differences in wording occur between the copy of a letter held in the Archivo General de la Nación Argentina, on which Ramos drew, and the letter sent from Gelly to Bonpland, the latter is almost certainly the unidentified recipient in Ramos's discussion.
92. Remarkably little concrete is known about Victoriana Cristaldo. See Hossard,

Bonpland . . . explorateur en Amérique du Sud, pp. 127–28. Even the supposed manner of their meeting in a field clinic, which Hossard relays, remains conjecture.

93. See Domingo Aldão to Bonpland, Santa Ana, 27 Jan. 1842; AAB, carpeta 6, MFJAD. Aldão's letters are property reports. He told Bonpland that Victoriana had been greatly cheered to learn he was well.

94. Bonpland to Ferré, Santa Ana, 7 May 1842; AAB, carpeta 1, MFJAD. Born in Minas Gerais, Ulhoa Cintra was the minister in the Riograndense Republic responsible for justice and for foreign affairs. See Spalding, *Revolução Farroupilha*, p. 124.

95. Bonpland, travel journals, "Diario de viaje à Santa Ana al Estado Oriental," 15 Oct. 1842, fol. 4.

96. Ibid., 6 Nov. 1842, fol. 7. On Garibaldi's fighting for the Unitarians, see McLean, "Garibaldi in Uruguay"; Adelman, *Republic of Capital*, p. 135. Garibaldi's efforts were not confined to Spanish America; he also fought on behalf of the Farrapos in Rio Grande do Sul.

97. Bonpland, "Diario de viaje à Santa Ana al Estado Oriental," early November 1842, fols. 8 and 8 verso.

98. Apollon de Mirbel to Bonpland, Santa Ana, 29 Sept. 1842; AAB, carpeta 3, MFJAD.

99. Whigham, *Paraguayan War*, 1:105. See also Adelman, *Republic of Capital*, pp. 125, 127.

100. Bonpland, "Journal d'agriculture," São Borja, 1843; AAB, carpeta 5, MFJAD.

101. Ibid.

102. Ibid., 1 Jan. 1844.

103. See Bonpland to Gregorio Maciel, Sargento Mor, São Borja, 6 Sept. 1847 (letter in Spanish); AAB, carpeta 8, MJFAD. Bonpland was trying to collect for curing Maciel's wife of herpes in June 1833 and for the treatment of "el negrito" in January 1844.

104. The broad pattern was repeated in Bonpland's vaccination records for 1853. On 28 February of that year, following work "in the house of Sousa's Indians," patients 33 and 34 were Bonpland's sons "Amadito of 4 to 5 years and Anastasio of 2 to 3 years."

105. Bonpland, travel journals, "Diario de viaje de Corrientes à São Borja, July 1844," Santa Ana, 4 Aug. 1844, fol. 5. The locations at the head of this manuscript should clearly be reversed.

106. Ibid., Restauración (Paso de los Libres), 11 Aug. 1844, fol. 6.

107. Ibid., São Borja, 20 Aug. 1844, fol. 6 verso.

108. The anti-Rosas actions of the Madariaga brothers were heavily backed by Brazil. See Whigham, *Paraguayan War*, 1:105.

109. See ibid., esp. 1:466n14.

110. See Bonpland's list of names of people at São Borja in 1848, mainly officials; ms. 212, MHN.

111. See B*** (Roy), *Mes voyages avec le docteur Philips*, esp. p. 259.

112. Ibid., pp. 314–15.

113. See Demersay, *Histoire physique, économique et politique du Paraguay*, 1:xl.

114. Ibid., 1:xxi.

115. José Antonio Pimenta Bueno, Asunción to Bonpland at São Borja (letter in Portuguese), 1 Nov. 1846; AAB, carpeta 2, MFJAD. The jurist and liberal politician Pimenta Bueno had a reputation for intelligence. It was said of him that he was brilliant enough "to enter the Pantheon through the front doors," a rare quality in imperial Brazil. See Pang, *Noblemen of the Southern Cross*, p. 63.

116. Bonpland to Pimenta Bueno, 8 Nov. 1846; AAB, carpeta 2, MFJAD. This draft contains a mass of corrections.

117. Bonpland to Pimenta Bueno, 21 Nov. 1846; AAB, carpeta 2, MFJAD. While the draft of this letter carries no date, this can be established from the recipient's reply on 15 December 1846.

118. Pimenta Bueno to Bonpland, 15 Dec. 1846; AAB, carpeta 6, MFJAD.

119. On the character of Carlos Antonio López's government, see especially Whigham, *Paraguayan War*, 1:68.

120. Contreras Roqué and Boccia Romañach, *Paraguay en 1857*, pp. 84–85.

121. José Francisco Xavier Sigaud (1796–1856) first came to Brazil in 1825. He served as one of the heads of the Sociedade de Medicina do Rio de Janeiro. His *Du climat et des maladies du Brésil, ou statistique médicale de cet empire* is a landmark in the history of Brazilian medical publications.

122. Sigaud, Rio de Janeiro, to Bonpland at São Borja, 1 Oct. 1849; AAB, MFJAD.

123. Sigaud proposed José dos Santos Carvalho, probably a student of pharmacy, to make the link between the capital and São Borja.

124. On the first occasion, in 1833, a French-educated South American medical doctor also was chosen to relay the award, Teodoro M. Vilardebó (1803–1857) of Montevideo. He was also a polymath, who studied in Paris at some of the same institutions as Bonpland. Mañé Garzón, *Vilardebó . . . primer médico uruguayo*; Schiaffino, *Vida y obra de Vilardebó*.

125. Sigaud to Bonpland, Rio de Janeiro, 11 Feb. 1854; AAB, MFJAD. This letter was probably a reply to a letter written by Bonpland to Sigaud from São Borja, 25 May 1853; AAB, carpeta 8, MFJAD. Its most interesting theme was that Demersay had begun the publication of his travel account and Bonpland hoped to see the first parts of this during a journey to Montevideo. While Sigaud sent his February 1854 letter to São Borja, Bonpland received it at Santa Ana on 1 May 1854, when he was no longer a resident of Brazil.

126. The certificate was sent from Rio de Janeiro on 21 Mar. 1851. Bonpland's reply to José Praxedes Pereira Pacheco, the president of the society, came from São Borja on 10 Oct. 1851; AAB, MFJAD.

127. Gay, *Invasão paraguaia*. Gay wrote much more widely than this, however, including an important study of the Jesuit missions. José Honório Rodrigues considered Gay perhaps one of the best exponents of regional history in nineteenth-century Brazil (*História e historiadores do Brasil*, pp. 73–90).

128. As can be inferred from Gay to Bonpland, São Francisco de Assis, 30 Sept. 1847; AAB, carpeta 4, MFJAD.

129. See the letters from Gay to Bonpland from Alegrete, 5 July, 14 Nov., and 7 Dec. 1848; AAB, carpeta 4, MFJAD. By the end of 1848, intellectual matters were already a theme of this correspondence. Gay had been asked by the French consul at Rio de Janeiro to supply books written in the Guaraní language, for which he turned to Bonpland for help.

130. Lynch, *Argentine Dictator*, p. 315.

131. Apollon de Mirbel, Uruguaiana to Bonpland at São Borja, 26 July 1847; AAB, carpeta 3, MFJAD. A further undated letter, but probably written later in 1847, continued the theme of discouraging Bonpland from agricultural speculations. Mirbel pronounced himself at ease upon hearing that Bonpland had a fine pharmacy under way at São Borja, because current rumor claimed that he was thinking of developing a yerba plantation. He asked Bonpland to remember all the problems with his land in Corrientes before launching into any further long-term agricultural schemes with unsure prospects. Mirbel moved from Uruguay to practice medicine at Uruguaiana. In a letter of 19 April 1847 to Bonpland, he sounded fairly optimistic about his decision, but Mirbel was soon describing Uruguaiana as a place of "dreadful gloom." In the 1850s, this Frenchman resettled in Uruguay, at Salto.

Chapter Five

1. Raffeneau-Delile to Bonpland, Montpellier, 4 Nov. 1848; AAB, MFJAD. Raffeneau-Delile joined Napoleon's expedition to Egypt in 1798, taking Bonpland's place. The author of numerous works, he is best known for the *Flore d'Égypte*. While consistently pessimistic, his letters to Bonpland offer a fascinating portrait of the gathering social tensions at Paris along the course of the first half of the nineteenth century.

2. Roguin to Bonpland, Montevideo, 24 Aug. 1852; AAB, carpeta 4, MFJAD. Bonpland had been projecting a return visit to Paraguay since 1846. He did not reach there before 1857, as part of a French naval expedition.

3. Baptista de Oliveira to Bonpland, Rio de Janeiro, 22 Mar. 1854; AAB, carpeta 4, MFJAD.

4. See Spalding, *Revolução Farroupilha*, esp. pp. 21–22.

5. Carvalho, *Nobiliário sul-rio-grandense*, pp. 207–8. Pedro Chaves was made Barão de Quaraí in 1855.

6. See Bonpland to Demersay, Porto Alegre, 10 June 1849, printed in Hamy, *Aimé Bonpland, médecin et naturaliste*, pp. 146–49.

7. Bonpland's portion of this sheep correspondence is made up of ten letters written from São Borja; manuscripts, I-2, 3, 36, BN. The reverse side of the correspondence is held in Buenos Aires at AAB, carpeta 3, MFJAD.

8. Bonpland to Chaves, 5 Aug. 1847 and 5 Mar. 1848, BN.

9. Ibid., 2 May 1848, BN.

10. Ibid., 25 Apr. 1848, BN.

11. Ibid., 24 June 1848, BN; on the character of Indian agriculture, see especially Auguste de Saint-Hilaire's description of the former mission at São Luís (*Viagem ao Rio Grande do Sul*, p. 148).

12. Bonpland to Chaves, 5 Oct. 1848, BN.

13. This becomes evident in ibid., 9 Oct. 1848, BN.
14. Francisco José de Sousa Soares de Andréa, later Barão de Caçapava (1781–1858), came to Brazil with the removal of the Portuguese court in 1808. He had an important career as a professional administrator.
15. Ibid.
16. Ibid., 24 June 1848, BN.
17. Ibid., 9 Oct. 1848, BN. See also Bonpland's notes from the *Jornal do Comércio* (Porto Alegre), 17 July 1848, about a project discussed in the provincial assembly of 1 July 1848. The outcome was hardly favorable for Bonpland's mission to convince a skeptic; AAB, carpeta 8, MFJAD.
18. Bonpland, *Journal voyage de Sn. Borja a la cierra y a Porto Alegre*, p. 3. This publication is based upon mss. 208 and 209 of the MHN.
19. Ibid., pp. 3–18.
20. There is a useful discussion of southern Brazil's physical environments in Waibel, "Princípios da colonização européia no sul do Brasil," pp. 227–28.
21. See Dean, "Latifundia and Land Policy in Nineteenth-Century Brazil," pp. 606–25.
22. Roche, *Colonização alemã e o Rio Grande do Sul*, 1:100–102, 109–12.
23. Roche, *l'administration . . . du Rio Grande do Sul*, pp. 229–30, 268n138.
24. Bonpland, *Journal voyage de Sn. Borja a la cierra y a Porto Alegre*, p. 18.
25. Ibid., pp. 20–21.
26. See Roche, *Colonização alemã e o Rio Grande do Sul*, 1:101.
27. Bonpland, *Journal voyage de Sn. Borja a la cierra y a Porto Alegre*, p. 25.
28. See "Herbe du Paraguay" in the scientific journal Bonpland kept at Buenos Aires, for March 1832, fols. 5 verso and 6; AAB, carpeta 7, MFJAD. Notes made subsequent to 1832 are in carpeta 5, legajo 13, MFJAD. See also Whigham, *Politics of River Trade*, 121–22.
29. Bonpland, *Journal voyage de Sn. Borja a la cierra y a Porto Alegre*, pp. 30–31.
30. On the return trip to Santa Cruz of November 1849, Bonpland became interested in the question of which types of woods worked best for drying the leaves (ibid., pp. 74–75).
31. See Miers, "On the History of the 'Mate' Plant," pp. 219–28, 389–401. Bonpland sent specimens and notes from Corrientes to Miers in London on 17 June 1857.
32. Raffeneau-Delile to Bonpland, Montpellier, 4 Nov. 1848. See also an earlier letter of 29 September; AAB, MFJAD.
33. Bonpland to Raffeneau-Delile, Porto Alegre, 10 June 1849, printed in Hamy, *Aimé Bonpland, médecin et naturaliste*, p. 149. Hamy was able to publish only a fragment of this letter. Another portion of it is in the French national archives.
34. Bonpland to Raffeneau-Delile, Porto Alegre, 10 June 1849; AJ[15], 570, AN.
35. Bonpland to the Delessert family, Porto Alegre, 10 June 1849; AAB, carpeta 4, MFJAD.
36. Bonpland to Demersay, Porto Alegre, 10 June 1849, printed in Hamy, *Aimé Bonpland, médecin et naturaliste*, pp. 146–49.

37. See the manuscript diagram of the colonial lots and their 39 petitioners, including Bonpland, along the trail from Paredão to the summit of the Serra in folder 18, "Nottes sur l'Ilex theezans"; ms. 215, MHN.
38. Isabelle, *Emigração e colonização*, pp. 65–66.
39. Bonpland, *Journal voyage de Sn. Borja a la cierra y a Porto Alegre*, p. 135.
40. Bonpland to François Arago, Montevideo, 28 Sept. 1849, printed in Hamy, *Aimé Bonpland, médecin et naturaliste*, pp. 150–51. On Arago's importance for Humboldt, see Botting, *Humboldt and the Cosmos*, pp. 195–97.
41. See Whigham, *Politics of River Trade*, pp. 65–66.
42. Carlos Creus, Montevideo, 29 Sept. 1849, printed in "Informes diplomáticos de los representantes de España en el Uruguay," *Revista Histórica* (Montevideo), nos. 139–41, 47 (1975): 854.
43. Bonpland, *Journal voyage de Sn. Borja a la cierra y a Porto Alegre*, pp. 65–66; Bonpland to Andréa, Porto Alegre, 28 Oct. 1849, "Note sur l'avantage de cultiver la plante qui fournit le maté, de former des bois de cette plante et d'améliorer la fabrication de l'herbe dite maté," printed in Hamy, *Aimé Bonpland, médecin et naturaliste*, pp. 152–56.
44. Andréa to Bonpland, Porto Alegre, 1 Nov. 1849; AJ[15], 570, AN.
45. Philip von Normann to Bonpland, Porto Alegre, 7 Nov. 1849; AAB, carpeta 3, MFJAD. Bonpland recorded that he answered this letter on 19 December of the same year. The civil engineer and architect Georg Karl Philip Theodor von Normann (1818–1862) was a fascinating figure in the historical development of Rio Grande do Sul. He arrived there in 1848, following a background of work on railroad construction in Sweden. The provincial engineers, most of them of German background, were responsible for an array of projects in the early 1850s, including colony design. Normann began his Riograndense career supplying tools and equipment to agricultural colonists. By mid-1850, among other projects, he was drafted to design and supervise the construction of the Teatro São Pedro, the most imposing building in Porto Alegre of the period. He ran into stiff political opposition during his work on this public project and was posted in 1855 into the interior to work on road construction. The challenges of working with a series of provincial administrations appear to have driven him to drink. Despite the high significance of the buildings he constructed in Rio Grande do Sul and the importance of his map collection, he died in poverty. See Barreto, *Bibliografia sul-riograndense*, 2:990–95; Weimer, "Engenheiros alemães no Rio Grande do Sul," esp. pp. 180–87.
46. Ms. 215, MHN.
47. Bonpland, *Journal voyage de Sn. Borja a la cierra y a Porto Alegre*, p. 71. Frederico Augusto de Vasconcellos de Almeida Pereira Cabral (1819–1886), of Portuguese origin, studied at the university in Coimbra. He came to Rio Grande do Sul initially as a mining engineer, brought to study the coal reserves there. See Barreto, *Bibliografia sul-riograndense*, 1:230–33. As the examples of von Normann and Vasconcellos show, the provincial engineers turned their skills toward many things while in provincial employ.
48. Vasconcellos to Bonpland, Rio Pardo, 20 Dec. 1849; AAB, carpeta 4,

MFJAD. Günter Weimer maintains that Peter Kleudgen (1813–1888) immigrated to Brazil in 1851 ("Engenheiros alemães no Rio Grande do Sul," p. 191) but the December 1849 reference from Vasconcellos calls that into question. Whatever his earlier career, Kleudgen's life was to be intimately connected with the development of the Santa Cruz colony, not least through his work as an immigration agent. See Barreto, *Bibliografia sul-riograndense*, 2:756–57, and Kleudgen, *Die deutsche Kolonie Santa Cruz*.

49. Bonpland to Andréa, São Borja, 24 Dec. 1849; correspondence of the presidents, *maço* (packet) 20, AHRGS.

50. The main problem, Bonpland noted, was that the forest workers stripped the maté leaves without regard to seasons (*Journal voyage de Sn. Borja a la cierra y a Porto Alegre*, pp. 37, 77).

51. Philip von Normann to Bonpland, Porto Alegre, 6 Mar. 1850; AAB, carpeta 3, MFJAD.

52. Vasconcellos to Bonpland, Picada de Santa Cruz, 16 and 24 Mar. 1850; AAB, carpeta 4, MFJAD. The letter arrived at São Borja on the evening of 22 April, when Bonpland began an immediate reply. Vasconcellos presents a clear case of somebody over whose life Bonpland had some influence. In 1853, he wrote to the Frenchman at São Borja from Entre Ríos, Argentina, where Vasconcellos was evaluating the condition of some local sheep flocks. He had married and taken up the project of breeding sheep in Uruguay, thinking that he would probably settle somewhere close to Colonia. One of his associates was Irineu Evangelista de Sousa, Barão and later Visconde de Mauá (1813–1889), the great capitalist of imperial Brazil. Vasconcellos to Bonpland, Concordia, 24 Mar. 1853; AAB, carpeta 4, MFJAD.

53. Bonpland to Vasconcellos, São Borja, 22, 23, 24, and 25 Apr. 1850; AAB, carpeta 4, MFJAD.

54. See Bell, *Campanha Gaúcha*, pp. 235n61, 240n12.

55. Avé-Lallemant, *Viagem pela província do Rio Grande do Sul*, p. 171.

56. Ibid., p. 172.

57. Roche, *Colonização alemã e o Rio Grande do Sul*, 1:102, 105–6, 274–76. Today it is the home to a rapidly developing university, the Universidade de Santa Cruz do Sul.

58. Data on maté exports from Rio Grande do Sul are printed in Whigham, *Politics of River Trade*, p. 128, and Silva, "Ligações externas da economia gaúcha," p. 86.

59. See Hensel, "Beiträge zur näheren Kenntniss," pp. 349–50.

60. See Macchi, *El ovino en la Argentina*, esp. pp. 33–56.

61. Rock, *Argentina, 1516–1987*, p. 112.

62. Bonpland, *Journal voyage de Sn. Borja a la cierra y a Porto Alegre*, pp. 84–86. See also Thomas Page's 1855 description of the Estancia Campbell (*La Plata . . . and Paraguay*, esp. p. 325).

63. The account of the visit of 13–14 July 1850 is in Bonpland, *Journal voyage de Sn. Borja a la cierra y a Porto Alegre*, p. 90. A sympathetic portrait of Urquiza's intellectual interests appears in Whigham, *Paraguayan War*, 1:120.

64. See Shumway, *Invention of Argentina*, esp. pp. 169–70, 174–75, 180, 217.

65. See Bonpland to Fidel Sagastume, Montevideo, 15 Aug. 1850, printed in Domínguez, "Urquiza y Bonpland," esp. pp. 14–15.

66. The others were Saturnino Masoni (1826–1892) and George Penabert. These three individuals are obvious candidates as sources for some of the unidentified photographic images of Bonpland.

67. See Bonpland, *Journal voyage de Sn. Borja a la cierra y a Porto Alegre*, p. 66. Fredricks is a key figure in the history of early South American photography. Traveling there between 1844 and 1853, his roving career touched Argentina, Brazil, Cuba, Uruguay, and Venezuela for certain, and possibly also Paraguay. Based at Buenos Aires in 1851–52, Fredricks is regarded as the most important of the photographers active there around the middle of the nineteenth century. Among other things, he was responsible for the first general view of that city. He later opened a well-regarded photographic studio in New York, The Temple of Art. Fortunately, examples of his South American work are reaching print. See Levine, *Cuba in the 1850s*, esp. pp. 23, 25, 26, 28, 32, 73, 80; Fundación Antorchas, *Años del daguerrotipo*, pp. 19, 52–53, 56–57, 62–63, 101, 102. The last contains an unidentified portrait of Bonpland from the collections of Argentina's Museo Histórico Nacional, reproduced on page 88.

68. "Nouvelles géographiques," *Bulletin de la Société de Géographie*, 4th ser., 1 (Jan. 1851), pp. 86–87.

69. Bonpland to Chaves, Montevideo, 12 Aug. 1850, BN.

70. Bonpland to Desmarest & Ducoing, Montevideo, 30 Aug. 1850; AAB, carpeta 4, MFJAD.

71. Desmarest & Ducoing to Bonpland, Paris, 7 Jan. 1851; AAB, carpeta 4, MFJAD.

72. Bonpland to Mirbel, Montevideo, 1 Sept. 1850, printed in Hamy, *Aimé Bonpland, médecin et naturaliste*, pp. 158–60.

73. Gavrelle was a French authority on medical substances, who was visiting Montevideo. He and Bonpland shared an interest in ethnobotany.

74. Bonpland to the Chevalier Gavrelle, Montevideo, 8 Sept. 1850; AAB, carpeta 5, MFJAD.

75. Bonpland, *Journal voyage de Sn. Borja a la cierra y a Porto Alegre*, p. 104.

76. Bonpland's notes are dated from Montevideo, 5 Oct. 1850; AAB, carpeta 6, MFJAD. The author of the illustrated work remains to be clarified. Today, it is in the collections of the Biblioteca Nacional del Ecuador and erroneously attributed to Bonpland, under the title "Floresta Americana—Atlas, Manuscrito," Montevideo, 1850. See Díaz Piedrahita, "Botánica . . . de Humboldt y Bonpland," p. 77.

77. Bonpland, "Diario de viaje de Montevideo à San Borja"; AAB, carpeta 7, MFJAD.

78. Bonpland to Alfred Demersay, São Borja, 10 Oct. 1851; AAB, carpeta 6, MFJAD.

79. Ibid.

80. See Whigham, *Paraguayan War*, 1:107–8. Bonpland also made reference in a letter of 1852 to the decadence of commerce at São Borja. This we infer from the

letter of reply Antônio Vicente Porto wrote from Porto Alegre to Bonpland, 14 Jan. 1853; AAB, carpeta 3, MFJAD. Porto was a pharmacist in Porto Alegre who supplied medicines for Bonpland. He was an admirer of Bonpland's "generous spirit" and sent regular letters to São Borja.

81. Bonpland to Pujol, São Borja, 30 Nov. 1852, printed in Pujol, *Corrientes en la organización nacional*, 2:257–59. Bonpland's notes on yerba formed an entire chapter in Vicente Quesada's 1857 description of Corrientes (*Provincia de Corrientes*, pp. 78–90). Following the stimulus of Pujol's interest in planting cotton, Bonpland requested two ploughs of French manufacture from São Borja to help with the cultivation of this crop on the Estancia Santa Ana; see Bonpland to Pujol, Restauración, 29 July 1853, printed in ibid., 3:189. He concluded within a few years from this empirical crop trial that cotton did not work in southeastern Corrientes; see Page, *La Plata . . . and Paraguay*, p. 296.

82. Bonpland to Pujol, São Borja, 30 Nov. 1852, printed in Pujol, *Corrientes en la organización nacional*, 2:258.

83. There are several references similar to the following in Bonpland's working notes: "From San Xavier you can see a very high hill, which is known by the name of the Cerro de las Doze Vueltas. Behind this mountain, they reckon there is a very large *yerbal* that was worked in the time of the Jesuits. They say further that there are *picadas* of which one still sees the vestiges." Folder 21, "Sur le *mate* et les bois de *mate*"; ms. 215, MHN.

84. Whigham, *Politics of River Trade*, pp. 126–27.

85. See Bonpland's extensive manuscripts on yerba, especially from around San Xavier, in folder 21, "Sur le *mate* et les bois de *mate*"; ms. 215, MHN. These include his research notes, frequently drawing on oral research.

86. Bonpland to Pujol, São Borja, 14 Jan. 1853, printed in Pujol, *Corrientes en la organización nacional*, 3:9–11.

87. Bonpland to Gay, São Borja, 19 Apr. 1853; AAB, carpeta 4, MFJAD.

88. Part of the idea was for Bonpland to become one of the founders of the lodge at São Borja. A copy of the Masonic records from there on 22 May 1853, recommending Doctor Amado Bonpland as a member, is held in the Bonpland archive at Buenos Aires; AAB, carpeta 4, MFJAD. His letter of acceptance carries three separate dates, the most convincing of which is 5 September 1853. In this, he noted he had been set to become a Freemason in 1808 before particular circumstances, left unspecified, stood in the way. He was flattered to join an association for which he had always had "the deepest respect and the fullest admiration." This note from Bonpland to Gay was signed from São Borja on 2 Dec. 1852; BBAW. Gay's letter accepting Bonpland as a Freemason is dated 28 September of Masonic year 5852 [1852]. This reveals that the priest was also an honorary member of a lodge at Rio de Janeiro. A list of the 18 members of the lodge Cordialidade no Oriente as of 15 June 1856 is found in the Bonpland manuscripts at Berlin; BBAW. Almost all of these were Brazilian. They included Manoel de Almeida Gama Lobo d'Eça, scion of a leading regional landowning family; like Bonpland, d'Eça held the third degree of membership. By 1856, Padre Gay had risen from the eighteenth degree to the thirtieth. The Greek-born doctor Marcos Christino

Fioravante also held this elevated degree of Masonry. According to Robert Avé-Lallemant, Fioravante served as a ship's surgeon in the British Royal Navy before emigrating to Brazil around 1808 (*Viagem pela província do Rio Grande do Sul*, p. 284).

89. See Gay to Bonpland, 6 June of Masonic year 5856 [1856]; AAB, carpeta 4, MFJAD.

90. Gay to Bonpland, São Borja, 1 Dec. 1853; AAB, carpeta 4, MFJAD.

91. See Barreto, *Bibliografia sul-riograndense*, 1:578.

92. See Bonpland's sworn legal testimony about animal losses made at Curuzú Cuatiá, 13 July 1853; AAB, carpeta 3, MFJAD. When Pujol sought a copy of Bonpland's testimony the following year, Bonpland told him he would send it as soon as he next returned to Santa Ana, where he kept the document well protected. Bonpland to Pujol, Restauración, 30 Sept. 1854, printed in Pujol, *Corrientes en la organización nacional*, 4: 197–99.

93. The matter is reviewed in detail in the letter from Bonpland to Pujol, Restauración, 30 Sept. 1854, printed in Pujol, ibid., 4:197–99. The draft of this letter also contains an aide-mémoire on the sheep problem. Bonpland recalled that working together with Virasoro began during the first days of the latter's administration. His own portion of the enterprise was a result of the 30 fine merino rams and some sheep bought from Peter Sheridan of Buenos Aires, who at the time of purchase held the finest and most numerous flock available. Bonpland argued that all the merinos scattered around the eastern fringes of Corrientes were his, since he was the only person to introduce the breed east of the Miriñay River; AAB, carpeta 1, MFJAD. Despite his squabbles with Virasoro over livestock, Bonpland used his links with the frontier commander in order to occupy more land around Santa Ana. He ran into difficulties with the Abalos family over this land in 1855; "Campo del General Abalos," AAB, carpeta 8, MFJAD.

94. See the written findings signed by Bartolomé Rolón and witnesses at Timboy, in the second section of the department of Curuzú Cuatiá, 19 July 1853; AAB, carpeta 3, MFJAD.

95. Bonpland to Pujol, Restauración, 29 July 1853, printed in Pujol, *Corrientes en la organización nacional*, 3:189.

96. See Bonpland, "Sur les moutons"; AAB, carpeta 8, legajo 1, MFJAD.

97. Bonpland to Gregorio Váldez, 1 Aug. 1853; AAB, carpeta 1, MFJAD. Váldez, secretary-general of the government of Corrientes, helped Bonpland with the legal business of recovering sheep. This letter also includes interesting medical news about the demise of Colonel Loureiro, a political leader at São Borja.

98. See Bonpland, "Journal d'agriculture," 19 Oct. 1853; AAB, carpeta 5, MJFAD. On the preceding day, Bonpland wrote a long note on manioc, comparing the Pernambucan and local methods of planting this crop. According to him, the Brazilian method was to plant the segments of manioc vertically or obliquely, while the Spanish planted them horizontally. In what could be his motto, he noted that only experience would tell which of the two methods was preferable. Bonpland seems to have drawn experience here from a Brazilian peon, Francisco, whom he described as a *Bayano*, or Bahian, in the entry for 4 June 1854.

99. Victor Martin de Moussy to Pujol, Restauración, 12 Dec. 1853, printed in Pujol, *Corrientes en la organización nacional*, 3:302.

100. Domínguez claimed that Bonpland arrived at Montevideo near the end of December (*Bonpland . . . en la República Argentina*, p. 56), but the latter was already dating letters from there in the first third of the month.

101. See this correspondence in Hamy, *Aimé Bonpland, médecin et naturaliste*, pp. 163–87.

102. Bonpland to Vasconcellos, Montevideo, 10 Dec. 1853, printed in ibid., esp. pp. 166–67.

103. Bonpland to François Delessert, Montevideo, 26 Dec. 1853, printed in ibid., pp. 176–81.

104. Bonpland to Desmarest & Ducoing, Montevideo, 26 Dec. 1853; AAB, carpeta 4, MFJAD.

105. See Bonpland to Humboldt, Corrientes, 7 June 1857, printed in Hamy, *Aimé Bonpland, médecin et naturaliste*, esp. p. 213.

106. See Jennifer Pitts's introduction in Tocqueville, *Writings on Empire and Slavery*, p. xxxvii. An interesting review of the different French ideas about North African colonization appears in Heffernan, "Parisian Poor and . . . Algeria."

107. Édouard Drouyn de Lhuys, the minster of foreign affairs, to Consul General Maillefer [Daniel-Pierre Martin-Maillefer], Paris, 30 Nov. 1853; CCC, Montevideo, 1843–1856, tome 5, fols. 279–80, MRE. Around this time Bonpland was also invited to accompany the United States' Plata-Paraná-Paraguay survey; see Page, *La Plata . . . and Paraguay*, pp. 295–98. As he was very positive about the idea, it remains unclear why he did not act upon it. Other work, including the new plant mission for Algeria, probably stood in the way. On the considerable significance of the U.S. naval survey of the Plata, see Fifer, *Perceptions of Latin America*, esp. pp. 13–18.

108. Bonpland to Napoleon III, Montevideo, 12 Jan. 1854; AAB, carpeta 2, MFJAD. Both a draft and a copy of the letter sent are found in the Bonpland archive at Buenos Aires. My wording is based on the draft. A transcription of the letter sent is printed in Hossard, *Bonpland . . . explorateur en Amérique du Sud*, pp. 195–96. Maillefer to Drouyn de Lhuys, Montevideo, 2 Feb. 1854; CCC, Montevideo, tome 5, fol. 282.

109. This is according to the testimony of Bonpland's close friend at São Borja, the French-born priest and scholar Gay. See his manuscript "Le naturaliste Mr. Aimé Bonpland," São Borja, 29 Aug. 1858. This manuscript of 19 numbered pages is in F^{17} 3974, AN.

110. Bonpland to Napoleon III, Montevideo, 12 January 1854; AAB, carpeta 2, MFJAD.

111. See Gay's ms., "Le naturaliste Mr. Aimé Bonpland"; F^{17}, 3974, AN. Gay also claimed to learn from Bonpland's oral testimony that the latter was present at Napoleon III's birth. Gay to the Baron d'Ornano, French vice consul at Porto Alegre, São Borja, 15 Oct. 1856; Affaires Diverses, République Argentine, 1841–1867, carton 2, MRE.

112. Bonpland to Maillefer, Montevideo, 21 Jan. 1854; CCC, Montevideo, tome 5, fols. 284–85 verso.

113. See Bonpland to Humboldt, Montevideo, 29 Jan. 1854, printed in Hamy, *Aimé Bonpland, médecin et naturaliste*, p. 182. In the following month, Bonpland already described the Algerian work to Humboldt as "an immense task," while in October he claimed there was nobody competent to whom he could delegate. Bonpland to Humboldt, Montevideo, 3 Feb. 1854, and Restauración, 2 Oct. 1854, printed in ibid., pp. 186, 188–89.

114. Bonpland to Maillefer, Montevideo, 21 Jan. 1854; CCC, Montevideo, tome 5, fols. 284–85 verso.

115. Maillefer to Drouyn de Lhuys, Montevideo, 2 Feb. 1854; CCC, Montevideo, tome 5, fol. 282.

116. Ibid.

117. Bonpland to Maillefer, Concordia, Entre Ríos, 4 Mar. 1854; CCC, Montevideo, tome 5, fols. 295–96.

118. This South American palm is today a focus for conservation in Argentina's Parque Nacional El Palmar, Entre Ríos.

119. Pedro Antonio Margat (1806–1890), a naturalized Uruguayan, arrived at Montevideo from Versailles in 1838. His career in the horticultural transformation of Montevideo's parks and gardens was important. See Pivel Devoto, "Diario . . . de Pedro Margat," pp. 473–501.

120. Maillefer to Drouyn de Lhuys, Montevideo, 4 July 1854; CCC, Montevideo, tome 5, fol. 305.

121. Maillefer to Drouyn de Lhys, Montevideo, 2 Oct. 1854; CCC, Montevideo, tome 5, fol. 338.

122. Maillefer to Alexandre, the Comte Walewski, Montevideo, 1 Jan. 1856; CCC, Montevideo, tome 5, fols. 384 and 384 verso.

123. Benjamin Poucel to Bonpland from on board the steamship *Progreso*, 14 Feb. 1854; AAB, carpeta 3, MFJAD. The letter was prompted by the fact Bonpland had forgotten some plants on board the ship. Along with his own good wishes, Poucel forwarded those of Samuel Lafone, the leading capitalist in Uruguay of the period. Poucel was the founder around 1838 of an important merino-breeding property in southern Uruguay, the Bergeries Mérinos, Naz du Pichinango. This fell foul to the conflict of the Guerra Grande, during part of which Poucel was imprisoned with other French and British foreign residents at Durazno, in the interior of Uruguay. However, in his 1854 note he made an invitation to Bonpland to visit his property at Pichinango. Parts of Poucel's South American career are summarized in Duprey, *Voyages aux origines françaises*, pp. 207–30.

124. See Hermann, *France en Amérique latine*, p. 259.

125. A detailed description of Bonpland's arrival at Santa Ana appears in his "Diario de viaje, 1854–55," 22 Mar. 1854, fol. 3 verso.

126. See Bonpland, "Journal d'agriculture," Santa Ana, June 1854; AAB, carpeta 5, MFJAD.

127. Wilhelmy's study in Corrientes concerned the German colony Neu-Karlsruhe (Liebig), founded in 1924 on the grasslands. Among its other economic activities, this colony drew fifty thousand maté plants from the government of Corrientes,

planting them on open land beginning in 1925. The results were disappointing in comparison with the yields from the forests (Wilhelmy, *Geographische Forschungen in Südamerika*, pp. 98, 103, 266 plate 7).

128. See Dean, *With Broadax and Firebrand*, pp. 127, 171–73.

129. Brazil, *Anais do Itamaratí*, 4:251.

130. See Bonpland to Cândido Baptista de Oliveira, director of the Rio de Janeiro Botanical Garden, Montevideo, 25 Jan. 1854; AAB, carpeta 4, MFJAD. Bonpland wrote to this Brazilian in Spanish. Cândido Baptista de Oliveira (1801–1865) had a very distinguished career. He was appointed director of the Rio de Janeiro Botanical Garden in 1851, telling Bonpland in a letter from Rio de Janeiro written on 19 November 1853 that he was happy to work beyond the *redemoinho* (whirlpool) of politics. He also sent south a catalog of the contents of the Rio garden, published in 1843. In addition, Baptista de Oliveira commented on the news that the last British mail boat had brought word of the death of his former teacher and friend Arago, "whose loss for France and the rest of the world could be compared with reason to the extinction of a *brilliant star* in the firmament of the sciences." On 22 March 1854, Baptista de Oliveira followed his earlier shipment of materials with "a specimen of Brazilian tea, cultivated in the province of São Paulo."

131. See Bonpland, "Journal d'agriculture," 6 Apr. 1854.

132. See the long letter from Bonpland to Baptista de Oliveira, Montevideo, 25 Dec. 1855; AAB, carpeta 4, MFJAD. This provides a detailed accounting of what Bonpland had done with the tea seeds. When he left Santa Ana on 16 October 1855, the two remaining tea plants were doing well. He asked for a further shipment of tea seeds and also, if possible, for indigo. While interested in the contents of the catalog of the Rio de Janeiro garden, Bonpland did not find this as rich as he had supposed (an impression Charles Darwin shared).

133. Bonpland developed a habit of sending seeds and plants to Urquiza for his garden. In 1856, for example, he sent him a hundred bulbs of an amaryllis set to bear flowers of what he considered an appropriate shade of red, the color of the Federalists in Argentina. See Bonpland to Urquiza, Restauración, 16 June and 17 Sept. 1856; AAB, carpeta 1, MFJAD.

134. Bonpland to Pujol, Santa Ana, 11 Oct. 1855, printed in Pujol, *Corrientes en la organización nacional*, 5:308.

135. Ibid., 6 May 1854, 4:92–93. The letter also contains much on planting and on seeds, including reference to the work Bonpland was then doing in connection with Algeria.

136. See Bonpland, "Journal d'Agriculture," Santa Ana, 4 June 1854; AAB, carpeta 5, MFJAD.

137. Bonpland to Pujol, Restauración, 12 June 1854, printed in Pujol, *Corrientes en la organización nacional*, 4:114. There are other mentions of viticulture and of Reboul in later letters to Pujol.

138. See the unsigned letter written from Queyrac, 19 Aug. 1854; AAB, carpeta 6, MFJAD.

139. See Bonpland to Pujol, Restauración, 30 Sept. 1854, printed in Pujol, *Corrientes en la organización nacional*, 4:197–99.

140. Ibid., 4:203.

141. Ibid, Santa Ana, 14 Oct. 1854, 4:225–26.

142. See the official letter from Pujol to Bonpland, nominating him as the director of the museum or permanent exposition of the province, Esquina, 10 Oct. 1854, printed in ibid., 4:220–21.

143. Pujol to the governor delegate Manuel Antonio Ferré, ibid., 14 Oct. 1854, 4:222–24.

144. Bonpland to Pujol, Santa Ana, 27 Oct. 1854, printed in ibid., 4:240–42. A French translation of the original Spanish is printed in Hamy, *Aimé Bonpland, médecin et naturaliste*, pp. 190–92. See also Quesada, *Provincia de Corrientes*, pp. 45–46.

145. Bonpland to Pujol, Santa Ana, 27 Oct. 1854, printed in Pujol, *Corrientes en la organización nacional*, 4:243–45. The French version appears in Hamy, *Aimé Bonpland, médecin et naturaliste*, pp. 192–94.

146. Bonpland to Pujol, Restauración, 6 Nov. 1854, printed in Pujol, *Corrientes en la organización nacional*, 4:253–57. The French version appears in Hamy, *Aimé Bonpland, médecin et naturaliste*, pp. 194–97.

147. Bonpland to Pujol, Santa Ana, 31 Dec. 1854, printed in ibid., 4:308–9. In this letter, Bonpland wrote about seven immense *yerbales* ("which I visited in all their splendor") in the vicinity of Santo Ângelo. He maintained that these were now destroyed through inappropriate management.

148. Bonpland to Gay, Santa Ana, 4 Jan. 1855, printed in Hamy, *Aimé Bonpland, médecin et naturaliste*, p. 198.

149. "He takes great care of his garden, in which he has growing some little of almost everything, even to the tea plant. The soil is light. Cotton, he says, is not worth cultivating on the Uruguay; neither is the land east of the Corrientes River adapted to it. His Irish potatoes are very good." Page, *La Plata . . . and Paraguay*, p. 296. While Bonpland's links with the U.S. naval survey of the Plata are clearly documented, another North American link from around this period remains shrouded in mystery. Sometime in 1855, George Catlin, one of the leading painters of the Indians of North America, set out from Berlin carrying a letter of recommendation from Humboldt to Bonpland. In one of his books, Catlin maintained that he subsequently met, in 1856, with "the Baron Bonpland," mistakenly elevating him to the aristocracy, at Santa Ana (*Lifted and Subsided Rocks of America*, p. 220); Manthorne, *Tropical Renaissance*, p. 87. Borrowing the phrasing of Marjorie Catlin Roehm, Catlin was "a vagabond artist" between 1853 and 1858, supposedly making more than one journey in South America (*Letters of George Catlin*, p. 326). In his impressive study, Brian Dippie has argued the following: "In the 1850s Catlin left few reliable guideposts and many that are misleading, but when his chronology is unscrambled and his actual itinerary traced, the lost years of America's greatest Indian painter should be full of revelations" (*Catlin and His Contemporaries*, p. 353). Given Bonpland's movement patterns, he was often a difficult man for the traveler

to track down. I have found no mention of Catlin in any of Bonpland's records. The most interesting aspect today in Catlin's South American career is his awareness of the rapid cultural change then affecting the indigenous peoples of the region, the stimulus that pulled him forward. On the way out from Europe to visit Bonpland, he stopped at Rio de Janeiro. He liked the city but chose not to tarry there, arguing "we travel to see the *perishable*, not the *eternal*" (Catlin, *Last Rambles amongst the Indians*, p. 207).

150. Bonpland to Pujol, Restauración, 13 Jan. 1855, printed in Pujol, *Corrientes en la organización nacional*, 5:6–7. In his impressive study of the Guaycuruan Indians, James Saeger makes the following interesting observation about their view of settled economic activities: "In the pre–mission era, cultivation was appropriate only for women or such ethnic inferiors as Guanás or Guaranis, whose very devotion to agriculture revealed their inferiority" (Saeger, *Chaco Mission Frontier*, p. 71). John Hemming points out a symbiotic relationship, "with the Guaicuru obtaining the agricultural labor they despised, and the Guaná the protection of a powerful warrior tribe" (*Red Gold*, p. 394).

151. See the ms. "Campo del General Abalos"; AAB, carpeta 8, MFJAD.

152. Bonpland to Pujol, Restauración, 15 May 1855, printed in Pujol, *Corrientes en la organización nacional*, 5:193–95.

153. Bonpland to Pujol, Restauración, 20 May 1855, printed in Pujol, ibid. 5:205. The semiweekly newspaper *El Comercio* published Pedro de Angelis's biography of Bonpland in sections, beginning in its 22 February 1855 issue, and printed his recent letters from Montevideo to Humboldt, beginning on 6 May. Bonpland kept very much abreast of the Correntino news and still followed recent developments across the region very closely.

154. Ibid., 20 May 1855, 5:205–7. The draft of this letter is at AAB, carpeta 1, MFJAD. Mentions of problems with Reboul appear in Bonpland's agricultural diary. On his links with the French colonists, see also Marceaux to Bonpland, Corrientes, 20 Sept. and 18 Oct. 1857; AAB, carpeta 3, MFJAD. Bonpland's experiments with viticulture are described in Quesada, *Provincia de Corrientes*, p. 58.

155. Bonpland, "Journal d'agriculture," 3 Sept. 1855; AAB, carpeta 5, MFJAD.

156. Bonpland to Pujol, Santa Ana, 11 Oct. 1855, printed in Pujol, *Corrientes en la organización nacional*, 5:307–10; Page, *La Plata . . . and Paraguay*, p. 296.

157. See Bonpland, "Diario de viaje, 1854–55," 13 Oct. 1855, fol. 3; AAB, carpeta 7, MFJAD.

158. See the Baron d'Ornano to Bonpland, Porto Alegre, 12 May 1855; AAB, carpeta 3, MFJAD.

159. Bonpland to the Baron d'Ornano, Montevideo, 25 Dec. 1855; AAB, carpeta 3, MFJAD.

160. See the Baron d'Ornano to Bonpland, Porto Alegre, 12 Aug. 1856; AAB, carpeta 3, MFJAD.

161. Bonpland to Pujol, Santa Ana, 30 Mar. 1856, printed in Pujol, *Corrientes en la organización nacional*, 6:72.

162. Ibid., Montevideo, 31 Oct. 1855, 5:316. The month given for this letter seems

to be in error. Since Bonpland had still to arrive in the Uruguayan capital, it was probably written in either November or December.

163. See Domínguez, *Bonpland . . . en la República Argentina*, p. 56.

164. Bonpland to Humboldt, Montevideo, 2 Dec. 1855, printed in Hamy, *Aimé Bonpland, médecin et naturaliste*, p. 199. Hamy's printed month of September on this letter is in error.

165. See Lynch, *Argentine Dictator*, esp. p. 265.

166. The character of Solano López's tour and its implications for Paraguayan development are outlined in Whigham, *Paraguayan War*, 1:176–80.

167. William Gore Ouseley to Bonpland (letter in French), Encarnación, 1 Apr. 1855; AAB, carpeta 3, MFJAD. Bonpland received this letter on 10 October 1855 at Restauración. He noted that he wrote on the same day to the Paraguayan diplomat Juan Andrés Gelly.

168. Bonpland to Ouseley, Montevideo, 18 Dec. 1855; AAB, carpeta 3, MFJAD.

169. See Gontier to Bonpland, Paris, 29 July 1855; AAB, carpeta 3, MFJAD. Bonpland noted he received this letter on 25 December 1855 and wrote an immediate reply. Gontier had tried to visit Bonpland at Le Havre in 1816, on the point of Bonpland's departure from France, but he arrived too late.

170. Bonpland to Demersay, Montevideo, 25 Dec. 1855, printed in Hamy, *Aimé Bonpland, médecin et naturaliste*, pp. 201–3. Demersay's comments upon receiving this letter are interesting. He noted that Bonpland was forgetting his age, claiming Bonpland's return to France would have been very profitable for the natural sciences, in particular for geography.

171. Bonpland to Baptista de Oliveira, Montevideo, 25 Dec. 1855; AAB, carpeta 4, MFJAD.

172. Bonpland to Wilhelm and Berthold Seemann, Montevideo, 26 Jan. 1856, printed in Hamy, *Aimé Bonpland, médecin et naturaliste*, pp. 205–6.

173. See Bonpland to Pujol, Montevideo, 10 Jan. and 16 Jan. 1856, printed in Pujol, *Corrientes en la organización nacional*, 6:16, 19.

174. Ibid., Restauración, 20 Apr. 1856, 6:88.

175. Bonpland to Urquiza, Concordia, 18 Feb. 1856; AAB, carpeta 1, MFJAD. Tordillo horses were famed for their willingness to cross water, an obviously useful attribute for a traveler.

176. Bonpland to Pujol, La Cruz, 7 July 1856, printed in Pujol, *Corrientes en la organización nacional*, 6:158–59.

177. Ibid., São Borja, 25 July 1856, 6:171–73.

178. See the pair of letters from Bonpland to Pujol, Restauración and São Borja, 1 Sept. 1856, printed in ibid., esp. 6:200, 201.

179. Bonpland to Pujol, Restauración, 28 Sept. 1856, printed in ibid., 6:217.

180. Bonpland to Friedrich von Gülich, São Borja, 8 Aug. 1856, printed in Hamy, *Aimé Bonpland, médecin et naturaliste*, esp. p. 207. Part of this letter also became an elegy to Pujol's capacities, notably with the design to develop a natural history museum.

181. Roguin to Bonpland, Montevideo, 20 Feb. 1857; AAB, carpeta 4, MFJAD.

182. Manuel Luís Osório, the Marquês do Herval (1808–1879), was a gaúcho and one of Brazil's most distinguished soldiers during the nineteenth century. As a Liberal, he played a major role in national politics after the Paraguayan War. See Love, *Rio Grande do Sul and Brazilian Regionalism*, pp. 21–22; Whigham, *Paraguayan War*, esp. 1:358–59. Osório is commemorated in permanency in Brazil, not least with a statue in Rio de Janeiro.

183. Gay to the Baron d'Ornano, São Borja, 15 Oct. 1856; République Argentine, Affaires Diverses, 1841–1867, carton 2, MRE.

184. See ms. 215, MHN.

185. Bonpland, "Journal d'agriculture," 30 Sept. 1856.

186. Ibid., 28 Oct. 1856.

187. Bonpland to Pujol, Restuaración, 28 Sept. 1856, printed in Pujol, *Corrientes en la organización nacional*, 6:217.

188. Bonpland, "Diario de viaje de Restauración à Corrientes, October 1856," 12–13 Oct. 1856; AAB, carpeta 7, MFJAD.

189. The instructions are printed in Pujol, *Corrientes en la organización nacional*, 6:247–48.

190. See ibid., pp. 245–47.

191. See Gómez, *Amado Bonpland*, p. 33.

192. See Gay's ms., "Le naturaliste Mr. Aimé Bonpland," p. 4; F[17], 3974, AN.

193. The manuscript of the journey from Corrientes to Asunción forms part of the collections of the Biblioteca Nacional in Lima, Peru. Julio Rafael Contreras Roqué and Alfredo Boccia Romañach have recently provided a painstaking edition of the work, translating the original French into Spanish (*Paraguay en 1857*).

194. Gay's ms., "Le naturaliste Mr. Aimé Bonpland," pp. 13–14; F[17], 3974, AN. See also Bonpland to Humboldt, Corrientes, 7 June 1857, printed in Hamy, *Aimé Bonpland, médecin et naturaliste*, p. 213.

195. Bonpland to Maillefer, Corrientes, 6 Apr. 1857; AAB, carpeta 4, MFJAD. Ernest Mouchez accomplished important hydrographic work along the Atlantic coast of South America. According to Maillefer, the idea of offering Bonpland an official passage to Paraguay was his; he enjoyed the notion that Bonpland could botanize for Algeria above the tomb of his former persecutor Francia. This missed the point that Francia did not have a tomb, since his body supposedly disappeared. See Maillefer to Walewski, Montevideo, 4 June 1857; CCC, Montevideo, 1857–1864, tome 6, fols. 26 and 26 verso; Paraguay, Ministerio de Interior, *Restos mortales del . . . Francia*.

196. Ernest Mouchez to Bonpland, Montevideo, 20 Nov. 1857; AAB, carpeta 4, MFJAD. There was an unsuccessful effort by Maillefer to send Bonpland on a repeat visit accompanying the *Bisson* to Paraguay in late 1857, with the hope that he could reach Mato Grosso, "so vast, so fertile and so little known." Illness prevented Bonpland from making this second journey. However, since Mouchez had been unable to ascend the rivers above Asunción, Maillefer later related to Paris, Bonpland would have less cause to miss "the virgin forests of Cuiabá" with which the consul "had nourished his botanical imagination." See Maillefer to Walewski, Montevideo,

1 Dec. 1857 and 27 Apr. 1858; CCC, Montevideo, tome 6, fols. 64 verso–65 and 82–84 verso.

197. Bonpland visited the Chamonix valley during August 1805 in the company of the famous botanist and biogeographer de Candolle; see the latter's *Mémoires et souvenirs*, p. 155.

198. Bonpland to Maillefer, Corrientes, 6 Apr. 1857; AAB, carpeta 4, MFJAD.

199. See Scobie, *Revolution on the Pampas*, pp. 32–33; Whigham, *Politics of River Trade*, p. 77.

200. Within Brougnes's writings, see his *Moyen de s'enrichir par la culture du sol en Uruguay*, dated from Montevideo on 1 July 1851. A copy of this rare pamphlet is housed in the Bonpland archive at Buenos Aires. See also his *Système de colonisation*. It remains unclear whether Brougnes and Bonpland had direct contact, but the former drew on the latter's authority in one of his emigration works designed to attract European immigrants. He claimed that Bonpland qualified the missions of Corrientes as the "Garden of South America" (Brougnes, *Extinction de paupérisme agricole*, p. 81). Similar logic animated the Nueva Burdeos colony in Paraguay, and similar problems of execution lay behind its failure. Bonpland was aware of the problems of this colony when he visited Asunción (Contreras Roqué and Boccia Romañach, *Paraguay en 1857*, p. 111).

201. Bonpland to Maillefer, Corrientes, 6 Apr. 1857; AAB, carpeta 4, MFJAD. Who Bonpland meant by the "entrepreneur," whether Brougnes (the overall architect of the scheme) or Victor de Sabater (director of the French agricultural colony), remains unclear. The latter met a violent death. Since their contract exempted the colonists from any military service, Sabater's 1855 offer to the governor that "we are always ready to shed our blood for our new country" was unlikely to meet universal support in the colony. See the correspondence between Sabater and Pujol printed in *El Comercio*, 8 Mar. 1855.

202. Bonpland to Maillefer, Corrientes, 30 May 1857; CCC, Montevideo, 1857–1865, tome 6, fols. 45 and 45 verso.

203. Maillefer to Walewski, Montevideo, 1 Sept. 1857; CCC, Montevideo, tome 6, fols. 48–49.

204. See Miers, "On the History of the 'Mate' Plant," esp. p. 389.

205. Bonpland to Normann, Corrientes, Mar. 1857, printed in Hamy, *Aimé Bonpland, médecin et naturaliste*, pp. 211–12.

206. See ms. 215, MHN.

207. See Gay to Bonpland, São Borja, 6 May 1857, and Bonpland to José Maria Rolón, Corrientes, 10 June 1857; AAB, carpeta 4, MFJAD. Rolón was a priest and later a governor of Corrientes.

208. Gay to Bonpland, São Borja, 19 July 1857; AAB, carpeta 4, MFJAD. These lands related to the Campo das Vacas Brancas of Indian legend in Missões. It was this *yerbal* that inspired the then–frontier commander Osório to later adopt the title "baron of Herval." See Rodrigues, *São Borja e sua história*, pp. 119–20. Nonoai was a frontier colony, designed to congregate "civilized" Indians. It had the considerable

indigenous population of 547 around this time. See Avé-Lallemant, *Viagem pela província do Rio Grande do Sul*, pp. 391–92.

209. Gay to Bonpland, 19 July 1857; AAB, carpeta 4, MFJAD.

210. The membership list is given in Mañé Garzón, *Vilardebó, primer médico uruguayo*, p. 204.

211. Bonpland to Humboldt, Corrientes, 7 June 1857, printed in Hamy, *Aimé Bonpland, médecin et naturaliste*, pp. 212–16.

Chapter Six

1. Bonpland to Pujol, Restauración, 20 July 1857, printed in Pujol, *Corrientes en la organización nacional*, 7:99–101.

2. Bonpland, "Diario, 1857," 29 July 1857, fol. 2 verso; AAB, carpeta 7, MFJAD.

3. Bonpland, "Journal d'agriculture," 29 July 1857.

4. Bonpland, "Diario, 1857," 30 July 1857, fol. 2 verso, and "Journal d'agriculture," 30 July 1857.

5. Bonpland, "Diario, 1857," 13 Aug. 1857, fol. 5; AAB, carpeta 7, MFJAD.

6. Louis Marceaux to Bonpland, Corrientes, 20 Sept. 1857; AAB, carpeta 3, MFJAD.

7. Marceaux to Bonpland, Corrientes, 18 Oct. 1857; AAB, carpeta 3, MFJAD.

8. Pujol to Bonpland, Corrientes (the date on the manuscript is torn but it is probably 7 Nov. 1857); AAB, carpeta 1, MFJAD. Bonpland's reply referred to letters from the governor written from Itatí, 30 Nov. 1856, and from Corrientes, 7 Nov. 1857.

9. Bonpland to Pujol, Paso de los Libres, 19 Nov. 1857, printed in Pujol, *Corrientes en la organización nacional*, 7:154–56.

10. Bonpland, "Journal d'agriculture," Nov. 1857; AAB, carpeta 5, MFJAD.

11. On Kasten, see Barreto, *Bibliografia sul-riograndense*, 2:741; Avé-Lallemant, *Viagem pela província do Rio Grande do Sul*, esp. pp. 299–300.

12. See Scobie, *Revolution on the Pampas*, esp. pp. 25, 75–76, 144–47.

13. Fortunato Francisco da Silva to Bonpland (letter in Portuguese), Uruguaiana, 1 Jan. 1857; AAB, carpeta 4, MFJAD.

14. Bonpland, "Journal d'agriculture," 25 Feb. 1858. The comment echoes the frustration of 11 October 1857, when he waited for two hours to receive his key to the inn. The local residents were at church.

15. Bonpland to Pujol, Santa Ana, 15 Feb. 1858, printed in Pujol, *Corrientes en la organización nacional*, 8:58–59.

16. On the expansionism of the Luso-Brazilian ranchers, see Bell, *Campanha Gaúcha*, esp. pp. 36, 83.

17. Bonpland to Pujol, Santa Ana, 20 Mar. 1858, printed in Pujol, *Corrientes en la organización nacional*, 8:75–76.

18. Marceaux to Bonpland, Goya, 28 Mar. 1858; AAB, carpeta 3, MFJAD.

19. Avé-Lallemant, *Reise durch Süd-Brasilien*. The parts of this book relating to Rio Grande do Sul were published in Portuguese translation as *Viagem pela província do Rio Grande do Sul*.

20. Avé-Lallemant to Humboldt, São Borja, 10 Apr. 1858, printed in Hamy, *Aimé Bonpland, médecin et naturaliste*, pp. 285–86.

21. Bruhns, *Life of Alexander von Humboldt*, 1:411.

22. Ibid.

23. Avé-Lallemant to Humboldt, Uruguaiana, 19 Apr. 1858, printed in Hamy, *Aimé Bonpland, médecin et naturaliste*, pp. 287–89.

24. Bruhns, *Life of Alexander von Humboldt*, 1:410.

25. See Bonpland's "Journal d'agriculture," 17 Apr. 1858; AAB, carpeta 5, MFJAD.

26. Bonpland to Karl Wilhelm Kasten, Santa Ana, 19 Apr. 1858; AvHF, BBAW.

27. See *Bonplandia* no. 13 (15 July 1858), p. 271.

28. Sarton, "Aimé Bonpland (1773–1858)," p. 394. An account of Avé-Lallemant's visit was forwarded from the French consulate in Rio de Janeiro to Paris as early as October 1858; it included the comment that this Prussian medical doctor was "very well known and much liked" in the former city. See the copy of the letter sent from Rio de Janeiro on 20 Oct. 1858; F[17], 3974, fol. 45, AN.

29. See, for example, Kellner, *Alexander von Humboldt*, pp. 90–91.

30. Bonpland's agricultural journal is disorganized in its chronology, but it records the entire period following his final return to Santa Ana; AAB, carpeta 5, MFJAD.

31. Gay's ms., "Le naturaliste Mr. Aimé Bonpland," pp. 14–15; F[17], 3974, AN.

32. Kasten to Friedrich von Gülich, Uruguaiana, 24 May 1858; AvHF, BBAW.

33. Ibid. See also, in the same Berlin archive, Pedro de Angelis to Humboldt, Buenos Aires, 18 June 1858. De Angelis's account contains a number of errors. First, the Santa Ana site where Bonpland died was not the same location as the place of the same name where he was taken by force into Paraguay in 1821. As well, Bonpland left three children in Argentina, not two. Pedro de Angelis had also taken steps to inquire about the state of Bonpland's manuscripts, although he seems to have been equally interested in obtaining the deceased's example of the Prussian order of the red eagle, the king of Prussia's order of chivalry recognizing excellence in both military and civilian fields, seeking to use this as a souvenir of his "excellent and old friend."

34. See the news from Britain in *Bonplandia* 22 (15 Nov. 1854), p. 264. At the end of 1862, the editor Seemann replaced the German serial *Bonplandia* with the English *Journal of Botany, British and Foreign*.

35. See Browne, *Charles Darwin*, 1:266, 454.

36. Humboldt to Bonpland, Berlin, 10 June 1858, printed in full in the original French in Schneppen, *Bonpland: Humboldts vegessener Gefährte?* pp. 31–34.

37. Ibid., p. 34.

38. Humboldt to François Delessert, Berlin, 14 July 1858, printed in Hamy, *Aimé Bonpland, médecin et naturaliste*, pp. 239–41.

39. The relationship stretched back to the early nineteenth century. Humboldt told the South American revolutionary Manuel Palacio to use the Paris address of the Delessert family as a sure way of communicating with him. See Manuel Palacio

to Bonpland, London, 29 Apr. 1815 (segment of this long letter written on 13 May) in *LCGE*. This interesting publication provides facsimilies of the correspondence Bonpland received from a series of South American revolutionaries.

40. See Hamy, *Aimé Bonpland, médecin et naturaliste*, p. 240. The Museo de Ciencias Naturales Dr. Amado Bonpland is today a valuable part of the cultural patrimony of Corrientes.

41. Sir Woodbine Parish to Humboldt, St. Leonards-on-Sea, 5 Aug. 1858, printed in ibid., p. 290.

42. Humboldt to Élie de Beaumont, 1858, printed in ibid., pp. 242–43.

43. See Humboldt to Alexander von Schleinitz, Berlin (a Prussian diplomat and minister), 12 Dec. 1858; AvHF, BBAW.

44. Walewski to Maillefer, Paris, 7 Apr. 1858; CCC, Montevideo, tome 6, fols. 80–81 verso.

45. Maillefer to Walewski, Montevideo, 28 June 1858; CCC, Montevideo, tome 6, fols. 89–91 verso. The comment about intellectual work was probably a reference to Brossard's 1850 study of the international relations of the Plata (*Considérations historiques*), a product of his attachment to the French extraordinary mission there of 1847. An impressive list of Bonpland's Paraguayan correspondents is given at the end of his travel diary to Asunción. They include British and French diplomats, the pharmacist Domingo Parodi (who shared membership of the Sociedad de Medicina Montevideana), and the Hungarian-born military engineer Wisner von Morgenstern (Contreras Roqué and Boccia Romañach, *Paraguay en 1857*, pp. 125–30).

46. Consul Brossard compared a recently published catalog prepared by Vicente Estigarribia, once Francia's doctor (and notable beyond his role in the history of Paraguayan science as the sole individual trusted with unlimited rights of access to the dictator's private rooms), with what he found in Bonpland's manuscripts. Although Brossard wrote patronizingly about the quality of Estigarribia's knowledge of indigenous plants, and with only lukewarm enthusiasm about Bonpland's, he sent a huge list of 206 species drawn from their manuscripts from Paraguay considered of potential value for acclimatization in Algeria. See Brossard to Walewski, Asunción, 4 Nov. 1858; CCC, Assomption, 1854–1862, tome 1, fols. 316–17. On Estigarribia, see Chaves, *El supremo dictador*, pp. 180–81.

Conclusion

1. Bruhns, *Life of Alexander von Humboldt*, 1:404.
2. See Lack, "Botanical Field Notes Prepared by Humboldt and Bonpland," esp. p. 502.
3. The French natural historian d'Orbigny traveled in South America between 1826 and 1833. His journeys were stimulated by a visit to Humboldt at Paris in 1825 (Rebok, "Expedición americana de Alexander von Humboldt," p. 452). The gifted d'Orbigny had a more conventional career than Bonpland. Based on the strength of both his collections and his publications, he was appointed to a chair at the Jardin des Plantes. On Darwin's rivalry with d'Orbigny, see Browne, *Charles Darwin*, 1:267, 454, 465.

4. Glick, "Science and Independence in Latin America," esp. p. 333.
5. See, for example, Kohlhepp, "Humboldt en los trópicos," p. 20.
6. Brunel, *Biographie d'Aimé Bonpland* (1871), p. 127.
7. Conde d'Eu, *Viagem militar ao Rio Grande do Sul*, pp. 114–15.
8. Pérez Acosta, *Francia y Bonpland*, pp. 45–46.
9. Domínguez, *Bonpland . . . en la República Argentina*, pp. 56–57.
10. See, on publishing plans, Domínguez's note to the reader in his institute's 1914 edition of Humboldt's letters to Bonpland (Trabajos del Instituto de Botánica y Farmacología, *Lettres inédites de Alexandre de Humboldt*).
11. Driver, *Geography Militant*, esp. p. 12.
12. See, for example, Martins, "Darwin and the Brazilian Landscape," and Naylor, "Natural Historians and the Landscapes of Argentina."
13. I take the view that the Rosen Stile in Bonpland's account of his visit to Asunción is a garbled version of Rosenschöld. Contreras Roqué and Boccia Romañach point to Bonpland's claim that Rosen Stile was not a qualified medical doctor, thinking this both an error and a sign that Rosen Stile and Rosenschöld were possibly not one and the same (*Paraguay en 1857*, p. 102). Like many, however, Munck af Rosenschöld practiced in South America based on his studies but without a medical certificate. See Mörner, *Eberhard Munck . . . en el Paraguay*, p. 4.
14. See Fittkau, "Spix, Zoologe und Brasilienforscher," esp. pp. 53–54. While Spix was the senior authority of the two during the field research, Martius outlived him by forty-two years.
15. Mauthe, "Die Österreichische Brasilien expedition 1817–1836," esp. p. 22.
16. See Dickenson, "Naturalist on the River Amazons," p. 213; Raffles, *In Amazonia*, pp. 114–49.
17. Hamy, *Aimé Bonpland, médecin et naturaliste*, p. xcv.
18. See Maillefer to Walewski, Montevideo, 1 Sept. 1857; CCC, Montevideo, tome 6, fol. 49.
19. It was an interest Bonpland shared with a more famous environmental pioneer, George Perkins Marsh.
20. Montoya, *La ganadería y la industria de salazón de carnes*, p. 14.
21. See Macchi, *El ovino en la Argentina*, esp. pp. 41–42, 105–36.
22. See Bell, *Campanha Gaúcha*, pp. 115–17.
23. Miers, "History of the 'Mate' Plant"; Demersay, *Étude économique sur le maté*; Bonpland, "Bemerkungen über die Verbreitungssphäre des Paraguay-Thee's."

Bibliography

Archives

Archives Nationales de France
Archivo Aimé Bonpland, Museo de Farmacobotánica "Juan Aníbal Domínguez," Facultad de Farmacia y Bioquímica, Universidad de Buenos Aires
Arquivo Histórico do Rio Grande do Sul
Berlin-Brandenburgische Akademie der Wissenschaften
Biblioteca Nacional, Rio de Janeiro (seção de manuscritos)
Bibliothèque Municipale de La Rochelle
LuEsther T. Mertz Library of the New York Botanical Garden, Bronx, New York
Ministère des Relations Extérieures, Paris
Muséum d'Histoire Naturelle, Paris
Public Record Office, London

Other Sources

Adelman, Jeremy. *Republic of Capital: Buenos Aires and the Legal Transformation of the Atlantic World*. Stanford, CA: Stanford University Press, 1999.
Anastasía, Luis Víctor. *Larrañaga: su oración inaugural de la Biblioteca Pública: visión y proyecto liberal de la historia y de la cultura para la formación humana*. Serie Educación-Sociedad-Economía. Montevideo: Fundación Prudencio Vázquez y Vega, 1989.
Araújo, Orestes. *Diccionario geográfico del Uruguay*. 2nd ed. Montevideo: Tipo-Litografía Moderna, 1912.
Argentine Republic. *Agricultural and Pastoral Census of the Nation*. Vol. 3, *Stockbreeding and Agriculture in 1908: Monographs*. Buenos Aires: Printing Works of the Argentine Meteorological Office, 1909.
Arnold, David. *The Problem of Nature: Environment, Culture and European Expansion*. Oxford and Cambridge, MA: Blackwell, 1996.
Aubouin, Isidore. *Banquet patriotique célébré par les français habitent à Buénos-Ayres, le 29 juillet 1832, a l'occasion du second anniversaire da la grande semaine de juillet (discours, pièces de vers et couplets composés pour cette circonstance)*. Buenos Aires, 1832.

Avé-Lallemant, Robert. *Reise durch Süd-Brasilien im Jahre 1858.* 2 vols. Leipzig: F.A. Brockhaus, 1859.

———. *Viagem pela província do Rio Grande do Sul.* Trans. Teodoro Cabral. Belo Horizonte: Editora Itatiaia; São Paulo: Editora da Universidade de São Paulo, 1980 [1859].

Avenel, Jean-David. *L'affaire du Rio de la Plata (1838–1852).* Collection campagnes & stratégies. Les grandes batailles, no. 26. Paris: Economica, 1998.

Azara, Félix de. *Voyages dans l'Amérique méridionale.* 4 vols. and a large-format atlas. Paris: Dentu, 1809.

B***, Armand de (Roy, Just-Jean-Étienne). *Mes voyages avec le docteur Philips dans les républiques de la Plata (Buenos-Ayres, Montevideo, la Bande-Orientale, etc.).* Tours: A. Mame, 1861.

Barreto, Abeillard. *Bibliografia sul-riograndense: a contribuição portuguesa e estrangeira para o conhecimento e a integração do Rio Grande do Sul.* 2 vols. Rio de Janeiro: Conselho Federal de Cultura, 1973–1976.

Beck, Hanno. *Alexander von Humboldt.* 2 vols. Wiesbaden: Franz Steiner, 1959–61.

Bell, Stephen. "Aimé Bonpland and Merinomania in Southern South America." *Americas* 51, no. 3 (Jan. 1995): 301–23.

———. "Aimé Bonpland e a avaliação de recursos em Santa Cruz, 1849–50." Trans. Carmen Vera Cirne Lima. *Estudos Ibero-Americanos* (Porto Alegre) 21 (1995): 63–79.

———. *Campanha Gaúcha: A Brazilian Ranching System, 1850–1920.* Stanford, CA: Stanford University Press, 1998.

Bertrand, Michel, and Laurent Vidal, eds. *À la redécouverte des Amériques: les voyageurs européens au siècle des indépendances.* Toulouse: Presses Universitaires du Mirail, 2002.

Beux, Armindo. *Franceses no Rio Grande do Sul.* Porto Alegre: Editora Metropole, 1976.

Bierck, Jr., Harold A., ed. *Selected Writings of Bolivar.* Compiled by Vicente Lecuna and trans. Lewis Bertrand. 2 vols. New York: Colonial Press, 1951 [published by Banco de Venezuela].

Boccia Romañach, Alfredo. *Amado Bonpland: caraí arandu.* Asunción: El Lector, 1999.

Bolívar, Simón. *Cartas del Libertador.* Tome 3 (1821–1823). 2d ed. Caracas: Banco de Venezuela; Fundación Vicente Lecuna, 1965.

Bonpland, Aimé. "Bemerkungen A. Bonpland's über die Verbreitungssphäre des Paraguay-Thee's." *Zeitschrift für allgemeine Erdkunde* 5 (1858): 76–83.

———. *Description des plantes rares cultivées à Malmaison et à Navarre.* Paris: Imprimerie de P. Didot l'aîné, 1813 [1812–1817].

———. *Journal voyage de Sn. Borja a la cierra y a Porto Alegre: Diário viagem de São Borja à Serra e a Porto Alegre.* Transcription of the original manuscripts, notes, and revision by Alicia Lourteig. Porto Alegre: Instituto de Biociências, Universidade Federal do Rio Grande do Sul; Paris: Centre National de la Recherche Scientifique, 1978.

———. *Bonplandia: Zeitschrift für die gesammte Botanik,* 10 vols. Edited by Berthold Seemann (1825–1871) (Hannover: Carl Rümpler, 1853–1862).

"Bonpland's Useful Exertions in the Region Watered by the River La Plata." *American Farmer* 2 (25 Aug. 1820).

Botting, Douglas. *Humboldt and the Cosmos.* London: Joseph, 1973.

Bowman, Charles Harwood. *Vicente Pazos Kanki: un boliviano en la libertad de América.* Trans. Raúl Mariaca G. and Samuel Mendoza. La Paz: Editorial Los Amigos del Libro, 1975.

Brackenridge, H[enry] M[arie]. *Voyage to South America Performed by Order of the American Government, in the Years 1817 and 1818, in the Frigate Congress.* 2 vols. Baltimore: Author; John D. Toy, printer, 1819.

Brazil. Ministério das Relações Exteriores. *Anais do Itamaratí,* vols. 1–4. Rio de Janeiro: Imprensa Nacional, 1936–1942.

Brossard, Alfred de. *Considérations historiques et politiques sur les républiques de La Plata dans leurs rapports avec la France et l'Angleterre.* Paris, 1850.

Brougnes, Auguste. *Extinction de paupérisme agricole par la colonisation dans les provinces de la Plata.* 2d ed. Bagnères-de-Bigorre: Typographie de J.-M. Dossun, 1855.

———. *Système de colonisation dans les provinces confédérées de la République Argentine par des familles agricoles européennes. Contrat passé entre M. Brougnes et le gouvernement de Corrientes.* Bagnéres-de-Bigorre: Imprimerie de J.-M. Dossun, 1854.

Browne, Janet. *Charles Darwin: A Biography.* Vol. 1, *Voyaging.* Princeton, NJ: Princeton University Press, 1995.

Bruhns, Karl, ed. *Life of Alexander von Humboldt.* Trans. Jane Lassell and Caroline Lassell. Compiled in commemoration of the centenary of his birth by J. Löwenberg, Robert Avé-Lallemant, and Alfred Dove. 2 vols. London: Longmans, Green, 1873.

Brunel, Adolphe. *Biographie d'Aimé Bonpland.* Paris: Rignoux, Imprimeur de la Faculté de Médecine, 1859.

———. *Biographie d'Aimé Bonpland: compagnon de voyage et collaborateur d'Al. de Humboldt.* 3d ed. Paris: L. Guérin & Cie.; London: Trubner & Co.; Montevideo: Lastaria y Cia., 1871.

Burkhardt, Frederick, and Sydney Smith, eds. *The Correspondence of Charles Darwin.* Vol. 1, *1821–1836.* Cambridge: Cambridge University Press, 1985.

Burton, Captain Richard F. *Letters from the Battle-Fields of Paraguay.* London: Tinsley Brothers, 1870.

Cady, John F. *Foreign Intervention in the Rio de la Plata, 1838–50: A Study of French, British, and American Policy in Relation to the Dictator Juan Manuel de Rosas.* New York: AMS Press, 1969 [1929].

Candolle, Augustin Pyramus de. *Mémoires et souvenirs.* Geneva: Joël Cherbuliez, 1862.

Carvalho, Mário Teixeira de. *Nobiliário sul-rio-grandense.* Porto Alegre: Globo, 1937.

Castellanos, A. "Bonpland en los paises del Plata." *Revista de la Academia Colombiana de Ciencias* 12, no. 45 (1963): 57–87.

Castellanos, Alfredo R. "La biblioteca científica del Padre Larrañaga." *Revista Histórica* (Montevideo) tome 16, nos. 46–48 (Dec. 1948 [1949]): 589–626.

Catlin, George. *Last Rambles amongst the Indians of the Rocky Mountains and the Andes by George Catlin, Author of Life amongst the Indians.* London: Sampson Low, Son and Marston, 1868.

———. *The Lifted and Subsided Rocks of America with their Influences on the Oceanic, Atmospheric, and Land Currents, and the Distribution of Races.* London: Trübner & Co., 1870.

Chassériau, F. *Vie de l'amiral Duperré.* Paris: Imprimerie Nationale, 1848.

Chastenay, [Victorine], Madame de. *Mémoires de Madame de Chastenay, 1771–1815.* Introduction and notes by Guy Chaussinand-Nogaret. Paris: Librairie Académique Perrin, 1987 [1896].

Chaves, Julio César. *El supremo dictador: biografía de José Gaspar de Francia.* 2d ed. Buenos Aires: Editorial Ayacucho, 1946.

Chonchol, Jacques, and Guy Martinière. *L'Amérique latine et le latino-américanisme en France.* Preface by Antoine Blanca. Travaux et Mémoires de L'Institut des Hautes Études de L'Amérique Latine, no. 37. Paris: L'Harmattan, 1985.

Compte Rendu du XVIe Congrès International de Géographie, Lisbonne, 1949. Lisbon: Centro Tip. Colonial, 1952.

Conde d'Eu (Prince Louis Gaston d'Orléans). *Viagem militar ao Rio Grande do Sul.* Belo Horizonte: Editora Itatiaia; São Paulo: Editora da Universidade de São Paulo, 1981 [reprint of 1936 edition].

Contreras Roqué, Julio Rafael, and Alfredo Boccia Romañach. *El Paraguay en 1857: un viaje inédito de Aimé Bonpland.* Universidad Nacional de Pilar, Colección Temas Universitarios, vol. 1. Asunción: Servilibro, 2006.

Cooney, Jerry W. "Hazards of the Carrera del Paraguay." *Derroteros de la Mar del Sud* 21, no. 2 (2003): 35–44.

Cordier, Henri. "Le docteur E.-T. Hamy." *Bulletin de Géographie Historique et Descriptive* no. 2 (1909): 165–66; also published in *La Géographie* (15 Jan. 1909): 1–14.

———. "Le Dr. Hamy: historien et géographe." In *Mélanges américaines.* Paris: J. Maisonneuve & Fils, 1913.

———. *Papiers inédits du naturaliste Aimé Bonpland conservés a Buenos Aires.* Trabajos del Instituto de Botánica y Farmacología, Facultad de Ciencias Médicas de Buenos Aires, no. 30. Buenos Aires: Jacobo Peuser, 1914.

Dacanal, José Hildebrando, and Sergius Gonzaga, eds. *RS: economia e política.* Porto Alegre: Mercado Aberto, 1979.

Darlington, William. *Reliquiae Baldwinianae: Selections from the Correspondence of the Late William Baldwin, M.D. Surgeon in the U.S. Navy.* Edited and with an introduction by Joseph Ewan. Classica Botanica Americana, Supplement II. New York and London: Hafner, 1969 [1843].

Darwin, Charles. *Journal of Researches into the Natural History and Geology of the Countries Visited During the Voyage of H.M.S. Beagle Around the World, Under the Command of Capt. Fitz Roy, R.N.* 2d ed. London: John Murray, 1845.

Dean, Warren. "Latifundia and Land Policy in Nineteenth-Century Brazil." *Hispanic American Historical Review* 51, no. 4 (Nov. 1971): 606–25.
———. *With Broadax and Fire: The Destruction of the Brazilian Atlantic Forest.* Berkeley and Los Angeles: University of California Press, 1995.
Deffontaines, Pierre. "Colonisation des basses terres du Paraná et Río de la Plata." In *Compte Rendu du XVIe Congrès International*, pp. 149–67.
Demersay, Alfred. *Étude économique sur le maté ou thé du Paraguay*. Société Impériale et Centrale d'Agriculture de France. Paris: Bouchard-Huzard, 1867.
———. *Histoire physique, économique et politique du Paraguay et des établissements des Jésuites.* 2 vols. with a large-format atlas. Paris: Librairie de L. Hachette, 1860–1864.
———. "Note sur les manuscrits et les collections de M. Aimé Bonpland." *Bulletin de la Societé de Géographie* 4th ser., 19 (1860): 426–29.
———. "Notice sur la vie et les travaux de M. Aimé Bonpland." *Bulletin de la Societé de Géographie* 4th ser., 5 (Apr. 1853): 240–54.
———. *Du tabac au Paraguay, culture, consommation et commerce.* Études Économiques sur l'Amérique mériodionales. Paris: Guillaumin, 1851.
Díaz Piedrahita, Santiago. "La botánica y el viaje de Humboldt y Bonpland." In Ecuador, *El Regreso de Humboldt*, pp. 67–78.
Dickenson, John. "The Naturalist on the River Amazons and a Wider World: Reflections on the Centenary of Henry Walter Bates." *Geographical Journal* 158 (1992): 207–14.
Dippie, Brian W. *Catlin and His Contemporaries: The Politics of Patronage.* Lincoln and London: University of Nebraska Press, 1990.
Domínguez, Juan A. *Aimé Bonpland: Su vida en la América del sur y principalmente en la República Argentina (1817–1858).* Buenos Aires: Imprenta y Casa Editorial Coni, 1929.
———. "Urquiza y Bonpland: antecedentes historicos. La disenteria en el Ejército Grande en formación, en 1850." *Trabajos del Instituto de Botánica y Farmacología* (Buenos Aires) 59 (Oct. 1938): 1–19.
Driver, Felix. *Geography Militant: Cultures of Exploration and Empire.* Oxford and Malden, MA: Blackwell, 2001.
Dubrunfaut, Auguste-Pierre. *Traité complet de l'art de la distillation.* 2 vols. Paris: Bachelier, 1824.
Duméril, Constant. *Élémens des sciences naturelles: ouvrage prescrit par arrêté et statut del'université pour l'enseignement dans les colléges royaux.* Paris: Deterville, 1825.
Dunbar, Gary S. "The Compass Follows the Flag: The French Scientific Mission to Mexico, 1864–1867." *Annals of the Association of American Geographers* 78, no. 2 (June 1988): 229–40.
Duprey, Jacques. *Voyage aux origines françaises de l'Uruguay: Montevideo et l'Uruguay vus par des voyageurs français entre 1708 et 1850.* Montevideo: Instituto Histórico y Geográfico del Uruguay, 1952.
Duviols, Pierre. "A propos d'une lettre d'Aimé Bonpland à Alexandre de Humboldt

et du secret de la culture du maté." In Potelet and Farré, eds., *Mundus Novus-Nouveaux Mondes*, pp. 131–43.

Ecuador. *El regreso de Humboldt: exposición en el museo da la ciudad de Quito, junio–agosto del 2001.* Quito: Imprenta Mariscal, 2001.

Fernández-Gómez, Emilio Manuel. *Argentina: gesta británica: revalorización de dos siglos de convivencia.* Vol. 1, *Los escenarios históricos y los grandes hechos.* Buenos Aires: Literature of Latin America (L.O.L.A.), 1993.

Fiedler, Horst, and Ulrike Leitner. *Alexander von Humboldts Schriften: Bibliographie der selbständig erschienenen Werke.* Beiträge zur Alexander-von-Humboldt-Forschung, vol. 20. Berlin: Akademie Verlag, 2000.

Fifer, J. Valerie. *United States Perceptions of Latin America, 1850–1930: A "New West" South of Capricorn?* Manchester and New York: Manchester University Press, 1991.

Fittkau, Ernst Josef. "Johann Baptist von Spix, Zoologe und Brasilienforscher." In Helbig, ed., *Brasilianische Reise*, pp. 53–74.

Forbes, John Murray. *Once años en Buenos Aires, 1820–1831; las crónicas diplomáticas de John Murray Forbes.* Compiled, translated, and annotated by Felipe A. Espil. Buenos Aires: Emecé Editores, 1956.

Foucault, Philippe. *Le pêcheur d'orchidées.* Paris: Seghers, 1990.

Fundación Antorchas. *Los años del daguerrotipo: primeras fotografías argentinas, 1843–1870.* Buenos Aires: Gaglianone Establecimiento Gráfico, 1995.

Furlong, Guillermo, S. J. "Nuevos datos sobre Bonpland en Buenos Aires (1818)." *Anales de la Universidad del Salvador* (Buenos Aires) 5 (1969): 159–71.

Galeano, Eduardo. *Memory of Fire.* Trans. Cedric Belfrage. Vol. 2, *Faces and Masks.* New York: Pantheon Books, 1987.

Gallo, Klaus. "Rivadavia y los ingleses." In Luna, ed., *Lo mejor de todo es historia*, 2:263–77.

Ganson, Barbara. *The Guaraní under Spanish Rule in the Río de la Plata.* Stanford, CA: Stanford University Press, 2003.

García Márquez, Gabriel. *The General in His Labyrinth.* Trans. Edith Grossman. New York: Knopf, 1990.

Gasulla, Luis. *El solitario de Santa Ana.* Buenos Aires: Santiago Rueda, 1978.

Gay, João Pedro [Jean-Pierre]. *Invasão paraguaia na fronteira brasileira do Uruguai.* Comments and additions by Major Sousa Docca. Porto Alegre and Caxias do Sul: Escola Superior de Teologia São Lourenço de Brindes, 1980.

Giberti, Gustavo Carlos. "Aspectos oscuros de la corología de *Ilex paraguariensis* St. Hil." In Winge and others, eds., *Erva-mate*, pp. 289–300.

———. "Bonpland's Manuscript Name for the Yerba Mate and *Ilex Theezans* C. Martius ex Reisseck (Aquifoliaceae). *Taxon* 39 (1990): 663–65.

Glick, Thomas F. "Science and Independence in Latin America (with Special Reference to New Granada)." *Hispanic American Historical Review* 71, no. 2 (1991): 307–34.

Gómez, Félix-Maria. *Amado Bonpland.* Corrientes: Cuaderno de Cultura, 1958.

Grierson, Cecilia. *Colonia de Monte Grande, Provincia de Buenos Aires: Primera y única colonia formada por escoceses en la Argentina*. Buenos Aires: Jacobo Peuser, 1925.

Guillemot, Eugène. *Affaires de la Plata: extraits de la correspondance de M. Eugène Guillemot pendant sa mission dans l'Amérique du Sud*. Paris, 1849.

Halperín-Donghi, Tulio. *Politics, Economics and Society in Argentina in the Revolutionary Period*. Cambridge: Cambridge University Press, 1975.

Hammerly Dupuy, Daniel. "Alejandro de Humboldt y las exploraciones científicas en América." *Historia: Revista Trimestral de Historia Argentina, Americana y Española* (Buenos Aires) año 5, no. 16 (Apr.–June 1959): 5–10.

———. "El naturalista Bonpland y la conspiración de José Carrera contra O'Higgins y San Martín." *Historia: Revista Trimestral de Historia Argentina, Americana y Española* 4, no. 13 (July–Sept. 1958): 83–94.

Hamy, E. T. [Ernest-Théodore]. *Aimé Bonpland, médecin et naturaliste, explorateur de l'Amérique du Sud. Sa vie, son oeuvre, sa correspondance*. Paris: Librairie Orientale & Américaine E. Guilmoto, 1906.

———. *Le centenaire du retour en Europe d'Alexandre de Humboldt et Aimé Goujaud de Bonpland (3 aout 1804)*. Angers: Imprimerie A. Burdin, 1904.

———, ed. *Lettres américaines d'Alexandre de Humboldt, 1798–1807, precédées d'une notice de J.C. Delamétherie et suivies d'un choix de documents en partie inédits*. Paris: E. Guilmoto, 1905.

Heffernan, Michael J. "The Parisian Poor and the Colonization of Algeria during the Second Republic." *French History* 3, no. 4 (1989): 377–403.

Helbig, Jörg, ed. *Brasilianische Reise, 1817–1820: Carl Friedrich Philipp von Martius zum 200. Geburtstag*. Munich: Hirmer, 1994.

Hemming, John. *Red Gold: The Conquest of the Brazilian Indians*. Cambridge, MA: Harvard University Press, 1978.

Hensel, Reinhold Friedrich. "Beiträge zur näheren Kenntniss der brasilianischen Provinz São Pedro do Rio Grande do Sul." *Zeitschrift der Gesellschaft für Erdkunde zu Berlin* 2 (1867): 227–69, 342–76.

Hermann, Christian. *La politique de la France en Amérique latine, 1826–1850: une rencontre manquée*. Collection de la Maison des Pays Ibériques, 67. Bordeaux: Maison des Pays Ibériques, 1996.

Holland, Charles. *Noticias de Buenos Aires, el Paraguay, Chile y el Peru: cartas del ciudadano inglés Charles Holland, 1820–1826*. Presentation and Introduction by Leon Tenenbaum; trans. Mabel Susana Godfrid de Tenenbaum and Leon Tenenbaum. Buenos Aires: Fundación Banco de Boston, 1990.

Holmberg, Eduardo L. "Correspondencia inédita de Humboldt y Bonpland: un hallazgo interesante." *Caras y Caretas* 8, no. 365 (30 Sept. 1905).

Hossard, Nicolas. *Aimé Bonpland (1773–1858), médecin, naturaliste, explorateur en Amérique du Sud: à l'ombre des arbres*. Preface by Bernard Lavallé. Collection Recherche et Documents - Amériques latines. Paris: L'Harmattan, 2001.

———, ed. *Alexander von Humboldt et Aimé Bonpland: Correspondance, 1805–1858*. Documents Amériques Latines. Paris: L'Harmattan, 2004.

Humboldt, Alexander von. *Briefe aus Amerika, 1799–1804*. Edited by Ulrike Moheit.

Beiträge zur Alexander-von-Humboldt-Forschung, vol. 16. Berlin: Akademie Verlag, 1993.

———. *Personal Narrative of a Journey to the Equinoctial Regions of the New Continent*. Abridged and trans. with an introduction by Jason Wilson, and a historical introduction by Malcolm Nicolson. Penguin Classics. London; New York: Penguin Books, 1995 [1814–1825].

———. *Reise durch Venezuela: Auswahl aus den amerikanischen Reisetagebüchern*. Edited by Margot Faak. Beiträge zur Alexander-von-Humboldt-Forschung, vol. 12. Berlin: Akademie Verlag, 2000.

———. *Tableaux de la nature, ou, Considerations sur les déserts, sur la physionomie des végétaux, et sur les cataractes de l'Orénoque*. 2 vols. Paris, 1828.

Humboldt, Alexander von, and Aimé Bonpland. *Monographie des mélastomacées*. 2 vols. Paris: Librairie Grecque-Latine-Allemande, [1806]–1816, and Paris: Chez Gide Fils, [1806]–1823.

———. *Plantes équinoxiales, recueillies au Mexique, dans l'île de Cuba, dans les provinces de Caracas, de Cumana et de Barcelone, aux Andes de la Nouvelle-Grenade, de Quito et duPérou, et sur les bords du Rio Negro, de l'Orénoque et de la rivière des Amazones*. 2 vols. Paris: F. Schoell; Tübingen: J.G. Cotta, [1805–] 1808, and Paris: F. Schoell, 1813 [1808–1817].

———. *Voyage aux régions équinoxiales du nouveau continent, fait en 1799, 1800, 1801, 1802, 1803, et 1804, par Al. de Humboldt et A. Bonpland*, vol. 5. Paris, 1820.

Humphreys, R. A. *Liberation in South America, 1806–1827: The Career of James Paroissien*. London: University of London and Athlone Press, 1952.

———. *Tradition and Revolt in Latin America and Other Essays*. New York: Columbia University Press, 1969.

Un inglés, *Cinco años en Buenos Aires [A Five Years' Residence in Buenos Ayres During the Years 1820 to 1825]*. 2d ed. Prologue by Alejo B. González Garaño. Colección El Pasado Argentino. Buenos Aires: Ediciones Solar, 1962.

Isabelle, Arsène. *Emigração e colonização na província brasileira do Rio Grande do Sul, na República Oriental do Uruguai e em toda a bacia do Prata*. Trans. Belfort de Oliveira and preface by Augusto Meyer. Rio de Janeiro, 1950 [1850].

———. *Voyage a Buénos-Ayres et a Porto-Alègre, par la Banda-Oriental, les Missions d'Uruguay et la Province de Rio-Grande-do-Sul*. Le Havre: Imprimerie de J. Morlent, 1835.

Jouanin, Christian. "Bonpland." In Musée National des Château de Malmaison & Bois-Préau, ed., *L'impératrice Joséphine*, pp. 54–67.

Kehlmann, Daniel. *Measuring the World*. Trans. from the German by Carol Brown Janeway. New York: Pantheon Books, 2006.

Kellner, L. *Alexander von Humboldt*. London: Oxford University Press, 1963.

Keynes, Richard Darwin, ed. *Charles Darwin's Beagle Diary*. Cambridge: Cambridge University Press, 1988.

Kirchheimer, Jean-Georges. "Bonpland et la conspiration française de 1818 à Buenos Aires." In Potelet and Farré, eds., *Mundus Novus-Nouveaux Mondes*, pp. 123–30.

———. "Narcisse Parchappe: un polytechnicien explore la Patagonie, 1838." In Laissus, ed., *Les naturalistes français en Amérique du Sud*, pp. 307–15.

———. "Voyageurs francophones en Amerique Hispanique au cours du XIX. siècle. Essai de constitution d'un fichier bio-bibliographique." Thèse de doctorat du 3ᵉᵐᵉ cycle, Univ. de Paris, X, Centre de Recherches Latino-Americaines, June 1984.

Kleudgen, Peter. *Die deutsche Kolonie Santa Cruz in der Provinz Rio Grande do Sul in Süd-Brasilien, nach den neuesten Nachrichten dargestellt*. Hamburg: R. Kittler, 1853.

Kohlhepp, Gerd. "Alexander von Humboldt en los trópicos del Nuevo Mundo. Reflexiones sobre el bicentenario del inicio de su 'Viaje a las regiones equinocciales' en 1799." *Diálogo Científico* 8, no. 2 (1999): 9–24.

Lack, H. Walter. "The Botanical Field Notes Prepared by Humboldt and Bonpland in Tropical America." *Taxon* 53 (2004): 501–10.

Laissus, Yves, ed. *Les naturalistes français en Amérique du Sud XVIᵉ-XIXᵉ siècles*. Paris: Comité des Travaux Historiques et Scientifiques, 1995.

Leitner, Ulrike. "The Botanical Results of Humboldt's Latin American Travels." Unpublished manuscript, BBAW.

Levine, Robert M. *Cuba in the 1850s: Through the Lens of Charles DeForest Fredricks*. Tampa: University of South Florida Press, 1990.

Linhares, Temístocles. *História econômica do mate*. Coleção documentos brasileiros, no. 138. Rio de Janeiro: J. Olympio, 1969.

Livingstone, David N., and Charles W. J. Withers, eds. *Geography and Enlightenment*. Chicago: University of Chicago Press, 1999.

López, Vicente Fidel. *Historia de la República Argentina: su origen, su revolución y su desarrollo político hasta 1852*. 4th ed., 10 vols. Buenos Aires: J. Roldán y Cia., 1926.

Lourteig, Alicia. "Aimé Bonpland." *Bonplandia* (Corrientes) 3 (1977): 269–317.

Love, Joseph L. *Rio Grande do Sul and Brazilian Regionalism, 1882–1930*. Stanford, CA: Stanford University Press, 1980.

Luna, Félix, ed. *Lo mejor de todo es historia*. Vol. 2, *Construyendo la Patria*. Buenos Aires: Taurus, 2002.

Lynch, John. *Argentine Dictator: Juan Manuel de Rosas, 1829–1852*. Oxford: Clarendon Press, 1981.

Macchi, Manuel E. *El ovino en la Argentina: acción de Urquiza, intento de desarrollismo: fábrica textil e inmigración catalana*. Colección Humanidades. Temas de Historia: 1, Trabajos originales, no. 8. Buenos Aires: Ediciones Macchi, 1974.

Maeder, Ernesto J. A. "La evolución de la gandería en Corrientes [1810–1854]." *Cuadernos de Estudios Regionales* 4 (1983): 7–21.

———. *Misiones del Paraguay: conflicto y disolución de la sociedad Guaraní (1768–1850)*. Colección Realidades Americanas. Madrid: Editorial MAPFRE, 1992.

Maeder, Ernesto J. A., and Ramon Gutierrez. *Atlas historico del nordeste argentino*. Resistencia: Instituto de Investigaciones Geohistóricas, Universidad Nacional del Nordeste, 1995.

Mañé Garzón, Fernando. *Vilardebó (1803–1857): primer médico uruguayo.* Montevideo: Talleres Gráficos Barreiro, 1989.
Manthorne, Katherine E. *Tropical Renaissance: North American Artists Exploring Latin America (1839–1879).* Washington, DC: Smithsonian, 1989.
Marshall, Oliver, ed. *English-Speaking Communities in Latin America.* Institute of Latin American Studies Series, University of London. Basingstoke and London: Macmillan, 2000.
Martin de Moussy, Victor. *Description géographique et statistique de la Confédération Argentine.* 3 vols. Paris: Firmin Didot, 1860–1864.
———. "Notice sur la vie de M. Bonpland en Amérique. Plata, Paraguay et Missions." *Bulletin de la Societé de Géographie* 4th ser., 19 (1860): 414–25.
Martins, Luciana L. "A Naturalist's Vision of the Tropics: Charles Darwin and the Brazilian Landscape." *Singapore Journal of Tropical Geography* 21, no. 1 (2000): 19–33.
Maudit, Fernando. "Arboriculture in Argentina." In Argentine Republic, *Agricultural and Pastoral Census*, pp. 267–93.
Mauthe, Gabriele. "Die Österreichische Brasilien expedition, 1817–1836." In Helbig, ed., *Brasilianische Reise*, pp. 13–27.
McLean, David. "Garibaldi in Uruguay: A Reputation Reconsidered." *English Historical Review* 113, no. 451 (Apr. 1998): 351–66.
———. *War, Diplomacy and Informal Empire: Britain and the Republics of La Plata, 1836–1853.* London and New York: British Academic Press, 1995.
Mier [Noriega y Guerra], José Servando Teresa de. *The Memoirs of Fray Servando Teresa de Mier.* Trans. from the Spanish by Helen Lane. Edited and with an introduction by Susana Rotker. New York: Oxford University Press, 1998.
Miers, John. "On the History of the 'Mate' Plant, and the Different Species of *Ilex* Employed in the Preparation of 'Yerba de Mate' or Paraguayan Tea." *Annals and Magazine of Natural History* 8 (1861): 219–28 and 398–401.
Minguet, Charles. *Alexandre de Humboldt, historien et géographe de l'Amérique espagnole.* La Découverte. Paris: François Maspero, 1969.
Miran, Joseph. *Un français au Chili, 1841–1853: correspondance et notes de voyage de Joseph Miran*, compiled and edited by Paul and Philippe Roudié. Collection de la Maison des pays ibériques, no. 30. Paris: Editions du Centre national de la recherche scientifique, 1987.
Monteil, Amans-Alexis. *Traité de matériaux des manuscrits de divers genres d'histoire*, vol. 1. Paris: Imprimerie de E. Duverger, 1836.
Montoya, Alfredo J. *La ganadería y la industria de salazón de carnes en el período 1810–1862.* Colección de temas de historia económica. Serie americana, no. 2. Buenos Aires: Editorial El Coloquio, 1971.
Morgan, Iwan. "French Ideas of a Civilizing Mission in South America, 1830–1848." *Canadian Journal of History/Annales canadiennes d'histoire* 16 (1981): 379–403.
———. "French Policy in Spanish America: 1830–1848." *Journal of Latin American Studies* 10, no. 2 (Nov. 1978): 309–28.
Mörner, Magnus, ed. *Algunas cartas del naturalista sueco Don Eberhard Munck af*

Rosenschöld escritas durante su estadía en el Paraguay, 1843–1869. Trans. from Swedish by Ernesto Dethorey. Stockholm: Biblioteca e Instituto de Estudios Ibero-Americanos de la Escuela de Ciencias Económicas, 1955.

Mújica Laínez, Manuel. *Misteriosa Buenos Aires*. Collección Piragua. Buenos Aires: Editorial Sudamericana, 1964.

Musée National des Château de Malmaison & Bois-Préau. *L'impératrice Joséphine et les sciences naturelles*. Paris: Éditions de la Réunion des Musées Nationaux, 1997.

Naylor, Simon. "Discovering Nature, Rediscovering the Self: Natural Historians and the Landscapes of Argentina." *Environment and Planning D: Society and Space* 19 (2001): 227–47.

Orbigny, Alcide Dessalines d'. *Viaje a la América meridional . . . realizado de 1826 a 1833*. 4 vols. Prologue by Ernesto Morales. Colección Eurindia. Buenos Aires: Editorial Futuro, 1945.

Ottone, Eduardo G. "Aimé Bonpland's Drawing of Itá Pucú, 1834, and the History of Early Geological Representations in Argentina." *Earth Sciences History* 23, no. 2 (2004): 121–33.

———. "The French Botanist Aimé Bonpland and Paleontology at Cuenca del Plata." *Earth Sciences History* 21, no. 2 (2002): 150–65.

Outram, Dorinda. "On Being Perseus: New Knowledge, Dislocation, and Enlightenment Exploration." In Livingstone and Withers, eds., *Geography and Enlightenment*, pp. 281–94.

Page, Thomas J. *La Plata, the Argentine Confederation, and Paraguay*. New York: Harper, 1859.

Pang, Eul-Soo. *In Pursuit of Honor and Power: Noblemen of the Southern Cross in Nineteenth Century Brazil*. Tuscaloosa: University of Alabama Press, 1988.

Papillaud, Henri. *Le journalisme français à Buenos Aires de 1818 jusqu' à nos jours*. Buenos Aires: Editorial Luis Lasserre, 1947.

Paraguay. Ministerio de Interior. *Los restos mortales del Dr. José Gaspar Rodríguez de Francia*. Asunción, Impr. Nacional, 1962.

Parish, Sir Woodbine. *Buenos Ayres and the Provinces of the Rio de la Plata: From Their Discovery and Conquest by the Spaniards to the Establishment of Their Political Independence, with Some Account of Their Present State, Trade, Debt, etc.* London: J. Murray, 1839.

Parsons, James J. "Giant American Bamboo in the Vernacular Architecture of Colombia and Ecuador." *Geographical Review* 81, no. 2 (Apr. 1991): 131–52.

Pérez Acosta, Juan F. *Francia y Bonpland*. Facultad de Filosofía y Letras [Universidad de Buenos Aires], Publicaciones del Instituto de Investigaciones Históricas, no. 79. Buenos Aires: Jacobo Peuser, 1942.

Pérez Petit, Victor. *En la Atenas del Plata*. Montevideo: Atlantida, 1944.

Piccirilli, Ricardo. *Rivadavia y su tiempo*. 2nd ed. 3 vols. Buenos Aires: Ediciones Peuser, 1960.

Pioli de Layerenza, Alicia, and María Isabel Artigas de Rebes. "Amado Bonpland en el Plata." *Hoy es Historia* (Montevideo) año 7, no. 41 (Sept.–Oct. 1990): 54–63.

Pivel Devoto, Juan E. "Diario del estabelecimiento de horticultura y aclimatación de Pedro Margat, 1846–1871." *Revista Histórica* (Montevideo) 50 (1977): 473–501.
Potelet, Jeanine, and Joseph M. Farré, eds. *Mundus Novus-Nouveaux Mondes (XVIe–XXe S.: Hommage à Charles Minguet*. Collection Archivos. Université de Paris X-Nanterre & Centre de Recherches Ibériques et Ibéro-Américaines, 1993.
Poucel, Benjamin. *Les bergeries Mérinos-Naz du Pichinango*. Paris: Imprimerie de Chassaignon, 1848.
——— . *Les otages de Durazno: souvenirs du Rio de la Plata pendant l'intervention anglo-française de 1845 à 1851*. Paris and Marseille: A. Faure, 1864.
Pratt, Mary Louise. *Imperial Eyes: Studies in Travel Writing and Transculturation*. London: Routledge, 1992.
Pujol, Juan. *Corrientes en la organización nacional*. 10 vols. Buenos Aires: Imprenta, Litografía y Encuadernación de G. Kraft, 1911.
Quesada, Vicente G. *La Provincia de Corrientes*. Buenos Aires: Imprenta de El Orden, 1857.
Racine, Karen. "A Community of Purpose: British Cultural Influence during the Spanish American Wars for Independence." In Marshall, ed., *English-Speaking Communities in Latin America*, pp. 3–32.
Raffles, Hugh. *In Amazonia: A Natural History*. Princeton, NJ: Princeton University Press, 2002.
Ramos, R. Antonio. *Juan Andrés Gelly*. Buenos Aires: Talleres Gráficos Lucania, 1972.
——— . *La política del Brasil en el Paraguay (bajo la dictadura de Francia)*. Buenos Aires: Editorial Ayacucho, 1944.
Rasmussen, Wayne D. "Diplomats and Plant Collectors: The South American Commission, 1817–1818." *Agricultural History* 29, no. 1 (Jan. 1955): 22–31.
Rebok, Sandra. "La expedición americana de Alexander von Humboldt y su contribución a la ciencia del siglo XIX. *Bulletin de l'Institut Français d'Études Andines* 32, no. 3 (2003): 441–58.
Rengger, Johann Rudolph, and Marceline Longchamps. *The Reign of Doctor Joseph Gaspard Roderick de Francia in Paraguay; Being an Account of a Six Years' Residence in that Republic from July 1819 to May 1825*. Trans. from the French. London: Thomas Hurst, Edward Chance & Co., 1827.
Rey, Auguste. *Le naturaliste Bosc, un Girondin herborisant*. Revue de L'Histoire de Versailles et de Seine-et-Oise. Versailles: Léon Bernard; Paris, Alphonse Picard, 1901.
Roa Bastos, Augusto. *I, the Supreme*. Trans. Helen Lane. New York: Knopf, 1986 [1974].
Robertson, John Parish, and William Parish Robertson. *Francia's Reign of Terror, Being a Sequel to Letters on Paraguay*. 2 vols. Philadelphia: E. L. Carey and A. Hart, 1839.
——— . *Letters on Paraguay: Comprising an Account of Four Years' Residence in That Republic Under the Government of the Dictator Francia*. 2d ed. 3 vols. New York: AMS Press, 1970 [London, 1839].

---. *Letters on South America; Comprising Travels on the Banks of the Paraná and Rio de la Plata*. 3 vols. London: John Murray, 1843.
Roche, Jean. *L'administration de la province du Rio Grande do Sul de 1829 à 1847, d'après les rapports inédits du Président du Rio Grande do Sul devant le Conseil Général, puis l'Assemblée Législative Provinciale*. Faculdade de Filosofía, Universidade do Rio Grande do Sul. Porto Alegre: Gráfica da Universidade do Rio Grande do Sul, 1961.
---. *La colonisation allemande et le Rio Grande do Sul*. Travaux et mémoires, vol. 3. Paris: Institut des Hautes Études de l'Amérique Latine, 1959.
---. *A colonização alemã e o Rio Grande do Sul*. 2 vols. Trans. Emery Ruas. Porto Alegre: Editôra Globo, 1969 [1959].
Rock, David. *Argentina, 1516–1987: From Spanish Colonization to Alfonsín*. Berkeley and Los Angeles: University of California Press, 1987.
Rodrigues, Cláudio Oraindi. *São Borja e sua história*. Coleção Tricentenário, no. 1. São Borja, 1982.
Rodrigues, José Honório. *História e historiadores do Brasil*. São Paulo: Fulgor, 1965.
---. "Padre Gay." *Provincia de São Pedro* (Porto Alegre) 19 (1954): 75–93.
Rodríguez Esteban, José Antonio. "El conocimiento geografico en Argentina. Siglos XIX y XX." *Ería. Revista de Geografía* (Oviedo) 24–25 (1991): 23–38.
Roehm, Marjorie Catlin. *The Letters of George Catlin and His Family; A Chronicle of the American West*. Berkeley and Los Angeles: University of California Press, 1966.
Ruiz Moreno, Aníbal, Vicente A. Risolía, and Rómulo d'Onofrio. *Aimé Bonpland: aportaciones de carácter inédito sobre su actividad científica en América del Sud*. Publicaciones del Instituto de Historia de la Medecina, vol. 17. Buenos Aires, 1955.
Rupke, Nicolaas A. *Alexander von Humboldt: A Metabiography*. Frankfurt am Main: Peter Lang, 2005.
Sabato, Hilda. *Agrarian Capitalism and the World Market: Buenos Aires in the Pastoral Age, 1840–1890*. Albuquerque: University of New Mexico Press, 1990.
Sabor, Josefa Emilia. *Pedro de Angelis y los origines de la bibliografía Argentina: ensayo bio-bibliográfico*. Biblioteca Dimensión Argentina. Buenos Aires: Ediciones Solar, 1995.
Sachs, Aaron. *The Humboldt Current: Nineteenth-Century Exploration and the Roots of American Environmentalism*. New York: Viking, 2006.
Saeger, James Schofield. *The Chaco Mission Frontier: The Guaycuruan Experience*. Tucson: University of Arizona Press, 2000.
Sáenz Quesada, María. "La Atenas del Plata." In Luna, ed., *Lo mejor de todo es historia*, pp. 257–61.
---. *Mariquita Sánchez: vida política y sentimental*. Buenos Aires: Editorial Sudamericana, 1995.
Saint-Hilaire, Auguste de. *Viagem ao Rio Grande do Sul, 1820–1821 [Voyage à Rio Grande do Sul, Brésil]*. Trans. Leonam de Azeredo Penna. Belo Horizonte: Editora Itatiaia; São Paulo: Editora da Universidade de São Paulo, 1974 [Orléans: H. Herluison, 1887].

———. *Voyage dans les provinces de Rio de Janeiro et Minas Geraes.* 2 vols. Paris: Grimbert et Dorez, 1830.
Sarton, George. "Aimé Bonpland (1773–1858)." *Isis* 34, pt. 5, no. 97 (Summer 1943): 385–99.
Schiaffino, Rafael. *Vida y obra de Teodoro M. Vilaredebo (1803–1857): médico y naturalista, higienista e historiador.* Montevideo: Imprenta El Siglo Ilustrado, 1940.
Schneppen, Heinz. "Aime Bonpland: ¿El olvidado compañero de Humboldt?" Trans. Carmen Livieres-Maynzhausen. *Historia Paraguaya* 39 (1999): 249–79.
———. *Aimé Bonpland: Humboldts vergessener Gefährte?* Berliner Manuskripte zur Alexander-von-Humboldt-Forschung, no. 14. Berlin: Akademie Verlag, 2000.
Schulz, Wilhelm. *Aimé Bonpland: Alexander von Humboldts Begleiter auf der Amerikareise, 1799–1804: Sein Leben und Wirken, besonders nach 1817 in Argentinien.* Abhandlungen der mathematisch-naturwissenschaftlichen Klasse der Akademie der Wissenschaften und der Literatur, Mainz, no. 9. Wiesbaden: Franz Steiner Verlag, 1960.
Scobie, James R. *Buenos Aires: Plaza to Suburb, 1870–1910.* New York: Oxford University Press, 1974.
———. *Revolution on the Pampas: A Social History of Argentine Wheat, 1860–1910.* Austin: University of Texas Press, 1964.
———. *Secondary Cities of Argentina: The Social History of Corrientes, Salta, and Mendoza, 1850–1910.* Completed and edited by Samuel L. Baily. Foreword by Ingrid Winther Scobie. Stanford, CA: Stanford University Press, 1988.
Seckinger, Ron. *The Brazilian Monarchy and the South American Republics, 1822–1831: Diplomacy and State Building.* Baton Rouge: Louisiana State University Press, 1984.
Shumway, Nicolas. *The Invention of Argentina.* Berkeley and Los Angeles: University of California Press, 1991.
Sigaud, Joseph-F. X. (José Francisco Xavier). *Du climat et des maladies du Brésil; ou statistique médicale de cet empire.* Paris: Fortin, Masson, 1844.
Silva, Elmar Manique da. "Ligações externas da economia gaúcha (1736–1890)." In Dacanal and Gonzaga, eds., *RS: economia e política,* pp. 55–91.
Silvestre, A.-F. *Notice biographique sur M. André Thouin, professeur de culture au jardin du roi, membre de l'institut, de la société royale et centrale d'agriculture, etc., etc.* Paris: Imprimerie de Madame Huzard, 1825.
Slatta, Richard W. *Gauchos and the Vanishing Frontier.* Lincoln: University of Nebraska Press, 1983.
Spalding, Walter. *A Revolução Farroupilha: história popular do grande decênio, seguida das efemérides principais de 1835–1845, fartamente documentadas.* 2d ed. São Paulo: Editora Nacional; Brasília: Instituto Nacional do Livro, 1980 [1939].
Stewart, Watt. "The South American Commission, 1817–1818." *Hispanic American Historical Review* 9 (1929): 31–59.
Stoddart, D. R. *On Geography and Its History.* Oxford: Blackwell, 1986.
Szuchman, Mark D., and Jonathan C. Brown, eds. *Revolution and Restoration: The*

Rearrangement of Power in Argentina, 1776–1860. Lincoln and London: University of Nebraska Press, 1994.
Taunay, Afonso de E. *A missão artística de 1816*. Coleção Temas Brasileiros, vol. 34. Brasília: Editora Universidade de Brasília, 1983 [Rio de Janeiro, 1956].
Tocqueville, Alexis de. *Writings on Empire and Slavery*. Edited and translated by Jennifer Pitts. Baltimore and London: Johns Hopkins University Press, 2001.
Thénard, Louis Jacques, baron. *Traité de chimie élémentaire, théorique et pratique*. 5 vols. 5th ed. Paris: Crochard, 1827.
Thésée, Françoise. *Auguste Plée, 1786–1825: un voyageur naturaliste, ses travaux et ses tribulations aux Antilles, au Canada, en Colombie*. Collection Kòd yanm. Paris: Editions Caribéenes, 1989.
Trabajos del Instituto de Botánica y Farmacología, Facultad de Ciencias Médicas de Buenos Aires, no. 31. *Archives inédites de Aimé Bonpland*. Tome 1, *Lettres inédites de Alexandre de Humboldt*. Preface by Henri Cordier and a note to the reader by Juan A. Domínguez. Buenos Aires, 1914.
―――, no. 42. *Archives inédites de Aimé Bonpland*. Tome 2, *Journal de botanique*. Prologue by Juan A. Domínguez. Buenos Aires: Jacobo Peuser, 1924.
Trabajos del Instituto Nacional de Botánica y Farmacología "Julio A. Roca," Facultad de Ciencias Médicas de Buenos Aires, ser. 2, no. 1. *Archivo de Aimé Bonpland*. Vol. 3, *Documentos para la historia de la República Entrerriana*. Prologue by Antonio Sagarna. Buenos Aires: Imprenta y Casa Editora Coni, 1939.
―――, ser. 2, no. 2. *Archivo de Aimé Bonpland*. Vol. 4, *Londres, cuartel general europeo de la emancipación americana*. Prologue by Guillermo Leguizamón. Buenos Aires: Editora Coni, 1940.
Trystram, Florence. "Aimé Bonpland (1773–1858) en Argentine." In Laissus, ed., *Les naturalistes français en Amérique du Sud*, pp. 227–34.
Vaillant, Auguste Nicolas. *Voyage autour du monde, exécuté pendant les années 1836 et 1837 sur la corvette La Bonite, commandé par M. Vaillant, capitaine de vaisseau; publié par ordre du gouvernement, sous les auspices du Département de la Marine*. Atlas, *Album historique*. Paris: A. Bertrand, 1840–1852.
Varese, Juan Antonio. *De las peripecias del artista César H. Bacle en las costas de Montevideo*. Montevideo: Torre del Vigía Ediciones, 2001.
Vidal, Emeric Essex. *Picturesque Illustrations of Buenos Ayres and Monte Video, Consisting of Twenty-Four Views: Accompanied with Descriptions of the Scenery, and of the Costumes, Manners, &c., of the Inhabitants of Those Cities and Their Environs*. London: R. Ackermann, 1820.
Waibel, Leo. *Capítulos de geografia tropical e do Brasil*. 2d. ed. with annotations. Rio de Janeiro: Secretaria de Planejamento da Presidência da República, Fundação Instituto Brasileiro de Geografia e Estatística, Superintendência de Recursos Naturais e Meio Ambiente, 1979 [1958].
―――. "Princípios da colonização européia no sul do Brasil." Trans. Orlando Valverde. In Waibel, *Capítulos de geografia tropical e do Brasil*, pp. 225–77.
Weimer, Günter. "Engenheiros alemães no Rio Grande do Sul, na década 1848–1858." *Estudos Ibero-Americanos* 5, no. 2 (Dec. 1979): 151–205.

Wendroth, Hermann Rudolf. *Album de aquarelas e desenhos, de cenas de viagem, vistas, tipos e costumes do Brasil, c. 1852*. Reproduced in the 1980s by the government of Rio Grande do Sul, n.p., n.d.; original unpublished manuscript in Arquivo da Casa Imperial do Brasil, Petrópolis, catalog C, no. 218.

Whigham, Thomas L. "Agriculture and the Upper Plata: The Tobacco Trade, 1780–1865." *Business History Review* 59 (Winter 1985): 563–96.

———. "Cattle Raising in the Argentine Northeast: Corrientes, c. 1750–1870." *Journal of Latin American Studies* 20, no. 2 (Nov. 1988): 313–35.

———. *The Paraguayan War*. Vol. 1, *Causes and Early Conduct*. Lincoln: University of Nebraska Press, 2002.

———. *The Politics of River Trade: Tradition and Development in the Upper Plata, 1780–1870*. Albuquerque: University of New Mexico Press, 1991.

———. "Some Reflections on Early Anglo-Paraguayan Commerce." *Americas* 44 (1987–88): 279–84.

———. "Trade and Conflict on the Rivers: Corrientes, 1780–1840." In Szuchman and Brown, eds., *Revolution and Restoration*, pp. 150–76.

———. *La yerba mate del Paraguay (1780–1870)*. Serie Historia Social. Asunción: Centro Paraguayo de Estudios Sociológicos, 1991.

Wilhelmy, Herbert. *Geographische Forschungen in Südamerika*. Kleine geographische Schriften, vol. 1. Berlin: Dietrich Reimer Verlag, 1980.

Williams, John Hoyt. "Paraguayan Isolation under Dr. Francia: A Re-evaluation." *Hispanic American Historical Review* 52 (1972): 102–22.

———. *The Rise and Fall of the Paraguayan Republic, 1800–1870*. Austin: University of Texas Press, 1979.

Wilson, Alexander. *American Ornithology*. 9 vols. Philadelphia: Bradford and Inskeep, 1808–14.

Wilson, Jason. "The Strange Fate of Aimé Bonpland." *London Magazine* (Apr.–May 1994): 36–48.

———. *Traveller's Literary Companion to South and Central America*. Traveller's Literary Companion. Series foreword by Margaret Drabble. Chicago: Passport Books, 1995.

Winge, Helga, and others, eds. *Erva-mate: biologia e cultura no Cone Sul*. Porto Alegre: Editora da Universidade Federal do Rio Grande do Sul, 1995.

Index

Note: Page numbers in italic type indicate illustrations.

Abalos, Remígio, 195, 211
Abalos family, 195
Academia Caesaro-Leopoldina, 1
Acosta family, 93
Aging, comments on, 85–86
Agriculture: in Algiers, 187; in Argentina, 32–33, 98–101; contributions to, 26, 29; during imprisonment, 72–74; Indians and, 47, 137–38; at Santa Ana ranch, 124–25, 202, 210–12. *See also* Botany; Resources, assessment of; Seeds
Agroforestry, 165
Aguilar, Victoriano, 46, 247*n*32
Alfalfa, 99, 101
Algarrobilla, 50, 140
Algeria, 165, 187–89, 203, 205–6, 219
Alibert, Jean-Louis, 51, 95, 111, 249*n*50, 258*n*25
Alsina, Valentín, 139, 269*n*40
The American Farmer (periodical), 34, 43
Andréa, Francisco José de Sousa Soares de, 167, 174–77, 184, 196, 201, 206, 276*n*14
Angelis, Pedro de, 11, 95–98, 106, 258*n*26, 286*n*53, 291*n*33; *Colección de obras y documentos relativos a la historia antigua y moderna de las provincias del Río de la Plata*, 106
Angola grass, 167
Arago, François, 174
Aráoz de La Madrid (general), 148
Araticu, 71
Araújo, José Joaquín de, 31, 50
Araújo, Luís, 116
Araújo, Mariano, 104
Argentina: agriculture in, 26, 29, 32–33, 98–101; botanical garden in, 29, 35; botanical work in, 26, 29, 33–36, 39–40, 42–44, 96–105; and civil war, 131–63; colonization of, 205; France and, 38, 40–41, 132–33, 136, 138–40, 142, 196; national library of, 25; Paraguay and, 65, 174, 246*n*121; plants in, 26; politics in, 38, 40–41, 129, 131–32, 178; reputation in, 236*n*48; Uruguay and, 130. *See also* Buenos Aires; Plata
Argerich, Cosme, 112, 264*n*99
Aripí, Nicolás, 52–62, 65
Arnold, David, 7
Arroyo Grande, battle of, 155
Artigas, Andresito, 84
Artigas, José Gervasio, 51, 62, 67, 249*n*59
Ash trees, 100
Asparagus, 29
Asunción, 68, 70–72, 77, 198, 202–3
Atalante (ship), 139, 140, 146
Atienza, Rafael de, 115–17, 119–21, 137
Atrevido (ship), 139
Australian pine, 142
Autonomists, 270*n*40
Autran, Eugène, 13
Avé-Lallemant, Robert, 177–78, 212, 213, 214–16, 220, 223, 224
Azara, Félix de, 31, 39, 109

Bacle, César-Hippolyte, 133, 268*n*11
Balcarce, Marcos, 45
Baldwin, William, 31–34
Bamboo, 43, 71, 253*m*28
Banks, Joseph, Sir, 13, 20, 21
Banville, Auguste, 26, 41, 102, 129, 246*m*10
Baptista de Oliveira, Cândido, 164, 175, 192, 198, 284*n*30
Baradère, Raymond, 142, 145, 147, 152
Barrère, B. (consul), 67, 245*m*105
Barrois, Charles, 95, 122, 258*n*25, 266*m*141
Basques, 141
Bates, Henry Walter, 226
Beck, Hanno, 14
Belgrano, Francisco, 39, 42
Belgrano, Manuel, 36, 42, 88
Benoit, Pierre, 36, 45, 95, 244*n*84
Bernal, Pablo, 123
Berón de Astrada, Genaro, 120, 125, 130, 134
Besse, Pierre, 102

Bethlehemite order, 29, 44
Bichat, Xavier, 3
Birds, 96–97
Bisson (ship), 202, 203
Blanc & Constantin, 96, 111, 120
Blancos, 132
Bolívar, Simón, 2, 10, 21–23, 27, 34, 74–75, 132, 254*n*43
Bombardera (ship), 45–46, 48
Bombo (ship), 48–49
Bonite (ship), 140
Bonpland, Adeline-Anne-Marguerite (née Delahaye) (wife), 26; English spoken by, 33; during imprisonment, 75, 85, 253*n*42; marriage to, 25, 240*n*25; political involvement of, 38; relationship with, 45, 48, 59, 90
Bonpland, Aimé: biographies of, 11–12, 14, 161, 286*m*53; confusion concerning life and achievements of, 1–2, 4–6, 8, 15–16, 216–17, 220, 291*n*33; life span of, 268*n*2; literature on, 10–11; name of, 3; portraits of, *ii*, 108, *110*, *204*, 262*n*86; scholarship on, 11–15, 225; value of studying, 15–19, 222–23
Bonpland, Amado (Amadito) (son), 184, 209, 212, 273*m*04
Bonpland, Anastasio (son), 184, 208, 273*m*04
Bonpland, Carmen (daughter), 155, 184, 208, 211, 217, 218
Bonpland, Emma (stepdaughter), 26, 33, 45, 59, 85, 240*n*25, 247*m*32
Bonpland, Michel-Simon (brother). *See* Goujaud-Bonpland, Michel-Simon
Bonpland, Pompeyo (grandson), 12
Bonpland, Simon-Jacques (alias Jean) (father), 2–3
Bonpland & Company, 106
Bonplandia (journal), 1, 198–99, 216, 217
Bordelaise (ship), 138, 139
Bosc, Louis-Augustin Guillaume, 79, 85, 95, 255*n*70, 258*n*25
Botanical gardens: plan for Argentine, 29, 35; Rio de Janeiro, 175, 191, 197, 206, 284*m*30
Botany: and Algeria, 187–90, 203, 205–6, 219; in Argentina, 26, 29, 33–36, 39–40, 42–44, 96–105; attraction to, 3–4; in Brazil, 161–62; cell theory of, 142; correspondence on, during civil wars, 142–45; Corrientes museum and, 206; economic, 142–43; education in, 4; during imprisonment, 69–72; manuscripts on, 9–10; in Montevideo, 187; in Paraguay, 69–72, 202–3; plant exchanges, 26, 34, 36, 79, 89, 94, 97, 162, 189–90, 206, 217–19; publishing of work on, 7–8, 21–22, 35–36, 89, 107, 109, 111, 142–45; at São Borja, 102–5; in Southern South America, 6, 9, 14, 18; in Uruguay, 187–92; vegetation and soil studies, 93. *See also* Agriculture; Seeds
Botijas Islands, 43

Botting, Douglas, 4
Bowles, William, 36
Brackenridge, Henry Marie, 31–33, 241*n*35
Brazil: Bonpland and, 125, 165–82, 206; botany in, 161–62; colonization of, 165, 169–70, 177–78; French cultural mission to, 244*n*87; Grandsire and, 75–76; land policies of, 169–70, 175; Paraguay and, 147–48, 153; possessions in, 184; retreat into, 155–62; tea cultivation in, 191; vegetation regions of, *169*. *See also* Rio Grande do Sul
Breard (business associate), 45, 48, 49, 53, 65, 85
Breeding: of mules, 211; in Rio Grande do Sul, 167–68; of sheep, 15, 99, 106, 113, 115, 122, 123, 154, 157–58, 160, 171, 186, 191. *See also* Merino sheep
Britain: and commerce, 241*n*44; efforts to gain Bonpland's release, 77–78; and Paraguay, 153
Brossard, Alfred de, Comte, 8, 203, 219, 292*n*46
Brougnes, Auguste, 205
Bruhns, Karl, 34, 220
Brunel, Adolphe, 11, 86, 224
Buchet de Martigny, Henri, 132
Buenos Aires: achievements in, 63; agriculture around, 32–33, 98–101; arrival in, 26–27; Bonpland on life in, 38–39; foreigners' impressions of, 27–29, 31–32, 241*n*35; French conspiracy in, 38, 40–41; Plaza de Toros, *32*; post-imprisonment return to, 94–96; post-imprisonment work in, 96–102; salons in, 28; yerba cultivation around, 39–40, 42
Burton, Richard, 68

Caacatí, 52–53, 59, 104
Caa miní, 55
Caa obí, 69–70
Caa-tay, 139
Cabañas (colonel), 92
Cabral, Pedro, 115
Cabrer, José María, 107, 262*n*81
Cáceres, Nicanor, 157
Caldas, Francisco José de, 22
Campbell (rancher), 157
Campe de Rosamel (admiral), 76
Candelaria, 51, 54–55, 61, 67
Candolle, Augustin Pyrame de, 86, 131, 142–45, 228; *Prodromus systematis universalis*, 144, 187
Capybaras, 43, 123
Carabí (insurgent leader), 148
Cardoso, José Mariano, 125, 138
Carob bean, 140
Carob trees, 27, 100
Carrera brothers, 40, 245*m*09
Carriego, Evaristo, 52–53
Carvalho e Mello, Luís José de, 77
Carvalho, José dos Santos, 274*m*24
Castelli, Pedro, 136

INDEX 313

Castro, José Ildefonso, 59
Casuarina, 266*m*42
Catigua, 72
Catlin, George, 285*m*49
Cattle ticks, 147
Cedar, 71
Ceibo tree, 43, 246*m*20
Cerrito, 72–74
Chaco, 114, 148
Chaco Indians, 148–49
Chairs, university. *See* University chairs
Chamorro (commander), 92, 127
Chastenay, Victorine de, Comtesse, 64, 81, 140–41, 251*m*2
Chaves, Antônio Rodrigues, 166–68, 171–73
Chaves, Pedro Rodrigues Fernandes, 166
Chaves family, 175, 179
Chemistry, 37, 96
Chevalier (business partner), 37, 49
Chilavert, Martiniano, 136, 147, 269*n*21
Childhood, 2–3
Children, Bonpland's, 10, 153, 155, 184, 218, 273*m*04
Chinese parasol tree, 71–72
Chinese tea, 180–81, 191–92
Christaldo, Juan Nicolás, 52, 58
Civilizing mission, 17
Civil wars, 131–63; activities during, 133–34; correspondence during, 142–46; political involvement during, 132–42, 145, 147–54; retreat into Brazil, 155–62; return to interior, 146–55; visits to Montevideo, 139–46, 149–52
Climate, 146
Collections: in Buenos Aires, 95–96; disposition of, after death, 217–18; during imprisonment, 85; sent to Jardin des Plantes, 102, 109; state of, 222
Colonization: of Algeria, 165, 187–89, 203, 205–6; of Argentina, 205; Bonpland and Santa Ana colony, 56, 58, 60–63, 68; of Brazil, 165, 169–70, 175, 177–78; Corrientes and, 165, 205, 209–10; French, 182, 196, 205; German, 165, 170, 176, 178, 196; Scottish, 97; Swiss, 209
Colorados, 132
Columbian Institute for the Promotion of Arts and Sciences, 31
El Comercio (newspaper), 196, 286*m*53
Commerce: Argentina and, 65, 68, 85; Britain and, 241*n*44; in Corrientes, 47–50; France and, 241*n*44; Paraguay and, 65, 68
Conceição Veloso, José Mariano da, 145
Concepción mission, 125
Concordia, 178
Congress (ship), 31, 34
Conservation, forest, 173, 176, 228
Contraband, 92, 124
Cordier, Henri, 12–13, 236*n*47
Corpus Christi mission, 56–57

Correa da Câmara, Antônio Manoel, 76–77, 81, 192, 254*n*52
Correio do Sul (newspaper), 206
Correspondence: from Buenos Aires (1836–1837), 108–9; with Chaves, 166–67; during civil wars, 142–46; with Humboldt, 13, 14, 21, 23, 34, 60, 85–86, 95, 111, 122, 187, 196, 198, 203, 207, 212, 217–18, 266*m*42; in later years, 181; post-imprisonment, 89–90; publication of, 12, 20
Corrientes: Bonpland and, 45–52, 61, 63, 88, 90–94, 104, 112–14, 120, 132, 146, 150, 152, 156–57, 165, 182–84, 202, 236*n*48; during civil wars, 147–55, 163; colonization of, 165, 205, 209–10; commerce in, 47–50, 119; descriptions of, 46, 89; development of, 122; and Entrerriano Republic, 45, 60; museum in, 193–94, 196, 202–3, 206, 209, 218, 291*n*39; optimism in, 117; politics in, 129–30, 133, 136, 174, 182; ranching potential of, 104; return from Misiones to, 59–60; and yerba, 125–26, 182–84, 192, 200
Corvisart, Jean, 3
Cotton, 74, 97–98, 100, 182–83
Creus, Carlos, 174
Cristaldo, Victoriana, 153, 155, 184, 272*n*92
Crossbreeding. *See* Breeding
Cuesta, Manuel Joaquín de la, 44
Cultivation. *See* Experimental cultivation
Curundey tree, 114
Curupay tree, 37
Curuzú Cuatiá, 93–94, 104, 115–16, 123–24, 130, 157
Cuvier, Georges, 77

Daguerreotypes, 179, *204*
Darwin, Charles, 102, 114, 217, 222, 260*n*51, 260*n*55, 264*m*10
Date palm trees, 203
Davison, Diego, 122
Davison, Roberto, 122
Dean, Warren, 191
Death of Bonpland, 217
Deforestation, 165
Delessert, Benjamin, 173
Delessert, François, 142–43, 179, 181, 187, 218
Delessert family, 41, 111, 122, 179–80, 222
Demersay, Alfred, *ii*, 11, *57*, *158*, *159*, 159–61, 173, 181–82, 198, 224
Desault, Pierre-Joseph, 3
Desbrosses, Frédéric, 17, 106, 114, 119, 121, 265*m*30
Desfontaines, René-Louiche, 4
Desmarest & Ducoing, 180
Desnoyers, Jules, 10
Devería, Achille, *ii*
Díaz de Vivar, Antonio, 93
Díaz de Vivar, Justo, 114–15

Dickson, George Frederick, 95–96
Domínguez, Juan A., 12, 13, 94, 134, 224
Driver, Felix, 225
Dubrunfaut, Augustin Pierre, 96
Dulgeon, Thomas, 124
Duméril, Constant, 109
Duperré, Guy-Victor, 140, 270*n*46
Dupotet (admiral), 140–41, 146, 151
Dupuy, Daniel Hammerly, 40
Dupuytren, Guillaume, 4, 95, 258*n*25
Duran, Alexandre, 49
Dysentery, 178–79

Echagüe, Pascual de, 134–35, 149
Economic botany, 142–43
Education, 3–4
Élie de Beaumont, Jean-Baptiste-Armand-Louis-Léonce, 218
Emma (Adeline Bonpland's daughter). *See* Bonpland, Emma (stepdaughter)
Encienso, 72
Endlicher, Stephan, *Genera plantarum*, 187
Enghien, duke of, 68, 252*n*8
Engineers, 175, 277*n*45, 277*n*47
England. *See* Britain
English potatoes, 167
English sheep, 123
Entre Ríos, 45, 59–60, 154–55, 178–79, 227
Entrerriano Republic, 45, 51, 53, 59–60
Environmental determinism, 146
Escoffier (hostage), 70
Espinillo trees, 112, 113, 125
Estancia Santa Ana. *See* Santa Ana ranch
Estigarribia, Vicente, 292*n*46
Eurocentrism, 2, 16
Europe: attitude toward, 16; departure from, 21–23, 25; reputation in, 1, 5, 65; seed exchanges with, 17, 29, 34, 36
Exotic species, introduction of, 26, 100–101, 142, 266*n*42. *See also* Botany: plant exchanges; Seeds: exchanges of
Explorations, *xiii*

Farroupilha Revolt, 118, 128–29, 135–36, 138, 150, 154, 163
Federalists, 129, 131–32
Ferré, Pedro, 90–92, 104, 105, 114, 120, 125, 127, 129, 133, 136–38, 148–51, 153–56, 186, 222, 257*n*8
Finances: book sales and, 25, 29–30; during civil wars, 142–43; and debt, 95; and French state pension, 5, 14, 25, 41, 89, 105–6, 119–20, 138, 142, 168, 173, 218; during imprisonment, 82, 89; means of supporting his family, 35; medical practice and, 184; obscurity concerning, 14; parental estate and, 25, 106, 240*n*26; tannery and, 37–38; and taxes, 199; work patterns affected by, 89, 221

Firewood, 43, 99, 100
A Five Years' Residence in Buenos Aires (Anonymous), 28
Flechilla, 93
"Flore des Provinces Unies de la Plata," 35–36
Forage, 99
Forest, F., 41
Forest conservation, 173, 176, 228
Fortune (ship), 147
Fossils, 114
Foucault, Philippe, 11, 15
Fox, Henry Stephen, 101, 260*n*51
France: and Algeria, 187–89, 219; and Argentina, 38, 40–41, 132–33, 136, 138–40, 142, 196; Bonpland and, 5–7, 17; colonization by, 182, 196, 205; and commerce, 241*n*44; and Corrientes, 205; influence of, in South America, 16–17; and Montevideo, 141; and Paraguay, 68; politics in, 102; and Uruguay, 17, 130, 132, 205
Francia, José Gaspar Rodríguez de: age of, 86, 131, 143, 144, 146; appeals to, on behalf of Bonpland, 74–78; character of, 64; death of, 86, 150; novel about, 10–11; portrait of, *66*; relationship with, 2, 43, 46, 61–62, 65, 70, 80–81, 83, 131, 148; release of Bonpland, 81–83; rule of, 51, 57, 67–68, 147–48, 254*n*43; tobacco cultivation under, 108; and *yerba*, 61, 125–26
Fredricks, Charles DeForest, 179, 279*n*67
Freemasonry, 184–85, 280*n*88
French Academy of Sciences, 96

Galeano, Eduardo, 16, 208
Gallocheau, Élisabeth-Olive (née Bonpland) (sister), 3, 21, 47, 146
Gallocheau, Pierre-Philippe-Amable-Honoré, 3, 21
Galup, José Manuel, 44, 46, 85
García de Cossio, José, 40
García Márquez, Gabriel, 10
Garibaldi, Giuseppe, 154, 273*n*96
Gasulla, Luis, 11, 236*n*42
Gauss, Carl Friedrich, 11
Gavrelle, Chevalier, 180
Gay, Jean-Pierre (João Pedro), 8–9, 12, 162, 184–85, 192, 194, 197, 199, 201, 206–7, 217, 224, 274*n*27, 275*n*29
Gay-Lussac, Joseph-Louis, 6–7
Gelly, Juan Andrés, 153, 271*n*76
Geology, publications on, 8
German colonization, 165, 170, 176, 178, 196
Giant water lilies, 36–37, 114, 180, 187
Gigaux (friend), 109
Glick, Thomas F., 223
Goethe, Johann Wolfgang von, 78
Gómez, Gregorio, 52
Gonçalves da Silva, Bento, 136, 154
Gontier (friend), 198

INDEX

Gordon, George J. R., 160
Goujaud-Bonpland, Michel-Simon (brother), 3; botanical collections of, 233*n*5, 240*n*26; character of, 238*n*7; correspondence with, 21, 25; and family finances, 25, 240*n*26; and medicine, 90, 97; relationship with, 3, 90
Grains, 167
Gramajo, Juan Francisco, 118
Granadilla, 179
Grandsire, Richard, 68, 73, 75–80, 83, 84, 254*n*44
Gray, Asa, 31, 204
Great Britain. *See* Britain
Griffiths, Charles, 260*n*51
Grigera, Tomás, 30–31
Grivel (rear admiral), 78
Guaicurú Indians, 139, 149
Guaicurú root, 94
Guana Indians, 108
Guanás Indians, 195
Guano, 37
Guaraní Indians, 51–52, 56, 58, 84, 180
Guaraní missions, 51
Guavas, 74
Guayana Indians, 122, 125
Guindet (ship captain), 146
Gülich, Friedrich von, 199, 200

Haenke, Tadeus, 34, 253*n*31
Halperín-Donghi, Tulio, 45
Hamy, Ernest-Théodore, 11–12, 20, 34, 76, 95, 133, 187, 226, 236*n*47
Hannah, John, 109
Hastrel, Adolphe d', 151
Herbarium, 9
Heredia, Alejandro, 91
L'Herminier, Félix Louis, 36
Hoker, Henry, 114
Honeylocust trees, 101
Honors received, 80, 161–62, 194, 198, 207, 217, 291*n*33
Hooker, William Jackson, 13, 86, 198, 228
Horsetail tree, 142
Hossard, Nicolas, 15
Hullet Brothers, 29
Humboldt, Alexander von, 11, 104, 161; association with, 1–2, 4–9, 5, 13, 21, 41–42, 98, 109, 216, 218–19, 220, 262*n*86; Avé-Lallemant and, 212, 214–15; correspondence with, 13, 14, 21, 23, 34, 60, 85–86, 95, 111, 122, 187, 196, 198, 203, 207, 212, 217–18, 266*n*142; difficulties with, 34, 42, 246*n*115; efforts to gain Bonpland's release, 74–78, 253*n*42; and French cultural mission to Brazil, 244*n*87; guano introduced by, 37; reputation of, 1–2, 7

Imprisonment, 62–87; agricultural activity during, 72–74; Bonpland's accounts of, 73, 86–87; Bonpland's capture, 62–63; botanical work during, 69–72; communication during, 79–80; conditions during, 68–69, 87; efforts to secure release from, 65, 74–78; fame resulting from, 7, 10, 65, 74; medicine during, 70–74; new family formed during, obscurity about, 73; reasons for, 65, 67–68, 77, 83; release from, 81–83
L'Independant du Sud (newspaper), 38
Indians: agriculture of, 137–38; attitude toward, 47, 53, 56, 149, 171, 195, 210; Chaco, 148–49; during civil wars, 148–49; Francia's attack on, 62–63, 68; Guaicurú, 139, 149; Guana, 108; Guanás, 195; Guaraní, 51–52, 56, 58, 84, 180; Guayana, 122, 125; as laborers, 171; pottery of, 137–38; of Santa Lucía, 137; near San Xavier, 210; Tobas, 137
Indigo, 36, 62, 251*n*200
Ingres, Jean-Auguste-Dominique, 112
Ingres, José, 112–13, 139, 147, 264*n*106
Ink, 140
International Congress of Americanists, 12
Isabelle, Arsène, 103, 174
Isasi, José Tomás, 61, 65
Isis (journal), 13
Italian immigrants, 132
Itapúa, 82–83, 147–48
Itatí, 47

Jaguars, 43, 83
Jardin des Plantes, Paris, 3–4, 41, 89, 94, 101, 102, 107, 109, 218
Jefferson, Thomas, 5
Jennerian Society, 160
Jesuit missions. *See* Missions
Jesús mission, 57, 72
Joséphine, Empress, 6, 10, 15, 21, 25–26, 158, 188, 220, 238*n*6, 240*n*25
Jussieu, Adrien de, 109
Jussieu, Antoine-Laurent de, 4

Kasten, Karl Wilhelm, 210–11, 215–17
Kehlmann, Daniel, 11
Kleudgen, Peter, 175, 278*n*48
Kunth, Karl Sigismund, 6, 79, 161

Lacour, Jean, 102
La Cruz mission, 92–93, 125, 148
Lagresse, Jean, 40
Lalande de Calan (captain), 138
Lamarck, Jean-Baptiste, 4
Land, plans for owning and using, 19, 29, 44, 89, 116, 119–21, 165, 173–77, 195, 211–12
Land rent, 98–99
Lange, Ambrose, 186
Largo, José, 139, 149
Larrañaga, Damaso Antonio, 30, 242*n*55, 242*n*56
Lavalle, Juan, 132, 136–40, 139, 147, 148, 153, 155
Lavaysse, Dauxion, 36
Lebreton, Joachim, 38–39

Lechêne, Gabriel, 26, 41
Ledesma, José, 195
Legalists, 129, 150
Legion of Honor, 161
Legumes, 167
Leitner, Ulrike, 6
Leloir, Antoine, 40
Leopoldina, empress of Brazil, 75
Levant cotton, 100
Liautaud (doctor), 180–81
Liberals, 129
Libraries: in Buenos Aires, 29–30, 88; in Montevideo, 30; in Uruguay, 242*n*56
Lima e Silva, João Manuel, 118
Lindau, João, 127–28
Livestock: and civil wars, 186; in Corrientes, 106; food for, 27, 100; grazing for, 112; from imprisonment, 74, 80, 82; at Santa Ana ranch, 128, 134–35. *See also* Ranching
Locusts, 210–11
London, 22
Longchamps, Marcel, 70–71
López, Carlos Antonio, 160, 182, 203
Lopez, Francisco, 123
López, Vicente Fidel, 28
López Jordán, José Ricardo, 59–60
Loreto, Marqués de, 39
Louis XVII, 244*n*84
Lozano, Pedro, 107
Lozano (business partner), 37
Luca, Don Tomás de, 28
El Lucero (newspaper), 98
Luchi, Louis de, 9
Luisamaria (ship), 139

Machado, Lucien, 103
Maciel, Gregorio, 156
Maciel, Santos, 116
Madariaga, Joaquín, 93, 163
Madariaga brothers, 157
Madison, James, 5
Magariños, Bernabé, 91, 257*n*9
Maillefer (consul). *See* Martin-Maillefer, Daniel-Pierre
Maize, 53, 99, 167, 193
Maler (colonel), 41
Malmaison, 6, 15, 25–26, 29, 36, 143, 188, 220, 240*n*25, 251*n*2
Mandeville, Henry, 111, 122
Mandioti, 53
Manioc, 47, 94, 167, 191, 193, 219, 281*n*98
Manuscripts, 24; from Buenos Aires, 36; French acquisition of, 8–10; from prison years, 65; uncertainty concerning, 8–9, 12, 36. *See also* Publications
Marceaux, Louis, 209, 212
Margat, Pedro Antonio, 190, 283*n*19
Maria (Indian companion), 73

Marijuana, 29
Marques family, 117
Martin de Moussy, Victor, 186
Martín García (island), 39, 42–43, 102–3, 140
Martin-Maillefer, Daniel-Pierre, 188–91, 203, 205, 219, 226–27, 282*n*107
Martins da Cruz Jobim, José, 161
Mártires mission, 125
Martius, Karl Friedrich Philip von, 104, 144–45, 161, 225
Masoni, Saturnino, 279*n*66
Masons, 184–85, 280*n*88
Maté consumption, 96, 171–72. *See also* Yerba maté
Mauthe, Gabriele, 226
Medicine: appointment to chair in, 50–51, 249*m*52; in Brazil, 161; correspondence concerning, 111; finances and, 184; Goujaud-Bonpland and, 90, 97; Guaicurú root as, 94; during imprisonment, 70–74; practice of, 73–74, 83, 91–92, 103–4, 115–16, 121–22, 124, 125, 127, 130, 136, 150, 154, 156, 178–79, 183, 208; and smallpox, 91–92; snakebite treatment, 83; studies in, 96
Melastomes, 6
Mendeville, Jean-Baptiste Washington de, 28, 78, 90
Mendeville, Mariquita, 90
Merino sheep, 15, 99, 106, 109, 111–12, 115, 117, 120, 123, 134, 145–46, 154, 160, 166–67, 171, 174, 178–79, 191, 227
Mexico, honorary citizenship in, 80
Michi, Maria, 184
Microscopes, 142–43
Mier Noriega y Guerra, Servando Teresa de, 239*m*3
Miers, John, 206
Military service, 3
Miller, Augustín, 156
Mirbel, Apollon de, 155, 163, 275*m*29
Mirbel, Charles François Brisseau de, 75, 122, 138, 142–43, 180
Misiones, 45, 50–62, 67, 68, 83–84, 174, 182, 183, 199–200, 210
Missions: in Brazil, 166–67; during civil wars, 148; Demersay's work on, 159; in Paraguay, 69–72; of Rio Grande do Sul, 103; in Upper Plata, 51–59, 84, 88, 90, 117–18; yerba maté cultivation in, 39, 55–56, 126–27, 194, 207. *See also individual missions*
Missões, 91
Modernity, 116
Modernization, 193–94
Le Moniteur (periodical), 79
Monte Grande, 97
Montevideo, 132–33; French influence in, 141, 174; landing place at, *141*; visits to, 138–46, 149–52, 174, 178–81, 187–207, 197–99

Morgan, Iwan, 132
Morínigo, Sebastian José, 61
Mouchez, Ernest, 203
Munck, Eberhard, 225
Murdaugh, William Henry, 194–95
Muséum d'Histoire Naturelle, Paris, 8. *See also* Jardin des Plantes
Mutis, José Celestino, 22
Mutis, Sinforoso, 22

El Nacional (newspaper), 150
Napoleon Bonaparte, 5, 14, 38, 40, 84, 158, 188
Napoleon III, 17, 188
Nascimbene, Luís, 128, 134–35
Natterer, Johann, 225–26
Natural history, Cochabamba chair in, 34–35
Navarre, 6, 15, 25–26, 188, 220
Nollet, Juan Francisco, 151, 272n80
Normann, Philip von, 175, 176, 206, 277n45
Nova genera et species plantarum, 79
Novara (ship), 212

Oak trees, 100
Odicini, Bartolomé, 181
O'Higgins, Bernardo, 245n109
Olivera, Domingo, 63
Ombú, 100
Orange trees, 43, 54, 55, 64, 74, 93, 125, 156, 184, 207
Orbigny, Alcide d', 104, 198, 217, 222, 261n63, 292n3
Oribe, Manuel, 132, 154
Ornano, Baron d', 197
Ortellado, Norberto, 62, 68
Osório, Manuel Luís, 201, 287n82
Ottone, Eduardo, 18
Ouseley, William Gore, 198

Page, Thomas Jefferson, 194, 212
Pago Largo, battle of, 89, 130, 134
Palacio Fajardo, Manuel, 22, 239n17
Palmeira, Conde, 76–77
Palm trees, 207
Palo de lanza tree, 114
Pampas, 33
Paraguay: Algerian plant exchange with, 219; approach to, 44–63; Argentina and, 65, 174, 246n121; botanical work in, 202–3; Brazil and, 147–48, 153; communication with, 61–62; Demersay's publication on, 159; departure from, 83–84; France and, 68; Francia's rule of, 51, 57, 67–68, 147–48, 254n43; imprisonment in, 7, 10, 62–87; isolation of, 67, 147–48; and Misiones, 174, 182; personal connections with, 88–89; post-Francia, 153, 160; tobacco cultivation in, 108; visits to, 165, 202–3
Paraguayan tea. *See* Yerba maté
Paraná islands, 42–43
Paraná River, 42, 45–46, 94
Parchappe (businessman), 85
Parental estate, 25, 106, 240n26
Paris: activities in, before departure for South America, 22–25; archival material in, 8–10; education in, 3; Humboldt and, 5–6, 41; materials sent to, 103, 105, 109, 189, 222; seed exchanges with, 29, 79, 180; thoughts of travel to, 64, 188, 201, 207
Paris, France, 64
Parish, Woodbine, 27, 77, 78, 218, 255n65
Paso de los Libres. *See* Restauración
Paspalum, 139
Pastures, 93, 101, 104, 112, 114, 115. *See also* Ranching
Paz, José María, 136–37, 149–52, 154, 271n76
Pazos Silva, Vicente (Pazos Kanki), 22, 239n14
Peach trees, 99
Peanuts, 74
Pedro I, emperor of Brazil, 75
Pedro II, emperor of Brazil, 159, 224
Pellegrini, Carlos, 108, *110*
Penabert, George, 279n66
Pension, 5, 14, 25, 41, 89, 105–6, 119–20, 138, 142, 168, 173, 218
Pentland, Joseph Barclay, 98
Pereira Pacheco, José Praxedes, 162
Pérez Acosta, Juan, 68, 224
Périchon, Estebán, 46, 115
Périchon, Pastora, 8, 47
Périchon family, 46, 146, 209, 224
Petitjean, Alphonse, 106, 121, 265n130
Phillips (doctor), 158
Photography, 179, *204*, 279n66, 279n67
Picada (colonial trail), 165, 173, 175–78, 183
Pimenta Bueno, José Antônio, 160, 176–77, 198, 274n115
Pineapples, 36
Pinto de Queros, Francisco, 129
Planalto, 170, 178
Plants. *See* Agriculture; Botany; Seeds; Trees
Plata: attraction to, 23; and civil war, 131–63; entry to, 25–42; France and, 17; independence of, 22; politics of, 181. *See also* Upper Plata
Plaza de Toros, Buenos Aires, 32
Pliny, 96
Poinsett, Joel Roberts, 80, 85
Politics: Adeline Bonpland and, 38; in Argentina, 38, 40–41, 129, 131–32, 178; Bonpland on South American, 181–82; during civil wars, 132–42, 145, 147–54; and contact with revolutionaries, 10, 22; in Corrientes, 129–30, 133, 136, 174, 182; Paraguay and geopolitics, 67; of the Plata, 181; post-imprisonment contacts in, 90–91; in Rio Grande do Sul, 128–29; in São Borja, 118; in Upper Plata, 129–30
Polygonum, 139

Porto Alegre, 168, 172, *172*, 206
Potatoes, 53, 74, 167, 181, 193. *See also* Sweet potatoes
Pottery, 137–38
Poucel, Benjamin, 17, 191, 283*m*23
Pratt, Mary Louise, 2; *Imperial Eyes*, 223
Proa (sublieutenant), 61
Publishing and publications: ambitions for, 7, 21–22, 35–36, 89, 107, 109, 111, 142–45, 173; on botany, 8; on geology, 8; Humboldt and Bonpland and, 6. *See also* Manuscripts
Pueyrredón, Juan Martín de, 23, 30, 36, 40, 42, 245*m*09
Pueyrredón (colonel), 139
Pujol, Juan, 8, 9, 121, 165, 182–84, 186–87, 192–203, 205, 206, 209–11, 222
Pumpkins, 99, 167

Quilombo (community of escaped slaves), 112

Raffeneau-Delile, Alire, 7, 36, 73–74, 79–80, 85, 95, 156, 164, 173, 244*n*85; *Flore d'Égypte*, 275*m*
Ramírez, Francisco, 45, 51, 53, 55, 58, 59, 67
Ramírez, José León, 81, 147
Ranching, 104, 113–17, 123. *See also* Livestock; Pastures
Razac (business associate), 45, 49
Reboul, Pierre, 192, 196
Rengger, Johann Rudolph, 70–71, 73, 83
Renovales (regrowth forests), 113–14
Reputation, Bonpland's: based on Avé-Lallemant's impressions, 215–17, 223; in Buenos Aires, 28, 50–51, 102; in Corrientes, 194; in Europe, 1, 5, 65; in Paraguay, 73; among scientists, 4–5, 7–8, 27, 79, 145, 217, 255*n*65; in South America, 1, 7–8; waning of, 2
Resources, assessment of, 19; in Argentina, 33, 43–44, 47, 88, 98–101, 126–27; in Brazil, 18, 165; for colonization, 210; in Corrientes, 197; during imprisonment, 65, 69–71; of missions, 53, 55–56; in Uruguay, 102–3, 183. *See also* Agriculture
Restauración, 135, 157, 183, 196, 197, 201, 210–11
Revista del Plata (periodical), 11
Ribeiro, Sebastião, 125
Ribeiro, Severino, 125
Rice, 201
Richard, Achille, 111
Rincón de las Gallinas, 103
Rio de Janeiro Botanical Garden, 175, 191, 197, 206, 284*m*30
Río de la Plata, 132–33, 182. *See also* Plata
Rio Grande do Sul, 14, 88, 90, 91, 103, 118, 128–29, 133–36, 150, 152, 155, 162–63, 165–73, *170*, 175–78, 206, 227, 277*n*45
Rio Pardo, 168–69
Rivadavia, Bernardino, 2, 17, 23, 25, 44, 63, 88, 222

Rivera, Fructuoso, 91, 131, 132, 136, 138, 140, 147, 148, 150–52, 154–55, 222, 257*n*9, 257*m*10
Róa Bastos, Augusto, *Yo, el Supremo*, 10–11
Robert de Connaut, Charles, 38, 40, 68, 83
Robertson, John Parish, 64, 71, 80–81, 97
Robertson, William Parish, 27–28, 46, 60–64, 80–81, 97
Rodney, Caesar Augustus, 34
Rodrigues, José Honório, 274*m*27
Roger, Aimé, 105–8, 133, 261*n*68, 265*m*30
Roguin, Dominique, 28, 41, 45, 53, 60, 63, 73–74, 82, 85, 90, 95, 102, 142, 152, 164, 196, 200–201, 246*m*15, 258*n*26
Roguin & Meyer, 29, 30, 46–50, 85
Romero (*subdelegado*), 70, 94
Rosa multiflora, 103
Rosas, Juan Manuel de, 13, 17, 94, 100, 101, 129–34, 136–40, 142, 153, 155, 164, 178, 186, 198
Roy, Just-Jean-Étienne (pseudonym: Armand de B.), 158
Royal Botanic Gardens, Kew, 198, 217

Sabbath, working on, 125, 156–57
Sabor, Josefa Emilia, 258*n*26
Sachs, Aaron, 7
Sáenz Quesada, María, 63
Saguier, Pedro (Pierre), 68
Saint-Hilaire, Auguste de, 30, 84, 91, 98, 104, 145, 161
Saint-Victor (ship), 26
Salons. *See* Tertulias
Salto, 103
San Carlos mission, 84, 125
Sánchez, Mariquita, 28, 142
San Ignacio Miní mission, 52, 53, 56, 62
San José mission, 125
San Juan, 196, 205, 209
San Marcos, 152–53
San Martín, José de, 36, 117, 245*m*09
San Roque, 94
Santa Ana, 116, 150
Santa Ana mission, 52, 55–63, 65, 68, 89
Santa Ana ranch: assessment of, 116, 124–25; boundaries of, 116, 195, 211–12; during civil wars, 152–55; cultivation practices at, 125, 189, 191–93, 196–97, 202, 210–12; drawing of, *213*; final months at, 208–16; as "general headquarters," 200; land claim for, 89, 120–23; management of, 138, 152–55, 191, 201, 208–9; ranching at, 128, 134–35, 153, 186, 211; scientific materials remaining at, 8, 12; taxes on, 199; visitors to, 126; willed to his children, 184
Santa Catalina, 97
Santa Cruz, 165–72, 175–78
Santa Fe, 154
Santa Lucía, Corrientes, 137
Santa Lucia, Uruguay, 151
Santa María de Fé mission, 68–69, 71–72

Santa María la Mayor mission, 125, 129
Santa Rosa mission, 68–69
Santos Maciel, José, 94
Santo Tomás mission, 84
Santo Tomé mission, 128
San Xavier mission, 125, 127, 183, 195, 210
São Borja, 112–13, 128; arrival in, 84, 89–90; during civil wars, 118; descriptions of, 84, 109, 182; farm in, 104; residence in, 88–92, 102–5, 155–63, *158*, 166–67, 181–82, 184–85, 199–201, 223, 224, 227; resources at, 206–7; as trade and travel hub, 84, 112–13, 158–59
São Borja mission, 162, 214
São João Mini mission, 103
São Leopoldo, 170, 196
São Miguel mission, *159*
São Xavier mission, 207
Sarmiento, Domingo F., 101
Sarratea, Manuel de, 123
Sarratea, Mariano de, 22, 88
Sarratea, Mariano de (son), 123
Sarton, George, 4–5, 6, 10, 13–14, 16, 41, 216, 240*n*25
Schleiden, Matthias Jacob, 142, 270*n*53
Schulz, Wilhelm, 14
Scientists: associations with, 3–4, 7–8, 13, 161–62, 165; reputation among, 4–5, 7–8, 27, 79, 145, 217, 255*n*65
Scobie, James, 98–99
Seeds: cultivation of, 189; exchanges of, 17, 29, 34, 36, 50, 79, 107, 142, 156, 180, 181, 187–90, 192, 203, 266*m*42; for Indians, 53. *See also* Exotic species, introduction of
Seemann, Berthold, 217
Sellow, Friedrich, 91, 145, 226
Serra, 14, 165, 168–70, *170*, 175–76, 227. *See also* Breeding, of sheep; English sheep; Merino sheep
Sheep, 122, 151, 152, 156–57, 160, 178. *See also* Breeding, of sheep; English sheep; Merino sheep
Sheridan, Peter (Pedro), 99, 109, 111, 120, 123, 153
Shumway, Nicolas, 129, 131, 145
Sigaud, José Francisco Xavier, 161, 274*m*121
Silva (colonel), 129
Silva, Francisco Fortunato da, 211
Silvero, José, 157
Sití, Francisco Xavier, 51
Slaves, 112, 171
Smallpox, 91–92, 156, 160
Snakebite, treatment of, 83
Soares da Silva, José Boaventura, 91
Sociedad de Medicina Montevideana, 181, 207
Sociedad Rural Argentina, 63
Sociedad Rural de Mejoramiento, 106
Société de Géographie, Paris, 159, 179
Solano López, Francisco, 198
South America: migration to, 21–23; reputation in, 7–8. *See also* Southern South America
South American Commission, 31–32, 43

Southern South America: Bonpland in, 1, 6, 15; botanical studies in, 6, 9, 14, 18; French influence in, 16–17; reputation in, 1, 8
Spix, Johann Baptist von, 104, 145, 225
Spy, Bonpland as, 133
Staples, Robert, 36
Starvation, 96
St. John's Bread, 27, 100
Strzelecki, Paul Edmond de, 105
Stuart, Charles, 253*n*42
Suárez, Francisco, 200
Subtropics. *See* Tropics and subtropics
Sugarcane, 74, 94
Sunday, working on, 125, 156–57
Sweet potatoes, 94, 99, 167, 191
Swiss colonization, 209
Symonds, Henry (Henrique), 104–5, 113, 123
Syphilis, 73, 103, 115–16, 136

Tacuarí (ship), 198
Tagle, Gregorio, 31
Tala, 100
Tanning, 37–38, 96
Tea, 180, 191–92
Tenore, Michel, 97, 100, 101
Tertulias (salons), 28, 40
Tetanus, 125
Theatins, 152–53
Thédy (merchant), 157
Thénard, Louis Jacques, 4, 96
Thompson, Evarista, 90
Thouin, André, 79
Timber, 48, 105, 153
Tobacco, 47, 52, 69, 96, 99, 100, 107–8, 147, 180, 182–83
Tobas Indians, 137
Trade. *See* Commerce
"Tragic fate," 2, 14, 223
Travelers and travel accounts, study of, 15–16, 18, 225–26
Trees: agroforestry, 165; conservation of, 173, 176, 228; cultivation of, in Argentina, 99–101; exotic species of, 100–101; on the pampas, 33; regrowth forests, 113–14; at Santa Ana ranch, 125. *See also specific types*
Tresserra, Juan Antonio, 146
Trinidad mission, 72
Tropics and subtropics: attraction to, 7, 43–44, 88, 100, 102–3, 131, 177, 203, 205, 224; cultivation in, 98, 156; Humboldt's impact on, 7; study of, 140
Tulips, 181

Ulhoa Cintra, José de, 154
Unitarians, 129, 132, 136, 145
United States, 31–32
University chairs: materia medica, 50–51, 249*m*52; natural history, 34–35

University of Greifswald, 217
Upper Plata, 13, 25; botanical work in, 35–36, 102–5; 1836–1839 stay in, 111–30; missions in, 51–59, 84, 88, 90; politics in, 17, 129–30; trade opportunities in, 44–45; woodcraft in, 33; yerba in, 39. *See also* Corrientes; Entre Ríos; Entrerriano Republic; Misiones
Urquiza, Justo José de, 13, 163, 178–79, 181, 192, 199, 222, 227
Urucu, 72, 253*n*31
Uruguay: and Argentina, 130; botanical work in, 187–92; and civil war, 131–63; descriptions of, 102–3; France and, 17, 130, 132, 205; national library of, 242*n*56. *See also* Montevideo
Uruguay River, 113, 124–25, 128

Vaccine, smallpox, 91–92, 156, 160
Vaillant, August Nicolas, 140
Vais, Angelo, 124–25
Vasconcellos, Frederico de, 175–77, 187, 277*n*47, 278*n*52
Vauquelin, Nicolas-Louis, 37, 96
Vázquez, Santiago, 145
Vedette (ship), 139
Vélez Sarsfield, Dalmacio, 270*n*51
Vences, battle of, 163, 181, 199
Verazzi, Baldassare, 151
Veron, Juan Andrés, 50
Vicuña Mackenna, Benjamín, 270*n*51
Vilardebó, Teodoro M., 274*m*124
Vilmorin (botanist), 181
Vins de Peysac, Marquis de, 107
Virasoro, Benjamín, 163, 186, 195
Virasoro, José Antonio, 186
Virasoro, Valentín, 112

Viticulture, 192–93, 196, 209
Vivielle, Léopold, 235*m*28
Voulquin, Feliberto, 48, 52, 54, 56, 58, 85

Water lilies. *See* Giant water lilies
Water Witch (ship), 212
Weitsch, Friedrich Georg, 5
Wheat, 99
Whigham, Thomas, 108, 183
Wilhelmy, Herbert, 191
Willdenow, Karl Ludwig, 6
Williams, John Hoyt, 51, 67, 78
Wilson, Alexander, 97
Wilson, Jason, 4, 10
Wilson, William, 112, 264*n*99
Wisner von Morgenstern, Franz, 174

Yapeyú mission, 117–18, 152, 194
Yatay palm trees, 52, 94, 123, 189–90, 203
Yerba maté, 15, 48; in Argentina, 39–40; in Brazil, 165–66, 168, 171–73, 175, 177–78, 183–84; in Corrientes, 125–26, 182–84, 192, 200; destruction of, 126, 183, 200; Francia and, 61, 125–26, 147; geography suitable for, 193; in Guaraní culture, 180; in Misiones, 51–63; in missions, 39, 55–56, 126–27, 194, 207; observations on, 202; in Paraguay, 74; preoccupation with, 32–33, 39–40, 42–44, 51–63, 192–98, 200–201, 228; preparation of, 57, 171–72; projects concerning, 58–63, 113, 126–27, 128–29, 136, 175, 183–84, 187, 194; trade in, 171–72

Zea, Francisco Antonio, 22, 51
Zeballos, Estanislao S., 236*n*48
Zénobie (ship), 180